*Edited by*
Taiwo Oloruntoba-Oju & Kirsten Holst Petersen

# CULTURE & THE CONTEMPORARY AFRICAN
*(A festschrift for Mai Palmberg)*

Utgiven av Recito Förlag
Tryckt av Bording i Borås år 2014

ISBN 978-91-7517-682-6

Bokutgivning.se
forlag@bokutgivning.se
www.bokutgivning.se

Recito Förlag AB
info@recito.se
www.recito.se

Första upplagan
Första tryckningen

Omslagsfoto: Mai Palmberg
Omslag: Namn Efternamn
Grafisk form och sättning: Emelie Jonsson

In Cooperation with Nordiska Afrikainstitutet
P O Box 1703, SE-75147 Uppsala, Sweden

*CULTURE & THE CONTEMPORARY AFRICAN*
*(A festschrift for Mai Palmberg)*

# Contents

# Acknowledgments

We acknowledge the sponsorship of this book by the Nordic African Institute, and the wholehearted support of both the former Director, Karin Nordberg, who agreed to the initial plans for the publication, and the present Director, Iina Soiri, who also gave unhesitant support even though she was not on ground when the initial agreement was reached.

Five of the papers edited for this volume had been presented at the *What's Culture Got to Do with it?* Conference organized by Mai Palmberg and held at the Nordic African Institute, Uppsala from June 15-18, 2009. Among them are the four keynote addresses at the Conference by Stefan Jonsson, Karin Barber, Elleke Boehmer and Signe Arnfred which had also been presented earlier on the web. The fifth, a paper by Taiwo Oloruntoba-Oju, had also been reviewed in the web presentation of the conference.

Friends of Mai's, especially Kirsten Petersen, Signe Arnfred and Susanne Linderos have also helped with behind the scenes calls and contacts, and sometimes with pictures, helpful information and other related materials. Birgitte Jansen, Librarian at NAI, Susanna Dukaric, Web Coordinator, and Research Administrator Inga-Britt Isaksson Faris also gave assistance in the course of the project. Anna Erikson-Trenter, also of the NAI family, gave assistance when we initially encountered language difficulties in our search for Swedish publishers.

Some of the pictures displayed in the book come from Mai's ubiquitous and inquisitive camera; those that accompany individual articles were supplied by the authors of those articles from a myriad of, sometimes discreet and sometimes nondescript, sources.

Many members of the *MAI and NAI Images List* were supportive and those who have contributed articles to this publication have been very patient even when the publication process appeared to be unduly delayed.

We thank all.

Taiwo Oloruntoba-Oju & Kirsten Petersen

# Mai, NAI and A Meeting of Minds
## (TRIBUTES)

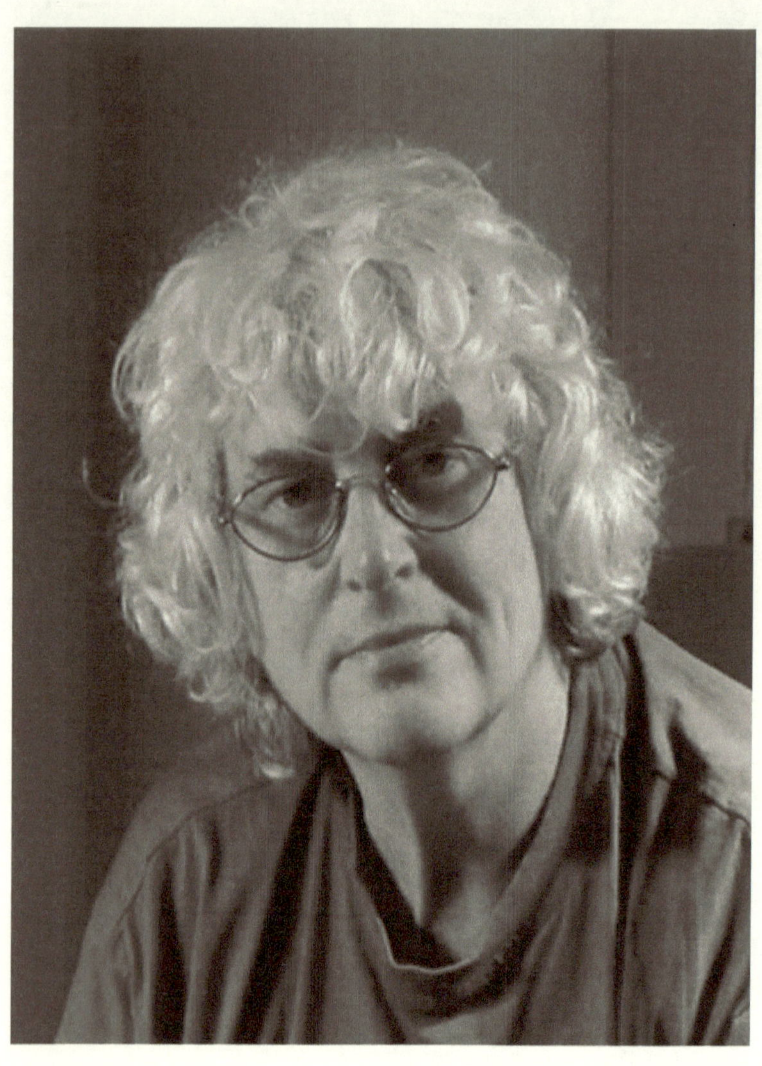

Mai palmberg
A festschrift

# Mai – en festskrift
## - Carin Nordberg

At the June 2009 "What's culture got to do with it?" conference which was Mai's last conference at the Nordic Africa Institute, I met many of those who had been engaged in her culture projects since their inception at NAI in 1995. I realized that her project on 'Cultural images in and of Africa' had become a symbol of the institute. Her work during all these years has contributed to many interesting and unexpected meetings. The scholars who came to the conference in June testified in their own ways to this effect.

When the project started it was from the beginning necessary to define what it was supposed to cover. Culture has, as we know, many different meanings. It was decided first of all, judging from some of the documents from this time, that culture would cover more the artistic and creative aspect of the term, rather than the anthropological understanding of the concept.

The project would also centre on culture as a modern phenomenon rather than as traditional culture. Mai was interested in literature, music, film, theatre, as well as the institutional framework for such cultural practices and products. Her project embraced the following thematic elements: Culture and identity; Image formation of and in Africa; Cultural dynamics of contemporary Africa, and Music.

She introduced at an early stage the programme called "The Writer's Africa," which involved Swedish, Finnish and African writers. During the last couple of years, the programme has, to my delight, focused on African writers, including an African Guest Writers Project. The first Guest Writer was Ama Ata Aidoo, followed by

Gabeba Baderoon, Tolu Ogunlesi and Shailja Patel. The focus on African writers inspired the initiative *Africa 2010*, which was to put African in focus for the Gothenburg Book and Library Fair in 2010.

In addition to the African Writers programme, Mai also invited African guest-researchers to come and work with the programme in Uppsala. She also set up an electronic forum which has linked together approximately 300 subscribers, as well as the website "The State of Arts in Zimbabwe." As a final contribution she has formulated ten statements on African Arts and Understanding Africa.

During 2009 we had on several occasions discussed what would happen to the programme once Mai left the institute in February 2010. The project had been evaluated in 2005[1] and we have a series of recommendations, some of which Mai has already attended to. There is also a recommendation to continue with a permanent focus on cultural studies in Africa at the institute. So far it has been decided to invite on an ad hoc basis Guest Writers to the institute and to continue the African Writers series. These activities would be handled by Dr. Stefan Helgesson on a part time basis for the institute.

If and how the institute will continue its engagement would continue to be a subject for further discussions. However, Mai has built up a unique resource. Potent seeds have been sown and I believe that we can expect a future harvest in the form of new and exciting initiatives.

Best wishes as she goes into a well-deserved retirement.

**Note**
[1]Rönning, Helge, "Assessment of the Project, 'Cultural Images in and of Africa,' at the Nordic Africa Institute." Maputo, March 22, 2005.

# MAI: SHE to whom
# this Honour is Due
# - Signe Arnfred

For fifteen years – from 1995 to 2010 – the *Cultural Images in and of Africa* research programme was an important part of the profile of the Nordic Africa Institute in Uppsala (NAI). From a humble start in 1962, the Institute was in the 1990s gradually growing into a place of international renown; the *Cultural Images* programme was a part in this process.

The program was set up and run by Mai Palmberg, and over the years a kind of synergy developed between the personality of Mai and the qualities of the program. Even if the program could be taken as a model for the particular kind of network based research communities, which during the period in question were flourishing at and around the Nordic Africa Institute, it was also very special due to the very special enthusiasm, engagement, capacity and devotion of Mai Palmberg. Similarly, to a certain extent the program grew into Mai's personal identity. The e-mail list, the *NAI-Images* list, which in many ways served as the backbone of the program was (by some) dubbed the *MAI-Images* list – the *Cultural Images* program and Mai Palmberg thus merging into one.

Mai's professional background is unusual for the kind of work in which she has excelled: she is a political scientist. One of her areas of interest during her years at university was, however, media studies, and thanks to her social science background the links and overlaps between culture studies and social sciences have been emphasized all through the program's life, along with an approach to cultural expression as connected to and reflecting social and political conditions.

Beyond her professional background as a political scientist Mai Palmberg is also a journalist; she likes reporting about things and events seen from her particular angle, and she is an active and capable photographer; her skills in this field have been used again and again by the Institute. Mai Palmberg's capabilities as a reporter and a photographer have also come to good use in program contexts, for example in her work with documenting contemporary art and its creators, the artists, in Africa.

In addition to all of this, Mai Palmberg is a scholar with an inquiring, critical mind and an ongoing interest in questions of epistemology and theory of knowledge related to African Studies. According to Mai herself, the fact that in her native Finland she belongs to a minority – the Swedish-speaking Finns – has made her extra alert to contemporary African post-colonial critique of dominant knowledge. I shared seven of Mai's fifteen years as a NAI researcher, 2000-2006 as a coordinator of a parallel research program, the *Gender, Sexuality and Society in Africa* program, and 2006-2007 as Acting Research Director. During that period we took many joint initiatives in terms of critical discussions of the epistemological basis for European knowledge of Africa, the limits of social science, merits and pitfalls of post-colonial theorizing and similar themes. To this extent I can very well claim a full measure of familiarity with Mai's endeavour at NAI.

For all of those years the *NAI-Images* e-mail list which I mentioned earlier served as the backbone of the program. The list, which in the end had as members some 300 scholars and/or artists in Africa and Europe, created out of this quite heterogeneous mass of people a virtual community of Africa-culture enthusiasts and devotees. Not 'African culture' in the old fashioned sense of masks and religious objects, but culture understood as contemporary culture in all of its manifestations, from literature and poetry to music and dance, theatre and film and to paintings, sculpture and installations.

In the Nordic countries the *Cultural Images* network has been of significant importance, creating and enhancing links between scholars, with a shared interest in African contemporary art and culture – scholars who have often felt isolated in their home institutions of English literature, musicology, or contemporary film, where they have been the only ones with research related to Africa. The e-mail list has created links not only between these scholars, but also between Nordic and African scholars of African culture – in addition to links with African creative artists: poets, painters, musicians etc. The e-mail list is interactive. It has been used for announcements of relevant conferences and publications, for reports from and reviews of the same, and for heated discussions, the discussions of 'African Music' and 'the role of museums in Africa' being some of the highlights.

All through the fifteen long years the *NAI-Images* list has been run by Mai, again with a firm and caring hand in her very personal style – the kind of hand-held care and nourishment which is so important in order for an e-mail list to develop beyond the mere function as a means of information, turning its subscribers into a community.

As a complement to and with a point of departure in the e-mail list, the *Cultural Images* program has sustained and invented a series of other institutions and events. First and foremost a number of conferences, workshops and publications have been organized, on a variety of themes, highlighting various aspects of the program's profile. Secondly the *Cultural Images* program has hosted a long series of African Guest Researchers, as a part of the NAI African Guest Researcher program. Being a very considerate person and always making that extra effort in her work, Mai has invariably invited 'her' African guest researchers to her home and/or (in the appropriate season) on a mushroom-picking excursion, followed by cooking and eating her trademark *Mai Palmberg mushroom soup*, the soup by the way not depending on the season, since Mai – as a Finn – has grown up in a culture of not only mushroom picking, but also mushroom drying and conservation!

Further, as a new creation in the context of the Nordic Africa Institute at some point in the early 2000s, the *Cultural Images* program (i.e. Mai Palmberg) invented the *African Guest Writer's* program – a program which immediately became such a success that its continuation beyond the closing down of the *Cultural Images* program has now been secured. As yet another activity in connection to the *Cultural Images* program Mai Palmberg has over the years been running an *African Writers' Meet the Author* series. Whenever an African writer had been invited to Stockholm or to Uppsala by somebody else for whatever reason, Mai Palmberg made sure to invite this person to an evening event in the library at NAI. Generally there would be an interview with the author, often with Mai herself as the interviewer, after which the author would read parts of her/his work. The *African Writers' Meet the Author* series was by its very nature a local event aimed at a Swedish audience. As such it is also characteristic for the way in which Mai Palmberg was running the program, always making sure to share her access to representatives of 'African culture' with a local Swedish and/or Nordic audience. All African guest researchers and guest writers have been taken on Nordic trips, making contacts, giving lectures or reading literature/poetry in other Nordic countries.

Even if communication between scholars and artists North-North, North-South, South-North and South-South has been at the core of the *Cultural Images* program, Mai has always also been concerned about communication beyond the closed circuits of scholarship, to non-scholarly audiences and consumers of culture. Some of Mai Palmberg's most well known and beloved publications born out of the program are of this nature, an example being her recent Swedish-language book on African contemporary culture, *Kultur I Africa*, co-authored with Karina Backstrom.

The *Cultural Images in and of Africa* program certainly has made a difference, in quite wide circles in the Nordic countries, to some extent in Europe and North America, and also among cultural scholars and practitioners in Africa. There are thus many good reasons for putting together a Festschrift for Mai Palmberg. She deserves it. The book certainly reflects in the various themes of the chapters the broad scope of the *Cultural Images* program. The diverse nationalities of the contributors – Nordic, British, Canadian, Zimbabwean, South African, Nigerian and Kenyan – also reflect the North-North, North-South, South-North and South-South impact and orientation of the program. This Festschrift will join the long list of books already published from and by the program, thus contributing to its life beyond death – with possibilities for resurrection at another time and place.

# To Mai: A Tribute
## - Robert Muponde

I agreed to write something on the occasion of Mai Palmberg's retirement but was not sure of what festschrift meant. So, I wrote to the *festschrift* editors and asked what this word might mean. I had never come across it. I told them that I thought festschrift meant facelift. They wrote back, and said, yah, there is something of that in the project or word. I was delighted. I accepted the invitation to misinterpret the word creatively by turning my mind to 'facelift' something I once thought of writing about on 28 February, the year 2000. It was meant to be an abstract for a potential paper destined to be read at a conference on music and identities which was organized by Mai Palmberg. I never managed to develop the paper or attend the conference. I became a different story. The wheel of fate directed me to other pastimes. But I still managed to catch up with the world of research. The selected conference papers were later co-edited and published by Mai in a volume with a very teasing title, *Playing with Identities in Contemporary Music in Africa.*

Mai has been a very keen and stubborn spirit where research in culture in Africa is concerned. She has also been able to accommodate the critical aspirations and talents of those African scholars who find their home institutions ill-equipped and stifling for the research projects they would like to do. However, I was an exception. When I visited the Nordic Africa Institute (NAI) as an African Guest Researcher on the 'Cultural Images in and of Africa' coordinated by Mai, I was coming from a top-of-the-range research institute in Africa called Witts Institute of Social and Economic Research (WISER). It was in September 2004, and I was in the middle of my Doctoral Fellowship at WISER as well as at the beginning of my term as a full-time Researcher at the same institute in South Africa.

At NAI, I met passionate, but disaffected and sometimes displaced African researchers who were trying as much as possible to catch up with the rest of the world in terms of reading and publishing. There was in these scholars bivouacked at NAI a fierce determination to make up for lost chances and time, and the NAI library and seminars provided the much-needed intellectual recuperation. I found Mai herself very helpful, always ready to lead through the snow a visiting African researcher to useful journals, new books, seminars, and also, invariably able to organize guest lectures for the often inexperienced scholar. I travelled to Finland and Denmark, where I met the leading professors in the fields of literature, culture and development studies. I also delivered guest lectures at Umea University and NAI. I have been to Sweden and Denmark a few times since then because of the vibrant research networks I built when I was at NAI.

These trips and experiences opened up new possibilities for African scholars who would ordinarily not have the opportunity to travel abroad and tell their story to a variegated but keen and intelligent audience. It is also Mai's ability to convene diverse communities of scholars on different aspects of culture in Africa that makes it possible to see her legacy is firmly settled in her ability to network and instigate intelligent conversations across cultures. Her talent has also been her ability to focus and intensify research in troubled areas of the continent such as Robert Mugabe's strife-torn Zimbabwe. Sometimes her passion and curiosity has been so unshakeable that at some point she was accused of being critically obsessed with Zimbabwean culture and politics. But, Mai being Mai, she has defiantly gone on to attempt an extended study of the country's politics and culture by organizing two workshops on Zimbabwean culture and politics, one in Harare and another in Oxford. To answer some of her critics in various disciplines and of various ideological persuasions, critics and cynics who perhaps question the raison d'être of her long-running project at NAI, she has staged a workshop provocatively and insolently titled 'What's Culture Got to Do with It'?. It was held in June 2009 in Uppsala, her intellectual home ground. The workshop itself is almost a tool of self-reflection, some kind of stocktaking on the part of the protagonist, and a multi-character analysis of the intellectual journey that Mai had undertaken, and concluded by retiring rather too soon. It is good that I will also be discussing different kinds of journeying in my paper article (in this volume).

It is good too that Mai had multiple voices answering the question in the venue where she has fought the most intense and extended intellectual and strategic battles for culture. Hers is not only a retort reminiscent of Tina Turner's 'What's love got to do with it?' but a riposte to those mindsets bent on trivializing the role of culture in development studies and politics. Above all, Mai has through her own agency and books and articles, made it possible for each cultural formation to find home in diversity and difference. I therefore find it easy to talk about two manifestations of culture in contemporary Zimbabwe in a book that is intended to celebrate the life of someone whose vision and experience can only be summed up as that of the proverbial whale. It is said that a whale contains all the meats of the world. When talking about choice in diversity, there is only an astounding expansiveness of possibilities when a gourmet contemplates the body of the whale, in Mai's case, the rich and variegated body of culture.

# A WORD FROM IINA SOIRI
## - Iina Soiri

To me, Mai Palmberg has always been synonymous with the Nordic Africa Institute. I first encountered her here when I arrived at NAI as a young student in the 1990s. We reconnected through the institute in 2011, when I returned to the Nordic countries from my 20-year sojourn in Africa. And when I started as NAI Director in 2013, Mai's legacy subsisted, even though she had already withdrawn from active service and returned to her home in Pargas, Finland. Yes, she has also been special to me as a fellow representative of our unique home culture in the Nordic region: we both hail from Finland.

One's sense of culture may be unique, but it is also relative and is often ignored until discovered, or re-discovered. In the Nordic countries, we have many languages and cultures, not to mention sub-cultures that transcend national boundaries. The same is true of the African continent. People often become aware of and identify more strongly with their own culture – be it in the anthropological or the creative and artistic understanding of the term – when they learn about other cultures. Meeting those from other cultures makes us more sensitive to and understanding of those cultures, their roots and representations. Sometimes, we are surprised to find not only differences, but also similarities between far flung cultures. Mai, with her research into and broad interest in literature, music, film and theatre and other cultural practices and products, made sure that we at NAI did not forget culture in our research, even though our research is predominantly politically and economically oriented.

Within itself, the Nordic Africa Institute also brings together different cultures. Its very purpose is the promotion and conduct of research into, and hence fostering of understanding of, modern development in Africa. And this is done within a Nordic setting, by exposing all of us here to a culturally diverse community of colleagues from all Nordic countries, and enriching our work in the process. Science and research is international, as culture is, and is not to be limited by national borders. But we often take internationalisation for granted and do not give it the emphasis and meaning it deserves. With her project *'What's culture got to do with it'* and book *KulTur i Afrika* Mai helped us to realise the many meanings of culture and the interplay between various cultures in our international work. Mai, coming from a country often known for silent and taciturn people, made us at NAI most vocal about African and Nordic cultures. She also created a network of people around NAI who are following her example, not least in the shape of this book.

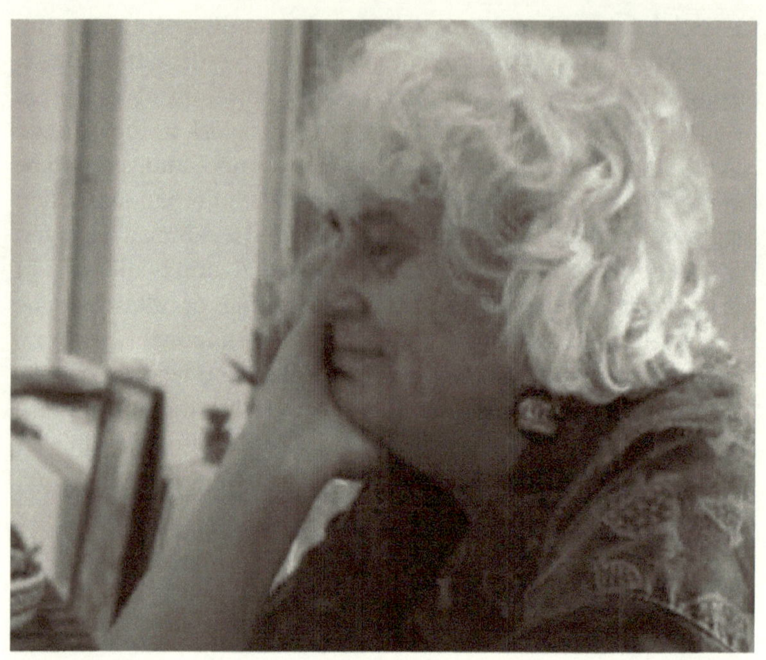

Mai & NAI

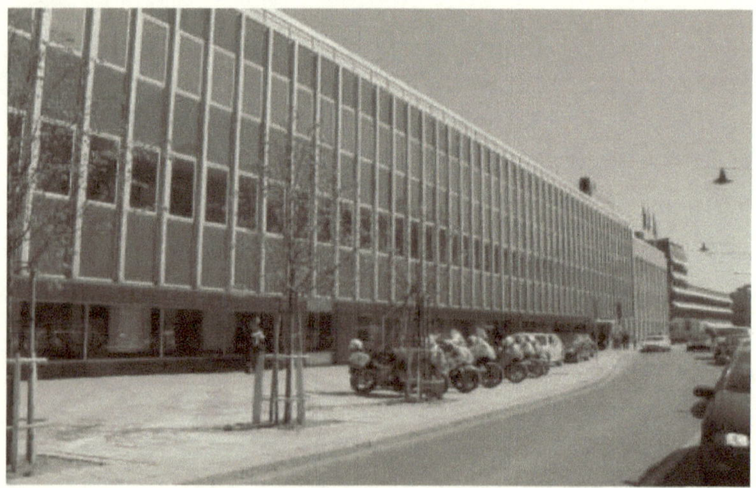

NAI Exterior, during Mai!

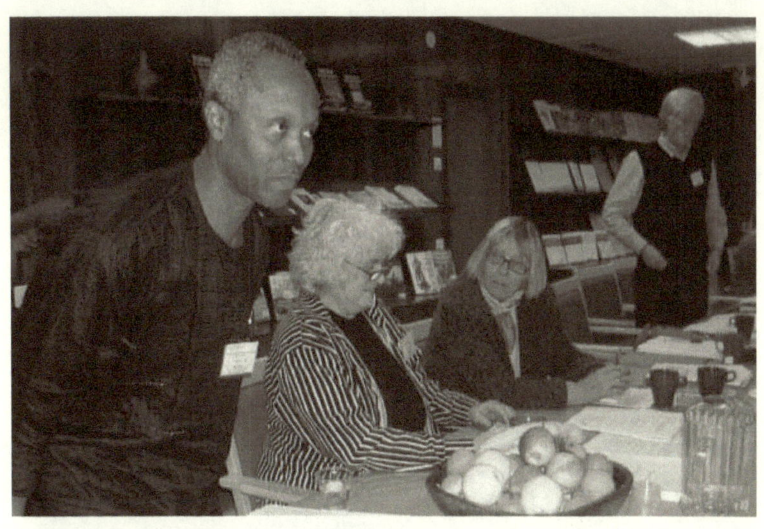

MP, Chairing a session
(with Kirsten Petersen, also seated)

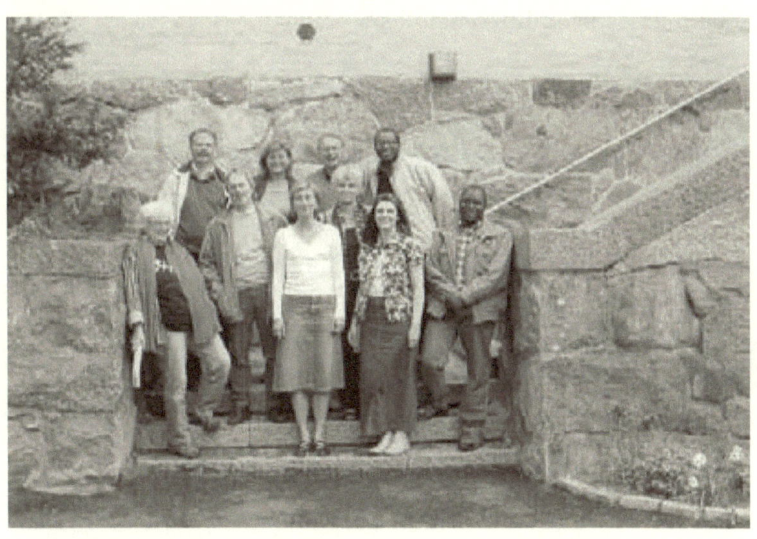

MP (left) outdooring with folks: Signe Arnfred (middle right);
Cyril Obi (back row right) and others

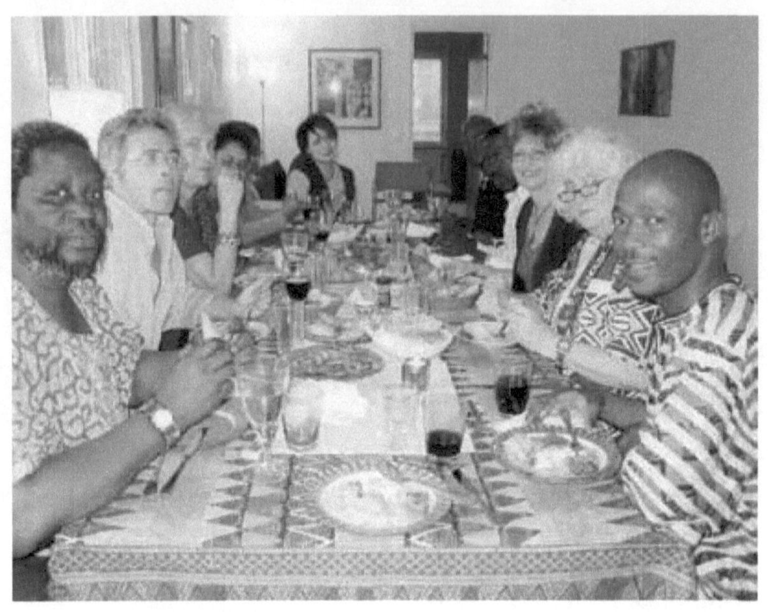

Different poses for different folks

Top: MP, second right, supping with folks

From left: Chenjerai Hove, Marc Epprecht, Signe Arnfred, ..., Akosua Adomako Ampofo, Lene Bull Christiansen

From right: Robert Muponde, Mai Palmberg, Deborah Posel, ..., Taiwo Oloruntoba-Oju

Behind the camera: Host: Amanda Hammar

Below: MP with Shailja Patel

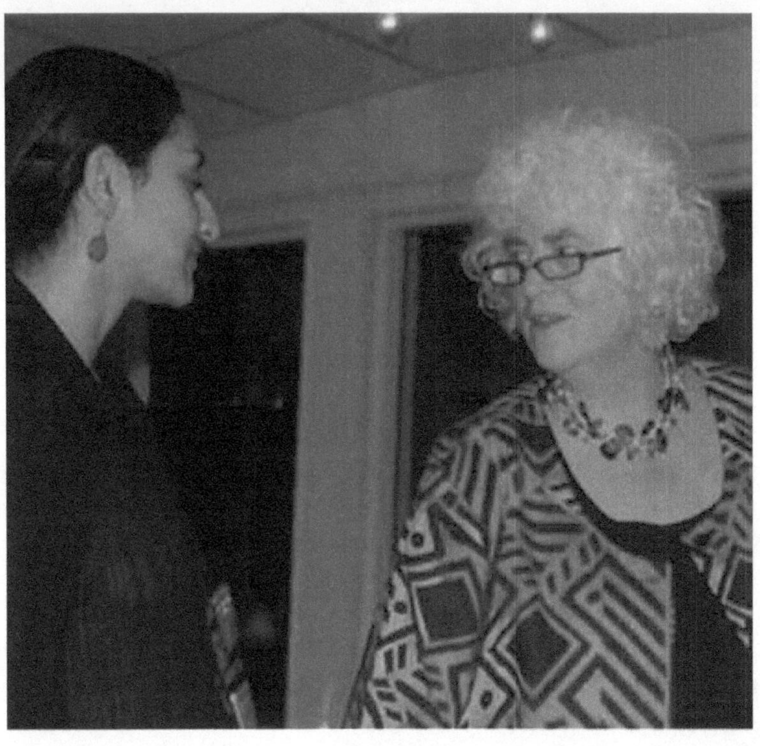

# INTRODUCTION:
## Mai and Nai: Arguments in African Culture
### - Taiwo Oloruntoba-Oju
### - Kirsten Petersen

This book offers a wide range of perspectives on African culture and its prospects, a topic that is very much dear to the heart of the honoree and her retinue – of friends, admirers, colleagues, and other researchers on Africa who have contributed to the volume. The book focuses largely on the unending *argument of culture* – what it really is and especially what it has meant for the development of Africa. The latter question was what Mai herself had in mind when she organised the "What's Culture Got to Do with it?" conference in Uppsala in June, 2009 at the twilight of her long sojourn at the Nordic Africa Institute. The keynote addresses presented at the conference have also been edited for this volume. The volume resonates with the vexed issue of *pastness* and *presentness*, of *narratives of originary* and their appropriate location within contemporary African culture. The role of history, ideology, language, literature and the arts in the formation and construction of cultures is central to the discursive trend in many of the contributions in the book.

We begin this anthology with the article by Stefan Jonsson, which initially derived from a larger project on the connection between post-world war European integration and European colonialism. Stefan writes that the colonisation, or re-colonisation, of Africa was phrased by Europe thinkers ostensibly as "what Europeans must and should do in order to have primitive and isolated Africa enter the circle of human culture." This argument of culture has analytic import within the context of this book, as it once again brings home the fact that the colonisation of Africa was motivated in part by a prescriptive and hegemonic view of the 'other' culture, and that the 'culture' argument is not always what it seems. Jonsson argues that the origins of the EU (European Union) cannot be separated from the perceived necessity to preserve and prolong the colonial system, and that the real motivation for European colonisation of Africa was less of an altruistic civilizing mission than a desire for domination and profit. (Compare Kipling's "the white man's burden," also highlighted in Signe Arnfred's chapter on "Africa Art and Gender.") As projected by Coudenhove-Kalergi during the relevant post world war one discourse, "Africa could provide Europe with raw material for its industry, nutrition for its population, land for its overpopulation, labour for its unemployed, and markets for its products."

Jonsson's historical excursion thus foregrounds "the inequality that obtains still today between Europe and Africa." His conclusion is that top European politicians continue to envision *Euroafrica* as a viable and necessary project, and that the hegemonic content of this vision continues to be disguised in the rhetoric of "unity," "peace and co-operation," as indicated in a 2007 speech by French Prime Minister Sarkozy cited by Jonsson. This theme of hegemony, inequality, and the uses and abuses of culture, is taken up from varied perspectives in this collection.

Karin Barber's *Moral Energy and what Looks like Life in African Popular Culture,* which the author considers to be "work in progress," examines the role of culture in the production and appreciation of literary forms. "What looks like life" is actually a code for the peculiar "realism" of certain products of African popular culture. Literary representations emerging in Africa from about the mid nineteenth century contain features that "look like life" and appear to conform to European standards of realism as espoused by Balzac, Ian Watt, Bakhtin, among others. However, another striking feature of African representations of the "realist" form is the feature Karin describes as "in-your-face 'moralising'": "Popular culture throughout Africa is saturated with moralising. Ordinary life is not depicted because it is worthy or interesting in itself, but because it provides a vehicle of great impact and immediacy for the purpose of driving home moral lessons which the audience can appropriate and apply to their own lives." Barber is concerned to highlight this apparently contradictory occurrence in African literary products compared with the West as a product of the intersection between culture, morality and the perception of realism. While literary or cultural moralism is boring, tedious and distasteful in Western critical reckoning, moral discourse permeates, and is well tolerated within, African aesthetics.

Evidence of the infusion of moral energy in African cultural products abounds. Barber draws detailed attention to examples from Yoruba (Nigerian) cultural products, including the "first Nigerian novel," the improvised Yoruba theatre the modern Yoruba newspaper. She also draws passing attention to examples from Igbo and Hausa (Nigerian) cultures, and from other African cultural environments such as Ghana, Kenya and Senegal. The purposeful life-likeness of these texts accentuates the moral imperative that seems so important to African cultural understanding. Within this "mode of moralising," the distinction between factual and fictional narrative becomes secondary. Barber also draws attention to what she considers the implication of this moral imperative in African popular culture for social, political and cultural conditions in Africa. "The apparently individual personal morality *encompasses* the political – reminding politicians that moral standards are shared, and apply to them as much as to us, and that no one is exempt from the requirements of decency and respect." Barber ultimately calls for a model of culture, of "realism" or of aesthetics that is "more sensitive to local perceptions and usages on the ground."

Elleke Boehmer's "Everything to do with it" examines the intertwining trajectory of literature as a form of culture that in turn impacts on culture. The article begins by dealing summarily with the old but vexed question mark regarding the utilitarian value of literature and the arts. Dismissing the idea that literature does not ever impact on real life, Elleke proceeds to elaborate on ways by which literature does add meaning to life by providing a means for the rhetorical interrogation of life processes. Especially by articulating the *unsaid* and *unsayable* (even if in "coded, oblique and disguised" ways), by traversing the *in-between* discourses (through "such techniques as implication, nuance, digression, and, in particular, as it is more random, unordered juxtaposition ... the activation of double meaning, *multivoicedness* and a plethora of significations, or, in short, complexity"), literature and other aesthetic forms provide a model, or at least suggestions, for dealing with some of the more difficult and apparently intractable real-life issues. Texts as disparate as Achebe's *Things Fall Apart* and Yvonne Vera's *The Stone Virgin*, Achmat's *The Bitter Fruit* and Dambudzo Marechera's works are used to exemplify sundry forms of articulating the complex, the horrifying, the unsaid and unsayable.

Elleke concludes by proposing that certain well known historical events and acute real life decisions are influenced as much by actual experiences as by inspiring encounters in literature. She offers as example the momentous decision by Nelson Mandela to come to rapprochement with the apartheid regime of South Africa. This decision, Elleke suggests, was an outcome of the combined inspiration received from his experience in prison and his close encounter with literature. Indeed, she privileges the latter, which she believes would have provided Mandela with "a model of thinking through reconciliation, or how to bring irreconcilables together." By this suggestion Elleke in a way also articulates a hitherto unsaid, if not itself an unsayable.

Signe Arnfred's "Africa, Art and Gender," examines four moments within African colonial and post-colonial history that also illustrate the western, hegemonic approach to the appreciation of "African tradition and culture," this time within the domain of gender and sexuality. What we have called the *argument of culture* or *contest of culture* trope is again rendered prominent here as Signe re-examines various scholarly and other contests regarding the history of contemporary African gender relations.

Signe's article begins by illustrating the manifestations of European colonial and patriarchal imagination in early European fictive and non-fictive narratives on Africa. The feminising and demonising images deployed in Rider Haggard's *King Solomon's Mines* ("Sheba's breasts"; "mother of evil," etc) fuelled negative European perception of Africa and subsequent imperialist designs. The article also analyses sundry manifests of gender exclusion, for example the absence of female artists at a certain points in African history, which, for Signe, are "an indication, not of patriarchal cultures in Africa or the African Diaspora, but of [the influence of] European patriarchal culture [as previously Simone de Beauvoir's work *The Second Sex*], in African mission and government schools."

Signe's excursion in this article takes us through prominent sites in the rise and development of African, and Africa inspired, gender discourse – from early European narratives, through the "Black Paris of the 20s and 30s" (a period and location that also feature independently in Carita Backström's article in this book), through the male and female writings of the 50s and beyond, to the rise and complexity of African feminism. Signe further argues that: "One of the tasks facing African feminists is a reinterpretation of [the] so-called "African tradition" [which] has been interpreted as patriarchal and oppressive of women [but which] perceptions have been discreetly undermined by women's fiction [and] are increasingly being questioned by African gender scholars."

Taiwo Oloruntoba-Oju's article, "Location of African Culture: Beyond Afroscepticism and the new Cosmopolitan Exotic," once again raises the unending controversy over the appropriate location of African culture in a world that is progressively globally referenced. Globalist discourse, Taiwo argues, fits sometimes unwittingly into the old but still ongoing imperialist "culture overwrite" programme aimed at suppressing other cultures and installing western hegemony disguised as "globalism." Sundry forms of African self-negation also fit into this programme. Taking Homi Bhabha's concept of the third space as his point of departure, Oloruntoba-Oju contends that, in reality, neither hybridity nor global in-betweenness could ever erase appreciation of the pastness that gives rise to presentness and without which the present lacks the appropriate frames of reference. Acknowledging that manifests of culture are frequently absorbed into an interstitial no man's land, he insists, however, that a committed cultural exegesis would always strive to "uncouple the hybrid" in contemporary manifests of culture and hoist the flag of the originating cultures at the various points of discovery. Taiwo raises the sceptre of culture as a key index of racial or ethnic survival and highlights the survival patterns of African cultures and the committed efforts of African statesmen and workers of culture. His concrete examples are drawn from contemporary Afro-pop and from African onomastic culture, both of which, even in their most exotic forms in different locales, still enable *recognisance* of the underlying *langue* of African culture and manifest the constant *renewal* of the culture and, ultimately, its *continuance* albeit in modified forms.

In "Call me by my Rightful Name ..." Wumi Raji, interrogates Paul Gilroy's theory of *the Black Atlantic* and its implicit presumption of the 'homelessness' of elements of the black Diaspora. In distancing itself from Africa, Gilroy theory avoids the term 'roots,' against which he posits the alternative term 'routes,' preferring a narrative of the interstistial space in which black elements found themselves, especially in the Caribbean, to any narrative of sources or origins. This is pretty much akin to Bhabha's implicit dismissal of 'sources,' or 'origination,' against which he posits terms like 'interstices,' 'in-between-ness' and 'the third space.' Raji expresses a preference for theory such as Stuart Hall's, which is illustrated with Black Caribbean identity constructed on the two poles of "similarity" and "continuity" on the one hand, and "difference" and "rupture" on the other hand. Because it ensures a relationship with the past, the pole of similarity and continuity constantly reminds a typical Caribbean of the manner of his/her arrival at his/her contemporary location. The second pole, on the other hand, emphasises the "broken" nature of this continuity. The paper emphasises that change and difference are facts of history: "Even before their departures from Africa, differences existed among the slaves," and "like everything which is historical, [situations] undergo [a] constant transformation."

Kirsten Petersen diachronically recalls the schism in literary works produced during the apartheid regime, in which racial trading of blames was the dominant form of expression. At this period, only Alan Paton's *Cry the Beloved Country* (1948) expressed the possibility and indeed foresight of peace and unity via humanistic and Christian values, but his proposition seemed unrealistic. The setting up of the Truth and Reconciliation Committee as a means of national reconciliation in the post-apartheid regime, thus also signals the prophetic role of literature. The establishment of this body spurred a new series of literary works by South African authors, out of which Mark Behr's *The Smell of Apples* and Antjie Krog's *Country of My Skull* appear exemplary. The authors are White South Africans and the central theme in their selected works is peace and reconciliation, albeit expressed with considerable ambiguity. Kirsten juxtaposes and exposes the ambiguity of these texts which were, in part, reflections on the proceedings of the Truth and Reconciliation Committee. She suggests that the ambiguity is deliberate as the texts are mainly concerned with "the dilemmas of reconciliation, and their intention is to problematise the concept through precisely ambiguity." The cathartic role of literature through a vicarious involvement is apposite; the literature not only records the throes of the moment but, for Kirsten, also "allows for a deeper involvement in one person's struggle with the complexities." The textual ambiguities of the post-apartheid texts (even with apartheid officially over and reconciliation generally within grasp) forces a positive reappraisal of Alan Paton's novel of three decades before: "Paton's liberal humanism expressed in his beloved cry to his country turned out to be a universally applicable culture that was only begging to be applied to the South African situation, and its derivative literature.

Robert Muponde's article, "*Chotemgunre* – Song Drama in Zimbabwe" interrogates the continued appropriation of ageless cultural texts by contemporary political formations in Zimbabwe and the implication of this for cultural development and for theories of culture. The Shona (Zimbabwean) folk songs, *Chomtengure* (the turning wheel of the ox-drawn cart) and *Uyo Ndiani* (Who is that one?), feature in dominant critical reckoning as protest song but can also energise labour force and double as a song of redemption. The many interpretive possibilities belie a rigid appropriation of its meaning. Robert rather sees in the songs a metaphor for the migrancy of culture. *Chomtengure* is ubiquitous and will be found at spaces that "range from protest at labour sites to play and entertainment in the classroom; restoration of the moral and social order through direct and indirect rebuke of those who wrong others or indulge in unproductive social activities; and the meting out of instant, socially approved justice by victims of social miscreants." This complexity recommends a dynamic reading of culture, and the reading offers a pedestal from which to roundly rebuke the "cultural nationalists in Zimbabwe," who apparently impose their own reading of the song as protest. According to Robert, they "celebrate stasis as stability, and traces of travel as stains." Robert's take on culture would appear somewhat opposed to Taiwo's, where an acknowledgment of the dynamism of culture does not lead to a repudiation of its lingering influence. A meeting point is however possible: the continued deployment of those Shona songs which are, in Robert's own appreciation, "as old as imagination itself" would appear to also support the thesis of the resilience of old cultural forms even when they wear exotic new garbs and facilitate sundry new interpretations.

In "Stories of Frozen Worlds ..." Ranka Primorac, argues that the official narratives of Zimbabwean colonial past and of anti-colonial wars are an attempt to re-inscribe the past based on "a certain understanding of time." The article sets this official understanding against the concept of time presented in the English-language novels of Zimbabwean Chenjerai Hove (*Bones*, *Shadows* and *Ancestors*). Ranka critically examines the narrative of "the three dovetailing *Chimurengas*," being the official version of Zimbabwe's history, dubbed "patriotic history" by the authorities. The narrative presents a paradox: a construction of history "for the future" based on a return to the past; a revalorisation and revalidation of war and veterans' tactics as acceptable politics within civil society. The concomitant linear concept of time and rigidification of identities provides a theoretical framework for the examination of the brutal dictatorship and suppression of opposition that characterises contemporary Zimbabwe. Hove's novels present, in Ranka's view, a different and liberating perspective of time. They construct a version of passage of time "as devourer ... as a test of endurance, and ... as an indicator of power relations - as variants of the theme of *curtailed movement*." In the process, Ranka concludes, the novels appear to "[articulate, and demand] certain basic spatio-temporal rights, whose realisation may be seen as going hand in hand with envisaging the forging of a new Zimbabwean consciousness."

Marc Epprecht's chapter examines the growth of literary and aesthetic texts authored by Africans, which challenge the cultural taboo of silence on non-normative sex on the African continent. The author identifies three phases of the new queer aesthetics, from the queer literature of the fifties and late eighties which largely associated homosexuality with "coloureds, foreigners, criminality and/or insanity," and portrayed Africans as "victims of homosexual rape or exploitation," through that of the late eighties to the nineties which coincided with and received impetus from the emergence of what Epprecht calls "political homophobia" that triggered the emergence of gay rights groups and explicit gay literature especially in South Africa, to the third phase, can be described as a period of explosion of gay aesthetics from the late nineties to 2009. In this third phase, the scope of expression widened considerable to include documentaries like *Woubi Chérie*, films like *Karmen Gei* and *Emotional Crack* and novels like Jude Dibia's *Walking with Shadows*, among many others. A common concern of the new wave of works (dubbed a "restorative queer aesthetic" by Elleke Boehmer) has been, Epprecht explains, "to demonstrate [that] continuities and compatibilities between traditional extended family values (*ubuntu*) and new expressions of non-normative sexuality would be truer to the spirit of African humanism than dogmatic and coercive notions of heteronormativity embedded in modern ideas around social respectability." Epprecht also makes the point, however, that while the sympathetic aesthetic depictions of same sex sexuality could be seen as a possible pointer to changing perceptions of the phenomenon on the African continent, their immediate cultural impact "should not be overstated."

In "Religion and Sexuality in Two Contemporary African Novels," Chima Anyadike explores the relationship between the development and expression of sexual awareness and the empowerment of young women in two cognate African cultures, as represented in Chimamanda Adichie's *Purple Hibiscus* (Nigerian) and Zakes Mda's *The Heart of Redness* (South Africa), among other novels. Chima's objective is to highlight the intersection between race and culture and the effect of the imposition of western colonial cultures on Africa. His suggestion, which many would consider controversial, but which he argues forcefully from the perspectives of the novels, is that the pre-colonial and traditional moral and religious orders constitute healthier contexts for women and men's sexual development and empowerment than the superimposed western cultures. Chima alludes to the Asian and Middle Eastern trajectory and the resilience of their traditional religions and cultures (and languages, we might add) to wonder why Africans have been so ready to dissolve their traditions into what the author considers dubious cultural offerings from the West. He also faults the general depiction of women from western feminist perspectives as if "the road to female sexual freedom and empowerment must go through the process of the rejection of socially approved rules of sexual conduct." Drawing examples from contrastive presentations in African novels, Chima insists that it should be possible to depict strong African women without "the taint of promiscuity, prostitution and 'alien' feminism." The imposition of celibacy on men and a permanent state of virginity on women the name of priesthood (especially in the Catholic religion) is another example of how alien, western derived, cultures are imposed on African societies. Interestingly, Chima also addresses what he calls the opportunistic appropriation by African men of certain western cultural values which has apparently allowed the systematic domination and oppression of women in ways that were not generally allowed in pre-colonial Africa.

Carita Backström's article, "Primitive, Essence, Fusion," traces the origin and development of the contemporary fusion of dances from two different and distinct cultures, European and African. Once considered poles apart, the classical ballet was to begin to accommodate forms of "primitive" African dance until eventually a *fusion* of both modes was achieved. Though the concept of cultural fusion (described as "the synthesis or integration or combination of two or more cultural forms of expression which have their roots or sources in different traditions or different countries") appears self-evident today, such a possibility used to be considered remote, and, at the beginning, it was a "daring political and aesthetic choice to make," as Carita explains. (A parallel exists in the world of music, with African-American jazz described as "no music at all" when it made its debut in Paris twixt the world wars, as highlighted in the chapter by Signe Arnfred).

Carita's paper zeroes in on three moments in dance history that produced the ideological/political and aesthetic momentum that led to contemporary fusion. The key personalities of these moments were western ballet dancers such as Cendrars, Léger and Börlin (who produced Birgit Åkesson Sylvia Glasser). Beginning as a search for authenticity, these pioneers were to discover in Africa what Glasser was to describe as "deeper roots for the dance." Carita carefully examines their passion and their commitment which was to result in contemporary *fusion*. Quite interesting too, from the perspective of culture, transition and change, Carita makes the point that the fusion of ancient African and modern western dance forms was made possible through a "respectful approach," by which the different forms could be combined "without violating or trivializing the origin."

This look-back-to-origins is also picked up in Reuben Chirambo's paper, "Dancing Banda's Dictatorship in Malawi…" Reuben first of all makes a case for dance as discourse, based on Foucault's analysis of discourse as statements made in general and specific domains, and as being constitutive of all social and political relationships and power relations. In his analysis, dance as discourse implicates more than just body movements; rather, it incorporates the totality of meanings emanating from a dance performance and its contexts. Within this discursive frame, dance performances during the dictatorship of Banda in Malawi carried a deeper meaning than mere entertainment. They were discursive practices that involved interaction between the leadership and the ordinary people, thus representing and re-presenting their power relations. Political power not only resides in but, crucially, is also reproduced by these dances, with the accompanying songs and chanting of the praise names of the dictator. Culture and artefacts of culture are classically appropriated by and in the service of dictatorship, as in this example. What is also interesting in this Malawi example, however, is the perhaps unwitting but certainly ironic collaboration of the oppressed folks in the reproduction and sustenance of discursive forms that gave Banda's dictatorship the guise of popular appeal. What we have then is a case of cultural forms producing and sustaining a culture of acquiescence in servitude.

Bode Omojola's article examines contradictory notions in modern African popular music and highlights the challenge faced by African musicians in dealing with received European cultural practices. It also highlights the complexity of locating these cultural practices in relation to African cultural heritage. According to the author, the syncretistic musical language of highlife, for example, speaks to the ways in which Yoruba and indeed Nigerian musicians in general responded to the imposition of Western musical practices in the country. By reworking Western harmonic elements in a manner that conforms to the cyclic character of Yoruba drumming, by adapting Western-type melodies to suit the tonal and inflectional features of Yoruba language, and by incorporating indigenous musical instruments into their musical performances, musicians like Olaiya, another prominent example, sought to "own" the western structures. The modern reworking of Western and indigenous elements illuminates the social dynamics and the constantly shifting social and political landscape of their environment, laying the foundation for the emergence of a new popular music tradition that would reflect emerging African social, political and urban experience. *Juju* music, developed by musicians like Ebenezer Obey, Sunnny Ade, Idowu Animasaun and Shina Peters, incorporates traditional Yoruba performance practices and styles in a manner that fundamentally differs from what obtains in *highlife* music, thus illustrating the strong neo-traditional basis of the classic *juju* form.

The impact of global media in shaping or misshaping culture, as manifested in the lives and experiences of young women in Tanzania and Zimbabwe, is the focus of Hilde Arntsen and Ylva Ekström in their article titled "Finding One's Feet in Modernity" Young People and the Media in Dar-es-Salaam and Harare." The international media has often been isolated as one of the catalysts of the cultural erosion noticed among African youths. However, drawing insights from media globalisation and media ethnography or media anthropology, and through field interviews of young women (represented here by Linda and Mary who were secondary school students), Hilde and Ylva argue the potential benefits of cultural interaction or even cultural symbiosis in the environment. The media no doubt played a vital role in deciding the appearances of the young women, their choice of careers, their popularity, their socialisation process into womanhood and how 'modern' they were perceived among their peers; in effect helping them to find their feet in modernity. On the other hand, the societal and cultural systems and the inherent traditional values inhibited how much of these 'foreign' ideas can be adapted. The authors make a case for the adaptation of ideas that accord with value systems of Tanzania and Zimbabwe, to ensure that their young women are not debarred from the advantages of globalisation, nor pursue the global culture to the extremes that may destroy important and progressive cultural values. Hilda and Ylva ultimately challenge the "grand theories of globalisation" and their fixation on systems and corporations while neglecting individuals: "Rather than adopting the position that all foreign media content is bad and that such material have detrimental influences on Tanzania and Zimbabwe" the authors opt for an approach that takes the media "as content with which the youth engage in a variety of ways." They also opt for "a concurrent analysis of media structures, media content and media audiences … to arrive at a more multi-faceted understanding of the processes at play."

Sola Ajibade's article examines the entrenchment of nativism in Yoruba literature. Linking this development with issues of society and polity, he argues that political independence is meaningful only when a people's pride in their positive cultural values is guaranteed. This is why, according to him, Yoruba writers generally advocate an African literature that represents an authentic African experience. Ajibade acknowledges the debt that Yoruba written literature owes to western colonial activities – which led to the emergence of the literature. D. O. Fagunwa marks a remarkable turn in literary writings in Yoruba with the publication of his first Yoruba novel, *Ogboju Ode Ninu Igbo Irumole*, in 1938. The novel attracted a massive appreciation from readers even as a hybrid of Yoruba folk tradition and Biblical injunctions. The article also focuses on Kola Akinlade, who adopts the detective fiction genre, a genre with few Yoruba literary writers, to echo the new transition trends in Yoruba language and culture. Akinlade's novels deal with the growth in crimes, the cause, and the resort to traditional methods of combating them when the contemporary agents of fighting crimes are unable to effectively perform this function. Akinlade, therefore, asks, through his works, for the activation of traditional institutions in maintaining law and order in the modern African society.

What's culture got to do with health? Makanjuola in his paper, "Health and the African Image" opines that people's attitudes, and the corresponding measures employed to combat ill-health, are closely connected to the peoples' culture and belief system. His examination of the Nigerian, especially Yoruba, response to mental health in particular demonstrates the resilience of age-long cultural attitudes which, for better or for ill, continue to dominate the response. The statistics (70%), is huge and, to the author, "embarrassing": "The transmission of this belief system into contemporary/modern health care practice is often an embarrasing fact that attests to the resilience of traditional African"ways of life" "notwithstanding the advancement of science and globalism and the pervasive influence of monotheistic religions." Indeed the new religions (Christianity and Islam) have only served to entrench the influence of spirituality in the aetiology of illness. Makanjuola also observes the paradox whereby orthodox western approaches are unable to meet many health needs, "notwithstanding advancement in science," and the traditional cultural methods achieved some astounding successes, notwithstanding the scepticism of science. Makanjuola concludes that the solution is not to dismiss traditional culture in relation to modern health care delivery, but to strive to understand it.

Adeyinka Banwo's review of Marc Epprecht's *Heterosexual Africa? The History of an Idea from the Age of Exploration to the Age of AIDS* explores the strengths and weaknesses of the text. The book is described as part of the continuing challenge to the stereotypical view that Africa is an exclusively heterosexual continent. Drawing from historical and non-historical fictional sources, Epprecht argues in the book that concepts of homosexuality and bisexuality were evident in Africa ever before the advent of western colonialists. The study also calls attention to the dearth of research into same sex sexuality on the continent, which, according to the author, is due to the reluctance of African researchers to accept the reality of the existence of homosexuality in Africa, and which in turn is one of the factors contributing indirectly to the spread of the HIV/AIDS pandemic in Africa. Banwo commends the depth of Epprecht's research, while however expressing the view that some examples cited by Epprecht to validate his arguments have been and remain quite contentious.

The book is divided into six uneven and in-exclusive sections, comprising a preface and five culture-themed parts. Inevitably, being a festschrift, there has also been an outpouring of tributes to Mai Palmberg, some of which we have accommodated in the prefa-

tory and concluding parts of the book. Finally, we have adopted an
'all about' approach to the indexing of the keywords of this book,
'Africa,' 'culture' and their sundry collocates. The comprehensive
indexing of these terms gives the reader a quick and easy access to
the various descriptions of and approaches to the terms from the
numerous perspectives of the various contributors.

# Part I
# African Culture: On a Keynote

# EUROPE THROUGH AFRICA,
# AFRICA THROUGH EUROPE
## - Stefan Jonsson

When did average Europeans first gain first degree contact with Africans? There is much to support that this first happened in period immediately following World War One, from 1919 to 1925. More than a million soldiers born in the colonies of the European states fought on European soil in the First World War, almost all of them on the French and the British sides.[1] Among the French troops that after the war continued the occupation of the Rhineland were thousands of soldiers from Madagascar, West Africa, Morocco, and Algeria.

The presence of non-white soldiers in the occupying forces bred strong emotions among the German public and intelligentsia. African soldiers were generally perceived as unreliable savages, who posed great danger especially for the German female and juvenile population. Newspapers were flooded with articles disseminating rumours of atrocities committed by the foreign troops. Talk of "the black danger," "the black disgrace," "the black shame," and "the black peril." was in everybody's mouth. When Germany's Reich chancellor Müller, the highest ranking politician of the nation and a social democrat, addressed the parliament in April 1920 he started by stating the unbelievable – "French militarism has marched across the Main into enemy country" – and then went on, in the next sentence, to state the unthinkable: "Senegal negroes are camping in the Frankfurt University, guarding the Goethe House."[2] This was the scandal: Johann Wolfgang von Goethe, the very monument of the European spirit, the very proof of German superiority – now soiled and disgraced by black hands.

World War One ended with Germany's dishonourable concession of defeat and the ensuing peace treaties of Versailles and Trianon, which forced Germany to admit being guilty for the aggressions that led to war and to carry the burden of enormous monetary retributions. In order to ensure Germany's payment of its war debts, French troops in 1923 assumed control of the strategically important Ruhr area, the major industrial region and most vital economic zone in mainland Europe. This time, the share of colonial troops was small. This did not prevent German politicians and opinion makers from feeling humiliated and even violated. That West-African and North-African soldiers presented a threat to women and children was common opinion, as was the belief that syphilis and other [sexual/venereal] diseases would follow in the tracks of the African troops, or that their depraved habits corrupted the virtues and morality of the locals. Germany's president, social democrat Friedrich Ebert, repeatedly stated his conviction, that "the deployment of coloured troops of the most inferior culture as overseers of a population of such high spiritual and economic importance as the Rhinelanders is an intolerable violation of the law of European civilization." [3]

Ebert's opinion was indeed shared by all political parties in Germany of the period, with the exception of the Communists (KPD) and independent social democrats (USPD). Visual images of the period illustrate that Germany regarded the presence of black and coloured troops as a humiliation so shameful that it rocked at the very fundaments of national identity. One poster from 1920 shows a happy-looking black man, all naked except for the helmet usually worn by French troops, standing like a huge colossus with his legs spread wide and his giant feet crushing the cross-framed houses of a German town, at the same time rubbing against his waist and sexual organ ivory-white female bodies that he has caught in his hands.[4] Yet another illustration is a commemorative coin, minted and sold to promote resistance against the French occupation. On one side of the coin is the facial profile of a black soldier, caricatured to look like a monkey, next to which are stamped the words "Liberté, Egalité, Fraternité" and "Die Wachtam Rhein," "Guard at the Rhine." On the other side of the coin we see a woman tied to a tree, the trunk of which, at closer scrutiny, turns out to be an enormous erect penis.

It is painful to look at these images today. Yet, such was the image of Africa and of the African at a time when they were transported right into Europe's fatigued and war-torn heart. In one sense, these statements and images are just a continuation of a long history of Europe's racial stereotyping of non-European peoples. My reason for returning to them now, however, is that they are also repressed parts of the origin and beginning of a new history, the history of inter-European cooperation and integration. For it is in this area and in this period that the story of what is today known as the EU, or the European Union, can be said to begin. This is so for many reasons. A first, more anecdotal but nonetheless significant reason is that Konrad Adenauer, the West-German prime minister who was instrumental to the construction of the European economic community (ECC) after World War Two, resided as vice mayor and mayor in Cologne during the whole Weimar period from 1919 to 1933. Adenauer's political world-view was largely shaped by the conflicts in the Rhineland during and after World War One. Another reason, as we shall see, is that the emergence of the European Union is far more intimately connected to Africa and to the question of Europe's dominance over Africa than we are led to believe by standard works on the history of modern Europe. In fact, this is a connection passed over in silence by the average historian. Thirdly, for those who first asserted the necessity of a European union, it was precisely this geographic area, the Rhineland and the Ruhr region, or the border zone between France and Germany and between Germany and the Benelux countries – that showed both the crux and proof of their argument. As we know, it was the attempts to resolve the centuries-long strife and conflicts about this region, blessed with stunning natural resources and a highly developed industrial infrastructure that initiated the first plans for a united Europe. These plans, in turn, formed the basis of what actually became the EU of today, which derives its origins from the so-called Schuman declaration of 1950, which led to the establishment of the European Coal and Steel Community (ECSC) a year later.

I have already mentioned that France's decision to march across the Ruhr and the Rhine with colonial troops turned Germany's political emotions to boiling point. However, smaller groups of intellectuals reached the opposite conclusion. In their view, France's occupation of the Ruhr area only demonstrated that the age-old animosity between France and Germany had led both states to a dead end. Henceforth, the survival of each country did not depend on its ability to defeat the other, but on the willingness and ability of both states to collaborate with one another. The best resolution of the Ruhr occupation and the sole possibility for a lasting peace consisted in some kind of political and economic union between the two countries. Out of Germany and France's unification, the rest of Europe would then follow. Or so they argued. "Anfänge Europas," "Beginning of Europe," was the title of an article published in May 1923 by German writer Heinrich Mann. He wrote: "Shall Europe ever become one: then the two of us first. We form the root. Out of us, the united continent – the others could not but follow us. We carry the responsibility for ourselves and the rest. Through us there will be a state above states and that state will last. Or else, no future will be valid for us, nor for Europe." [5]

That same year, and in the similar idealistic spirit, Richard Coudenhove-Kalergi published his pamphlet, *Paneuropa*. Coudenhove-Kalergi was born in the Habsburg Empire and was inspired by its supra-national constitution. For him, too, the Ruhr occupation and the apparently irresolvable border conflict between France and Germany were causes of alarm. "Out of the terrifying crisis, in which Germany and France are locked today, they will either emerge as united Europeans – or they will, biting at each others' throats, bleed to death from their mutually inflicted wounds." In order to prevent these once so powerful European states from being squashed between the growing superpowers to the east and the west, the states of Europe must unite in a pan-European union, and the first step in this process must be taken by France and Germany, Coudenhove-Kalergi argued. [6]

Coudenhove-Kalergi's pamphlet contains roughly the same argument, but elaborated in greater detail, as did many other proposals for European collaboration presented during the 1920s. "After 1923 whole staff of periodicals, associated pressure groups in many countries, and at least two dozen books published every year pursued this aim", writes Walter Lipgens, one of the principal historians of the European integration process. [7] According to Lipgens, five such proposals were more influential than others.

He mentions Demangeon and Delaisi from France, Alfred Weber from Germany, Ortegay Gasset from Spain, and, most important of all, Coudenhove-Kalergi's *Paneuropa*. To be sure, this Czech-Austrian thinker did not devote himself only to thinking, writing, and research, but organized a huge Pan-European movement that opened branches in most European states and gathered influential intellectual and political support from the best and brightest of his generation, including Selma Lagerlöf, the brothers - Heinrich and Thomas Mann - as well as statesmen like Winston Churchill, Konrad Adenauer and Aristide Briand, the latter serving for a long time as chairman of the Pan-European Union.

Coudenhove-Kalergi's argument for a European Union mirrors the world view of internationalists and liberal progressives of his era. A united Europe was paramount for political reasons, or simply to prevent a repetition of World War One. This was the argument for peace. A united Europe was desirable also for cultural reasons, as history seemed to indicate that Europe made up some sort of civilizational unity. This was the argument for civilization. In addition, the 1920s added a third, economic argument, for as Europeans compared their own states to the rapidly growing economies of the United States and the Soviet Union, they concluded that both enjoyed the advantage of being able to organize their economies on a continental scale, whereas Europe was torn apart and its economic dynamism, suffering and lagging behind because of trade and customs barriers, export prohibitions, and also the large scale debt owned by Germany to other states. The superpowers of the period – the British Empire, the Soviet Union, Japan and China, and the United States, profited from their sheer imperial largeness. They were self-sufficient in most raw materials and had greater markets for the sale of their products. This economic perspective then gradually turned into a geopolitical one, which touched the sensitive issue as to whether Europe would ever again be able to regain its place as a superpower on a par with the other ones. From this perspective, Africa was seen as a natural or necessary part of Europe's economic sphere, a part that needed to be more strongly connected to Europe, and one that needed to be exploited by united European forces in order to be properly and adequately used. As the intellectuals of the 1920s argued in favour of a European Union or federation, their arguments implicitly or explicitly addressed Africa. Europe could develop its fullest economic potential only through Africa.

Africa was mainly looked upon as a great provider of natural resources and agricultural produce, but also as a reservoir for hydroelectric power. Sometimes, Africa was seen as the solution to Europe's demographic problems; it was widely agreed that Europe was overcrowded and overpopulated, and the continent would be greatly helped if surplus population could emigrate and settle in the "empty" territory south of the Mediterranean. As Coudenhove-Kalergi stated in his essay titled "Africa," "Africa could provide Europe with raw materials for its industry, nutrition for its population, land for its overpopulation, labor for its unemployed, and markets for its products."[8]

What is important is that all these arguments for an assimilation of Africa into Europe then formed yet another strong argument for the unification of Europe. The common exploitation or use of Africa appeared as an aim so unquestionable, so attractive and beneficial, that it in itself would be a reason for the European states to forge a common cause; they simply had so many profits to harvest from it. A geopolitical calculation emerged in which two good things reinforced one other: by uniting Europe a new geopolitical sphere would emerge that, thanks to its inclusion of Africa, would be sustainable and prosperous; and by together developing Europe, the bonds of peace and collaboration would grow stronger between once antagonistic European states. In short, a unification of Europe and a unified European effort to colonize Africa were two processes that presupposed one another. As Coudenhove-Kalergi wrote: "The African problem thus brings us back to Europe. Africa cannot be made available, if Europe does not unite."[9]

This argument won support especially in Germany, which, through an arrangement of this kind, would regain access to its former colonial territories that it had lost in the First World War.[10] A co-European colonialism was also promoted as a higher form of colonialism, all adherents agreed. This would be a colonialism not governed by narrow nationalistic greed, but by the high ideals of European civilization. A few, among them Heinrich Mann, feared that Pan-Europe amounted to a new form of imperialism, which he nonetheless accepted as a lesser evil than its old form.[11] Interwar politicians, intellectuals, and visionaries also gave a name to the new superpower that would again raise the star of Europe. The geopolitical bloc was called Euro-Africa, a notion so prevalent in these years that it is difficult, if not impossible to find out who actually coined it. Contrary to a common understanding and standard historiography of the roots of today's European Union – in which Coudenhove-Kalergi is seen as the father figure of the founding fathers – Pan-Europe was not a project limited to Europe alone, but one which included Africa in its entirety, except for its British possessions. From 1920 to 1960 the European project was launched and developed, yet it is almost always forgotten that this European project was in fact always a Eurafrican project.

Let me make a digression here to give you a feel of the ideas and visions at stake, by looking at the Eurafrican project of the German architect, Hermann Sörgel's, his blueprint for what he called *Atlantropa*, which he considered a better alternative than Coudenhove-Kalergi's *Paneuropa*. Sörgel's basic idea was to dam up and contain the net inflow of water into the Mediterranean Sea. A great dam was to be built across the Gibraltar sound and a network of huge hydroelectric plants at the outlets of all the great rivers flowing into the Mediterranean, the Nile, the Rhône, the Po, the Tiber, the Ebro, as well as the rivers going into the Black Sea, the Danube, the Dnepr, and others. These immense technical works – on the same scale or greater as Stalin's plan to redirect Russia's major rivers toward the south – would then lower the sea level of the Mediterranean and also create a territorial bridge between Africa and Europe. His idea was to have the sea level decrease by 0.8 meters per year for more than a hundred years, until it would be 200 meters lower than it is today in the eastern part of the Mediterranean, and 100 meters lower in the western parts, the two parts being separated by yet another dam, the Messina dam, stretching from Sicily to Tripoli.

The benefits of this project would be enormous, Sörgel thought. The project would create large areas of new agricultural land. For instance, to the west of Palestine a stretch of land would rise out of the waters and would be made available to Jewish settlers, thus creating a new Israel, and thus also – as we may be allowed to say in retrospect – pre-empting the Israeli-Palestinian conflict. The project would also provide Europe with all the energy it could use, and even more so; as the surplus energy would be used to pump water from the Congo River, led by way of a system of channels through Lake Chad, in order to irrigate the Sahara, which would thus become agricultural land. The project would also join the continents, creating a territorial connection across which Africa's natural resources would flow into Europe, while Europe's surplus population would move into and colonize the African continent. The crowning infrastructural accomplishment would be a railroad connecting Berlin to Cape Town. Of course, the African people also figured in the equation, as a vast supply of labor for European industry. That the sovereignty over the newly created continent was on the side of Europe is signalled by its name; the unified territories of Africa and Europe would be called "*Atlantropa.*" Sörgel's technological vision was in his view the only possible solution to the problems facing Europe: unemployment, overpopulation, lack of energy and natural resources. At one stroke, these difficulties would be resolved. Indeed, the future of the West depended on the project: "Either: the fall of the West (*Untergang des Abendlandes*), or: Atlantropa as a turning point and new goal."[12]

The Decline of Europe, the Fall of Europe – this was the ominous scenario that had to be prevented by drawing on the continent to the South. That Europe was in decline was a fact proven by the war, by the inflation, by the depression. What was needed as a remedy was something that, in the German jargon of those years, was called "Lebensraum." This term may be properly translated into current jargon as "opportunities for investment and growth."

As I have already stressed, most people took it as self-evident that Africa could and would provide Europe with the Lebensraum – with the "opportunities for investment and growth" – that Europe needed.

Another influential exponent of this geopolitical theory is E. L. Guernier, Frenchman and author of numerous works on colonialism, among them *L'Afrique – Champ d'expansion de l'Europe* from 1932. In the preface, Guernier remarks that there is now a new kind of colonialism, most beautifully illustrated by the International Colonial exposition in Paris in 1931, and powerfully realized in the development of North Africa by the great French social planner and colonial administrator Hubert Luautey. Guernier explains the idea behind this new colonialism: "Today's colonization is the synthesis of a moral and highly civilizing endeavour – the gradual elevation of the standing of life of the non-developed races – and the no less human endeavour of the continuous maintenance, if not improvement of the conditions of life of an industrious Europe."[13] Guernier asserts that both continents stand to benefit from a thorough unification. Europe offers to Africa morality, culture, and civilization. Africa offers Europe raw materials, territory, resources, or, in short, opportunities for investment and growth. The result of Europe's expansion in Africa is not just the unification of Europe, but the emergence of a third geopolitical power sphere, that creates equilibrium in the global world system. For Guernier, as for Coudenhove-Kalergi, the unification of Europe and the colonization of Africa are projects that presuppose one another.[14]

I could go on mentioning a number of other works containing similar arguments. All of them assert that Europe and Africa are two halves, each of them helpless on its own, but together forming a glorious whole, or even a new super power. However, nobody suggests that there is any symmetry between the halves, much less any equality. "Africa is the only continent without history," writes Guernier, after which he goes on to show what Europeans must and should do in order to have primitive and isolated Africa enter the circle of human culture.[15] As for Coudenhove-Kalergi, justifiably known as pacifist, internationalist, and anti-Nazi, he comes across as a full-fledged biological racist when he speaks about Africa. Not only does he state that Africa should be Europe's plantation, but also that "Africa is a tropical Europe," and that "Europe is Eurafrica's head, Africa its body." Coudenhove-Kalergi explains that this is because of the inherent difference between the black and white races. "As long as the black race is unable to develop and civilize its part of the earth, the white race must do it."[16] At the same time, he states that Europe must at all costs prevent "that great numbers of black workers and soldiers immigrate to Europe."[17]

We must note here that Coudenhove-Kalergi speaks of soldiers. He is probably thinking of France's disputed use of black troops in its occupations of the Rhineland and the Ruhr region. For just as unthinkable as it was having black soldiers operate as law keepers and masters of Germany's cities and towns, so was it on the other hand self-evidently necessary to have European physicians and engineers developing Africa. And just as natural as it was to fear these African troops for introducing disease, criminality, and vice, for raping women and children, so was it natural it was to believe that Africa, if left on its own, would self-destruct. Coudenhove-Kalergi asks what would become of Africa if Europe pulled out from it: "The answer is: chaos, anarchy, misery, war of all tribes against one another." [18]

This is where we are able to locate the deep structure of the interwar discourse on Eurafrica. It is a racist discourse that allows its user to reject African presence in Europe as an absurdity with the same ease as he affirms European presence in Africa as a necessity, without even having to consider the *possibility* that the position is self-contradictory.

All the above may strike the reader as curiosities or anecdotal history without any relevance to the present world order. However, during World War Two and after, Eurafrica remained a primary and often evoked aim for many European politicians and intellectuals. Within the so-called European movement, Eurafrica emerges as the very key to the economic rehabilitation of the European continent after 1945. Programs for Euro-African unity are developed by all the political camps within the European movement, from the socialists to the conservatives – and their ideas are picked up and assimilated in the so-called Strasbourg plan, which consists of a detailed investigation of all the benefits that the European states would enjoy if they made Africa, and the development of Africa, a common European cause.

In this new situation after World War Two, as European unification begins and institutions are founded for the purpose of European inter-state collaboration, the arguments persist from the interwar era, although the importance of the demographic argument, that Africa was to be settled by Europe's surplus population, is diminished. In many blueprints and sketches, Africa comes across as an engineer's dream, as a science-fiction utopia, or as a new planet to be claimed and cultivated, just as has happened in the Americas, and in the great technological leaps in Mao's China and Stalin's and Chrushev's Russia. For it is above all with the help of modern technology that Africa is now to be colonized and developed – or be made valuable, as the French expression has it: "la mise en valuer de l'Afrique." Also, the political and geopolitical arguments have lost none of their appeal by the 1950s. Those writing about this issue in the late 1940s and early 1950s see Eurafrica as the possibility for Western Europe to vie with the super powers. For them, Eurafrica means a third way – or what the British foreign minister Ernst Bevin called a "third force" – in the increasingly polarized world order of the cold war. It is even probable that the notion of the "third world", when it was coined by the French demographer, Alfred Sauvy in 1952, did not refer to the colonized and so-called "under-developed" world, but to all states and people – including Sauvy's own France and large parts of Europe – that were not yet aligned to either the United States or the Soviet Union. [19]

As I have stated earlier, however, this idea of Eurafrica as a third sphere is not a product of the cold war, but rather of the geopolitical paradigm in a more general sense, in which the world was divided into several spheres of influence or power blocks, and in which Eurafrica was already in the 1920s presented as an entity of its own, besides the British Empire, America, the Soviet Union, and Japan/China. The post-war image of Eurafrica as a third force entails a slight transformation of this paradigm. From the left, a European-African community is now presented as a genuine alternative to the two enemies of the cold war, in the sense that it consists of independent European states along with now independent former colonies – all of this in the spirit of the Bandung conference and the non-aligned movement. From the right, Eurafrica is presented as the great opportunity for the states of Western Europe: that the European states, through a more progressive and concerted colonialism, will contain Africa in their own sphere of influence and prevent it from falling prey to pan-Arabism and communism. Regardless of its variety, the idea of Eurafrica strongly influences intra-European debate and discussion on the possible means and ends of European integration.

What modified the discussion about Eurafrica was not just World War Two but also the decolonization process as such. In this new situation, Eurafrica becomes from a European perspective the solution to the problem as to how to accept the increasing autonomy or self-government of the colonies, while at the same time continuing to gain from them economically and strategically. To this scenario we must also add a specifically French perspective: in order to preserve its remaining empire and acquire funds for investment in the colonies, France wanted the support and aid of the other European states. In reality, this meant that France, around 1950, entered the negotiations on the creation of a European economic community on the explicit condition that the community should also include European collaboration in the French and Belgian colonial dominions, and also to some extent those of Italy and the Netherlands. Economic collaboration means that the other European states will get access to France's markets, including its overseas territories and dominions, or the whole area called Union Française. Thereby, however, France would lose the economic advantage it enjoyed through its monopoly position in trading with these territories, and in order to compensate for this it is only reasonable and fair that the European states would also share the costs for investing in the colonies of the French union. Some German opinion makers welcomed this prospect, because there are strong economic actors in West Germany that want access to the raw materials that have been difficult to attain ever since Germany's loss of its colonies in 1919.

All of this amounts to a complex structural and long-term political process. The result is that the negotiations about the integration of Europe, the formation of the European Economic Community and its predecessors, directly become connected to the negotiations on how to establish Eurafrica – and in these negotiations and the talk surrounding them, many factors are involved: the future of French and Belgian colonialism, the European efforts for enduring peace, the vitalization of Europe's economy, the effort to consolidate West-Africa as a military strategic zone, and – as a nice wrapping around all this – the effort to realize the highest ideals of European civilization by unselfishly disseminating European culture and learning to allegedly inferior peoples.

Africa was mentioned once in the so-called Schuman Declaration of 1950, which was confirmed as the foundation for the European Coal and Steel Community between France, Germany, Italy, and the Benelux countries, and which is commonly seen as the seed of the European Economic Community, or EEC, that was constituted through the Rome Treaty of 1957. The Rome Treaty, in turn, is today considered as the birth of the EU, the European Union.

Let me quote this important document by French foreign minister Schuman in 1950:

> The solidarity in production [of coal and steel] thus established will make it plain that any war between France and Germany becomes not merely unthinkable, but materially impossible. The setting up of this powerful productive unit, open to all countries willing to take part and bound ultimately to provide all the member countries with the basic elements of industrial production on the same terms, will lay a true foundation for their economic unification. This production will be offered to the world as a whole without distinction or exception, with the aim of contributing to raising living standards and to promoting peaceful achievements. With increased resources Europe will be able to pursue the achievement of one of its essential tasks, namely, the development of the African continent.

Why, we should ask, was it important to mention Africa in this document dealing with the regulation and monitoring of the production of coal and steel in six West European states? The answer, I claim, lies in the historical pattern I have sketched above. Since the 1920s, community and collaboration of Europe's states had presupposed their collaboration in Africa as well. Now, as this community of Coal and Steel was established, it was, according to the authors of the declaration important also to signal that it enabled the more far-reaching collaboration that had for long occupied debates on foreign policy and geopolitics.

Thus, the Coal and Steel Community was not just the seed of today's EU, but also of Eurafrica.

People in the 1950s were well aware of this. An influential German writer on foreign policy, Anton Zischka, remarked in a book from 1951 that the Ruhr area and the Rhineland is the "kernel of crystallization" of European integration.[20] The process once begun there as France and Germany realized that the future of both states depended on a mutual agreement and collaboration in the production of steel and coal would, according to Zischka, seamlessly lead to a similar agreement and collaboration as regards the exploitation of Africa's resources. Africa, argued Zischka in the title of his book, is thus "Europas Gemeinschaftsaufgabe Nr. 1", "Europe's common priority number one." Like many political thinkers and intellectuals, Zischka took it for granted that there was a direct connection between European integration and European colonization of Africa. It was the two sides of one and the same process, with Eurafrica as the result. Moreover, Zischka asserts that Eurafrica is a force of disarmament, which will appease the nuclear combatants of the cold war. Indeed, fate and nature are on Eurafrica's side, says Zischka. The creation of Eurafrica is simply the meaning of history, it is not a question of *if*, but *when*, it will come into existence.[21]

I have made a sketch in the foregoing, a sketch of a political, intellectual, and academic discourse that played a considerable role in European debate between 1920 and 1960. In this debate, a future European community or union was inseparable from a common and unified colonization of Africa. This is work in progress. Our thesis is that these ideas were instrumental in the actual, diplomatic and political constitution of the EU, or of Europe as a political subject. The origins of the EU cannot be separated from the perceived necessity to preserve and prolong the colonial system. The support of this hypothesis, however, I will have to save for a different occasion. What I wanted to do, here, was to give a sense of the history of the inequality that obtains still today between Europe and Africa. And the essentials remain as they were then: at least on the political level, just as self-evident that Europe must do everything to prevent African migrants from entering, just as self-evident it is that Europe feels the right to enter Africa. Let me conclude, then, with a more contemporary reference. Speaking in Dakar in 2007, French Nicholas Sarkozy demonstrated that Eurafrica still remains, in the visions of the most high-ranking European politicians, the manifest destiny of two continents.

La France souhaite l'unité de l'Afrique, car l'unité de l'Afrique rendra l'Afrique aux Africains.

Ce que veut faire la France avec l'Afrique, c'est regarder en face les réalités. C'est faire la politique des réalités et non plus la politique des mythes.

Ce que la France veut faire avec l'Afrique, c'est le co-développement, c'est-à-dire le développement partagé.

La France veut avec l'Afrique des projets communs, des pôles de compétitivité communs, des universités communes, des laboratoires communs.

Ce que la France veut faire avec l'Afrique, c'est élaborer une stratégie commune dans la mondialisation.

Ce que la France veut faire avec l'Afrique, c'est une politique d'immigration négociée ensemble, décidée ensemble pour que la jeunesse africaine puisse être accueillie en France et dans toute l'Europe avec dignité et avec respect.. Ce que la France veut faire avec l'Afrique, c'est une alliance de la jeunesse française et de la jeunesse africaine pour que le monde de demain soit un monde meilleur.

Ce que veut faire la France avec l'Afrique, c'est préparer l'avènement de *l'Eurafrique*, ce grand destin commun qui attend l'Europe et l'Afrique. A ceux qui, en Afrique, regardent avec méfiance ce grand projet de l'Union Méditerranéenne que la France a proposé à tous les pays riverains de la Méditerranée, je veux dire que, dans l'esprit de la France, il ne s'agit nullement de mettre à l'écart l'Afrique, qui s'étend au sud du Sahara mais, qu'au contraire, il s'agit de faire de cette Union le pivot de *l'Eurafrique*, la première étapelus grand rêve de paix et de prospérité qu'Européens et Africains sont capables de concevoir ensemble.

------

* This article is part of a larger research project under the directorship of Professor Peo Hansen at Linköping University. I thank Peo for having rediscovered the repressed connection between European integration and European colonialism. Thanks also to the Swedish Research Council – Vetenskapsrådet – which is supporting this project.

**Notes and References**

[1] C. Koller, *'Von Wilden aller Rassen niedergemetzelt: Die Diskussion um die Verwendung von Kolonialtruppen in Europa zwischen Rassismus, Kolonial- und Militärpolitik (1914–1930)*. Stuttgart: Franz Steiner Verlag 2001, pp.476.

[2] Cited in C. Koller 2001: 213 ("Am Main ist der französische Militarismus eingerückt wie in Feindesland. Senegalneger liegen in der Frankfurter Universität und bewachen das Goethehaus.")

[3] Friedrich Ebert, 2001, *Schriften, Aufzeichnungen, Reden*, vol. 2 (Darmstadt, 1926), 290. Citerad I. Koller, 2001: 324, "Dass die Verwendung farbiger Truppen niederster Kultur als Aufseher über eine Bevölkerung von der hohen geistigen und wirtschaftlichen Bedeutung der Rheinländer eine herausfordernde Verletzung der Gesetze der europäischer Zivilisation ist, […]."

[4] Klaus Theweleit, *Männerphantasien*, vol. 1, Frauen, Fluten, Körper, Geschichte (2:a upplagan, München & Zürich: Piper Verlag, 2000), 1001.

[5] Heinrich Mann, "Anfänge Europas", *Sieben Jahre Chronik der Gedanken und Vorgänge: Essays*, red. Peter-Paul Schneider (Frankfurt am Main: Fischer Taschebuch Verlag, 1994), 114: "Will Europa denn eins werden: zuerst wir Beide! Wir sind die Wurzel. Aus uns der geeinte Kontinent, die anderen können nicht anders, als uns folgen. Wir tragen die Verantwortung für uns und für den Rest. Durch uns wird ein Reich sein über den Reichen, und das Reich wird dauern. Oder keine Zukunft gilt mehr für uns, noch für Europa."

[6] Richard N. Coudenhove-Kalergi, *Paneuro pa* [1923] (andra upplagan, Wien & Leipzig: Paneuropa-Verlag, 1926), 107-122: "Aus derfurchtbaren Krise, in der sich heute Deutschland und Frankreich befinden, werden sie entweder als verbündete Europäer hervorgehen – oder aber sie werden, ineinander verbissen, an den gegenseitigen Wunden verbluten."

[7] Walter Lipgens, *A History of European Integration*, vol. 1, 1945-47: The Formation of the European Unity Movement, övers. från tyskan P.S. Falla och A. J. Ryder (Oxford: Clarendon Press, 1982), 38.

[8] Richard N. Coudenhove-Kalergi, "Afrika", *Paneuropa* 5 (nr. 2, 1929), 3: "Afrika könnte Europa Rohstoffe für seine Industrie, Nahrungsmittel für seine Bevölkerung, Siedlungsraum für seine Übervölkerung, Arbeitsmöglichkeiten für seine Arbeitslosigkeit, Märkte für seinen Absatz bieten."

[9] Richard N. Coudenhove-Kalergi, "Afrika", *Paneuropa* 5 (1929), nr. 2, 18: "So führt uns das afrikanische Problem zurück zu Europa. Afrika kann nicht erschlossen werden, wenn Europa sich nicht einigt."

[10] See, for example, Richard N. Coudenhove-Kalergi, "Reparationen und Kolonien", *Paneuropa* 8 (1932), nr. 1, 7-11.

[11] Heinrich Mann, "Paneuropa, Traum und Wirklichkeit," *Sieben JahrebChronik der Gedanken und Vorgänge: Essays*, red. Peter-Paul Schneider (Frankfurt am Main: Fischer Taschebuch Verlag, 1994), 347-348.

[12] Herman Sörgel, *Atlantropa* (Munich: Piloty and Loehle; Zürich: Fretz and Wasmuth, 1932), 106. For an analysis of Sörgel's project, see Alexander Gall, *Das Atlantropa-Projekt: Die Geschichte einer gescheiterten Vision. Herman Sörgel und die Absenkung des Mittelmeers* (Frankfurt am Main: Campus Verlag, 1998).

[13] E. L. Guernier, *L'Afrique: Champ d'expansion de l'Europe* (Paris: Armand Colin, 1933), vii: "La colonisation d'aujourd'hui est la synthèse d'une oeuvre morale et hautement civilisatrice: l'élévation graduelle du *standing* de vie des races non évoluées, - et d'une oeuvre non moins humaine: le maintien, sinon l'améliriation constante des conditions de vie d'une Europe au travail."

[14] The correspondence between Guernier's and Coudenhove-Kalergi's ideas are underlined by the fact that Guernier publishes

in Coudenhove-Kalergi's journal. See E. L. Guernier, "Afrika als Kolonisationsland," *Paneuropa* 11 (nr. 1, 1935), 7-11.

15 E.-L. Guernier, *L'Afrique: Champ d'expansion de l'Europe* (Paris: Armand Colin, 1933), 55.

16 Richard N. Coudenhove-Kalergi, "Afrika," *Paneuropa* 5 (nr. 2, 1929), 5: "Afrika ist das tropische Europa" – "Afrika ist der Kopf Eurafrikas – Afrika dessen Körper." – "Solange der schwarze rasse nicht in der Lage ist, ihren Erdteil zu erschließen und zu zivilisieren, muß die weiße Rasse es tun."

17 Richard N. Coudenhove-Kalergi, "Afrika", *Paneuropa* 5 (nr. 2, 1929), 5: "daß schwarze Arbeiter und Soldaten in größerer Zahl nach Europa einwandern."

18 Richard N. Coudenhove-Kalergi, "Afrika", *Paneuropa* 5 (nr. 2, 1929), 6: "Die Antwort ist: Chaos, Anarchie, Seuchen, Kampf der Stämme untereinander."

19 Albert Sauvy, "Trois mondes, une planète", *L'Observateur* 1952 (August 14).

20 Anton Zischka, *Afrika: Europas Gemeinschaftsaufgabe Nr. 1.* Oldenburg: Gerhard Stalling Verlag, 1951), 312.

21 Anton Zischka, *Afrika: Europas Gemeinschaftsaufgabe Nr. 1* Oldenburg: Gerhard Stalling Verlag, 1951), 325.

# Moral Energy and What Looks Like Life in African Popular Culture*
## - Karin Barber

I want to speak about two striking and interrelated features that I have noted in accounts of popular culture right across the African continent, and over a long time span of more than a hundred years. My purpose is to explore the relationship between these two features. The first is the well-documented emergence, from the second half of the nineteenth century onwards, of new styles of representation which look, at least at first sight, like "realism". That is to say, narratives are often set in recognisable everyday life, revolve around recognisable everyday people – not gods and heroes – and unfold according to everyday logics of cause and effect, not bizarre coincidence or the operations of a *deus ex machina*. More importantly, these new styles of representation dwell on the *details* of that everyday life, using specific techniques of representation to produce lifelikeness. The emergence of this style went hand in hand with the appearance of new genres: the novel; the newspaper; rectangular two-dimensional figurative portable paintings; stage and television dramas where an extended, elaborate narrative is carried entirely through the speech and actions of the characters, not by a narrator. All these forms were new, and appeared in Africa only from the late nineteenth century onwards. And they seem strikingly similar across the continent. In Europe and America, the counterparts of these forms wereall associated with realism.

Balzac inaugurated a particular tradition of discussions of realism in the nineteenth century by proclaiming, in the opening pages of *Le Père Goriot*, "Ah! sachez-le: ce drame n'est ni une fiction, ni un roman. *All is true,* il est si véritable que chacun peut en reconnoitre les élé-ments chez soi, dans son coeur peut-etre". I'll come back to this theme of *recognition* of the truth of the text in one's own experience. The point for the moment is that Balzac's apparently naive (but actually very cunning) claim soon led to a discussion of the *artifices* of realism, the rhetorical means by which an illusion of reality is created, and the numerous ways in which this effect of reality can be combined with symbolic, archetypal or melodramatic modes.[1] Realism is a literary style – or a spectrum of related styles; like other literary styles, it makes claims about what is worth representing and what representation consists of. For my purposes, the most useful discussion is still Ian Watt's, in his great book *The Rise of the Novel* (1957), in which he identifies as the hallmarks of realism *particularities of time, place and characterisation:* realistic novels offer specific, plausible details which seem to correspond to real experience: narratives are set, by implication, in a particular year, a particular city; the characters speak with the idiosyncrasies that characterise individual personal expression, not (for example) in the uniformly elevated poetic diction deemed appropriate to heroic drama. The emergence of this style has been linked, by (among others) Charles Taylor in his *Sources of the Self: the Making of the Modern Identity,* to a new Enlightenment focus on the interiority and personal experience of the individual, on the one hand, and a new interest in and positive valuation of ordinary life and the everyday for its own sake on the other.

In Africa, representations that "look like life" are well known throughout the continent. Onitsha market literature's graphic evocations of modern city life in Nigeria, depicting the lives of clerks and schoolgirls and the expansion of the cash economy; Tanzanian and Malawian popular plays, depicting the familiar predicaments of ordinary families (money worries, keeping up with the neighbours, a drunken husband, trouble with the in-laws); popular painting in Shaba, Zaire, with its meticulous attention to details of clothing, furniture, wristwatches, where a high value is apparently placed on exactitude.

The second feature, however, is at odds with the Western nineteenth-century aesthetic of realism, insofar as this concerns a positive evaluation of individual specificity and the details of ordinary life *for their own sake.* Popular culture throughout Africa is saturated with moralising. Ordinary life is not depicted because it is worthy or interesting in itself, but because it provides a vehicle of great impact and immediacy for the purpose of driving home moral lessons which the audience can appropriate and apply to their own lives. The moralising imperative is generally ignored by Western scholars of African popular culture because it is distasteful, boring or embarrassing. Yes: moralising can be tedious. But it is everywhere. Both performers and audiences insist, over and over again in relation to numerous genres, on the central place of the moral lesson that the text or performance imparts. In northern Nigeria, according to Graham Furniss, a key factor in the "dynamic, expanding, adaptive nature of Hausa culture is … the strength of its moral discourse" (Furniss 1996:214). In Ghana, television audiences overwhelmingly assert that they watch TV drama for the sake of the moral lesson (Ametewee 1993). And it is touching to learn that the young rap artists innovatively producing Bongo Flava in Tanzania and *le rap Dakarois* in Senegal, though outwardly modelled on the aggressive, anti-social styles of American gangsta rap, are often actually warning even younger fans of the dangers of promiscuity, or calling on public-spirited citizens to clean up the streets.

My purpose here is to draw attention to the relationship in African popular culture between apparent "realism" and in-your-face "moralising". This leads to the question: What difference does this mode of discourse make? What implications does it have for social, political and cultural conditions in Africa?

To develop my theme I will look at three examples. I could have drawn these from the rich and detailed documentation now being produced by scholars in all parts of Africa. As it happens, however, all three come from my own work on Yoruba print and performance genres: if only because these examples are the ones I have reflected upon longest and feel most familiar with. They date from three successive moments in the history of Yoruba oral and written textual production.

### The "first" Yoruba novel

The text usually described as the first Yoruba novel stands at the head of what is now a huge, diverse written literature in Yoruba. *Itan Emi Segilola* was written by a newspaper editor-proprietor, Isaac B.

Thomas, in Lagos, and published in weekly instalments in Thomas's newspaper *Akede Eko* from July 1929 to March 1930. The full title was *Itan Emi Segilola, Eleyinju Ege, Elegberun Oko Laiye* (The Life story of me, Segilola, endowed with fascinating eyes, the lover of a thousand men). It purports to be a series of letters to the editor from an ageing and repentant adventuress or harlot. Now stricken with disease and destitution and facing imminent death, she recounts the story of her youthful exploits with glee as well as with pious regret.

The reality effect of this narrative is overwhelming: so much so, that many readers were apparently convinced that the letters were literally true and really written by an ageing seductress. Yet I.B.Thomas is playing a cunning game of revelation and concealment, procrastination and teasing, hinting at scandalous true information which he constantly dangles and withholds.

The story is set in Lagos, then the commercial and administrative capital of Nigeria, full of immigrants pursuing trade rather than agriculture, and with an exceptionally high literacy rate and large white-collar population. Particularities of time and place abound.

First, the narrative evokes the city with numerous references to real street names, buildings, churches and local personalities. Segilola says she was born and still lives in Popo Imaro; she loses her virginity, shockingly, to a medicine man who lived "on Oke Popo road near the Durosinmi compound" (and "some of the elders who are still alive today will not fail to recall a medicine man called Olojo on Oke-Popo Road"); she got married in the Cathedral Church at Ehingbeti, and so on.

Second, the narrative is locked into real time. One of the things Lagos newspaper editors saw as a key innovation and benefit of the newspaper was its secure dating of events as they happened – as this would nail things down and provide reliable data for future historians. The temporality of Segilola's story coincides with the actual dates of publication: thus, for instance, she states that she was born on 9 September 1882, and in an episode published during the autumn of 1929 she mentions having recently passed her 47th birthday. She also teases the readers with dates: she reveals that her wedding was on 6th November, but that she cannot give the year, for if she did, lots of people, especially older people, would remember the wedding and would be able to identify her and expose her to public humiliation. However, she will give us a hint – it was ten years before a famous incident when a man called Yesufa climbed onto his roof and shot at passers-by, giving rise to a popular song "An old man becomes a hunter, a murderous hunter of human beings".

Third, this last example illustrates another technique of I.B.Thomas's, the planting in the narrative of episodes from living popular memory. Presumably Yesufa's murderous outburst was something people did remember (this could be checked, by searching the newspapers of c.1912: something I have yet to do) and the popular song which commemorated it was one of many such which would have been remembered by I.B.Thomas's readers, and which were often re-published as free-standing items of cultural interest in the various Yoruba-language newspapers, having been sent in by readers.

Fourth, as we have seen, Segilola continually hints that real, still-living, prominent Lagosians were involved in her sleazy tale: and threatens that if she revealed their identity she would cause a major scandal. And finally, the epistolary form itself participates in the texture of the current public discourse of the time. The newspapers were largely made up of letter-like texts. I.B.Thomas wrote an open letter to a different prominent Lagos personality each week, urging him or her to take action on various points of public concern; contributors of regular columns almost always presented them in the form of letters to the editor; there were also letters from readers. The Segilola sequence, therefore, would strike readers as the normal, and indeed main, mode of communicating information and opinion – rather than as a fictional device.

This was not the first serialised narrative in the history of Yoruba print culture – the editor of *Eleti Ofe* had produced twelve episodes of a first-person narrative in 1924, which then came to an abrupt stop mid-stream and was apparently never finished (though, tantalisingly, I have found an advertisement in *Akede Eko* for a pamphlet version of this story in 1931, which suggests that it was eventually completed). But *Segilola* was the first work of fiction to take epistolary form. It was inserted into a context where the letter – self-evidently associated with literacy and the new clerkly and professional classes emerging in Lagos – was the principal vehicle for the discussion of local on-going political, social and cultural events in the city (and, increasingly through the 1920s, in the "provinces" too).

I.B.Thomas went out of his way to reinforce the effect of reality. In an editorial of August 22, 1929, when the Segilola story was entering its seventh week, he describes how the narrative came to be published in his paper:

> *Awa ko fi igbakan lo be alagba obinrin yi l'owe lati ma wa ko itan igbesi-aiye re sinu iwe irohin wa yi fun gbogbo araiye ka, sugbon funrare ni obinrin na to wa wa l'asale ale ojo Saturday kan ninu Office wa ti o si mu imoran nato wa wa lati ma se be; anu obinrin na si se wa pupo l'asale ojo na nigbati o t'enu bo oro lati ma so ohun ti mu on lati fo ma ko itan igbesi-aiye on na sinu iwe irohin....*[2]

We didn't at any time go to ask this elderly woman to write the story of her life in our newspaper for the whole world to read, but the woman came looking for us in our *Office* one Saturday evening of her own accord, and she was the one who proposed the idea; we felt very sorry for the woman that evening when she began to explain why she wanted to write the story of her life in the newspaper...

Moreover, he personally testifies to the truth of her story, asserting that he himself was not too young to be able to remember the days when Segilola's beauty was dazzling, "in this city of Lagos where both of us were born".

It seems that readers were taken in. One correspondent, signing herself "Jumoke" but emphasising that this was a pseudonym, states that all the details of Segilola's story were true: she can confirm this, because she too was a prostitute in Lagos before she repented and reformed. Moved by Segilola's plight she sends 10/- to the editor to pass on to her for the alleviation of her sufferings. A correspondent calling himself "D.A.L." writes an open letter to Segilola in November 1929: he takes his hat off to her, thanks her for her story, prays that God will forgive her; and observes that when the letters first began to come out, he thought the editor of Akede Eko was having a joke; but then he began to notice the names, places times and all kinds of other things, and this banished all his doubts and convinced him that it was all true. He has some questions for her, but they are not things that can be asked in this letter, so he would be very happy if she would allow him to meet her, if he undertakes not to reveal her name… Several other readers wrote in begging to be told the secret of Segilola's real identity. One, a well-known Ijêbu popular poet, even wrote a song, pleading "Akede Eko mo be nyin l'owe k'oruko Segilola to mi lowo" (Akede Eko, I ask you as a favour to write down Segilola's name and send it to me). But I.B.Thomas reports that he is not at liberty to divulge this information:

Aimoye awon ore wa yala ni'le tabi ni idale ni nwon to wa wa tabi ti nwon ko iwe si wa lati be wa pe awon fe lati mo oruko abiso tabi adugbo ti "Segilola Eleyin'ju ege na ngbe ni igboro ilu Eko wa yi? Sugbon anu nla lo se wa pupo fun pe awa to se ileri pelu ibura wa fun alagba obinrin to nko itan igbesi-aiye re na pe bi osan fe pada di oru, awa ko ni fi igbakan tuna asiri oruko abiso alagba obinrin na si eti 'gbo enikan…

Countless friends whether at home or abroad have been seeking us out or writing to us to beg us to tell them the first name or the neigh-bourhood where "Segilola of the Fascinating Eyes" lives in this city of Lagos of ours. But we're very sorry to say that we promised and indeed solemnly swore to this elderly woman who is writing her life-story that even if day turns to night we will never expose the secret of her name to anyone…[3]

This story was a sensational success. It spawned numerous letters, commentaries, columns criticising Lagos women, and a clamour for a translation into English, which I.B.Thomas duly produced and serialised the following year. The Yoruba version, immediately after the end of its serialisation, was also republished as a book, generating further controversy and a denunciation from the conservative English language *Nigerian Daily Times*. This novel, though long out of print, has influenced three generations of Yoruba writers, is still fondly remembered by elderly readers, and was recently broadcast in serial form on radio. The effect of reality that it pioneered was not immediately taken up by succeeding writers: D.O.Fagunwa's mesmerisingly imaginative heroic fantasies dominated the Yoruba prose tradition from the late 1930s to the late 1950s. But then the depiction of everyday actuality – including the seamy side of life that featured so strongly in *Segilola* – became fashionable again, and for the last fifty years has coexisted with an ever-expanding range of other modes and styles.

So this mimicry of the real was a major innovation which, at the very beginning of the history of the Yoruba novel, was extraordinarily intense – to the extent that readers were actually taken in. But that is only half the story. Equally intense is Segilola's moralising. She announces in her very first letter that she is telling her shameful story "for the whole world to read" for only one reason: the hope that

> *emi le se ore kan sile nigb'ehin ojo aiye mi yi to kun fun osi on are nipa pe boya emi yio ri awon ologbon die, yala ninu awon odomo-kunrin tabi papa gidi ninu awon odomobinrin ti nwon yio wo apere emi "Segilola Eleyinju Ege" k'ogbon, ki nwon ma ba kedun igbehin ojo aiye won na pelu omi'je kikoro l'oju won, gegebi emi "Segilola Eleyin'ju Ege" ti nke abamo l'oni yi: sugbon ti epa abamo kike mi na ko tun ba oro fun mi mo.*

> I may be able to do a good deed at the close of this life of mine which is full of misery and wretchedness, in that I may find a few wise ones, either among the young boys or more particularly among the young girls who will learn wisdom from the example of me, "Segilola of the Fascinating Eyes", so that they do not lament in their last days with bitter tears in their eyes, as I "Segilola of the Fascinating Eyes" am repenting today: but in vain, for in my case the antidote of my regret can no longer neutralise the poison [of my misspent life].

And she reiterates this pious hope in virtually every episode. The impression of reality that I.B.Thomas so successfully creates does not seem to be a depiction of Lagos life and times for its own sake, as an object inherently worthy of attention and interest. Rather, it seems intended to create a vivid impact in order to impress the urgency of the moral lesson on the mind of the reader. It's real! It's true! It's horrifying! and, above all, it could happen to you if you don't mend your ways. Lifelikeness serves to make the truth of the moral example stare you in the face.

And this interpretation was warmly endorsed by all the readers and commentators who wrote about it. In his letter, "D.A.L.", who said the real-life detail convinced him the story was all true, added that it also convinced him "that her life-story is full of lessons – lessons for parents, both mothers and fathers – for old and young, and above all for those who call themselves prominent ladies, high-lifers, good-timers – in due course they'll be forgotten, they'll be people we look at to spit upon… a great lesson for girls and married women, and even more for our young ladies, I can't say how delighted I am with your story…"[4] In this and other responses, the life-likeness and moral lesson seem to be absolutely inseparable.

So how do people take up these moral lessons they so eagerly identify? My second example, the Yoruba popular travelling theatre, sheds some light.

### The improvised popular theatre

Modern Yoruba popular travelling theatre emerged in the 1940s from "Native Air Operas", that is, dramatisations of Biblical stories with a predominantly or entirely sung text and stylised movements, staged by church choirs to attract people to the congregation and to raise funds for religious purposes. So successful were these dramas that enterprising actor-managers, chief among them Hubert Ogunde, were able very quickly to move out of the church and establish secular, professional, commercial travelling theatres producing plays on a wide variety of themes, ranging from folkloric tales to anti-colonial polemics and crime thrillers set in the contemporary underworld. By the early 1980s, when this theatre was in its heyday, there were over a hundred travelling theatre companies, each with a repertoire of half a dozen or more plays and a company of actors, actresses, drummers, drivers, and technicians (for the stage lights and sound system, vital to the success of any production) numbering ten, twenty or more members. In the process of secularisation and expansion, spoken dialogue gradually replaced most of the sung text, and fluid, lifelike representations of everyday characters replaced the stylised and ratherstatic cho-reographed Biblical characters.

Sêgilôla is lifelike because of her individual, urgent speaking voice, addressing the newspaper editor and, over his shoulder, the newspaper's reading public; the popular theatre was lifelike because it portrayed the interaction of characters as if their lives were conducted independently of the audience, and existed before and after the moment of the spectacle – creating the illusion of an on-going process on which the audience were merely eavesdropping. This illusionistic mode always co-existed with and was often thoroughly shot through by more presentational and openly theatrical styles, and some theatre companies developed it further than others. But all of them used the flow of natural-sounding speech to establish character and unfold the narrative, so that it seemed as if the people on stage were authoring themselves.

The Oyin Adejobi Theatre Company, one of the longest-established and most successful companies, excelled at generating a flowing, rippling stream of detail, some of which was necessary to the development of the plot, and some of which was not, but was extraneous, introduced by the improvisation of actors who drew on details of their own experience and memory to create effects resembling ordinary, recognisable local life. One of their most popular and long-lived plays, *Kuye,* which was originally created in about 1964 and which was still in their repertoire in the early 1980s, having undergone countless revisions and transformations over the years, opens with the entrance of an old woman, followed by a young boy. The old woman stops in the middle of the stage and says (my translation):

> What a bloody fool I am, what on earth am I thinking of? I've gone and forgotten the very thing I was supposed to be bringing along with me. Look, Kuye, you run back home and fetch it for me. When you get there, you'll see those clothes there. Look, Kuye! Kuye!! [Barber 2000:353]

Thus the play starts right in the middle of an existing situation. Only gradually do we, the audience, deduce that the woman is the unkind aunt of the deaf and dumb orphan Kuyê, planning to sell Kuyê's father's only legacy, his valuable handwoven robes, to an itinerant trader. This opening creates the unmistakable sense that the situation we encounter when the curtain opens pre-existed the moment of depiction. We start in the middle, and the preceding story is artfully introduced as if through the spontaneous remarks of the interacting characters. This is the effect of the "fourth wall", a central characteristic of nineteenth-century realism in the theatre, where the action unfolds as if in a private room, one wall of which has been removed so that the audience can eavesdrop. It is significant that the Yoruba theatre companies, although they also used a host of nonrealist modes and techniques of presentation, always performed on a front-facing platform stage in a bicameral auditorium (never in the round), and always used space as if they were behind a proscenium arch even when the church hall or hotel yard offered no such amenity. Their fundamental mode, which they emphasised in contradistinction to the older but still thriving art of the masquerade, was the conventional representation of lifelike situations, presented in the form of a picture to an audience who sat in rows facing the stage.

Bakhtin, in a wonderfully fresh discussion of early Greek prose romances, suggested that the unreal time and featureless abstract expanses of space against which the narratives unfolded was intimately connected to the plots full of coincidences and discontinuities. Concretisation – embedding a narrative in specific time, place and culture – limits the operation of chance in the later development of the novel. The representation of "the indigenous reality surrounding one" eliminates the possibility of free-wheeling plots where effects are unrelated to causes (Bakhtin 1981:100). This suggests the possibility that the Oyin Adejobi Theatre Company set their plays in a rich environment of recognisable, everyday detail precisely to eliminate randomness and to demonstrate that every action has determinate, unavoidable effects. This made the narrative more effective as a moral example. The more specific, local and idiosyncratic the detail, the more generically the moral could be applied.

And audiences unanimously spoke of the Yoruba popular theatre as, above all, sources of moral example. Everyone said "Others may come to laugh and have a good time, but *I* come to pick a lesson I can use in my life". Audience members took responsibility for their own edification: they did not receive wisdom so much as quarry it our of the narrative by their own efforts, and each segment of a mixed audience would extract the lesson that applied most closely to their own personal circumstances.

Thus, in a rather unpleasant play called *Oko Iyawo* (Bridegroom), the married men in the audience said that the most important character in the play was the husband (the "bridegroom" of the title) who rashly marries a second, younger, very wealthy and domineering wife whose greed and disrespect for the elders of her family leads to a catastrophic outcome for her husband as well as herself. The moral of the narrative, in the view of these men, was that one should investigate carefully before marrying a second wife, and should certainly never favour the junior wife over the senior. A young married woman told me that the most important character was Mosun, the second wife: "she is the one who makes everything happen", and that her actions embodied an important lesson for all young women: "we must respect our senior wives, and not use our husband's favour to domineer over them". A young unmarried man, however, told me emphatically that the lesson of the play for him was that one should not marry at all! Each of these respondents began their commentaryby saying "The play was very important, particularly for us married men [or young wives, unmarried men etc.], and especially for *me…*"

And in this mode of moralising, the distinction between factual and fictional narrative becomes secondary, as my final example shows.

**The modern Yoruba newspaper**
*Alaroye,* one of several Yoruba-language weekly newspapers flourishing in the 1990s and 2000s, purports to be reporting factual items – accounts of things that actually happened in local communities. No doubt most of the things they reported did happen. But that does not affect the function of the narrative, which is very often, like that of *The Life-story of me, Segilola* and *Oko Iyawo,* to anchor a moral paradigm. A report on a fatal accident in a local school begins (my

translation) "Bad times tend to pass by every day, they go round, they circulate; the prayer of young and old is that they don't come face to face with misfortune". It continues

> When Mrs Grace Adedoyin Ayankoya woke up early on Thursday morning last week, her prayer was that when she went out she should not meet trouble, that God would grant that she came back safely home. But fate and destiny never miss their mark...

The report then describes what happened: a man was mowing the grass outside the school building, watched by some of the teachers. The lawnmower was defective; a blade became detached, flew out and struck Mrs Ayankoya, killing her. Having briefly explained this, the newspaper report goes on to describe Mrs Ayankoya's husband's forebodings caused by a dream about death – but which he wrongly interpreted as applying to his mother not his wife – and his philosophical comments after the event. Thus the terrible incident reported in this newspaper item serves as the exemplification of a wider truth which applies to us all. Whether it is fact or fiction is secondary: its main function is to furnish an example.

### Morals and examples

In all three cases, the effect of lifelikeness cannot be understood as "realism" in the standard sense of a representation of the quotidian for its own sake; rather, the purpose of lifelikeness is to make an example of behaviour and its consequences more telling, more incontrovertible, to anchor it more firmly in a recognisable world in order to sustain a moral interpretation of the world. In all three cases, members of the audience must produce meaning for themselves by applying the example to their own situations. This means that the lifelike specificity is first converted to a generic model and then re-specified by application to a concrete situation – like a proverb.

So what is the nature of the morality that these genres are structured to impart, and that audiences are primed to extract? At first sight, it looks like a narrowly personal morality: individuals extract it to apply to their own lives. And often it looks specifically like a sexual morality, and a conservative one at that. The trend is to blame the woman (Segilola deserved what she got because she ignored her mother's advice; Mosun's greed and disrespect was what brought disaster on the whole family); to blame the poor (they deserve their poverty because they are lazy); and to counsel patient acceptance of fate (the article on the lawnmower accident, in striking contrast to the way such an accident would be reported in the British press, for example, does not ask "Why was that defective lawnmower not fixed?"). The causes of bad situations are often traced to the behaviour and attitudes of individuals, rather than to collective or structural causes such as social injustice, deprivation, lack of education or inequality.

This pattern brings to mind a distinction made by Latin American conscientisation theorists between two terms, sometimes translated as "people's" and "truly popular". People's culture emanates spontaneously from the ordinary people but is not in their true interests; truly popular culture usually needs to be catalysed by radical intellectuals from outside the community, but because it opens people's eyes to the causes of their oppression it is in their real interests.

If we were to apply this distinction to the form of moral representation that I have been discussing, I don't think there's much doubt that we would place it in the "people's culture" category. Forms like the Yoruba popular newspaper and theatre – along with Onitsha market literature, the Nairobi popular novel, the Tanzanian variety show, the Ghanaian concert party and innumerable other well-documented genres – all seem to mobilise lifelikeness in order to furnish a conservative, personal morality. In this they are sharply distinguishable from those more radical, critical genres that confront power, inequality and injustice head-on and call for collective effort to bring about change: the *chimurenga* songs of the Zimbabwean liberation war, the Kamiriithu conscientisation theatre in Kenya, outright political attacks on military dictators launched by Yoruba media poets in the 1990s. Within the framework of conscientisation theory, there is quite a tradition of examining "people's" culture genres and finding them wanting – unless covert or oblique social criticism can be detected within them.

However, we may need to rethink this distinction – as we have already rethought distinctions between "traditional", "popular"

and "elite" – in order to produce a model which is more sensitive
to local perceptions and usages on the ground. My impression from
talking to the producers and consumers of popular cultural forms
in Africa is that, almost always, the apparently individual personal morality *encompasses* the political – reminding politicians that
moral standards are shared, and apply to them as much as to us,
and that no one is exempt from the requirements of decency and
respect. Leaders are accountable for their own actions – the blame
cannot be shifted onto history or circumstances – and it is their
responsibility to find the right path and follow it. James Ferguson,
in his wonderful book *Global Shadows*, comments on "an idea that
keeps cropping up in the ethnography of Africa": the idea "that all
of the world, even the natural, bears the traces of human agency".
He cites the famous example, from Evans-Pritchard's *Witchcraft,
Oracles and Magic among the Azande*, of the person sitting under a
granary which collapses and kills him. Of course people know that
the granary collapsed because it had been eaten away by termites;
but why at that particular moment? Why was this man killed and
not another? "Who sent the termites?" The Azande seek a human
explanation underlying the perfectly-well understood natural or
mechanical causes of events in the environment. Ferguson goes
on to say:

> ...what is true of mortal fate is also true of economic and politi-
> cal destinies. Not only among the Azande, but throughout the
> region, disparities of power and wealth, like fluke accidents,
> never "just happen"; they demand to be explained in terms of
> meaningful human agency (Ferguson 2006:74).

And this search for human causes is not confined to "traditional"
settings: "Capitalist forms of accumulation and modern state economic activities are very widely understood in similar terms" (*ibid.*).
Those who "eat power" and grow fat at others' expense are held
responsible for their own actions.

This human-centred morality clearly has its drawbacks. Anyone
who has seen road accidents consistently attributed to witchcraft
will know this. Why can't people forget about the putative malevo-

lence of their fellow-road users, and just drive more carefully?[5] But at its most positive, this human-centric morality is of a piece with the determined efforts of self-development undertaken by communities who expect no support from the state – home town associations that tax their members to build a local dispensary, bridge or school. It is a "do-it-yourself ", "start-from-home" morality which says that everyone is responsible because everyone is human. And this is why there is such emphasis on the active work of the audience. It is up to them to find the lesson and apply it to their lives: they do not expect anyone else to do it for them. That is how moral examples work. Like a proverb, an example is only half the story: the other half is its appropriation and application.

Popular culture's moralising offers a perspective on the conditions in which we live which is weak on structural analysis. It is not, after all, true that corruption is purely the aggregate outcome of indivi-dual, personal moral failings: as Dan Smith has shown, it is syste-matic, a pervasive environment from which it may be impossible for even the best-intentioned individual to break free (Smith 2007). Living chastely will not make the state less unjust. But in British popular culture we experience the opposite weakness. In a feature on shoplifting in a national British newspaper a few months ago, a female interviewee, explaining that she wanted to provide her son with electronic games and clothes, told the interviewer, with ob-vious sincerity, "I'm not a thief. If the state had provided support, this would not have happened. It was a cry for help". If blaming the individual for systemic ills is one cliché, blaming the system for individual misbehaviour is another – its mirror-image.

### Notes
[1] It's important to note that even the representatives of the high point of 19th century European realism incorporated strong non-realist dimensions. In drama, Ibsen's representations of middle class life, evoked with a fidelity that astonished his audiences, nonetheless served increasingly symbolic purposes. In fiction, Henry James's almost excruciating attention to social nuance was, Peter Brooks has argued, fundamentally melodramatic (Brooks 1976).

[2] In all quotations, I reproduce the original orthography of *Akede Eko*. This rarely used tone-marks, and its conventions for word-breaks and elisions were slightly different from those of modern orthography.

[3] The question arises as to how many of these "readers' letters" were actually written by I.B.Thomas himself. This is difficult to judge. However, some of them use slightly different orthographic conventions and dialect forms from I.B.Thomas's own, suggesting independent authorship. They could still have been written at his instigation or with his encouragement – and given his energetic cultivation of correspondents all over the country, and his urgent need to make *Akede Eko* the centre of attention when he was in financial difficulties, this is certainly a strong possibility. It's unlikely, however, that he dictated the terms in which these correspondents expressed themselves, and that is the point at issue here.

[4] Most readers follow Segilola's own lead in affirming that the story contains moral lessons for everyone – men as well as women. Perhaps the lesson to men is primarily that they should avoid women like Segilola. But the connotations of the term *panságà*, which is the one most often applied to Segilola, are not confined to prostitution alone: its wider meaning includes loose living, debauchery, and womanising, and there are strong suggestions that men as well as women engaged in sex for money or other material gain in 1920s Lagos. However, the massive weight of condemnation is undoubtedly tilted towards women, whose deceitful exploitation of their sexuality is treated as both the symptom and the cause of the corruption of modern life.

[5] This example also reveals a further conundrum concerning responsibility. Blaming witches for road accidents does seek a human cause, as Ferguson's argument suggests: but it shifts the blame away from another human cause – the bad driving. And it substitutes a mystical remedy (divination, sacrifice, *juju*) for a non-mystical one (driving more carefully).

**References**

Ametewee, Awo Mana 1993 "Akan drama on GBC television as a tool for the education of adults in selected parts of the Accra metropolis". M.Phil dissertation, University of Ghana, Legon.

Balzac, Honoré de 1961 [1834] *Le Père Goriot*. Paris: Éditions Gallimard.

Barber, Karin 2000 *The Generation of Plays: Yoruba popular life in theatre*. Bloomington, IndianaUniversity Press.

Bakhtin, M.M. 1981 "Forms of time and of the chronotope in the novel: notes toward a Historical Poetics." In *The Dialogic Imagination*, ed. Michael Holquist, trans. Caryl Emerson and Michael Holquist. Austin, Texas: University of Texas Press (84-258).

Brooks, Peter 1976 *The Melodramatic Imagination: Balzac, Henry James, melodrama and the mode of excess*. New Haven CT: Yale University Press.

Ferguson, James 2006 *Global Shadows: Africa in the neo-liberal world order*. Durham, NC: Duke University Press.

Furniss, Graham 1996 *Poetry, Prose and Popular Culture in Hausa*. Edinburgh: Edinburgh University Press for the IAI.

Smith, Dan 2007 *A Culture of Corruption: everyday deception and popular discontent in Nigeria*. Princeton NJ: Princeton University Press.

Taylor, Charles 1989 *Sources of the self: the making of the modern identity*. Cambridge: Cambridge University Press.

Watt, Ian 1957 *The rise of the novel: studies in Defoe, Richardson and Fielding*. London: Chatto and Windus.

*NOT TO BE CITED WITHOUT THE PERMISSION OF THE AUTHOR.

# Everything to do with it:
## Articulating the Unsaid and the Unsayable
### - Elleke Boehmer

In this presentation I want to pick up on two ideas that are implicit or explicit in discussions of culture and which seem to be ideas in contradiction, and which contradictions may be a function of rhetoric, more than anything. The one is the idea that poetry, culture, writing, literature, all that aesthetic stuff, makes nothing happen, to quote Auden's well tried phrase; that it has no effect in the real world. The other is that, on the contrary, culture is what makes us. Through writing we discover what we are up to. Literature makes the political meaningful, resonant; it gives us a grasp not so much on the real world, as on the *otherness*, the singularity, the incommensurability, that leads us to develop an understanding of further worlds – political, social, cultural – in addition to our own.

This last idea – that culture, and for me specifically in this discussion, literature, adds meaning – is the one that I want to think about more carefully in what follows. I will aim also to acknowledge that it may not be in contradiction with the first. As we will all know, in postcolonial as well as in area studies it is an idea that has often come under pressure. In both domains the alleged functionlessness of the literary and the aesthetic has been deemed a problem, especially in situations of deprivation, loss and hardship, where people are illiterate, and lack the means to even gain access to books.

What I want to offer, to the contrary, is the thought that to see the cultural, the literary and the political as making the same kinds of meanings, in more or less the same discursive domain, is to make a category mistake. The cultural and the political denote different kinds of activities, and different kinds of meaning making that may however elucidate one another. As the cultural and the textual are my concerns here, I would like to extend this into saying that the power of the literary – or perhaps specifically of writing, of forms of writing, or formed writing – is that it allows us to begin to conceive of meanings not yet spoken. It allows us to shadow forth significations, and configurations of ideas, perhaps not yet even thought. The literary then is not programmatic, not directive, not merely denotative.

From this it follows that the literary may be a powerful, though necessarily not purposeful tool for change. Writing as an aspect of the literary can articulate the as yet unsaid. But, in addition to this, writing allows the unsayable, the taboo, the forbidden, to be articulated, though in coded, oblique, and disguised ways. And by articulating the unsayable, writing can provide a way forward, a means to open the future, such as for those under taboo, for those who are forbidden or excluded in some way, for the wretched of the earth.

To bring these two points together. By means of what it makes possible, for example, by its joining together of oddities and incommensurabilities, by its juxtaposition of the unlikelihoods, writing allows the reader/the writer to conceive of what has not yet been conceived. It also encourages that which till now has been silenced or subdued, even when it was conceived, to be imagined. It allows the silenced to be thought in a new, perhaps digressive, evasive, oblique, yet still meaningful and memorable way (see, for example, Nussbaum 2001; Attridge 2004).

As this implies, my suggestion here is that aesthetic forms – here, the structures and codes of writing – offer us a mode of addressing, interrogating and thinking through some of the most difficult preoccupations and challenges of our postcolonial realities.

As Fredric Jameson contended some time back, reality – and I would add alternative realities – can only become available to us in language (Jameson 1981). As we see from the ways in which it persists amongst us, literature offers 'at least some degree of creative detachment from material circumstances' (Hallward 2001: 334). And not only that. Writing is also an inventive and highly malleable, and thus adaptive, mode of thinking beyond those realities, those material circumstances. It escapes censuring and censoring, and it projects into the future. To summarise Ato Quayson in *Calibrations*, though citing him out of context, writing is a construct that is intercalated with, ca-

librated, with the real world, which is however also a set of constructions (Quayson 2003). Writing therefore can through the medium of
those calibrations with the real world, offer a series of more and less
actual and more and less imagined constructions and reconstructions
of that real world. In cultural forms – visual media, musical expression, but also textual representations – connections between peoples are forged, ventured and fantasized, and critiques made. These
would be impossible outside of these forms because of the scope for
calibrated meaning and nuance they offer, and the imagined alternatives and wide-ranging shades of opinion to be explored.

Writing in the sense in which I am speaking of it here does involve
resistance, as we know well in postcolonial and related disciplines.
But it also entails what Ahdaf Soueif in a recent review called the
resisting of resistance. Writing animates an interrogation of the status quo, yet it casts beyond it also. It projects worlds beyond even
those that are being resisted (Soueif 2009).

To underline this point, here is a quote from J.M. Coetzee. It will
be immediately clear that the quotation is apt for the purposes of
developing my case. As we know, for Coetzee writing has always
been more eloquent, more pregnant with meaning, than other forms
of language. In his view, writing articulates what cannot be expressed outside of writing. And that means that writing by definition
will work to shift the boundaries of the known, the expected, the
respectable. Coetzee in *Doubling the Point* writes:

> Writing reveals to you what you wanted to say in the first place.
> In fact, it sometimes constructs what you want or wanted to
> say. What it reveals (or asserts) may be quite different from
> what you thought (or half-thought) you wanted to say in the
> first place. That is the sense in which one can say that writing
> writes us. Writing shows or creates (and we are not always sure
> we can tell one from the other) what our desire was, a moment
> ago (Coetzee 1992: 10).

In short, writing writes us; writing reveals what had not yet been
thought; writing illuminates our desire, though by the time we
understand it, it has vanished from us. An interestingly related ex-

ample of the reconstructive, but also constructive possibilities opened in writing – here, in particular, of the representation of gradual change set against abrupt breaks with tradition, be it oral or otherwise – comes to us from Chinua Achebe's *Things Fall Apart* (1958) whose fascinating complexity, lightly worn, speaks eloquently in this context (Achebe 1982). Colonial history was, when Achebe's novel was published, still highly polarised into coloniser and colonised perspectives: the heuristic focus was on the African versus the European, on Manichean opposition. From this we appreciate the difficulty involved in the attempt of *Things Fall Apart* to tell the story of colonial penetration into Igbo, which is not as a straightforward historical narrative, chronologically arranged. Rather, it tells that story with regard for the refrains, loopings back, and repetition-with-a-difference, of myth-based narration, and for the grey tones and paradoxes brought into play by any text.

In the novel, in contrast with what the historical narrative might have represented, we have a mixed moral picture of how incursion is produced by both sides, and how Igbo society has weakened itself by having become too divided along gender-symbolic lines. The final indictment of the colonial system is offered at the end of a long process of Igbo self-indictment, and makes the first indictment that much more powerful and iconoclastic by contrast. This is very evidently an example, though rooted in a specific context, of a resistance of resistance writing.

Now to follow through an important assumption on which rests this valorization of writing as bringing into being new meanings … The recognition of the importance of writing qua writing, whether in a postcolonial context or elsewhere, implies giving due recognition also to reading as a creative process, to the literariness and the individuality of a text, or a piece of writing, that choreographs that reading. Moreover, to spell out, it means doing so separately from attending to its socio-historical context, to which its appellation as postcolonial or African may disproportionately draw our attention. As this will suggest, I agree with Nick Harrison in his book *Postcolonial Criticism* (111) when he observes that our treatment of postcolonial literature requires us to attend to that literature as literature, as well as to what in historical terms makes up its post/coloniality

(Harrison 2003: 111). The literary text, even the postcolonial literary text, is to be valued precisely because it disrupts and interrogates through the reading process the dynamics of representativity that connects a text to an identity, a country, a voice. So we attend to a Nigerian text like Flora Nwapa's *Efuru*, say, not for its Nigerianness only or for the fact that it is written by a woman only (Nwapa 1966). We attend to it because its complexities ravel and dishevel such obvious and ultimately not very revealing one-to-one connections.

The writing of terror in a postcolonial context, in particular writing concerned with processing the pain and fear generated by state commandment, gives a further illustrative insight into the distancing, adaptive and transformative powers of writing, or of the literary text. Such powers emphasize for us how as-yet-unimaginable significations – in this case, terror – can often only be mediated to the conscious through metaphor, connotation, digression, distortion, implication, and what I will call unordered, as opposed to disordered, and random juxtaposition, and of all or some of these techniques working together. And this is yet another way of saying that the fictional or poetic text gives access, though it may be aslant or deflected, to the unspeakable: to the unsaid – the expression of extreme levels of violence in a terror situation, and the unsayable – pain, sorrow, fear.

Writing, as suggested, has the power to draw attention to places of refuge and reconstruction both within and outside of the terror-stricken state. It also supplies a fuller understanding of the painful losses as well as strategic gains of such acts. So it might, for example, explore the human inwardness that inheres to situations of extreme decimation, carnage and grief, through say, off-beat, even off colour and inappropriate humour, or through vivid, expressionist utterances of emotion. It might show, in the words of Kader Asmal *et al*, that 'humanism [travels] always with … resistance' (Asmal 1996: 50). By narrating historical division and pain, but also recovery and endurance, writing thus powerfully posits futurity in relation to the futureless (that is: terror, necropolitics). Paradoxically, it also reminds us of colonial 'pasts,' of the 'regeneration of colonialism through other means,' and hence of the need to remain vigilant about and to survive such regeneration (Frankenburg and Mani 322-34).

Zimbabwean Yvonne Vera's 2002 novella, *The Stone Virgins*, for instance, tells in disturbingly poetic terms, of quirky, unordered juxtaposition, not only of a horrifying terroristic act perpetrated upon village-dweller Nonceba and her sister during Zimbabwe's post-independence civil war. It also tells of the restorative processes of mourning and healing which, for Nonceba, eventually follow. Moreover, the narrative casts a coldly penetrating eye into the frozen mind of the terroristic (and terrorized) soldier and attacker himself, representing him, by contrast with survivor Nonceba, as suspended in a place outside of history. Relatedly, Achmat Dangor's *Bitter Fruit* (2004) is concerned more with a family's attempts to come to terms with the 'ordinariness' of life in the post-apartheid city, and with one another, than it is with the state-inflicted act of violent rape that, years before, first distanced them from one another. In these ways postcolonial narrative maps a chronology on to the 'moment of danger,' the moment- in-and-out-of time, of terror, registering through a plethora of human detail not only the past history but also the future consequences and repercussions of necropolitical acts for human subjects.

Having planted such a close focus on the culture that is writing, I'd like to query some of the assumptions underlying my prioritization. I'd then like to move on to two further examples that will illustrate my contention that writing allows new meanings to be shadowed forth through putting in play interesting attractions between unordered objects.

My first question then is to ask – and at once to concede to the contrary – whether writing necessarily articulates the unsaid and the unsayable. No it does not; it often describes the world as it is, and in factual, empirical terms. A second question, linked to this one, is to ask how, when it does articulate the unsaid and the unsayable, it goes about this. I've already suggested certain answers to this question, by outlining such techniques as implication, nuance, digression, and, in particular, as it is more random, unordered juxtaposition. In addition we might mention the activation of double meaning, multivoicedness and a plethora of significations, or, in short, complexity.

However, the reason I am returning to the question has to do with the concentration of such techniques in European modernist writing, and with how such writing was calibrated with a particularly reactionary politics in many writers. Of course, since Salman Rushdie wrote that we/writers from the empire were the first modernists, modernist techniques have been widely valorised, in postcolonial criticism, as the means of writing against a colonial grain, Dambudzo Marechera, for example, has been acclaimed for the subversive potential of his juddery, sometimes incoherent, glossolalia. Yet, as is also widely known and commented on, writing of complexity, indirection and ambiguity, too – fragmented collage writing – has been used to express views less than progressive as much as progressive. Right-wing opinions of the early 20th century experimental modernists come to mind.

So when we speak of writing qua writing as bodying forth new meanings, do we need to think again?

To confront this difficult question I suggest we need to bring the idea of silence or the unspoken, the as yet-unsaid, back into the frame. Moreover, we may need to deflect our attention away from the *mix* of objects that we find in a modernist type bricolage, away from hybridity, and all its dynamically connotative assemblage of random objects, and towards the spaces between the objects, the interstices. We may need to think about the spaces of possibility created by the unordered juxtaposition itself. And this is another way of saying we may need again to think differentially, to think between, to think otherness.

For, as Paul Gilroy says, the exposure to otherness is creatively unsettling. And again: 'The repudiation of dualistic pairings … can be accomplished via a concept of relation' (Gilroy 2004: 45, 77). To this I would add that unordered juxtaposition suggests relationality, or in Gilroy's terms: 'complex, tangled, profane and sometimes inconvenient forms of interdependency.'

Dipesh Chakrabarty's 'Historical Belatedness as Possibility' offers the insight that it is through finding and offering broad and vague new names for the revolutionary subject of history, that the radical historian invokes a new historical agent into being (Chakrabarty 2010). Note that he says names, not just one name, but a list, which again implies suggestive spaces between the words. For Chakrabarty, the names stretch and displace the original terms of analysis, drawn from Europe. So the radical historian turns from the too-specific-proletariat, and towards the more poetic phrase, 'the wretched of the earth.' To reinforce his point, Chakrabarty reminds us of Fanon's well-known observation: 'the terms of analysis have to be stretched every time we have to do with the colonial problem.' Rhetorical imprecision allows newness to come into the world.

With these ideas in mind I'd like now to move to my two closing examples, drawn from historical situations of encounter, negotiation, and the forging of interdependency, where writing or text allowed and encouraged relationality to emerge. The first example has to do with how late 19th century Indian travellers in London, who felt alien and displaced in its strange streets, were also aware of themselves as citizens of the empire. Though they brought to the city a set of standard expectations, articulated through received images of crowds, commotion, frenetic activity, and, above all, advanced industrial and commercial modernity, yet, far from positioning themselves as removed from that energy and modernity, they described themselves as forming part of it and blending in with the crowds, even quite criticizing its more socially derelict aspects. They located themselves as part of the unordered, creative juxtapositions that the city fostered, and not as forces or presences accentuating London's divisions and separations, but as part of its entanglements, as a part of its complex texture. They wrote a place for themselves into London through the very process of composing their travel narratives (Ahmed, Boehmer, Mukherjee, Nasta, Stadtler 2007-10).

My second example again looks at juxtaposition, yet focuses more on the spaces between texts in juxtaposition – and on how meaning is created between those jagged edges. The example has to do with the interesting question of how Nelson Mandela arrived at both his decision to negotiate with the apartheid regime, and at his techniques for negotiation. A range of different answers have been given to this question – for example, pointing to his experience of often polarized discussion in prison; and of nationalists joining together in conversation. I want to suggest in addition that Mandela came to this highly sophisticated stance in part through the chemistry between the widely differing texts that inspired him. A poem by G.A. Henty, 'Invictus,' his favourite Shakespeare, *Julius* Caesar, and Nadine

Gordimer's *Burger's Daughter*, allowed Mandela to think his way out of a polarised politics, and towards his negotiating strategy of give and take, or give on the basis of a shrewd anticipation of how much the other party was prepared to give. Disparate aesthetic forms, and the interplay between them, the relations between difference, provided Mandela with a model of thinking through reconciliation, or how to bring irreconcilables together.

Put differently, Robben Island confined Mandela to the *realm of the symbolic*, which earlier he had already learned skillfully to manipulate for the purposes of legal advocacy. Now he found it a medium in which his political intellect could move with special facility, as when he attempted to approach others' perspectives, including his warders,' on their own merits, or identified at different levels with both and Antigone in an Island production of Sophocles's eponymous play, or drew his necessarily random favourite reads into juxtaposition. Among prisoner friends he was well known for his tendency to meditate on a move in chess for days at a time: his style 'deliberate,' his strategy 'conservative,' as he himself admitted. He was noted, too, for the patience with which he pursued discussion with an interlocutor, relying on his capacity for listening and avoiding judgment, corroborating the other speaker's position with occasional remarks, pushing them gradually to concede common ground. It was an approach in which he resisted straightforward resistance through activating the spaces between words (Boehmer 2008).

Once, when inducting the SWAPO leader Toivo ya Toivo into how argument worked on the Island, Mandela provocatively advised him to 'engage all and sundry in conversation, during which he could make political points'; that is, to put relationality into play. Particularly difficult debates, as between the ANC and PAC or, later, with Black Consciousness adherents, Mandela liked to imagine literally in 3-D, as a drama played out in a theatre. This capacity to focus at length, if anything, deepened over the years, as he learned a new sensitivity to others' needs.

Mandela's example draws our attention to how difference comes together, how life is expressed through entanglements.

**References**

Achebe, Chinua. *Things Fall Apart* [1958]. London: Heinemann, 1982. Print.

Asmal, Kader, Louise Asmal and Robert Suresh Roberts. *Reconciliation through Truth*. Cape Town: David Philip, 1996. Print.

Attridge, Derek. *The Singularity of Literature*. London: Routledge, 2004. Print.

Boehmer, Elleke. *Nelson Mandela*. Oxford: Oxford UP, 2008. Print.

Chakrabarty, Dipesh. 'Historical Belatedness as Possibility.' *The Indian Postcolonial: A Critical Reader*. Ed. Elleke Boehmer and Rosinka Chaudhuri. London: Routledge, 2010. Print.

Coetzee, JM. *Doubling the Point: Essays and Interviews*. Cambridge, Mass.: Harvard UP, 1992. Print.

Dangor, Achmat. *Bitter Fruit*. London: Faber, 2004. Print.

Gilroy, Paul. *After Empire: Melancholia or Convivial Culture?* London: Routledge, 2004. Print.

Hallward, Peter. *Absolutely Postcolonial: Writing between the Singular and the*
 *Specific*. Manchester: Manchester UP, 2001. Print.

Harrison, Nicholas. *Postcolonial Criticism: History, Theory and the Work of Criticism*. Cambridge: Polity, 2003. Print.

Jameson, Fredric. *The Political Unconscious: Narrative as a Socially Symbolic Act*. London: Methuen, 1981. Print.

Nasta, Susheila; Ahmed, Rehana; Stadtler, Florian; Mukherjee, Sumita; Boehmer, Elleke and Ranasinha, Ruvani (2010). *Making Britain: discover how South Asians shaped the nation, 1870-1950*. The Open University, Milton Keynes, UK. Print.

Nussbaum, Martha. *Upheavals of Thought: The Intelligence of the Emotions*. Cambridge: Cambridge UP, 2001. Print.

Nwapa, Flora. *Efuru*. London: Heinemann, 1966. Print.

Quayson, Ato. *Calibrations: Reading for the Social*. Minneapolis: University of Minnesota Press, 2003. Print.

Soueif, Ahdaf. 'Reflect and Resist,' *Guardian Review* (Saturday 13 June 2009), p. 18.

Vera, Yvonne. *Stone Virgins*. Harare: Weaver Press, 2002.

# Africa, Art and Gender: Four Moments of Colonial/Post-colonial History
## - Signe Arnfred

'Africa, Art and Gender' is a very broad agenda, with possibilities for widely different approaches to very different bodies of material. In this essay I will visit four moments of colonial/post-colonial history, which I find fascinating and illustrative of different conceptions of relations and intersections between Africa and Gender, Africa and Art, and Africa, Art and Gender. The four moments are first the heydays of European colonial expansion, the very time of the Berlin Conference (1884-85) when Africa was being divided between European powers by lines drawn on maps, like the cutting of a cake. The issue here is colonial fantasies, as expressed in contemporary fiction: images of Africa in European minds. The second moment occurs some 40 years later, Paris in the period between the first and the second world wars. Influenced by the devastating war and the general atmosphere expressed in *Untergang des Abendlandes* (Oswald Spengler 1918-22), the derogatory image of places like Africa as having no civilization was partly replaced by curiosity and fascination – maybe one could find here inspiration for renewal and revitalization of European spirits? Vibrant African-American music (jazz) and a new interest in African traditional art point in that direction. Still, however, it is all about European fantasies and ideas. Few real Africans and African-Americans appear on the (European) scene; the few who do feed into myth and magic. The general template for European thinking is still the dichotomy of us/the Other(s); where in the late 19th and early 20th centuries the colonized Other was imagined as childish, inferior, not-yet civilized – the civilizing quest ("The White Man's Burden" as put by Rudyard Kipling 1901) being a major legitimation for the very act of colonization – in this period between the wars the othering turns, partly at least, to a positive othering. Africans are now imagined as free, sensual and unchained by the burdens of a tired, destructive European civilization.

Moments one and two are both about imaginations, and thus also about art. Gender appears as sexuality, not (at all) as gender equality or as women's rights. Such issues were only the concern of very limited groups is in the context of the third moment, the late 1940s and 1950s, the period after the Second World War, when changes in the Western hemisphere (USA emerging as a world power) and political movements in colonized countries caused a general de-colonization of black African countries from 1957 (Ghana) onwards. Among Black intellectuals (African, African American and Caribbean) invited to Paris for the First Black Writers and Artists' Congress 1956, women only appeared as wives; all delegates were men. Colonial education (however poor) and Christian missions have done their work: reading and writing in European languages are embedded in notions of male domination/female subordination as the normal (civilized) state of affairs.

The fourth moment in this tale of intersections between Africa, art and gender, is postcolonial feminist literature, scholarship and art from the 1990s onwards. This period is characterized not only by the appearance of an increasing number of women writers, artists and intellectuals/scholars on the scene, but also by African revisions of European conceptions of gender.

**Colonial Fantasies – 1885 Onwards**
By the end of the 19th century, European culture was inherently patriarchal. It had not always been like that. Feminist historians writing about the so-called 'dark middle ages' (Jacobsen 1986) bring evidence of gender relations different from the male domination/ female subordination that has later been considered the 'normal' state of affairs, and against which the First as well as the Second Wave of Women's Movements in Europe and the US have been struggling. At this point in time, however, European patriarchy was only marginally questioned (the first women's unions in the likewise patriarchal labour movement had just been formed), and the colonial patriarchs could depict themselves as valiant heroes

rushing to the rescue of poor oppressed women in faraway corners of the world. In the first decades of colonization, however, it was the general civilizing mission, which was emphasized as the driving force and motivation for colonization.

The colonizing enterprise was accompanied by a rich production of fantasies about colonized people and colonized lands. As is often the case in 'dynamics of Othering' (Hall 1992) fantasies of 'the Other' are characterized by projection of repressed and forbidden desires. The heydays of colonization coincided with the heydays of Victorian morality in Imperial Europe, with men (of the bourgeoisie) as staunch family heads, and women as wives and mothers, and as a-sexual Angels of the Home. Sexual desire was repressed and projected to the working class, and to the colonized populations (McClintock 1995). African women and men were imagined as promiscuous, licentious, sexually inviting – and dangerous and frightening at the same time. The fiction story, which in this section I shall use as an example of this fantasy production, is characterized by a projection of sexual fantasies to the act of discovery and penetration of foreign continents, *in casu* Africa.

The story *King Solomon's Mines* was written by Rider Haggard (1856-1925), published 1885, at the very time of the Berlin Conference. As a young man, Haggard had spent some years (1875-1882) at the bottom range of British civil service in the Colony of Natal, in present day South Africa. After his return to UK 1882 he never again set foot on African soil. Nevertheless, for the rest of his life as a writer Africa fuelled his imagination. *King Solomon's Mines* was the first English fiction adventure novel set in Africa. It became an immediate bestseller, and (more surprisingly) it has remained so ever since. It has been adapted to film at least four times (1937, 1950, 1985, and 2004 as a television series) and allegedly the *King Solomon's Mines* protagonist, the British adventurer and hero Alan Quaitermain, has inspired a later US incarnation, Indiana Jones. The story is about three British explorers, who set out on a journey guided by an old treasure map showing the location of 'King Solomon's Mines', an underground cavern replete with gold, ivory and precious stones. After many perilous adventures on the way they finally reach the location. The treasure is guarded by Gagool, an incredibly ancient witch (as they see her) and only after a life-and-death struggle with her (in which she dies), do they manage to grasp parts of the treasure and escape.

Of interest in this context are the treasure map, and the figure of Gagool. The treasure map *(fig 1)* shows a path leading across a plain to a mountain ridge, which must be crossed through a pass between two snow-clad peaks (named Sheba's Breasts). At the other side the path continues – now called 'Solomon's Road' and paved by an ancient civilization – to three heather-clad hills among which the mouth of the treasure cave is located. As pointed out by feminist researchers (Stott 1989; McClintock 1995) the treasure map turned upside-down depicts the body of a woman. The woman has no head, but the arms (the mountain range) and the breasts are there, and further down, in the midst of the triangle of heather-clad hills we find the hole, the entry-point to the interior, the goal of the men's desire, but also the location of risk and danger and possible death.

An illustration from a 1950s edition of King Solomon's Mines *(fig 2)* shows our heroes with their native helpers on an escarpment overlooking a vast stretch of land, beyond which we see the mountain range with 'Sheba's Breasts'. The illustration shows 'the imperial gaze': representatives of the imperial power posed in an elevated position from where the land can be overlooked and commanded. This land, which in colonial contexts and later is often named 'virgin land' is land where Europeans had not (yet) settled; virgin land passively awaiting (colonial, masculine) penetration. When eventually they reach the location where the treasure is hidden, they'll have to venture into underground caves, inhabited and protected by dark and dangerous forces in the shape of the old woman Gagool. She is ten generations old, maybe more, with eyes like a snake, "the mother of evil" (Haggard 1885/1994, 233). In European cultural tradition there are standard ways of demonizing female power, perceived as threatening by men; Gagool is classified as a witch.

Sigmund Freud, father of psychoanalysis, is Rider Haggard's contemporary. Freud, too, was a child of the imperial age. The language of psychoanalysis is characterized by colonial metaphors,

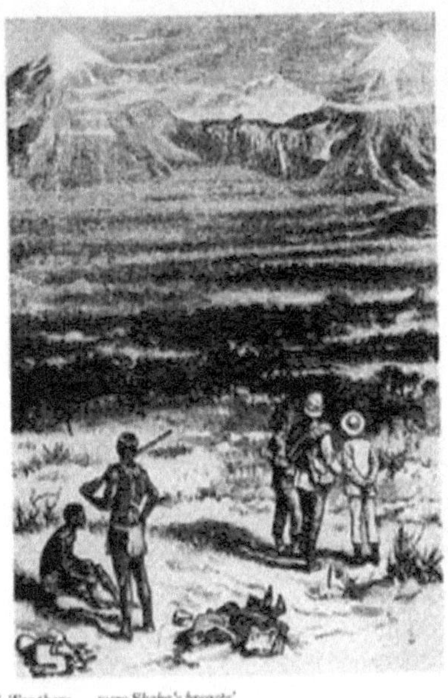


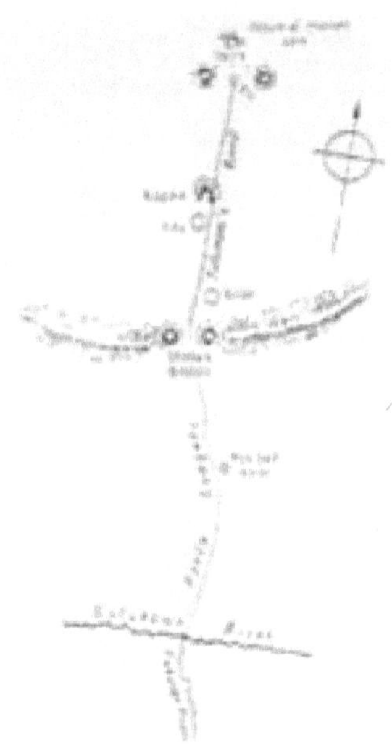


Fig. 1. Map of King Solomon Mines.
Fig 2. *'For there…were Sheba's breasts!'*

such as, for example, Freud's description of the female psyche as 'a dark continent' to be penetrated by the male/scientific gaze (Stott 1989).

Haggard's vision of the passive, innocent (female) 'virgin land' to be conquered by the active male explorer, as a contrast to the dark and dangerous forces underground, can be read as a parallel to Freud's ideas of the orderly, rational and controlled (male) 'ego', as a contrast to the wild and undomesticated desires of the unconscious, underground, the 'id'.

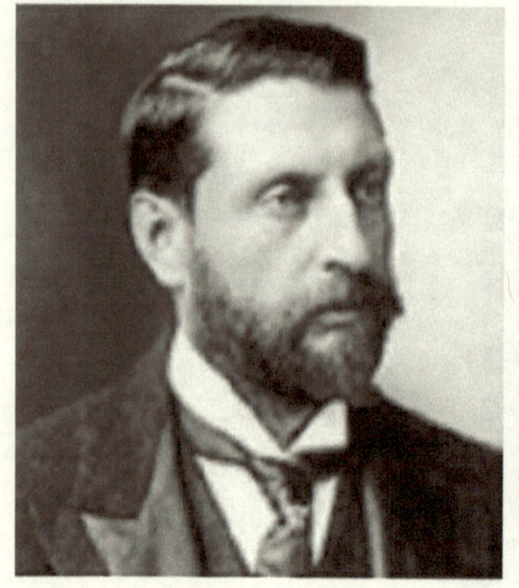
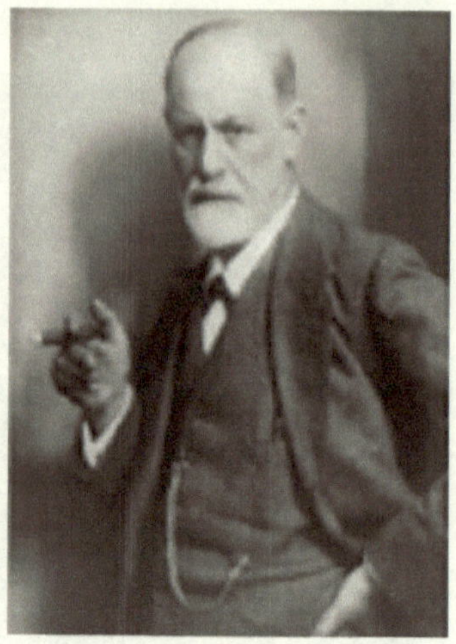

Rider Haggard 1856-1925
African landscape = female body

Sigmund Freud 1856-1939
Female psyche = dark continent

Fig.3. European gentlemen: Rider Haggard and Sigmund Freud.

This partial overlap between colonial fantasies replete with sexual metaphors on the one hand and the scientific language of psychoanalysis drawing on colonial, imperial metaphors on the other hand is an interesting sign of the general mood of the time. Colonialism was perfectly legitimate; there was a general faith in the superiority of Western civilization; issues of sexuality were only beginning to be conceptualized. Freud was indeed a radical and innovative thinker, his *Drei Abhandlungen zur Sexualtheorie* about child sexuality caused scandal when it was published in 1905. But Freud too believed in colonialism, and he took the hierarchies between races, and between men and women, for granted.

### Black Paris of the 1920s and 1930s

During the First World War, 180,000 African soldiers had been part of the French army, about 120,000 serving in Europe. For many Europeans this was their first encounter with black people; in the 1919 July 14th military parade on Champs Elysées *les Tirailleurs Senegalais* were hailed as heroes (Wendl and von Lintig, 2006). Other black sol-

diers, too, came to Paris during and after the war: black regiments of
the US army. "According to the French the jazz band was an equally
integrated part of the equipment of the American troop transport
trains as were arms of fire, and the dissemination of the new music
was an equally important task for the Americans as victory over the
Germans" (Blake 2006, 101). Jazz music, brought to Europe by Black
Americans, broke with all musical convention. It has been compared
to contemporary movements in art such as *Dada*. "The Great War
1914-1918 created the conditions for the breakthrough of Dada as
well as for the explosion of jazz. (…) Jazz music, which was critizi-
sed for breaking all rules, and about which it was said this was no
music at all, was the musical parallel to the anti-art activities of the
Dadaists (Blake 2006, 101). Paris between the wars seems to have
been a hotbed of musical and artistic innovations, with inspiration
from Africa looming large.

African inspiration in art actually dates further back, one of
the very first incarnations being Picasso's painting *Les Demoiselles
d'Avignon* from 1907 *(fig 4)*, where the faces of three of the ladies have
been turned into African masks.

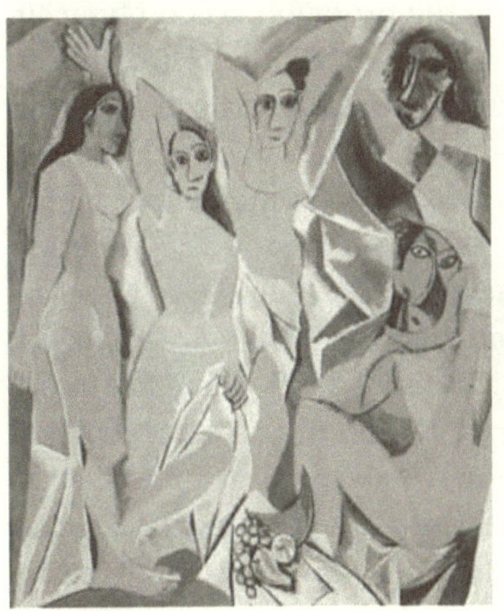
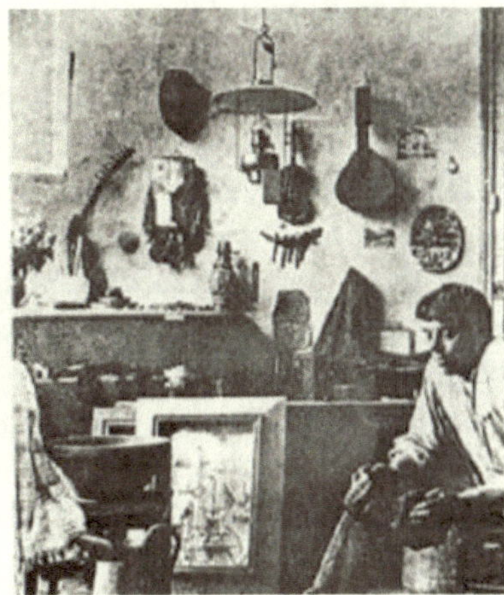

Fig. 4. Pablo Picasso *Les Demoiselles d'Avignon.*
Fig. 5. Georges Braque in his studio.

As the story goes, Picasso, while working on this picture, had happened to visit the collection of African masks at the Paris Ethnographic Museum at Trocadéro. Impressed by what he had seen, he had returned to his studio and finished the painting (Wivel 1986). Picasso over the years assembled quite a collection of African sculpture, and so did his friend and fellow painter George Braque. A photo of Braque in his studio 1911 playing the accordion shows African masks and artifacts on the studio wall *(fig 5)*.

After the war and fuelled by jazz music, African inspirations multiplied. Into this Paris environment arrived in 1925 *La Revue Négre*, a jazz revue from New Orleans, with musicians such as Sydney Bechet, and a young woman dancer, Josephine Baker. The revue consisted of a series of tableaux and dances, one of them *Le Dance Savage*, based on a fiction figure, a Senegalese seductress, Fatou-gaye, from a French colonial fantasy novel authored by Pierre Loti (Jules-Rosette 2007). The novel in which Fatou-gaye appears is from 1881, titled *Le Romand'un Spahi*. The novel was very popular in France at the time; like Loti's other fiction books it is based on his own life (in fantasy edition) and like his other books it has at its center a strongly erotic, sexually attractive young woman of a different race, with whom the protagonist (Loti himself ) falls in love (Hargreaves 1981). When in 1925 Josephine Baker performed this part in a wildly erotic dance dressed in an outfit of feathers and beads *(fig 6)* she became famous overnight. In her role as Fatou-gaye she somehow managed to combine the stereotype of a pre-World War 1 sexualized/eroticized racially inferior African woman with a different image of a free, unfettered, attractive sexuality, an image which matched the post-War sentiment of tired European culture and civilization having come to a dead end. Josephine Baker's performance fed on old stereotypes, but transformed them into something new and exciting, in tune with jazz music and modern art. Significantly the poster for *La Revue Négre (fig 7)* was designed by a well known Paris artist, Paul Colin.

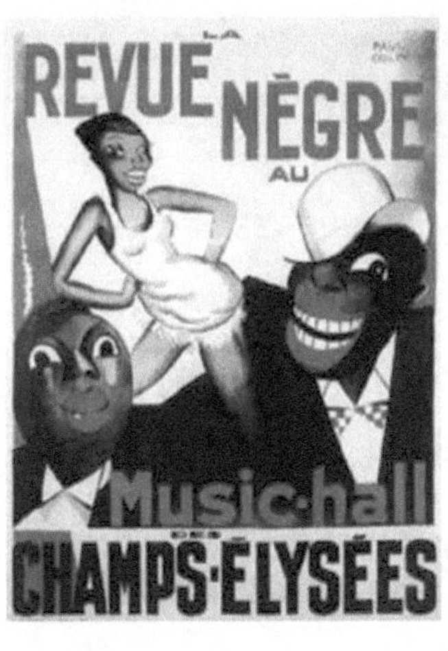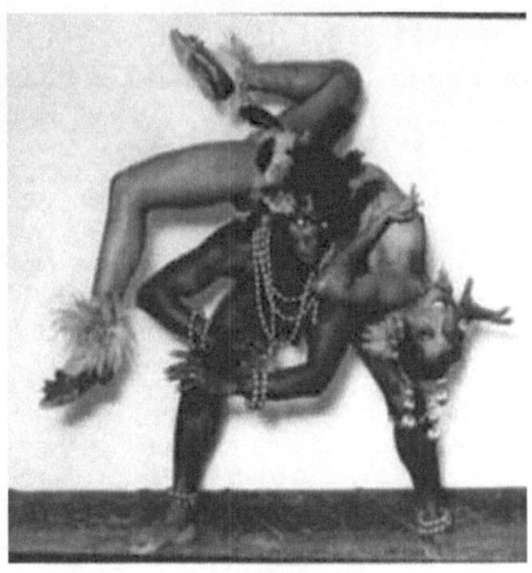

Fig. 6 (left) Josephine Baker with Georges Henri Riviers.
Fig. 7. La Revue Nègre.

The poster plays more on modernity than on the Fatou-gaye myth, its style is early jazz, but also with music hall/minstrel stereotypes (colours black, white, red; black men with big lips etc). Josephine Baker seems to have been a very clever and determined young person. Born 1906 she was barely 19 years old when she came to Paris and turned famous overnight. Three years later, in 1928, she embarked on a world tour, now with a different show (Jules-Rosette 2007). On this tour she also came to Copenhagen, enthusiastically received by the budding so-called culture-radical left, the group which spearheaded the anti-fascist struggle in Denmark, and in which the architect/designer/poet Poul Henningsen was a central force. A 1928 cartoon in the Denmark satirical annual review Blæksprutten *(fig. 8)*, titled: "On the way home from school" refers to Poul Henningsen's challenge to young Danish women that they should learn from Josephine Baker; "Why should it be considered a perversion to feel inspired by meeting the fundamentally natural human being?" Poul Henningsen is reported to have asked (Graugaard 2008, 100). What the Danish as well as the Parisian left wing saw in blackness was not so much black *culture* as black *nature*. "The black bodies were marked by nature; it was in their nature to be expressive, excessive and sensual" (Jamin 1996, 34). They were perceived as having rhythm in their bodies, dance in their blood.

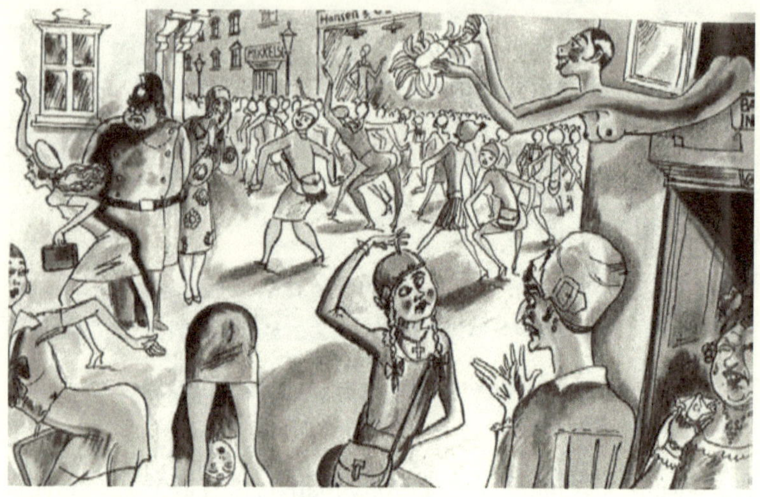

Fig.8: Danish satire *Blacksprutten*, 1928.

Josephine Baker remained a centre of radical activity in Paris throughout the 1920s and 1930s. For some years she ran her own night spot in Montmartre, *Chez Josephine*, and she was close to the centre of activities in the particular Paris mix of Africa, anthropology and art. In this capacity she also participated in raising funds for the colonial anthropological expedition *Mission Dakar-Djibouti* 1931-1933. The expedition was in itself an expression of the mix of influences and trends in Paris at the time. The organizing force was George Henri Riviére, at the time vice-director of the old *Museé d'Ethnographie de Trocadéro*, in the process of being transformed to *Museé d'Homme*. Riviére played cleverly on the general Africa-craze in Paris, organizing fund-raising events for the expedition, such as a boxing match featuring the African American boxer Al Brown.

The expedition itself was a French prestige project, with a mix of scientific, colonial and artistic, aims. The scientific aims had to do with a French interest in establishing an ethnographic tradition based on fieldwork (in this *metiér* the British were far advanced compared to the French) and also to establish French colonial presence in most of the areas covered by the expedition, the route of which went from east to west of Africa just south of the Sahara, through Senegal, Mali, Niger, Cameroun and further inland through what was then French Equatorial Africa to Sudan and Ethiopia. The expedition team was a bunch of young men of different professions: anthropologists, linguists, a musicologist, etc, led by anthropologist/linguist Marchel Griaule. Griaule had recruited Michel Leiris, poet, writer and previous member of the Surrealist movement, as secretary/archivist for the expedition. A woman linguist later joined the crew (Jamin 1996).

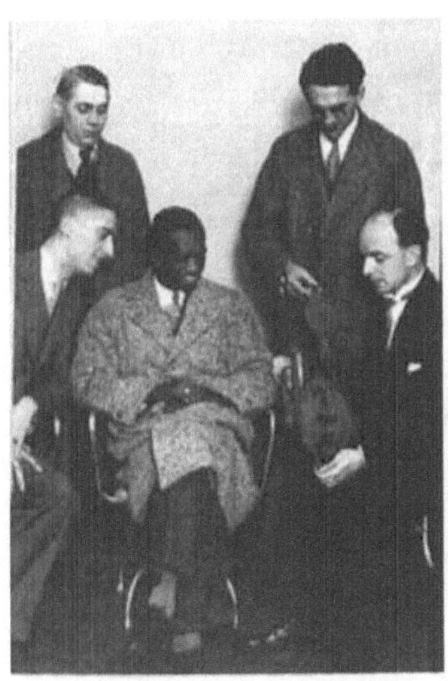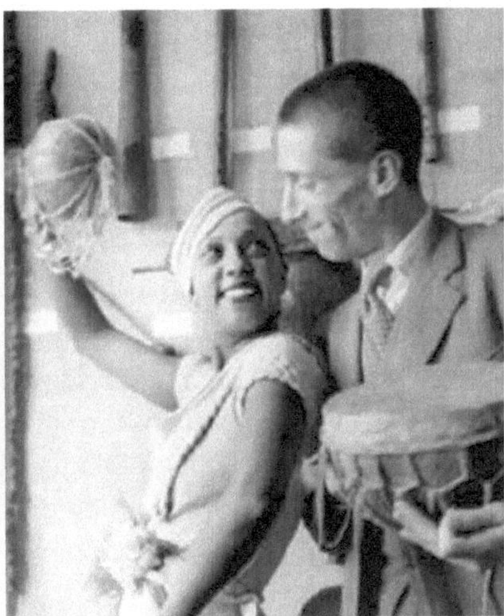

Fig. 9. Al Brown admiring an African mask held by Marcel Griaule, head anthropologist of the Dakar-Djibouti mission, with George Henri Riviére to the left.

Fig. 10. Josephine Baker with Georges Henri Riviers.

Leiris' book based on his diaries from the expedition is titled *l'Afrique Fantôme* ('Imagined Africa, Africa of Dreams,' published 1934).[1] Leiris was well aware of his own double inclinations of anthropological investigation on one hand, and artistic, spiritual fascination on the other. He writes in the preamble of the book of his fascination with the fantastic, spectacular and mysterious mask processions and dances, and of his own position as a European ill at ease, who initially had stupidly hoped that this long journey to faraway places, along with the scientific investigations, would also – through contact with the inhabitants of these exotic locations – turn himself into another type of person, more open and cured of his obsessions (Leiris 1996, 87). Leiris is interesting because he is aware of and acknowledges this double inclination for a desire for knowledge and a longing for revelation. He may be seen as an incarnation of the special inter-war Paris mix of ethnography and art, modernity and dreams.

The return of the expedition was celebrated in1933 with an exposition, for the opening of which Josephine Baker was present. Figure 10 above shows her with Georges Henri Riviere brandishing music instruments collected by the expedition. The expedition boasted of having brought back to Paris 3.500 pieces of artifacts, 6.000 photos, 3.500 meter film, 200 music recordings and 15.000 registered notes (Albers 2006, 171). The musicologist, André Schaeffner, had brought a travel grammophone and stacks of jazz records to play for the natives. To his disappointment there was no particular response (Jamin 1996, 31). A special issue of the art magazine Minotaur was published in celebration of the opening of the exposition *(fig 11)*. The fact that findings of the anthropological expeditions are celebrated in a magazine of art is characteristic of the time and place.

As a difference compared to a scientific journal, an art magazine such as Minotaur (it seems to be Leiris who had established the contact) offered the possibility to give an intermediate presentation, which could do justice to the anthropological meaning and importance of the objects and photos – the aspect which Griaule emphasized – while also making possible an artistic reception, and leaving space for fascination" (Albers 2006, 171).

In the inter-war period in Paris Africa, art and gender were entangled in new ways. 'African art' was taken seriously as art, admired and elevated. All the same a certain prejudice remained, in as far as what was appreciated was 'traditional art', not pieces produced by individual artists, and thus very different from 'European art'. Important, nevertheless, was the fact that 'Africa' in this period, in this context, was cast in a positive light, as a source of authenticity and 'naturalness' (eg Poul Henningsen) something from which Europeans could learn and draw inspiration.

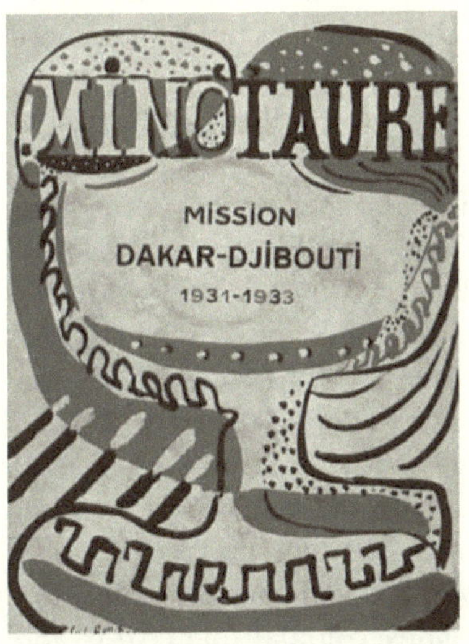


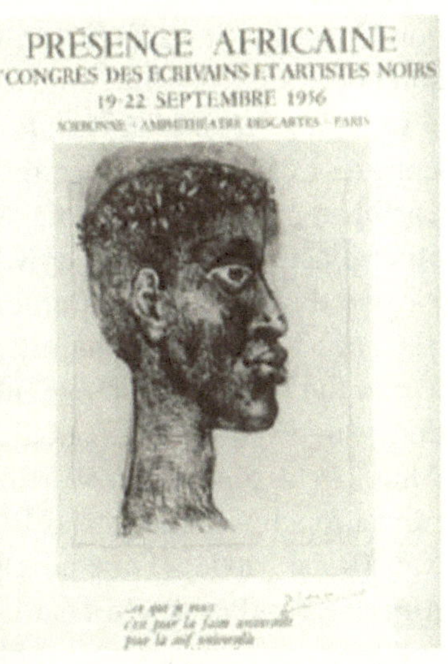


Fig. 11. Art magazine Minotaure 1933.
Fig. 12. Poster by Pablo Picasso, 1956.

As for 'gender,' nothing much had changed since the early days of colonial fantasies. Many European countries now had liberal and socialist women's movements, in the art world you would find some active women, but very few. African women were still seen as sexual objects.

**African Writers: Male/Female: 1950s Onwards**
In Paris, progressive intellectuals regained their forces after the end of the Second World War. Simone de Beauvoir and Frantz Fanon were part of the same circles. De Beauvoir, a woman, writing critically about gender; Fanon, an African, writing critically about colonialism and race. While the inter-war Africa fascination had been ambiguous regarding colonialism, the post-war scene of pro-

gressive intellectuals was clearly anti-colonial. This was true also of the African cultural/political/literary quarterly, *Presence Africaine*, started in 1947 in Paris. The driving force was Alioune Diop, a Senegalese professor of philosophy in Paris, the contributors counted, among others, Aimé Cesare, Léopold Senghor, Albert Camus, André Gide, Jean-Paul Sartre and Michel Leiris. In 1949 *Presence Africaine* expanded to include a publishing house and a bookstore (Wendl, von Lintig, Pinther 2006, 83). All of these – review, publishing house and bookstore – are still functioning.

In 1956, *Presence Africaine* organized the First International Congress of Black Writers and Artists. Delegates came from the Caribbean, the US and from Africa, and included Africans from other places, who would now be known as the African Diaspora. Picasso designed the poster for the event (fig 12). At the time the issue of blackness was mainly a cultural and epistemological one, like in the *Négritude* movement, started by three young black students/poets in Paris: Leopold Senghor (1901-2006) from Senegal, Aimé (1913-2008) from Martinique and Léon Damas (1912-1978) from French Guiana in the 1930s, with the magazine *L'Etudiant Noir* (Riesz, 2006). They now joined Alioune Diop and *Presence Africaine*. Blackness was a matter of shared culture, shared ancestry and (increasingly) joint struggle against colonialism in Africa and against racism in the US.

Seen from a gender point of view it is impossible not to notice that this whole movement was all male. The more than sixty delegates to the First International Congress of Black Writers and Artists, coming from twenty different countries, were all men *(fig 13)*. Not a single woman writer or artist.[2] I see this as an indication, not of patriarchal cultures in Africa or the African Diaspora, but of European patriarchal culture in African mission and government schools. All of these (male) writers had gone to school, of course, and had learnt to express themselves in French, English or Portuguese – the colonial languages. European, inherently patriarchal, culture is described for instance in Simone de Beauvoir's work, *The Second Sex*.

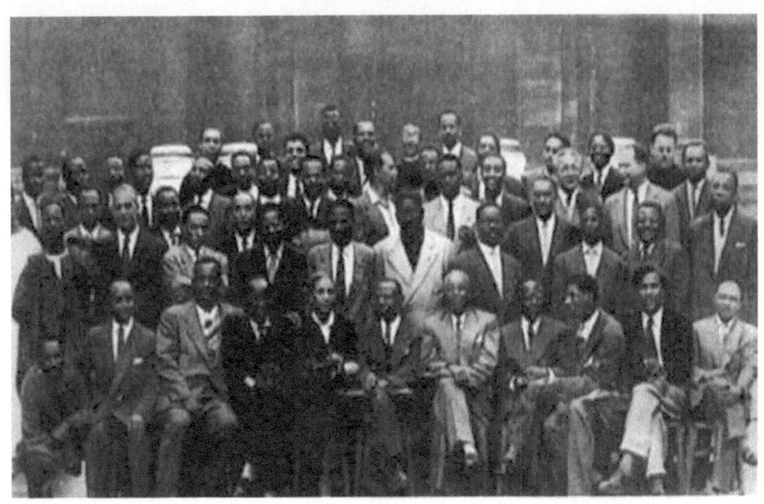

Fig. 13. The First International Congress of Black Writers and Artists.

The view of women in the early works of male African literature has been criticized as romantic and essentialized. According to Nfah-Abbenyi, women are described in *Négritude* poetry as "the symbol of the Earth, of the Nation, as Mother Africa. [...] The African woman was spoken for; she herself was not a speaking subject" (Nfah-Abbenyi 1997, 5).

African literature was a male phenomenon, and when, from the late 1960s onwards, the new women's movement appeared in US and Europe, the women of this movement were implicitly white. Early opponents to this state of affairs were black women in the US. "They rejected the hegemonic and totalizing conceptualizations of 'Woman' by Anglo-American feminists, as well as those presented by African American men" (Nfah-Abbenyi 1997, 1).

After this first all-male congress of black writers and artists in Paris 1956, it would take about a quarter of a century before African women writers would be acknowledged in their own right, as speaking and being listened to, talking with their own voices. Across the Channel, in London, the Heinemann African Writers' Series started in 1962, in the midst of the wave of decolonization and creation of independent African states. The first published volume was Chinua

Achebe's first novel, *Things Fall Apart*, originally published 1958 in a hardback edition. The African Writers Series was innovative, experimental and carried by enthusiasm. In the early 1960s it was received wisdom in British publishing houses that the only books that would sell in Africa were school textbooks; the colonial authorities saw books as a means of education of the new elite, "books for enjoyment which enhance understanding of other African's ways of love and death were not on their agenda" (Currey 2008, 2).

The African Writers Series, published in paperback (fairly innovative at the time), and being an offshoot from an educational publisher of British schoolbooks for use in the colonies, they were the only publisher at the time with the necessary business set-up to sell books in Africa. The African Writers Series continued to sell books for use in schools. "For the first time in history," Chinua Achebe is quoted to have said,

> Africa's *future* generations of readers and writers – youngsters in schools and colleges – began to read, not only *David Copperfield* and other English classics that I and my generation had read, but also works by their own writers about their own people (Achebe, quoted in Currey 2008, 1).[3]

Chinua Achebe's view of women in his native Igboland has been debated by feminist African scholars. Some see him as idealizing and romanticizing African women (Nfah-Abbenyi 1997, 35), while others are of the opinion that in his early novels Achebe is blind to the important roles played by women in Igbo society (Kolawole 1997, Nzegwu 2004). Yet others see him as very deliberately constructing his first novels according to the existing blueprint from Western classics:

Achebe's *Things Fall Apart* provided an avenue for his entrance into the arena of normal literary practice, allowing him to test the existing Western classics paradigm which presented the male as the authentic heroic model in the world of Chaucer, Milton, Shakespeare, Yeats, Eliot, Hawthorne, Poe and so forth. Form this viewpoint, Okonkwo's story begins the exploration of African thought from the position of a colonial heritage that emphasised and insisted on male dominance" (Kalu 2001, 70; Okonkwo is the protagonist of *Things Fall Apart*).

Kalu further points out that "Achebe continues to test the issue of male dominance in Africa based on the existing and validated Western paradigm. (…) [He] is using male social dysfunction to explore possibilities for the reinstatement of the female viewpoint in the discussion of contemporary Africa's experience" (Kalu 2001, 71). Kolawole agrees regarding a kind of progression in Achebe's treatment of issues regarding women, from the early to the later novels (Kolawole 1997, 111-125). According to Kalu, in order to understand male dominance on the African literary scene, and in African novels, Africa's colonial inheritance should be taken into consideration. Despite an overt male development story one may be able to decipher other layers of meaning with different gender connotations. This way of reading may be applied to male authors as well as to female ones. Unique to female authors, however, is the possibility of "depicting women and women's experiences, women's ways of knowing in women's spaces and locations" (Nfah-Abbenyi 1997, 35). The main difference between male and female authors, Nfah-Abbenyi says, lies not only in the fact that frequently women are the centre of woman authors' stories, but also that "we are led into her thought processes as she battles with the contradictions inherent in her life and the multiple demands that these same contradictions make of her as a wife, as a senior wife, as a mother and [...] as a mother of sons" (Nfah-Abbenyi 1997, 46).

During the first twenty years of its existence, the African Writer's Series published very few books by women authors. Of 250 titles published 1962 – 1981, only ten were written by women. Figure I4 shows the front cover of James Currey's recent book on the African Writer's Series, in which he himself was active right from the start. The number of women on the cover photo reflects the percentage of books by women authors published in the series: two out of sixteen = 12.5 %. The list of published books shows more or less 370 books (between 1962 and 2003) out of which about 43 are written by women. The chosen female faces to grace the cover are also not selected by chance; they are the most-published African women authors in the series. Buchi Emecheta has published 10 titles in AWS, Bessie Head 8 titles. Women's writing was fairly late in coming.

There were obstacles which had to be overcome. There was a double difficulty: on the one hand a colonial and post-colonial education system which gave preference to men, "while fewer women were sent to school or obtained university educations that have traditionally been prerequisites for the writing of African literature in European languages" (Nfah-Abbenyi 1997, 3); and on the other hand a women's movement which tended to universalize the experience of white Western women as being *the* female experience worldwide. According to Ama Ata Aidoo there is a long tradition of women's struggles in Africa; the role of African women authors is to give voice to perspectives and ideas rooted in this struggle.

African women struggling both on behalf of themselves and on behalf of the wider community is very much a part of our heritage. […] Africa has produced much more concrete tradition of strong women fighters than most other societies. So when we say that we are refusing to be overlooked we are only acting today as daughters and grand-daughters of women who always refused to keep quiet" (Aidoo, in Holst Petersen (ed) 1988, quoted in Nfah-Abbenyi 1997, 10).

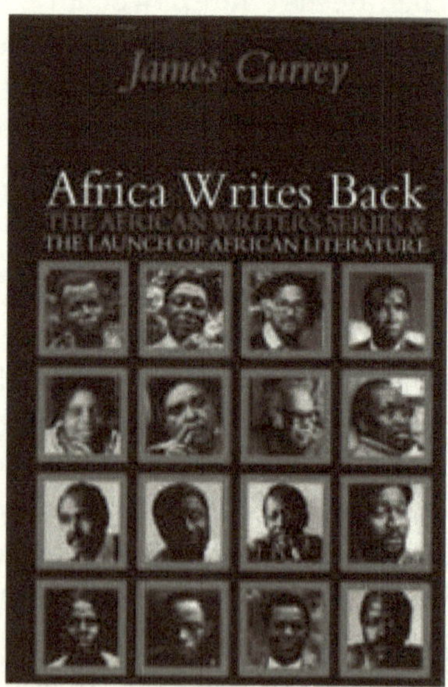


Fig. 14. James Currey's account of the African Writers' Series

Nfah-Abbenyi sees African women writers as pioneers in the formulation of perspectives and ideas based on the experience of African women. Even before feminism became a movement with a global agenda, she says, "African women both 'theorized' and practiced what for them was crucial to the development of women, although no terminology was used to describe what these women were actively doing, and are still practicing on a day-to-day basis" (Nfah-Abbenyi 1997, 10). Thus, according to her African feminist theory is embedded in women writers' fictional texts. "After reading these texts both as 'fictionalized theory' and as 'theorized fiction', finding and naming African indigenous theory that is autonomous and self-determining, I will conclude that these women writers have used their writing as a weapon to delve into the African woman question, concurrently offering reconstructive insights into feminist and postcolonial theories" (Nfah-Abbenyi 1997, 15).

**Postcolonial Feminist Literature, Scholarship, Art – 1990s Onwards**
From a situation in the 1950s, 1960s and 1970s where African women writers and artists were non-existent/invisible due to colonial ideologies and systems of education, there was in the 1990s a breakthrough for African women in literature, scholarship and art. In this decade the women's movement in the Western world at last has an impact, much through a series of UN organized World conferences on gender-related issues. [4] The impact is ambiguous; on the one hand the conceptions of Gender-and-Development are rooted in fixed gender dichotomies and standard notions of male dominance/female subordination, which do not necessarily fit African conditions; on the other hand, the international push to include gender in development issues creates a new focus on women in Africa, also on the African continent itself. In this decade many African universities opened centres for gender studies. Spearheaded by early women's fiction, questions regarding understanding of women's positions in African societies, of gender power relationships and male/female dynamics now start to be debated by (some) African (women) sociologists, anthropologists, scholars of literature – and acted upon by creative artists.

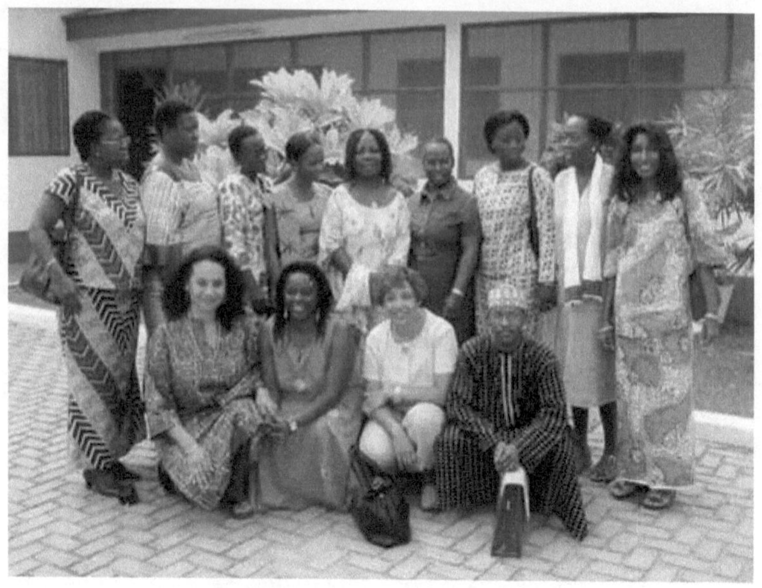

Fig. 15. At the African Gender Institute at the University of Cape Town.

The term 'feminism' was initially regarded with skepticism by African women writers and intellectuals – 'feminism' was considered too Western, too middle-class, and polarizing men and women (Nfah-Abbenyi 1997, 6-10, Ogundipe-Leslie 1994, 205-241). But 'feminism' has gradually been accepted and is now a name adopted by African feminists themselves for rethinking basic conceptualizations regarding women, men and gender relations (Lewis 2001). Some examples: several issues of the important South African journal *Agenda* have since 2001 been devoted to discussions of African Feminisms; since 2002 the electronic journal *Feminist Africa* has been published from the African Gender Institute at the University of Cape Town *(fig 15)*.

One of the tasks facing African feminists is a reinterpretation of so-called 'African tradition.' Western perceptions have imposed androcentric models on African literature, as discussed above in the case of Chinua Achebe. Western perceptions have also influenced ethnographic research on Africa, and in colonial and missionary interventions, 'African tradition' has been interpreted as patriarchal and oppressive of women. Such perceptions have, however, been discreetly undermined by women's fiction (Flora Nwapa's *Efuru*, 1966, is an early example), and they are increasingly being questioned by African gender scholars. These scholars acknowledge that present gender relations of power in most African contexts are patriarchal and male-dominated – but they suggest a different historical trajectory; rather than seeing the roots of contemporary African patriarchal structures in 'African culture,' these scholars point to "the new and growing patriarchal systems imposed on our societies through colonialism and Western religious and educational influences" (Amadiume 1987, 9). In their eyes, much of what is claimed by development agencies and by African leaders to be 'traditional African culture' is in fact *invented tradition*. In a certain sense, these feminists reverse the timeline. Where development discourse sees gender oppression in the past and gender equality in the future, these feminists say: No, this is not what things are like. Gender oppression in its present form has been imported to Africa from the West through colonialism and Christianity, and from the East through Islam. Before these interventions, social relations were different. There was hierarchy and oppression, yes, but gender did not necessarily play an important role. Hierarchies of age, of lineage and/or along the lines of master/slave were much more important. Gender hierarchies have been imposed on these societies through Western influence, these scholars say.

Thus an important line of investigation in this context is the critique of Western *patriarchalizing* views. One has to de-construct existing conceptualizations in order to be able to come up with new ones. It has become increasingly clear to African feminist thinkers that Western interpretations of African social life and Western influences through Christian missions and colonial institutions – from educational systems to state structures, and laws – have been inherently androcentric, and patriarchalizing, in as far as they put men at the centre (standard anthropological kinship diagrams are all constructed with a male ego), all of this combined with assumptions of male dominance/female subordination. Both Ifi Amadiume as an anthropologist and Oyeronke Oyéwùmí as a sociologist have attempted, in studies of their own native societies, Igbo and Yoruba respectively, to de-gender their approaches. Instead of taking man/woman dichotomies and gender hierarchies with men at the top for granted, they pose questions regarding what gender actually means in their respective societies. They come up with slightly different but equally radical answers. Amadiume finds that in Igbo society gender does not necessarily depend on the biology of bodies. Gender is situational; under certain conditions a daughter (biological woman) will be considered a son, a male heir; and under certain conditions a woman may turn herself into a 'husband' marrying another woman (Amadiume 1987).

Oyéwùmí finds that prior to colonization "the fundamental category 'woman' – which is foundational in Western gender discourses – simply did not exist in Yorubaland," as she writes with deliberate provocation (Oyéwùmí 1997, ix). What she means is that the concept of 'woman' is Western thinking and everyday use is so overloaded with implications and associations that are irrelevant and disturbing in African contexts, that analysis with 'woman' as a conceptual tool inevitably will lead investigations off the tracks. Meanwhile important objects of study remain unseen.

Nevertheless, over the years, Yoruba society has been interpreted in male/female terms. Lists of 'rulers' have been read as lists of 'kings' – even if not all of these 'rulers' were men. Yoruba personal names do not indicate the gender of a person; whenever the British saw a throne they imagined a man sitting on it. It didn't occur to them that some 'rulers' might have been women (Oyéwùmí 1997). Because of this type of misunderstandings a huge work of de-construction is needed. The apparently familiar must be scrutinized and questioned. Western concepts and lines of thought must be tested to see if they work. What is needed is a development of home-grown theories, as Amina Mama argues:

> There is a pressing need for 'home grown theory, particularly in view of the fact that the experience of African women differs so much from that of Western women. [...] While it may be incumbent upon us to draw on theories formulated elsewhere, perhaps it is necessary to re-operationalise some of the basic concepts used in women's studies, so as to ground them in our own experience and local conditions (Mama 1996, 67).

Women's experience and local conditions are also the raw material of women's fiction. In a certain sense African women's fiction have spearheaded development of African feminist thinking, and literary analysis has played and still plays an important role in the development of African feminist ideas, as many African scholars point out (cf Ogundipe-Leslie 1994; Kolawole 1997; Nfah-Abbenyi 1997; Nnaemeka 1997).

African women pictorial artists have also emerged on the scene. In the important and influential *Africa remix* exhibition, which from 2004 to 2007 toured Düsseldorf, London, Paris, Tokyo, Stockholm and Johannesburg, among 82 artists from 56 different African countries, 22 were women. Many of the women's works (and some of the men's) deal with gender issues.

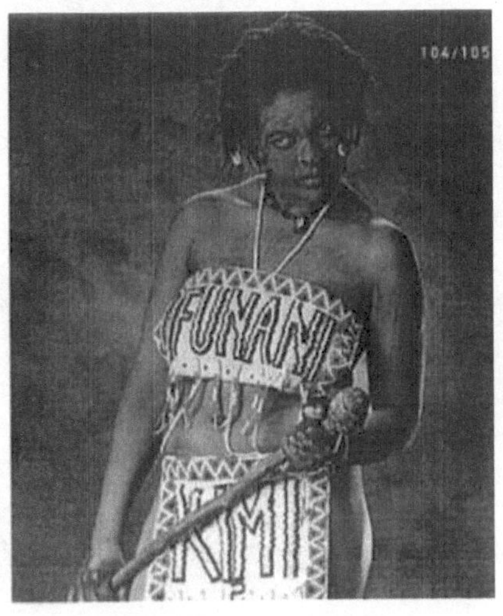


Fig. 16. Zamalo Dunywa's work Ufunani Kimi.

In order to wind up this essay on Africa, Art and Gender with examples of African pictorial art, I have chosen three works, which show artistic expressions matching some of the topics discussed above. Zamalo Dunywa's work *Ufunani Kimi* – "What do you want from me?" *(fig 16)* is a talking back/looking back picture. 'Talking back' is a term coined by African American feminist writer Bell

Hooks. The young woman in the photograph is dressed in the Zulu maidens' virginity costume, but she does not at all look submissive. She carries a club, and with an investigative and threatening gaze she not only looks back – she seems ready to strike back as well.

Wangechi Mutu's work *Mask (fig 17)* speaks about identities and re-interpretations of tradition. The young smart urban woman, with well manicured hands and polished nails (obviously cut from a magazine of sorts; many of Mutu's works are collage pieces including cuttings from women's magazines) has got herself entangled into an old African iron mask with traditionally combed hair and ugly teeth. Where does she belong? Or is she creating something new and previously unknown based on a mix of iron masks and magazines?

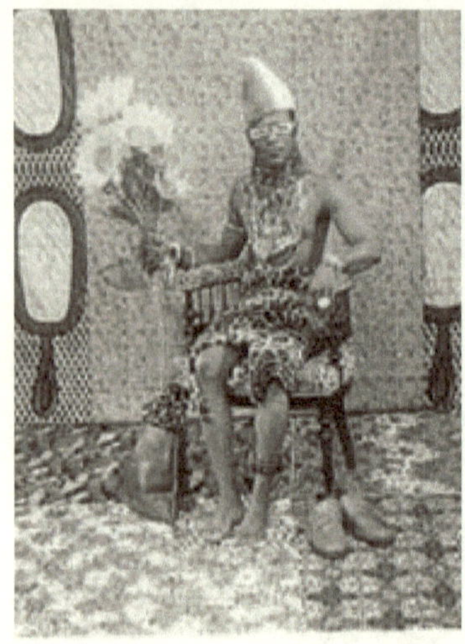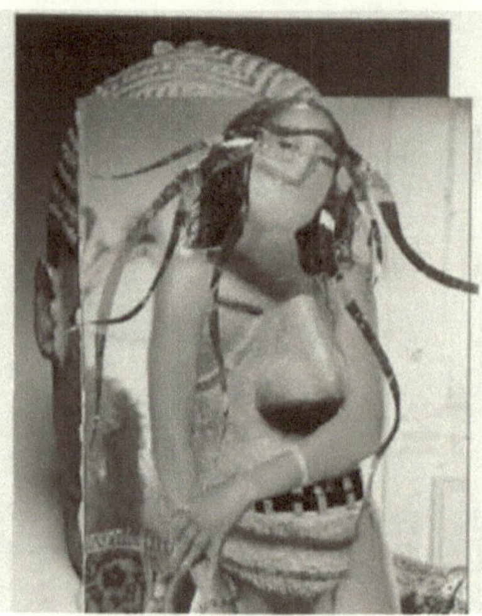

Fig. 17. Wangechi Mutu's work Mask
Fig. 18. Samuel F osso, Le chef: celui qui a vendu l'Afrique aux colon

The third picture is also a staged photograph, the artist is a man, Samuel Fosso, and the title is *Le chef: celui qui a vendu l'Afrique aux colons (fig 18)*. Samuel Fosso is dressed up according to Western stereotypes of an African chief, dressed in leopard hides with heavy golden necklaces and bracelets. But he also wears a funny set of smart sunglasses, and his brand new red leather shoes are neatly placed next to his fur clad throne. In his hand he holds a bunch of huge (artificial) sunflowers. The wall behind the throne, as well as the floor, are covered with brightly-coloured Afro-prints, one of these decorated with printed mirrors. The chief himself is a lean, small fragile body, almost feminine. In other of Fosso's photographs he pictures himself in drag. This is almost an inverted drag picture: a feminine man parading as a (supposedly) patriarchal chief. The picture turns stereotypes about Africa and about gender upside down a couple of times. It reflects certain expectations about what an African chief looks like (leopard hides, the throne) but then again it mocks those expectations (the feeble small feminine body, the sunflowers). Gender-wise it shows a supposed patriarch, who does not at all look like a patriarch. The mirrors in the background, some of them turned upside down, give away the key to this reading of the picture.

**Conclusion**
Winding up this essay on relations between (ideas of) Africa, Art and Gender, seen through four moments in a history of over more than 100 years – what can be said? From European art produced on myths, dreams and images of Africa (which had frequently more to do with Europe than with Africa as such), where the story line is clearly androcentric, and where with only few exceptions women appear as incarnations of sexuality (or motherhood) under the historical conditions of colonization, the situation slowly changes with the budding anti-colonial movements after the Second World War to one where African voices are heard and listened to. In the beginning these voices are still all male, and the situations they describe are seen from male points of view. African women fiction writers appear on the scene only in the 1960s, and African women pictorial artists only decades later.[5] Once African woman writers and artists do appear, however, their alternative descriptions of African social worlds are picked up by feminist scholars, laying the ground and clearing the way for African postcolonial feminist thinking about men, women, gender and sexuality.

**Notes**

[1] *L'Afrique Fantôme* has been republished several times, latest 1996 as part of a full collection of Leiris' work *Miroir de l'Afrique*.

[2] In the photograph there seems to be a woman sitting in the middle of the first row. Presumably this is Mme Yandé Christiane Diop, wife of Alioune Diop. Mme Diop has been the Director of *Presence Africaine* after her husband's death. The list of delegates for the conference is available on the website for W.E.B. Du Bois Institute for African and African American Research, Harvard University.

[3] Chinua Achebe was also the first editor of the series (1962-1972).

[4] In addition to the UN World Conferences on Women 1985 in Nairobi and 1995 in Beijing, there was also the Conference on Environment and Development in Rio 1992, the Conference on Human Rights in Vienna 1993, the Conference on Population and Development in Cairo 1994, and the Social Summit in Copenhagen 1995.

[5] I am in this context not counting white African writers like Olive Schreiner (born 1855), Doris Lessing (1919), Nadine Gordimer (1923), or white woman painters like Irma Stern (born 1894).

**References**

Albers, Irene (2006): '"Passion Dogo": Marcel Griaule und Michel Leiris.' Die Geheimnisse der Dogon (und der Franzosen), in Wendl, Tobias, Bettina von Lintig and Kerstin Pinther (eds) (2006): *Black Paris. Kunst und Geschichte einer Schwarzen Diaspora*, Peter Hammer Verlag.

Amadiume, Ify (1987). *Male Daughters, Female Husbands*. London: Zed Books.

Blake, Jody (2006): 'Modernistische Kunst und populäre Unterhalting im Paris der Jazz-Ära, 1900-1930,' in Wendl, Tobias, Bettina von Lintig and Kerstin Pinther (eds) 2006: *Black Paris. Kunst und Geschichte einer Schwarzen Diaspora*, Peter Hammer Verlag.

Currey, James (2008): *Africa Writes Back*, James Currey.

Graugaard, Christian (2008): 'Fire postkort fra minefelterne,' in Golden Days in Copenhagen (ed): *København i en Jazztid*, Politikens Forlag.

Haggard, Rider (1885/1994): *King Solomon's Mines*, Penguin.

Hall, Stuart (ed) (1922): *Formations of Modernity*, Open University Polity Press.

Hargreaves, Alec (1981): *The Colonial Experience in French Fiction*, Macmillan Press.

Jacobsen, Grethe (1986): *Kvindeskikkelser og kvindeliv i Danmarks middelalder*, Gad.

Jamin, Jean (1996): 'Introduction,' in Michel Leiris: *Miroir de l'Afrique*, Gallimard.

Jules-Rosette (2007): *Josephine Baker in Art and Life*, University of Illinois Press.

Kalu, Anthonia (2001): *Women, Literature and Development in Africa*, Africa World Press.

Kolawole, Mary Modupe (1997): *Womanism and African Consciousness*, Africa World Press.

Leiris, Michel (1996): *Miroir de l'Afrique*, Gallimard. Lewis, Desiree (2001): Introduction, African Feminisms, *Agenda* no 50, (2001).

Mama, Amina (1996): 'Gender Research and Women's Studies in Africa,' in Amina Mama (ed): *Setting an Agenda for Gender and Women's Studies in Nigeria*, Tamaza Publishing Company.

McClintock, Anne (1995): *Imperial Leather. Race, Gender and Sexuality in the Colonial Contest*, Routledge.

Nfah-Abbenyi, Juliana Makuchi (1997): *Gender in African Women's Writing*, Indiana University Press.

Nnaemeka, Obioma (1997): *The Politics of (M)Othering*, Routledge.

Nzegwu, Nkiru (2004): *Family Matters*, State University of New York Press.

Ogundipe-Leslie, Molara (1994): *Re-creating Ourselves. African Women and Critical Transformations*, Africa World Press.

Petersen, Kirsten Holst (ed) (1988): *Criticism and Ideology: Second African Writers' Conference*, Stockholm 1986. Nordiska Afrikainstitutet, Uppsala.

Riesz, János (2006): Verlohrene shone und Propheten kommenden Unheils. Gemeinsamkeiten und Unterschiede der frühen Négritude-Dichter, in Wendl, Tobias, Bettina von Lintig and Kerstin Pinther (eds) (2006): *Black Paris. Kunst und Geschichte einer Schwarzen Diaspora*, Peter Hammer Verlag.

Stott, Rebecca (1989): 'The Dark Continent: Africa as a Female Body in Haggard's Adventure Fiction,' in *Feminist Review* no 32.

Wendl, Tobias and Bettina von Lintig (2006): 'Das Schwarze Paris. 'Geschichte, Kunst und Mythos,' in Wendl, Tobias, von Lintig and Kerstin Pinther (2006).

Wendl, Tobias, Bettina von Lintig and Kerstin Pinther (eds), (2006): *Black Paris. Kunst und Geschichte einer Schwarzen Diaspora*, Peter Hammer Verlag.

Wivel, Mikael (1986): Manden med øjnene, in *Louisiana Revy*, vol 26, no 3.

# Part II
## Culture, Conflict & Controversy

# Location of African Culture: Beyond Afroscepticism and the New Cosmopolitan Exotic
## - Taiwo Oloruntoba-Oju

"What is theoretically innovative, and politically crucial, is the need to think beyond narratives of originary and initial subjectivities and to focus on those moments and processes that are produced in the articulation of cultural differences." **(Homi Bhabha,** *Location of Culture* 32)

"That wench within the human psyche which we vaguely call tragedy is the most insistent voice that bids us return to our sources; there, illusively, hovers the key to the human paradox, the key to our being or non-being." **(Wole Soyinka**, *Myth, Literature and the African World* 147)

*Bi ọmọdé ba subú a wo iwaju, bi agba ba subú a wo ẹyìn*

("When a child stumbles, he looks to the fore; when an elder stumbles, he glances behind [for the cause]").
**(A Yoruba proverb)**

**Pastness, Presentness, In-Between-ness and Culture Survival**
The title of this chapter is deliberately set as an echo of Homi Bhabha's (1994) postcolonial classic, and as an implied criticism of aspects of his long-running advocacy of a "third space" of culture, or of cultural in-between-ess. The criticism is not of the notion of cultural in-between-ness per se, since cultural in-between-ness is an inevitable consequence of transnational or other contacts, hence an age-long and a not-at-all-controversial notion in itself. However, certain collateral assumptions that recur in sundry formulations of *the third space* do collide unrelentingly with some of culture's well

established socio-political and affective imperatives as they relate to colonized or displaced peoples. The problem here has been the appropriate location of narratives of originary within the rubric of postcolonial discourse, and particularly in issue is the formulation of "the third space of culture" formed in the process of transnational contact as one that is, among others, "not part of the continuum of the past or present" (*Location* 7). The contention has been whether indeed cultural products of "the third space," to which Africa and its Diasporas are also consigned in such formulations, can be validly theorized in isolation of "the continuum of the past or present," and whether it would not rather indeed be politically crucial for Africans to continually confront those discourses that threaten to annihilate their own narratives of originary and their concomitant sense of being.

 The socio-political and affective imperative of culture that Bhabha's formulation collides with is easily appreciable. Culture, as aptly captured in Wole Soyinka's theorization, is "an instrument of self-definition," and therefore "a primary target of assault by an invading force" ("Survival Patterns" 190); conversely, the preservation of culture or its artifacts has always been a prime objective in the struggle for liberation, survival and a continued sense of selfhood on the part of the colonized and the displaced. Whereas the creation of new transcultural or hybridized forms in the process of colonial and transnational contact (and resistance) is always to be acknowledged, and indeed has been variously theorized (for example as typically involving the "appropriation" and "abrogation" of aspects of colonialist language and culture (Aschroft et al 2), or as involving strategies of "pidginisation," "relexification," "contextualization" (Zabus 102), etc), what is contentious is the formulation of the resulting "third space" of culture as a place where, as Bhabha continues to insist, arguably in postmodernist fervour, "[it would not be important] to trace the original moments from which the third emerges" (Rutherford 211).

By impliedly consigning all narratives of originary (where we came from, how we have lived, our language/culture, and how we got here – in Chinua Achebe's parlance: "where the rain began to beat us" (*Morning Yet* 29) – to the dustbin of insignificant history, such formulations do play even if unwittingly into a perpetual western attitude and frequent imperialist design to overwrite other, especially African, cultures, ultimately obstructing what Asante ("New Understanding") has termed the "recentering of Africans in a human place." The counter struggle for African cultural and socio-political survival continues to be provoked by, among others, the now fashionable articulation of *change* in the African socio-historical and cultural clime as a death-knell of African culture, or of *Africanity*,[1] in the wake of a new and presumably supplanting cosmopolitan imaginary. This article is in furtherance of the debate between a conception of culture as *continuous* or as *discontinuous*, and a further expression of the reality that the African cultural present can hardly discountenance its past, more so a past that is continually attested in the continent's new, sometimes exotic, languages and in the cognate cultures at home and abroad. And this is in spite of the sundry and growing expressions of *Afroscepticism* in discourses on African culture.[2]

It is important to clarify that Bhabha does appreciate and make allowance for the socio-political and affective imperatives of culture noted above. He does in fact reiterate that "any group or society that has been oppressed wants an acknowledgment of its own history, a history which has been hidden or denied" (Makos "Rethinking Experience"). And indeed Bhabha's intervention comes from a political perspective and concern to destabilize certain discursive binaries (*civilized/savage, enlightened/ignorant*, etc) by which the west justified its attitude towards, and domination of, colonized peoples and cultures.[3] But he does this by way of a somewhat universal attack on the concept of culture originaries and a sense of homogenous identities. For him, the complex negotiation of language and culture that occurs in the colonial process draws attention retrospectively to the processes involved in the formation of all cultures and all identities. This process, in which the colonizers' culture does not solely act upon, but is also acted upon by, the culture of the colonized, shows that "no culture is full unto itself," which thus "[challenges] our sense of the historical identity of culture as homogenizing, unifying force, authenticated by originary Past, kept alive in the national tradition of the People" (*Location* 37).

The alternative posited by Bhabha, then, is to "think beyond narratives of originary and initial subjectivities and to focus on those moments and processes that are produced in the articulation of cultural differences." However, the dilemma that such propositions have always posed for all subdued cultures, and the discursive conflict here, is that the interstistial existence of colonized and displaced peoples, which the people themselves well understand, is precisely the condition that continuously urges upon them the consciousness of history and of the difference of cultures; this is what has always triggered those recollections of the Past, of their originating moments, providing at least affective if not material comforts as they luxuriate in the real or imagined narratives of their self-hood and of grand gone-by days.

Bhabha's "third space" postulation has been variously criticized for, among others, its inability to account for the different types of Diasporas (Mitchell, "Hype of Hybridity"), or for the "material conditions that would emerge within a colonial discourse analysis" (Parry, "Problems," cited in Meredith, "Hybridity"); its privileging of literary texts above material experience, and hence its doubtful applicability to the flesh and blood, real life, migrant (Gikandi, "Globalisation" 644), or to the *resident* and *resilient* cultural products of Africa" (Oloruntoba-Oju, "Irreducible Africanness"); for "[repeating] and [rehearsing] (sic) the falsities and dominant tendencies of an Anglo-American, eurocentric approach to knowledge production on Africa and the Black world, despite setting out initially to point out the dangers of such an approach" (Osei-Nyame 73), etc. It has also been criticized for its doubtful novelty, originality or utility (Majorie Perloff; Mark Miller, cited by Eakin, "Havard's Catch"), and even its turgidity (The Bad Writing Contest, "Press Releases").

The endeavour in this article is additionally to locate Bhabha's postulations within what I call the colonial *African culture overwrite* continuum, that is, the apparent and continued imperialist (and neo-imperialist) project of overwriting the cultures of Africa and the cultures of other worlds, as a continuing strategy to advance western hegemony, now fashionably disguised as an all-embracing "globalism." I would also argue that Bhabha's illustrations and metaphors need not have led to his conclusions, and that any "third space" postulate that discounts original moments of culture is inappropriate to African literature, culture and aesthetics. I would further advance that, even while the dynamism of the cultural process, characterized by Appadurai in terms of what he called "deterritorialization" and the "growing disjunctures between ethnoscapes, technoscapes, finanscapes, mediascapes and ideoscapes" ("Disjuncture") is to be constantly acknowledged, it is equally true that African languages and cultures, by continuing to thrive in some of their ancient forms, sometimes in hidden ways, respond positively to narratives of originary far more than is acknowledged by those potentially castrating perspectives of "in-betweenness" that presume to dispense with the past. I would reiterate finally that the panacea for the socially and culturally dispossessed has always been and remains to continually rev up recollections of those originaries of culture that stood for their, in this case African, sense of being.

It must be disclaimed that the insistence here is not the same as an extreme nativist or essentialist advocacy for a lived return to the past (as if that were even a remote possibility), or a view of the past as a pristine idyll and the only bridge to the future. The instability of the cultural process as it mimics the undulating ebb and flow of life is a pre-historic given that is already known to, and accounted for by, even the *hardiest* nativist[4] – *ìgbà kan n lọ ìgbà kan n bọ̀ ìgbà kan o lo ilé ayé gbó*, as the ancient Yoruba put it ("a period goes, another comes; no single clime could ever exhaust existence"). Nonetheless, the creation of hybrid forms, resulting typically but not exclusively from the contact and clashes of different languages and cultures, should not compel us to discountenance the historicity involved in the process, or to discountenance the pastness that feeds the presentness. Rejecting the notion of a *third space* of culture as one that is "not part of the continuum of the past or present," this paper reaffirms instead a continuing and pervasive *renewal* process, sometimes conflictual and sometimes consensual, by which the African cultural parole continues to mimic its langue in various domains.

This *continuance* reading of culture – the position that hybridity does not necessarily dissolve its components into insignificance or nothingness, and that its *newness* does not blunt the appreciation of the continued presence of the old – has been presented in different forms in postcolonial discourses. This article proposes to further advance the reality of a continuing Africanity in various dimensions of culture on the continent, and in its numerous Diasporas in which what we describe here as the *new cosmopolitan exotic* is progressively located. What we call for in the final analysis is a new vocabulary for the concept of "change" in postcolonial African culture.

**In-Between the *African Culture Overwrite* Continuum**
Interventions such as Bhabha's could be located, albeit with a sense of irony, within the *African culture overwrite continuum*. The old colonial *overwrite* assault on indigenous African history and culture into which the new discourse fits is established knowledge. The catalogue includes not just the *dark colonial narratives*[5] in which Africa supposedly had no history, no culture and no language, but also the actual culture castration policies and practices of colonial authorities – for example, the banning, as "heathenish," of various forms of indigenous African aesthetic expressions (masks and masquerades, indigenous musical instruments such as gongs, drums and castanets, folk performances and the like), in favour of Christian and Islamic forms, being the supplanting religions and civilizations of the colonialists.

The attack on indigenous African languages has undoubtedly been the most devastating instrument of the culture overwrite programme. Since language is the ultimate tool of self-expression, self-identification/authentication, and of the performance of culture, to cut off the indigenous mother tongue (pun intended) was to slash a vital artery of identity and culture. In place of it, the colonialists largely substituted garbled forms of European languages in the production of the new African, resulting in a devastating "in-betweenness" (including a Caliban loss of competence in both the indigenous and the new, colonial, languages, witness among others the fits and stumbles of African nations' foreign language speeches at the United Nations where, on the other hand, the nations that do have languages speak them. Also involved was a "fundamental collateral damage to cognitive development caused by the absence of a systematic mother tongue input, which is otherwise so crucial to the formative stages of child education" (Oloruntoba-Oju, "Irreducible

Africanness." See also Chumbow, "Place of Mother tongue"; Adegbija, "Language Attitudes"; Oloruntoba-Oju, "Communication"; Cummins, "Language, Power and Pedagogy"). This programme of cutting off the mother tongue continues insidiously to date in many "postcolonial" schools and colleges in Africa, in some of which the sign, "Speak English *Always*" (my emphasis), continues to be displayed (Fig 1).

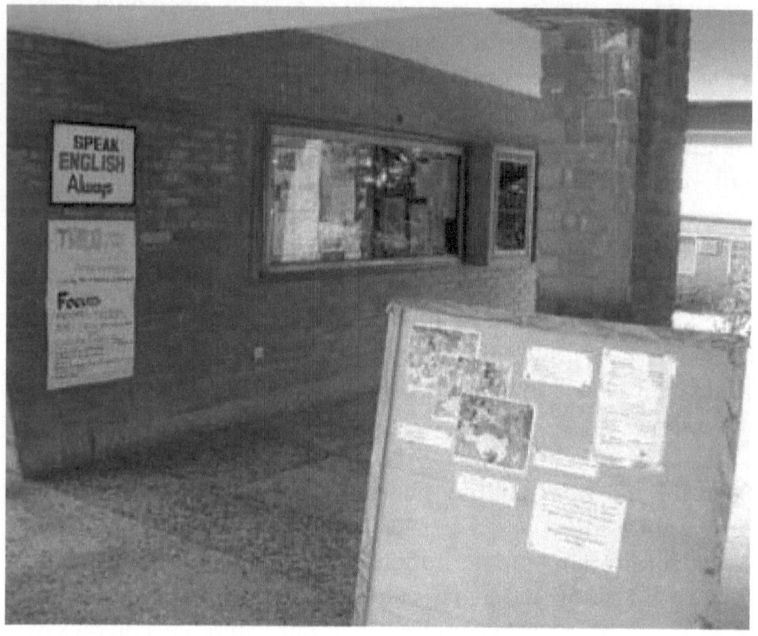



Fig.1. Thomas Adewumi International College, Oko, Omuaran, Nigeria (TAICO): *"Speak English Always"*

However, what may not be so well established is the contemporary reality of the imperialist programme as a continuing project. As a number of historians and theorists have affirmed (see Jonnson "The Western View," and in this volume), the continuation of the neo-imperialist project to re-colonize Africa is not a figment of the imagination of the African nationalist, or some variant of "nativist" alarmism. The enthronement of an apparent "global" (but in reality Anglo-global) culture has also continued through the work of multinational corporations, through continued economic impoverishment that ensures the continued dependence of the erstwhile colonies and its populations on western economies, and through the obtrusive and imposing media and satellite outposts of neo-colonial cultures (see also Wallerstein, "Culture as Ideological Battleground"). More subtly still, the *culture overwrite* programme may be observed enacted, not exclusively but often through language, at sundry informal and sometimes nondescript sites, such as dictionaries; in humanistic disciplines, where negatively valued "cultural thought patterns" are typically assigned to non-Western, especially non-English rhetoric (see Oloruntoba-Oju, "Perspectives"); in computer word-processing, and sometimes *word-dispossessing* softwares (in which you may comfortably write "Americanism" and "Europeanism," for example, but not "Africanism," notwithstanding that the latter term is no more "homogenizing" than the former), etc. Against such a background, any insinuation of the non-existence, non-relevance or absolute dissolution of an African original culture within a migrant "in-between-ness" can be justifiably described as a complicit theory, even if unwittingly so.

The point here is to locate interventions such as Bhabha's within this continuum, since the contention in this paper is set in contradiction to some of the postulates that power the continuum. Whether in the hands of conscious colonial/imperial activists, or of concurring elements among the once colonized, the objective, or at least the effect, of the *African culture overwrite* programme is always the same – the dissolution of African claims to an original indigenous culture, and to its rightful cultural suzerainty over African-derived meanings and aesthetics within the African Diaspora and within the new, 'global,' cosmopolis. Concomitantly, we must conclude, a theory of "in-between-ness" such as Bhabha's that purports to write off or discount the claims of African cultural originaries (or other culture originaries) on, or contribution to, African-derived migrant cultures does fit into a continued imperialist programme to *overwrite* the cultures of dominated populations.

The *African culture overwrite* programme has often involved a *culture rewrite* process, that is, the *rewriting* of sundry manifests of indigenous African cultures by witting and unwitting alienating hands, to suit hegemonic and propaganda objectives. The *rewriting* of African history and culture as non-existent (or as sub-human) in western anthropological narratives provided the original justification for actualizing the *culture overwrite* programme. While the formal abolition of slavery and the granting of forms of "independence" to once colonized entities did not thereby dissolve this programme, again, the subtle forms by which the programme has continued to be activated or *performed* into contemporary times have not always been obvious. One of such is through intellectualist *rewrites* or figment *location* of culture originaries.

The illustrative fragments by which Bhabha exemplifies the "new" "in-between-ness" of culture manifests are classic examples of idiosyncratic *rewrites* and figment locations of the cultures of the once colonized. Interpretive idiosyncrasy and a neo-Baudrillardian simulacrum is the hallmark of such *rewriting*. For example, Bhabha's borrowed metaphors of transition could also be deployed with comparable if not greater comfort in support of opposing views of in-between-ness – the "bridge," or "staircase," wherever and however "in-between" it may hang, is also a signifying index of some origin (of source, or starting place), and of potential destination, just as the "sailing ship" (another of Bhabha's metaphors for in-between-ness) presupposes the co-referentiality of source and destination ports. The point here is that meaning is typically anaphoric, hence anchored always on some known quantity or frame of reference; and where cataphoric, its significance must be recoverable within the scope of signification or of reading expectation, or it falls in void. It is therefore not helpful to deploy the term "alternative," as Bhabha does, while denying or discounting its presupposition, the "native" in "alternative," without which our understanding of the latter term cannot be complete. Similarly, Bhabha's "non-presence" (of "in-betweenness") can only take its reference from both the "presence" and the "pastness" from which the so called "non-presence" inevitably derives. In short, the recognition of "in-between-ness" relies precisely on the relation of the "in-between" to adjacent locales, and hence the postmodernist paradox. To strip "in-between-ness" of its adjacent cultural frames is to upturn the system of meaning that is necessary to apprehend its presuppositions. The resulting language can only be discordant, and sometimes incoherent.

Third space propositions are sometimes goaded by a somewhat opportunistic analysis of data that is otherwise innocent of or incidental to the propositions. One such piece of data in *Location of Culture* is the American (English) radio broadcast of a performance artist, "from the hot deserts of Nogales," which data includes insertions of Mexican (language). This simple code-switching/mixing (a sociolinguistic phenomenon long recognized and abundantly theorized) becomes, in Bhabha's *rewriting*, a symbol of the "beyond," of the "intervening space," and a "'newness' that is not part of the continuum of the past of the present." In reality, however, the data, a combination of English and Mexican, *is* certainly part of the continuum of the past, with a definite history, and part of the present, with a definite socio-cultural momentum. The broadcaster referred to by Bhabha, Guillermo Gomez-Peria, did not have to live in or broadcast from the Arizona desert for such an insertion of minority codes, a regular fare even in USA presidential campaigns, to occur. Nor does this or other even more intertwining code mixtures dissolve appreciation of the original sources of the code-mixed parts. Hybridity maintains rather than dissolve the perennial tension between pastness and newness; the components of the new exhibit forms that are recognizable as belonging to the old and new. The forms thereby project the contestant social, and other, values of the different climes that they represent.

A close look at other data deployed by Bhabha affords a glimpse of the obfuscation process that apparently sustains those culture *diminutions*, that is, his downgrading *rewrite* of original situations, cultures, and their true historical course. Often, we find a sheer reification of the artistic impulse in these *rewrites*, and an elevation of idiosyncratic aesthetic *splashes on canvas* to the status of undying truth. For example, Nadine Gordimer's attention to detail, which no doubt is aesthetically captivating, is however disproportionately draped in halo imageries in Bhabha's *rewrite*. Gordimer describes in the novel the moment when Aila, the main character, who has

been under guard for her crime, comes face to face with her aggrie-
ved husband. Among other gestures described by Gordimer, Aila
"placed the outer edge of each hand, fingers extended and close together, as a frame on either side of the sheets of testimony in front
of her. And she placed herself before him, to be judged by him."
This picturesque scenario can be replicated a hundredfold (in similar scenes of crime, in police charge rooms, in seminar/conference
rooms as paper presenters compose themselves and their papers,
and at sundry sites of similar engagements); however, in Bhabha's
idiosyncratic *rewrite*, this common enough gesture becomes: "the
in-between hybridity of the history of sexuality and race," "a boun-
dary that is at once inside and outside, the inside's outsideness."
This fairly common kinesis, Bhabha insists, designates "Aila's in-
between identity" and affirms "the borders of culture's insurgent
and interstitial existence," etc, etc! (*Location*, 16-19).
 The tragic confrontation in Toni Morrison's *Beloved* would also be
treated under the theme of in-between-ness by Bhabha. Hoewver,
the non-compliant dynamism of the text would appear to force him
into at least a string of ambivalences on the issue. Seith's oxymoro-
nic infanticide in Morrison's novel (Seith loves her babies so much
that she kills them to prevent their falling into the hands of the slave
master and into slavery) is historically attested in plantation slave
life and in the corresponding, reportorial, narratives. As an aside,
the historical Black (slave period) infanticide cannot be placed on
the same ethical plane as Chinese female infanticide; however, the
Chinese version does represent the same tragic impetus that powers the cyclical motion of personal and communal catastrophes
throughout human history. Chinese female infanticide has accounted for the destruction of some 39% of female children, and is now
increasingly replaced with other forms of gendercide such as female
deselection (abortion of female fetuses). The analogy with historical
black infanticide, which I cautiously propose here, is imperfect but
useful in emphasizing that the tragic is not resident in any specific
so and so domains, not least the "interstitial" locale of Bhabha's
("third space") theoretical beloved. Rather, tragedy belongs with
the perennial and it as much encompasses tales of dislodgement
as myriad other human disasters, cataclysmic consequences, and

what Wole Soyinka famously describes as "the recurrent cycle of human stupidity."

Morrison's *Beloved*, then, isolates such a tragic moment in black history, indexing a pastness that, tragic as it was, continues to feed into the present even if as a narrative of remembrance. Bhabha would acknowledge, almost in momentary Freudian amnesia of the thesis of "in-between-ness," the novel's inherent call for continuity, for "social solidarity" and a sense of belonging that carries the past along. Even in Bhabha's hands, therefore, Morrison's *Beloved* resists the attempt to *rewrite* it in a manner to deny or downplay a past that begs so evidently, in the novel as elsewhere, to be recognized and be therapeutically re-inscribed with the present: "I want you to touch me on my inside part and call me by my name … I am looking for the join … I am loving my face so much … my dark face is close to me … I want to join." Beloved's plaint in this novel is to carry forward her sense of being, to continue with her name, her fundamental identity, her Blackness, into new dwellings and new forms of identity. Not to bury the past, but to acknowledge it into the present, and deal with it progressively in terms of the demands of the present and the future. Same as Barack Obama would say decades later even in the throes of an uncertain presidential election: *You just gotta deal with the past.*

Morrison's novel thus leaves Bhabha no option but to acknowledge the insistence of history and, not only its compelling intrusions but also its frequent footholds in the present. For once, "in-between-ness" is subordinated to locatives of pastness in Bhabha's apparently foiled *rewriting*:

The women speak in tongues, form a space "in-between" each other which is a communal space. They explore an interpersonal reality: a social reality that appears within the poetic image as if it were in parenthesis – aesthetically distanced, held back, *and yet historically framed*. It is difficult to convey the rhythm and the improvisation of those chapters, but *it is impossible not to see in them the healing of history, a community reclaimed in the making of a name* (*Location*, 17; my emphases).

The focus on Bhabha in criticisms of the "globalist" fixation of some postcolonial theorists is only the price often paid for prominence in a field. In reality, the refutation of the continuing presence of the past and denial of culture's established legacy is a rapidly growing pastime of many of "our own brothers and sisters." The question of African "culture" has long been compromised, when even "joint heirs" of the culture deny its legacies. On this, Chinua Achebe's Obierika, has always been irresistible: "Our own men and sons have joined the ranks of the stranger … [The white man] says that our customs are bad; and our own brothers who have taken up his religion also say that our customs are bad." (Achebe, *Things Fall Apart* 115)

And good old Frantz Fanon:

Having judged, condemned, abandoned his cultural forms, his language, his food habits, his sexual behaviour, his way of sitting down, of resting, of laughing, of enjoying himself, the oppressed flings himself open upon the imposed culture with the desperation of a drowning man." (Fanon 39)

The concomitant self-denial or denial of self, by a horde of "new" Africans has been variously theorized (Compare the terms, "self-negation" and "self betrayal" (Soyinka, *Myth*, viii), or "self-dispossession" (Oyewumi 2001), "self erasure" or "self-deracing,"[6] etc deployed in similar contexts). The proliferation of such denial today is taking place against the background of a growing globalism or cosmopolitanism and the intensifying heterogeneity, noted earlier and elaborated below, of various aspects of African spiritual and material culture – culinary, vestment, sexual, literary, musical, kinetic, etc. That the authors and proprietors of the 'global' culture hardly let go of their own language, culture or positive traditional values, but relentlessly promote them, is a moral apparently lost on the rather enthusiastic African Afrosceptics, the African deniers of an African heritage. The immutable lyric of legendary Nigerian musician Fela Anikulapo Kuti, in his song *Colo-mentality*, is relentlessly apposite about the Africans he considered trapped within a colonial mentality:

*Dem don release you now, but you never release yourself.* ("They have since released you [from slavery], but you have not released yourself")

**The African Grand Possessive and the New Cosmopolitan Exotic**
As noted in the foregoing, a cornerstone of Bhabha's (and related) formulations on the question of identity is the idea that so much heterogeneity is framed in each culture as to apparently confound any idea of the homogeneity of identities. What is 'local' is invariably a mix, and this complex mixture is a global phenomenon, thus setting, according to Bhabha (and rightly too), "new rules of cultural understanding." "I'm attempting with my work to shift notions of what it means to belong to a culture, to have an identity -- to show how limited it is to cling onto rigidly defined imperialist or nationalist ideas" (cited in Makos "Rethinking Experience).

Heterogeneity has also been the presumed foil of any notion of Africanity and the most important principle behind the growing *Afroscepticism* in discussions of culture within the African context (see note 2). In sample formulations, what is called "African" art or music is nothing but "a hybrid blend of global sentiments…" (Bessire 185); Africa being "home to a thousand peoples … there are many styles that have not been touched by Africa and most of the rest have had many non-African hands on them as well" (Benzon 119, 203), etc. One of the *illustrants* of the determined *Afroscepticism* noted above is the Dutch wax whose alleged "trajectory from Indonesia to Holland to England and then to Africa and other parts of the world challenges the very notion of Africanicity" (Bessire 185). However, apart from not citing the historical or critical sources of this "trajectory," Bessire's skepticism here fails to appreciate the distinction between the wax technology of the fabric and the coloured patterns enabled by the technology, or interrogate why the Dutch do not strictly use the fabric themselves and who they rather make them for. The sceptic also fails to acknowledge the *adire* fabrics which have Yoruba and some other West African locations, notably Mali, as their undisputed homeland, and from which Ankara and Dutch wax and Indonesian patterns were copied for the purpose of trade.

More to our point here is that ancient African and other cultures themselves expressed a better understanding of the interface between heterogeneity and identity, and they frequently framed both in sayings that accommodate the potential ambivalence of identity, without undermining its basic recognisance. The Yoruba certainly understood identity as occurring within variable contexts, hence for example acknowledging sub-fields of heterogeneity within otherwise close-knit units, but without dislodging the conceptual homorganic frames that constitute larger, common ties of being. Heterogeneity is identified between households, and even amongst siblings and kin, let alone beyond borders:

*Báyi làá se n'ìlé wa, èèwọ̀ ibomìì*
("'Thus we behave in our house;' [is] a taboo elsewhere.")

*Èyí wù mí ò wù ọ́; ọmọ iyá méji jẹun lọ̀tọ̀ọ̀tọ̀*
("What appeals to me does not to you; [hence] two siblings sup differently")

Tí a bá ní ká fi ọmọ wé ọmọ, a ó lu ọmọ pa
("If we should compare sibling to sibling [demanding similar behaviour], we would end up clobbering one to death")

*Kìí jẹ́ ti baba t'ọmọ kó má láàlà*
("It cannot belong so uniformly to father and son as to have no demarcation")

Etc.

The ancient Yoruba were not disturbed, either, by the anonymity of those miniscule and indeterminate occurrences that have mixed or combined over time to constitute the present state of affairs. The lines of the palm (hand) offered a paradigm of unknown or obscure sources (*àtẹ́wọ́labálà a o m'ẹni o kọọ́* – "we only found lines on the palm; we do not know who drew them"); and periodicity a paradigm of the dynamism of history and culture (*ìgbà kan n lọ ìgbà kan n bọ̀ ìgbà kan o lo ilé ayé gbó* – "a period goes, another comes; no single clime could ever exhaust existence"). They recognize *àsà ìsẹ̀mbáyé* (age-old tradition or *culture immemorial*), *àsà ode ìsìn* or *àsà ode ìwoyí* (modernity; literally, "habits of today") and what they call, often pejoratively, (hybrids, mixtures). Locating the time of "entanglement" to employ a recurrent notion in Archille Mbembe's *On the Postcolony*, may seem tough, if not impossible; however, for the Yoruba, identity is constituted by those peculiarities established in terms of their stability over time and in terms of sustained distinction from other peculiarities. Modes of expression that are sufficiently peculiar to constitute a noticeable difference relative to others, or a difference that is sufficiently significant to constitute a peculiarity – these are the precise constituents of identity. The determination of the hybrid relies precisely on the recognition of adjacent and temporal identity frames, notwithstanding their liability to change, transmutation and transformation.

## Recognition and Recognisance

A twin process of *recognition* (of *self* and the *other*, as different, new or "exotic") and the simultaneous insertion of *recognisance* codes (those markers of continuity of an indigenous cultural self-hood) can always be identified within prevalent cultural practices in Africa and the cognate literature. Such recognition, and the representation of 'new,' cosmopolitan, western derived cultural forms as different, and sometimes as "exotic," has been a regular fare in African literature of hybrid expression (Chinua Achebe's *No Longer at Ease*, Wole Soyinka's *The Lion and the Jewel*, Gabriel Okara's "The Piano and the Drum," Okot P'Bitek's *Song of Lawino* and *Song of Ocol*, and Ama Ata Aidoo's *The Dilemma of a Ghost* as well as Zulu Sofola's *The Sweet Trap* being among early precursors).

In Achebe's *No longer at Ease*, the people of Umuofia "whistled in unbelief" to learn that, in Lagos, then a new African Cosmopolis brimming with "alien" cultural infusions, you could no longer attend your neighbour's ceremony without one of those papers (invitation cards) on which *RSVP* (promptly translated by the innovative indigenes as "rice and stew very plenty") is written. In Soyinka's *The Lion and the Jewel*, Sidi flays Lakunle's imported courtship manners, which not only seems designed to avoid the traditional bride wealth, but also comes with "this strange mouthing of yours," an intriguing description of kissing by a native girl. In his *The Interpreters*, the behaviour of the Oguazors provokes a mirthful satire on the importation of Victorian habits and colonial speech mannerisms on to African soil. In *The Childe Internationale* occurs a clash of culinary cultures, also a regular fare in many early African satires on western habits: Politician in the play takes one look at the "continental dish" prepared by his "been-to [Europe or America]" wife and pushes it aside, with an explanation that he does not mind eating it, "especially when I'm not hungry." In yet another example: the indigenous African gastric tract seems indifferent to hot peppery stuff, but in Zulu Sofola's *The Sweet Trap*, the educated wife cries her heart out after the indigenous peppery food sends several guests at her party (cosmopolitan elite also called "big men," and women) choking. Obi Okonkwo in Achebe's *No Longer at Ease* also complains of four years of nothing but "boiled potatotes" in the white man's land. The language of "othering" western culinary culture, as "exotic," is often dysphemistic in African literature. The examples can be multiplied.

Such examples no doubt draw attention again and again to the undeniably contestant nature of the process by which "culture" emerges and is articulated. It may of course be retorted that these examples occurred earlier on at a transitive juncture when colonial contact was relatively new and the contest of cultures was still raging (these are, after all, texts of the 50s and 60s through the 70s), and that new cultural equilibriums have since emerged. It may also be retorted that these are fictional representations rather than real life expressions, a criticism akin to that noted earlier in relation to Bhabha's formulations.

However, continued and real life culinary contestations are what you would find articulated in the numerous African, Pakistani and Indian cuisine shops that dot the heartland of European and American cities, and on the high seas in ships that bear "home food" to the stranded elements of the Diaspora. A few years ago, 2006, Olusegun Obasanjo, President of Nigeria at the time, was on CNN and he found occasion to talk about African culinary delights (how he especially loved pounded yam and not only that, loved to eat it the traditional way with his fingers). Flash back to Achebe's novel of 1960: "The second generation of educated Nigerians had gone back to eating *pounded* yam ("pound yam") or *garri* with their fingers for the good reason that it tasted better that way. Also for the even better reason that they were not as scared as the first generation of being called uncivilized" (*No Longer at Ease,* 18). And if Obasanjo's statement appeared like the tantrum of a doubtlessly maverick (ex) president, visit the weekend *owambe* African parties at home and abroad and see guests push aside Euro-continental culinary stuff for: "the real thing." Contemporary multinational billboards dotting the Nigerian skyline also acknowledge the continued resilience of traditional culinary habits, while advocating a "peaceful co-existence" and appealing to a sense of compatibility (Fig 2).

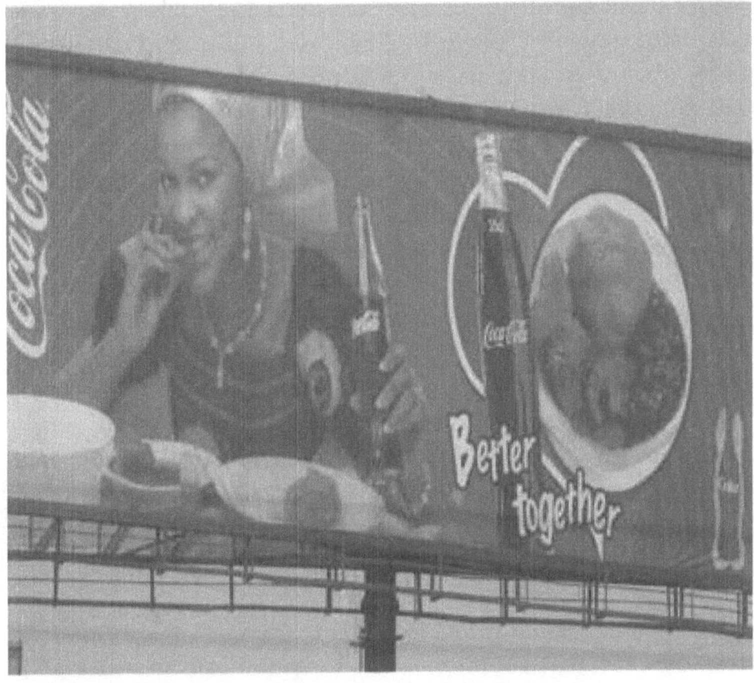


Fig. 2: Contemporary multinational billboards advertise new global/exotic products in Africa by acknowledging the resilience of old cultural habits

What contemporary cultural equilibriums show in reality therefore is a contest in which the "old" continues to reassert itself, albeit in new forms. Indeed, the new Cosmopolitan exotic, including colonial languages and their code-mixed varieties, western hippie culture, hip-hop music, western "high fashion," culinary mixtures and so on, have over time become an integral part of "native" African "in-between" life; the question, however, has been whether such "in-between-ness" justifies a questioning of more traditional forms of Africanness as a viable or continued identity.

The sundry denial of the African self noted by Fanon and others above is matched in intensity by the affirmation, by notable African literati, statesmen, musicians, dramatists and sundry culture workers, of an African identity, and of "a cultural entity which we define as the African world" (Soyinka, *Myth*, viii). In the affirmative utterances of these individuals, we find distinctive echoes of the old declaration of an African self both on the continent – from Negritude's formulations, albeit imperfect, through sundry "nativist" postcolonial pronouncements, and in the African Diasporas, represented in the Pan-Africanist philosophies of Du Bois and Marcus Garvey; in such iconic black consciousness utterances as the Afro-Cuban Arsenio Rodriguez's *Yo naci del Africa* ("I was born of Africa"); James Brown's "Say it loud, I m black and proud," or the Jamaican Peter Tosh's "Don't care where you come from; as long as you are a Black man you re an African," a call reloaded more recently in Lord Laro's "Though I'm Caribbean, I am African."

The African grand possessive (this is ours; this is African, I am/we are African/s) is continually expressed up to contemporary times in a language that is at once assertive and contestatory, as much in political speeches:

> "Being part of all these people, and in the knowledge that none dare contest that assertion, I shall claim that I am an African."
> - Mbeki, "South Africa"

as in satirical musical lyrics:

> *A no be gentul man at all …*
> *A be Africa man original*
> *A no what to wear*
> *But my friend don know*
> He put im coat, he put im tie …

"I'm not a Gentle man at all …
I am an original African man,
I know what to wear
But my friend doesn't.
He wears a coat, dons a tie …"
   - Fela Anikulapo Kuti (*Gentleman* 1973);


and sometimes in superlative tones:


*Ko si fasan kan to ju ti a lo*


"There is no fashion that is higher than *ours*"
   - Lagbaja (*Skentele Skontolo* 2004).


The Nigerian international masked musician, Lagbaja, has pursued
the same theme in the quote above in his latest "Dress with Sense"
track in the album *Sharp Sharp*, in which he also claims an African
originary for some of the more exotic 'new' cosmopolitan fashion
habits, such as the modern braid and labyrinthine tattoo marks that
have become a new fad in the west. Palimpsest traces of an African
originary continue be found at every level of cultural expression
*from hair to toe* (Fig 3).

Also important is the continued expression of *root impulse* by
contemporary elements within the Diaspora. Though such root impulse is not new, the deep expression of an African consciousness
and need for root-identification by some of these cosmopolitan or
"modern" elements could be quite startling (and here we are not
talking about the conscious workers of culture amongst them or
even about those formal, neo-Garvey, 'return to Africa' or 'Africa
for Africa' movements represented on today's world wide web, but
about the numerous everyday people who are not publicly identified
"nativists"): 'It was time to come back home and I packed my load
and headed straight to Nigeria. It was not that I got tired of working
with the BBC or living in the UK […] I have kids and wanted them
to come home and get some grounding on who they are, which for
me, was very important' (Azuh 2009). Some of these returnees also

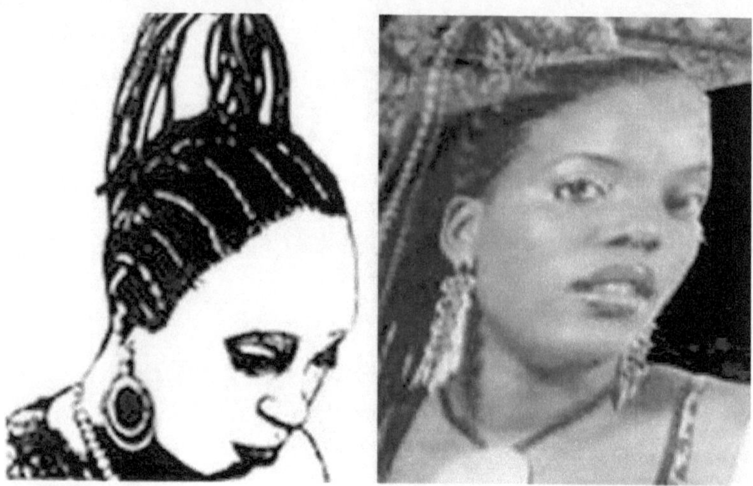

Fig. 3: Palimpsest traces of an African originary from hair to toe

express an acute understanding of identity that is not at all confused by the heterogeneous mass that the African world has become:
"Africa is important to me in terms of who I am. ... I do realize that
all those different countries within the continent have various different cultures that all vary within themselves, but they're also different from being African-American cultures" (quoted in Dent 115).

The daily activities and decisions of such people in the African
Diaspora emphasize the need to absorb the affective domains of
daily living into the theorization of contemporary African culture.
A thousand and one anecdotes of migrancy reveal gaps and dents
in the theory of "in-between-ness" as a death-knell of culture originaries. "What do we do," asks Gikandi (644), "when we discover
that the subaltern of the new Diasporas, instead of adopting the
cosmopolitan beloved of the new postcolonial elite, continue to
demand the most fundamentalist forms of cultural identification?"
Gikandi would also chide the new globalist discourse (the variety
prominently championed by Bhabha and Appadurai) for the "rather
optimistic claim that the institutions of cultural production provide
irrefutable evidence of new global relations." He contends further
that "it is premature to argue that the images and narratives that
denote the new global culture are connected to a global structure or

that they are disconnected from earlier or older forms of identity." Continuing syncretistic practices in imported religions and the resilience of traditional rituals and observances in day to day living certainly confound any view of 'change' as implying a death-knell of original cultures.

The numerous statements of affirmation from such a broad spectrum of contemporary African and Diaspora life provide basis for the emergence of a renewed vocabulary for the appreciation and categorisation of emergent African cultural phenomena. The new vocabulary avoids the pulverising insinuations of "change" or "newness" as the death-knell of African culture or of an African sense of being. From an Africanist perspective, the new vocabulary would speak, instead, of *continuance, recognisance, re-affirmation, renewal, re-integration.*

The task of the relevant culture work is to continue to elicit concomitant features at the level of language and symbol from all relevant texts. Cultural Africanity indeed requires a level of commitment akin to Molefi Asante's five part Afrocentrist manifesto, including: "an intense interest in psychological location as determined by symbols, motifs, rituals, and signs;" "a commitment to finding the subject-place of Africans in any social, political, economic, or religious phenomenon with implications for questions of sex, gender, and class," and "a defence of African cultural elements as historically valid in the context of art, music, and literature," among others.

The affirmation of *continuance* of African culture in contemporary cosmopolitan, even exotic, aesthetics is based precisely on the fact, which has been noted elsewhere, that "the vast folk literature is not only alive but [is] vigorously contemporary, providing constant support for new forms for the literate culture developing within the language itself as a result of its reduction to writing" (Irele 96). The continued presence of Yoruba oral forms "some of them of great antiquity" in contemporary discourse (Barber 357) is a situation that is replicated in many African cultures. At the same time, the assimilation of "foreign elements" into the gut of African culture does not lead to the dissolution of the base codes of the culture. The hybridity that characterises examples such as the above (from Fela Anikulapo-Kuti and Lagbaja), had, as noted earlier, been well located within the theorisation of African literature and cultures, in terms of the "appropriation" and "abrogation" rights of colonized entities over the colonizing languages and cultures (Achebe, *Morning Yet*; Soyinka, *Myth*; Aschroft et al, *Empire*, among others).

**Codes of Recognisance: Hybridity and Committed Cultural Exegesis**
Often identifiable within the new Africa related or Africa derived cultural products are what may be called the *base codes* of African culture, that is, those elements that bear the mark of African philosophical, psychological and cultural orientation and which underlie the various surface forms in which this orientation is expressed. These underlying elements constitute the *langue* of the culture, for which the surface elements are sundry, individuated and contextually formed *paroles*. Eliciting the various forms by which the African cultural langue continues to be evident in the new, especially cosmopolitan, paroles is a critical arm of African culture affirmation and re-affirmation.

Numerous examples from contemporary African music on the international scene show that the base codes of culture may often become hybridized or even suffer from anonymity within specific uses. This may be an effect of *encoder unawareness* or of *indifferent tooling* (in this case a disinterested "free translation" of elements of an original culture). Consider the lyrics of Àsá (Bukola Elemide), the Nigerian international singer, in the song "Jailer." The music is Afro-pop and reggae, with elements of African drum polyrhythm dominating the background. This rhythm undeniably reflects the African cultural langue. However, ignoring the rhythm for a moment, the lyrics are dominated by English enunciation codes, with a sprinkling of pidgin lexis and syntax (underlined below). Like the English component, the pidgin inserts also serve as *recognizance codes* that draw attention to the respective component languages of the song. Interestingly, the enunciation codes of Yoruba, Asà's mother tongue, do not feature at all in the song:

> I'm in chains, you`re in chains too
> I wear uniforms and you wear uniforms too
> I'm a prisoner, you`re a prisoner too Mr Jailer
> …

I'm talking to you jailer
Stop calling me a prisoner
*Let he who is without sin*
*Be the first to cast the stone* Mr Jailer

…

*You see if you [re] walking in a market place*
*Don't throw stones*
*Even if you do you just might hit*
*One of your own*

…

I hear my baby say I *wanna* be president
<u>I wan chop money, from my *govument*</u>

…

While the song's enunciation codes are largely English, with a sprinkling of pidgin, including the socio-linguistically analyzable slang, *wanna,* which is a distinct Americanism, the lyrics show no *base code* or no underlying cultural code that is distinctly English. There are a couple of internationally recognizable inputs from other cultural sources, especially the exhortatory item "let he who is without sin be the first to cast a stone," which bears a definitive sign of *recognisance* in relation to the Judeo-Christian religion and the related Biblical moral. The statement's direct lexical and structural echo assists with the *recognisance* of its cultural source, an originary that is not rendered invalid by the hybridity of the new expression.

On the other hand, even though as noted the enunciation codes of Yoruba, Àsá's mother tongue, do not feature in the song, the gnomic item *if you [re] walking in a market place/Don`t throw stones/Even if you do you just might hit/One of your own* is distinctly of Yoruba origin. It derives directly from the Yoruba proverb and philosophy, *tí a bá sòkò lójà ará ilé ẹni ló n bá* ("if you throw a stone in a market it would hit someone from your own household"). The proverb indexes not only the issue of human and social solidarity, which is also the overall philosophy of Àsá's song, but also the intense communality that continues to characterize traditional Yoruba culture and metaphysical world view. It is this intense communality that ensures the retributive chain indicated in the proverb. However, the source of this base or underlying cultural input to the song is rendered anonymous in the course of *rewriting* or translating the original. Not only is the enunciation code in which the song is rendered English, none of the formal elements associated with the rendition of proverbs in Yoruba culture (e.g. introductory or closing acknowledgment formulas), etc, is inserted to encourage any recognition of the source.

In essence, the translation by Àsá is not culturally committed[7]; it is disinterested, as a result of which the item takes on a life of its own, becoming anonymous, its origin to all intents and purposes unknown. In truth this proverb becomes "deterritorialized." However, while the resultant "anonymity" may well be a tribute to the "newness" of "in-between-ness" that characterizes migrant cultures (indeed, Àsá's halting, migrant Yoruba in her songs creates a sometimes hilarious hybrid), it certainly does not indicate a complete severance from, or dissolution of, the pastness that has transmuted into the newness, as any rigorous analysis would often show. The originary *never disappears*, to borrow Appadurai's dictum of acknowledgment. A *linguistic culturology* may sometimes be necessary to "uncouple the hybrid" ("Oloruntoba-Oju, "Irreducible Africanness") in artifacts of culture.

There is yet another applicable and possibly disturbing trajectory to the analysis above. On the one hand, the Yoruba proverbial as rendered in the song may be seen as having been absorbed into an anonymous "global" community of proverbs, within an interstistial no man's land and as a tribute to the anonymity of the gnomic code. On the other hand, however, the song's enunciation codes, being English (language), would by and by, albeit wrongly, confer de facto suzerainty over the proverb on the cognate culture (English). In time and away from conscious memory, the status of English as a surrogate language or surrogate culture bearing the proverb to the global world would appreciate; the surrogate mother appropriates the baby as its own, assuming a 'universalist' propriety over conception, parturition and nurture. This is another area in which cultural activism asserts its relevance. It is the duty of committed cultural exegeses to elicit palimpsest marks of an original culture from contemporary manifests of the culture, and establish appropriate communal proprietary rights, triumphantly hoisting the flag of the originating culture. Whatever little that Africa has it should preserve.

## The Resilience of African Onomasis[8]

The African name, whether in its home ground or the Diasporas, in ancient form or in modified versions and appellations, continues to be the most treasured expression of identity and the most resilient expression of an ancient African culture. Some of its features include its intense communality and ethnology, and an all too common referentiality with metaphysics and mythology, history, appellation and praise. It continually functions as a culture performative, sharing deep linguistic and semantic features with its cognate African language and occurring as a conspicuous artifact of culture within multiple new sites of cultural expression. Though not resistant to transformations (e.g. through abbreviation, compounding, anglicizing, etc), the African name often manifests a preservation instinct, functioning as a virtual check on hybrid mutations.

The insertion of the African name as untranslated forms in African literatures in English and other colonial languages, and its continued dispersal in sundry sites of cultural intersection, also function as cultural *recognizance*, and a mark of the *continuance* of culture within the densest of metropolitan locales. Onomasis thus provides yet another basis for the location of African culture, even contemporary African culture, within narratives of originary. It becomes one of those perplexing phenomena that confound insinuations of 'in-betweenness,' or of 'newness' as a death knell for African culture.

## Conclusion

Is there any such thing as "African Culture"? Indeed, is there anything that may be called "African" – African history, African language, African art, African music, African sexuality, African body and, more tendentiously, African future?

Scepticism about the notion "African" is perhaps more prevalent in discourses on cultural forms relating to Africa than in anything else. The growing *Afroscepticism* is powered not only by the vast and continuing heterogeneity of aspects of life in Africa and in the Black Diasporas, but also by theories of hybridity and their often selective emphases on *illustrants* of the present. However, neither such heterogeneity nor the presence of hybridity is sufficient to dislodge the reality of Africanity, or of African-derived forms, which can always be established through a critical engagement with the past in relation to the present.

Contemporary African culture both at home and abroad continues to be defined by a constant search for ancient African meanings and significances, and the *continuance* of these meanings and significances in numerous guises in contemporary forms. While the dynamism of culture and the constant creation of hybridized transnational forms is beyond question, such hybridity does not dissolve the claims of culture originaries on contemporary culture derivatives, nor does it support a definition of contemporary interstitial space in terms of a "'newness' that is not part of the continuum of the past or present." The task continually confronting committed workers of culture is to elicit, indeed disentangle, from the cultural forms that represent the new cosmopolitan exotic, those items and substances at every level of language and culture that continue to enable the continent's narratives of originary.

Globalism or not, the civilized world does encourage appropriate proprietary acknowledgments of artifacts of culture. There is no reason for Africans to deny themselves the cultural pride and the sense of worth and belonging that derives from such proprietary relations to culture. When even the most advanced societies of the West continually protect the records of their culture and relish the memories of their glorious past, why should Africans be so easily persuaded to throw away theirs? The task for African workers of culture is to relate elements of contemporary cultural output to their cultural fount, thus enhancing the knowledge of African history and culture and the appropriate proprietary acknowledgments.

**Notes**

[1]Molefi Asante (*Manifesto* 16-17) distinguishes between the terms "Afrocentricity," "Afrocentrism" and "Africanity." He rejects the latter two on the basis that "Afrocentrism" tends to insinuate the clannishness connoted by all "centrisms" especially "Eurocentrism." On the other hand, he rejects the term Africanity on the basis that, to him, it connotes a mere affectation ("simply affecting African styles and manners"), whereas Afrocentricity is "something deeper" in the form of "conscientization related to the agency of African people." However, the term Africanity could also be used to cover the areas covered by Asante's five part "Afrocentricity" manifesto. Furthermore, Asante's preferred term "Afrocentricity" does not appear, linguistically at least, to avoid the insinuation of centrism either, while Africanity may well do. The term Africanity is therefore preferred and used here to cover issues and concerns relating to the African heritage and African agency.

[2] The works of Stuart Hall, especially "Cultural Identity and Diaspora" (1990) and "The Local and the Global: Globalization and Ethnicity" (1991), as well as Paul Gilroy's *The Black Atlantic: Modernity and Double Consciousness* (1993) are prominently bracketed in what we term here the *Afrosceptic* category, along with the works of Homi Bhabha, Aryun Appadurai, Anthony Appiah and Archille Mbembe. Two anthologies, *Ways of Seeing the World: Beyond the New Nativism* (ed. Archille Mbembe) and *The Future of Africa* (ed. Major and Major 2003) are among those that also project considerable scepticism about the concept of an African culture, while some, like Palmberg's (2001) *Encounter Images in the Meetings between Africa and Europe,* steer a middle course by exploring narratives of African heterogeneity of African images but without dismissing the possibility of certain core African values. The works of Afrocentrists and Africanists (Asante, 1980; 2000, among others) provide a definitive and resilient counter discourse to the general run of what we describe here as *Afroscepticism.* Mbembe (3) was to comment in apparent frustration that "the relentless critique of [nativist discourse] has not succeeded in putting it to rest"! See Olaniyan (2006) for a discussion of *Afrocentrism* and its antecedents.

[3] Archille Mbembe (*On the Postcolony*) would go further to propose to 'destabilize' binaries such as resistance/passivity, autonomy/subjection, hegemony/counter-hegemony, etc, quite as if these binaries were only a figment of "nativist" imagining.

[4] Hardly a typology, this! Adeeko (1998) projects an interesting typology of nativist perspectives into 'classical,' 'structuralist' and linguistic 'nativisms' and proffers a "critical reading" of nativist aesthetics. He cautions, however, that this reading should "not be taken as a repudiation of either nativism in criticism or its rhetoric of difference" (p. xi).

[5] My preferred term for the more established but pejorative tag, *Dark Continent Narratives*.

[6] I have taken the liberty to coin the latter terms from Cooper's (2004) reference to "[t]hese new tragic mulattoes, victims of an old-fashioned Euro-American racism that masquerades as newly-fashioned cultural theory, [who] derace and erase themselves."

[7] I am being careful to distinguish here between Àsá (whose artist name actually means "tradition" or "custom," and who has shown overall commitment to matters of culture) and this translation of hers.

[8] A fuller discussion of this segment was presented at the "What's culture Got to do with it?" conference at the Nordic African Institute, Uppsala, in June 2009, and is in further preparation for a separate publication.

**References**

Adegbija, E. *Language Attitudes in Sub-saharan Africa: A Sociolinguistic Overview*. Clevedon, Avon: Multilingual Matters Ltd, 1994. Print.

Adeeko, A. *Proverbs, Textuality and Nativism in African Literature*. Gamesville: University Press of Florida, 1998. Print.

Achebe, Chinua. *Things Fall Apart*. London: Heinemann, 1958.
---. *No Longer at Ease*. London: Heinemann, 1960.
---. *Morning Yet on Creation Day*. New York: Garden City, 1975.

Amatus, A. "Meet Kadaira, Managing Editor, Next Newspaper." *The Sunnews Online*. Web. 28 -03- 2009. http://www.sunnewsonline.com/sunstyle-28-03-2009-002.htm.

Appadurai, Arjun. "Disjuncture and Difference in the Global Cultural Economy." *Public Culture* (1990) (2.2): 1-24.

Asante, Molefi Kete. *An Afrocentric Manifesto*. Cambridge and Malden: Polity Press, 2007. Print.
---. "Afrocentricity: Toward a New Understanding of African Thought in this Millenium." University of Liverpool. Web. 2 Aug 2000, accessed 03 Mar 2007.

Ashcroft, Bill, et al. *The Empire Writes Back: Theory and Practice in Postcolonial Literatures*. London & New York: Routledge, 1989. Print.

Bad Writing Contest. "The Philosophy and Literature Bad Writing Contest Press Releases1996-1998." *Denis Dutton Web*. N.p. N.d. 5 April 2009. http://denisdutton.com/bad_writing.htm.

Barber, K. "Literature in Yoruba: Poetry and Prose, Travelling Theatre and Modern Drama." *The Cambridge History of African and Caribbean Literature, Vol. 1*. Ed. Abiola Irele & Simon Gikandi. Cambridge: Cambridge University Press, 2004. 357 378. Print.

Benzon, William, L. "African Music in the World." *The Future of Africa.* Ed. David C. Major and John S. Major. The New York Society for International Affairs, 2003. 199 208. Print.

Bessire, Aimee. "Critical Voices in African Contemporary Art." *The Future of Africa.* Ed. David C. Major and John S. Major. The New York Society for International Affairs, 2003. 175-186. Print.

Bhabha, Homi. *The Location of Culture.* London: Routledge, 1994. Print.
---. "Cultures in Between." *Questions of Cultural Identity.* Ed. S.Hall and P. Du Gay.London: Sage Publications, 1996. Print.

Chinweizu, et al. *Toward the Decolonization of African Literature.* Enugu: Fourth Dimension Publishers, 1980. Print.

Chukwukere, B. Ibe. "The Problem of Language in African Literature." *African Literature Today* 3 (1963): 15-26. Print.

Chumbow, B. S. "The Place of the Mother Tongue in the National Policy on Education." *Multilingualism, Minority Languages and Language Policy in Nigeria.* Ed. E.N. Emenanjo. Agbor: Central Books, in Association with The Linguistic Association Nigeria, 1990. 61-70. Print.

Cooper, Carolyn, "'No Matter Where You Come From': Pan-Africanist Consciousness in Caribbean Popular Culture." Third NBD/ UWI Open Campus Dominica Distinguished National Lecture Series (May 5-6, 2010). Retrieved 13 September,
 2010. http://www.cob.edu.bs/News/COOPER_PANAFRICAN_ LECTURE.pdf.

Cummins, J. *Language, Power, and Pedagogy. Bilingual Children in the Crossfire.* Clevedon, England: Multilingual Matters, 2000. Web. 12. 2. 2006.

Dent, David, J. "African-Americans and Africa." *The Future of Africa.* Ed. David C. Major and John S. Major. The New York Society for International Affairs, 2003. 209-216. Print.

Eakin, Emily. "Harvard's Prize Catch a Delphic Postcolonialist." *The New York Times Web*. N.p. Nov 17, 2001. Web. 5 Apr 2009. http://www.nytimes.com/2001/11/17/arts/harvard-s-prize-catch-a-delphicpostcolonialist.html

Fanon, Frantz. *Towards the African Revolution*. New York: Grove, 1967. Print.

Gikandi, Simon. "Globalization and the Claims of Postcoloniality" *The South Atlantic Quarterly* 100.3 (2000): 627-658. Print.

Gilroy, Paul. *The Black Atlantic: Modernity and Double Consciousness*. London: Verso, 1993. Print.

Hall, Stuart. "Cultural Identity and Diaspora" [1990]. *Colonial Discourse and Post- colonial Theory: A Reader*. Ed. Patrick Williams and Laura Chrisman. New York: Harvester, 1993. 392-403. Print.
---. "The Local and the Global: Globalization and Ethnicity." *Culture, Globalization and the World System*. Ed. Anthony King. Basingstoke and Birmingham: Macmillan/Department of Art and Art History, State University of New York at Binghamton, 1919. 19-39.

Jonnson, Stefan. "The Western World View and the Rest." Paper presented at the "What's Culture Got to do with it?" conference held at the Nordic African Institute, Uppsala, Sweden, June 15-18, 2009. (Edited version in this volume).

Makos, Jeff. "Rethinking Experience of Countries with Colonial Past." Web. 18 November, 2006. Http://Chronicle.Uchicago.Edu/950216/Bhabha.Shtml.

Mbeki, Thambo. "The Republic of South Africa Constitution Bill 1996" (Presentation), 8 May 1996. http://www.gov.za/awards/mbekiafrican.htm

Mbembe, Achille. *On the Postcolony*. Berkeley: University of California, 2001.

---. "Ways of Seeing: Beyond the New Nativism, Introduction to *African Studies Review*," 44.2 (2001): 1-14. Print.

Meredith, P. "Hybridity in the Third Space: Rethinking Bi-Cultural Politics in Aotearoa/New Zealand." Paper presented at the Oru Raugahau Research and Development Conference 7–9 July 1998, Massey University, New Zealand.

Mitchell, K. "Different Diasporas and the Hype of Hybridity." *Environment and Planning D.: Society and Space* 15 (1997): 53-553. Print.

Olaniyan, Tejumola. "From Black Aesthetics to Afrocentrism (Or A Small History of an African and African American Discursive Practice)." Web. *West Africa Review*, Issue 9. 4 September 2006. Http://www.westafricareview.com/issue9/olaniyan2.html.

Oloruntoba-Oju, T. "Communication and the Colonial Legacy in Nigeria. *Issues in Contemporary African Social and Political Thought*. Eds. O. Obafemi & A. Lawal. Lagos/Ilorin: Academia Publications, 1994, 109-125. Print.

---. "Perspectives on Rhetorical Patterns in Nigeria: Contrastive Rhetoric and the Politics of Culture." *Issues in Intercultural Communication* 2.1 (2008): 41-61. Print.

---. "Irreducible Africanness and Nigerian Postcoloniality from Drama to Video." *West Africa Review* Issue 11 (2007). Web. 4.2. 2009.

Osei-Nyame, Kwadwo. "Toward the Decolonization of African Postcolonial Theory: The Example of Kwame Appiah's *In My Father's House* vis-à-vis Ama Ata Aidoo's *Our Sister Killjoy*, Helon Habila's *Waiting for an Angel* and Ike Oguine's *A Squatter's Tale*. In Tobias Robert Klein, Ulrike Auga and Viola Pruschenk (Ed.). *Texts Tasks and Theories: Versions and Subversions of African Literature 3. Matatu* 35. Amsterdam and New York: Editions Rodopi, 2002, 69 – 92. Print.

Oyewumi, Oyeronke. "Ties That (Un)Bind: Feminism, Sisterhood and Other Foreign Relations." *Jenda: A Journal of Culture and African Women Studies* 1. 1. (2001).Web. 22. 4. 2005.

Palmberg, Mai. *Encounter Images in the Meetings between Africa and Europe.* Uppsala: The Nordic African Institute, 2001. Print.
Parry, B. "Problems in Current Theories of Colonial Discourse." *The Post-Colonial Studies Reader,* Eds. Bill Ashcroft, et al. London: Routledge, 1996, 36-44. Print.

Rutherford, J. "The Third Space: Interview with Homi Bhabha." *Identity, Community, Culture, Difference.* Ed. J. Rutherford. London: Lawrence And Wishart, 1990, 207- 221. Print.

Soyinka, Wole. *Myth, Literature and the African World.* Cambridge University Press, 1976. Print.
---. "Theatre in African Traditional Cultures: Survival Patterns" (1982) *Art, Dialogue and Outrage, Art, Dialogue and Outrage: Essays on Literature and Culture,* Ed. B. Jeyifo. Ibadan: New Horn Press, 1988, 190-203. Print.

Wallerstein, Immanuel. "Culture as the Ideological Battleground of the Modern World System." *Global Culture: Nationalism, Globalization and Modernity.* Ed. Mike Featherstone. London: Sage Publications Ltd. 31-56. Print.

Wali, Obi. "The Dead End of African Literature?" *Transition* 10 (1963): 13-15. Print.

Wa Thiongo, Ngugi. *Decolonising the Mind: The Politics of Language in African Literature.* London: James Currey, 1981. Print.

Zabus, Chantal. *The African Palimpsest: Indigenization of Language in the West African Europhone Novel.* Amsterdam, Atlanta, Ga, Éditions Rodopi, 1991. Print.

# Call me by my Rightful Name: Paul Gilroy's Black Atlantic and African Literature of the Trans-Atlantic Imagination
## - Wumi Raji

The first half of the title of my paper is actually the full title of a recent novel by Isidore Okpewho. *Call me by my Rightful Name* focuses on an African American's quest for self definition. Otis, the protagonist of the story has a habit of falling into fits, speaking a tongue nobody understands. Through the assistance of language experts, the tongue he speaks is eventually discovered to be the praise chant of a parti-cular sub-group among the Yorubas of South Western Nigeria. Our protagonist thus finds himself undertaking a return journey to the very place where his ancestors were uprooted from, completing the rites that were interrupted when they were captured in a raid and transported by force across the Atlantic. Otis afterwards returns to the United States to join the frontline in the Black nationalist agita-tion of the sixties.

Isidore Okpewho's *Call me by my Rightful Name* was published in 2005, twelve full years after Paul Gilroy's *The Black Atlantic* was first rolled out of the press. However, even if the novel had been publis-hed twenty years before, the possibility of it making the reference list in Gilroy's book is very doubtful. This directly is due to the fun-damental difference in the perspective of the two Black intellectuals. Because while the one is interested in the concept of roots and the inspiration it can provide for an individual or a group's struggle for self - definition, Gilroy's concern is simply and *only* with what he himself describes as the word's "homonym" – routes!

Gilroy's book is much discussed. Its pre-occupation is with the identity of blacks dispersed in the Western hemisphere as a conse-quence of the Trans-Atlantic slave trade. The expression "double consciousness" which appears in the sub-title is appropriated from W.E.B Du Bois' *The Souls of Black Folk* and is used to capture the tension inherent in the reality of being simultaneously black and a citizen of the West. The two "great cultural assemblages" between which black English or African Americans stand have "mutated" in the course of time and Paul Gilroy is unhappy with the way different groups have continued to fall back "on the idea of cultural nationalism, on the over-integrated conceptions of culture which present immutable, ethnic differences as an absolute break in the histories and experiences of 'black' and 'white' people." (2) Against this reality, the author sets for himself in the book, the task of demonstrating the continuity between the two identities, and specifically to oppose to the idea of "ethnic absolutism" and "cultural nationalism" a theoretical position which celebrates hybridity, creolisation and cultural mutation.

Gilroy identifies two major orientations in black cultural discourse. The first he describes as "essentialist" or "ontological" and the second as "pluralist." The ontological, according to Gilroy is characterised by a "brute" defence of what is perceived as an unchanging essence of black cultural identity. In cultural criticism, as Gilroy further states, the approach of this group is to downplay "the substantive political and philosophical issues involved in the process of artistic representation" (p.31) while laying total emphasis on aesthetic matter. Gilroy concedes that the group is very popular and this even when it is unable to point out exactly where "the highly prized... essence of black artistic and political sensibility" which it continues to defend is located. Here the intellectual or the artist is a leader and part of his/her duty is to provide guidance on the appropriate cultural choices for black people. "The community is felt to be on the wrong road," says Gilroy, "and it is the intellectual's job to give them a new direction, firstly by recovering and then by donating the racial awareness that the masses seem to lack."(32)
The pluralist perspective, which opposes the essentialist, represents identity as both open and complex. Blackness as a signifier, is perceived as heterogeneous, sundered, as it were, by multiple factors which include political affiliation, class status, sexuality, gender and even ethnicity. "There is no unitary idea of black community here,"

says Gilroy, "and the authoritarian tendencies of those who would police black cultural expression in the name of their own particular history or priorities are rightly repudiated"(p.32). The group receives influences and inspiration from different kinds of sources and also demonstrates a readiness to fuse "modernist" techniques and styles with received, traditional aesthetic forms.

Earlier, as he sets out to highlight the features of the two standpoints, Gilroy has dismissed both of them as "two different varieties of essentialism." Finally, while hailing the way the second outlook – which he sometimes describes as "strategic" – has projected race as a social construction, he still dismisses it for being "insufficiently alive to the lingering power of specifically racialised forms of power and subordination" (p.32). If the truth must be told, Gilroy's problem with especially the second perspective lies in its implicit deference to the concept of national identity or the nation state. Throughout the book, the author demonstrates complete impatience with anything that resembles what he often describes as "cultural nationalism" or "ethnic absolutism." He argues fiercely against the idea of "modern borders or pre-modern frontiers."(32) As he argues, his theory of the black Atlantic seeks to move beyond the constraints of ethnic difference and the inhibitions of national borders. Gilroy proposes instead an intercultural, transnational and hybridised perspective of identity, which perspective, as he argues, represents the only way to capture the restless, ever-evolving, diasporic reality of black political culture. "Routes," the concept which Gilroy would rather stress in place of "roots," has direct bearing with the image of the ship standing at the centre of his argument. Floating on the Atlantic, eternally on sail, the ship of black cultural identity is projected as a "living entity," forever criss-crossing the sea, connecting the different points that constitute the areas of the black Diaspora. "They were something more," says Gilroy – "a means to conduct political dissent and possibly distinct mode of cultural production." He writes further:

Ships also refer us back to the middle passage, to the half-remembered micro-politics of the slave trade and its relationship to both industrialisation and modernisation. As it were, getting on board promises a means to reconceptualise the orthodox relationship between modernity and what passes for its prehistory. It provides a different sense of where modernity might itself be thought to begin in the constitutive relationships with outsiders that both found and temper a self conscious sense of western civilisation.

Gilroy's concern in *The Black Atlantic* is intensely ambitious and wide-ranging. The work privileges the experience of travels, displacement, transformation, circulation and consumption. Chapter one delineates his conceptual perspective and is illustrated with the works and journeys of Martin Delany. Delany was a well-known Africanist but this does not represent part of Gilroy's interest. He would rather present the man as a very complex personality whose "political trajectory through abolitionisms and emigrationisms,… dissolves any simple attempts to fix him as consistently either conservative or radical" (p.20) Chapter two utilises the extraordinary stories of Frederick Douglas and Margaret Garner to articulate the complex struggles of black slaves for freedom and, thereafter, citizenship. Gilroy also underlines here the complicity of Western modernity, consistently described throughout the book as "rationality," with a racial tenor. Exploring black music in chapter three, Gilroy's concern is to dispel the notion that this black expressive form harbours a pristine essence of authenticity which has remained untouched through time. On the contrary, the author of *The Black Atlantic* would rather argue, following a suggestion by Le Roi Jones, that the form ought to be seen as "a *changing* rather than an unchanging same"(author's emphasis, p.101). Together, chapters four and five seem to stand at the centre of the book. Here Gilroy works to illustrate in concrete terms his ideas of trans-national or "outernational" identity. The chapters undertake a sustained exploration of the impacts of travels and of modernist philosophies on W.E.B Du Bois and Richard Wright, two prominent African American intellectuals and thinkers. Exploring the works of the former also provides the author with the opportunity to give sustained treatment to his concept of "double consciousness" which provides his analysis with a major frame of reference. While affirming the positive influence of Enlightenment philosophy on the overall identity of the two, Laura Chrisman has pointed out in an insightful critique of *The Black Atlantic* how "Gilroy's exclusive focus on Europe as a space of liberation for New World blacks... overlooks entirely the experience of Europe as historically and structurally oppressive for blacks from colonies" (*Black British Culture*, p.458). In the final chapter, Gilroy underlines the parallels and correspondences between the experience of blacks in the Diaspora and those of the Jews and he points out aspects of antagonistic relationships as well. In the end, he locates the factor linking the two groups together in the idea of Diaspora. As he seems to suggest, this fact of dispersal of the two peoples and their experience of suffering can provide the basis on which future political cooperation between them can be based. The book closes with a brief discussion of Toni Morrison's *Beloved*, especially its manner of transforming the Garner story. Gilroy warns that the novel's imaginative re-articulation of history should not be taken as an attempt to "recover hermetically sealed and culturally absolute racial traditions that would be content forever to invoke the pre-modern as the anti-modern." Rather:

> It is proposed here above all as a means to figure the inescapability and legitimate value of mutation, hybridity, and intermixture en route to better theories of racism and of black political culture than those so far offered by cultural absolutists of various phenotypical hues. (223)

Gilroy's theory of the Black Atlantic can be destabilized from different points but perhaps the best way to start is to point out that his so-called transnational theory is no more than another form of nationalism. Gilroy claims to be interested in hybridity, in cultural inter-mixture, creolisation and mutation, yet he wants blacks in the West to sail only in black ships or, for that matter, on the Black Atlantic. What this implies is that citizens of these different countries and different racial identities would have to travel in different ships and/or follow different routes. Passengers on each of the ships will not be able to interact with each other. They will be hermetically sealed off from one another. The theory of black solidarity across the Atlantic may have its own merits but it has to be recognized for what it is – another form of "brute pan-Africanism."

Another issue that I would like to take with Gilroy has to do with his tendency to dismiss any pre-occupation with national identity as a concern with ethnic absolutism or ethnic particularity. In this age of consistent travels and constant interactions and inter mixtures, every single nation state is necessarily a deeply heterogeneous space. And this is even more so of the nations that fall within Gilroy's definition of the Black Atlantic. Trinidad and Tobago, if I may illustrate with an example of a Caribbean state, has as its citizens an inter-mixture of people of African, Indian, European and Chinese descent. Should a Black indigene of such a country be concerned only with people of his or her complexion located within and across the Atlantic?

But honesty demands also that I admit that part of my problem with *The Black Atlantic* lies in its author's attitude towards Africa. Going by the way he develops his theory of the Black Atlantic, Gilroy's pre-occupation seems to be mainly with blacks located in Britain and the United States of America. Yes, Gilroy delineates clearly his point of departure in the book, making it clear that his concern mainly is with the Blacks in the Diaspora. But then that word can only make sense if there is a homeland. Shouldn't there be a relationship between a Diaspora and its homeland? Again, the point may be raised that the author has made it clear that his theory is concerned less – if at all – with "roots" as it is with "routes." In my view, this kind of position will only make his situation more difficult, because the question that may then be posed is whether Africa is not, in reality, part of the Black Atlantic. The slave ship of old used to set sail from Europe going down to Africa to collect slaves. It then sets off for the Americas where it discharges its human cargo. Thereafter, it returns to its point of origination in Europe. Throughout the book, Gilroy consistently refers to black people located in Europe and the Americas as being "in modernity" and this in a way that seems to suggest that he believes that those located elsewhere are outside of it. A similar sense of deliberate ambiguity on the part of the author is discernible in the way he now and again employs the term rationality in place of Western modernity. Again, it seems suggestive that any mode of existence that falls outside of the model that has been held up is either "irrational" or "pre-rational."

The above seems to be the only way to explain why Gilroy avoids

Africa like a plague in his work. Otherwise many of the subjects with whom he illustrates his position did have complex, multi-dimensional relationships with Africa. Martin Delany for one is an obvious Africanist. When, however, our author settles on him, what interests him more in the man's work is the way it affirms the "intercultural and the transnational" which, as he argues, is "more than enough to move discussion of black political culture beyond the binary opposition between national and Diaspora perspectives" (p.29). W.E.B Du Bois, who constitutes the focus of a chapter in Gilroy's book, took the decision later in life to settle down in Ghana. Indeed Du Bois' theory of double consciousness which Gilroy appropriates in his book was postulated directly in relation to the question of Africa vis-à-vis her Diaspora.

It is against this background of deliberate recoil from the homeland that this essay investigates the perspective in African literature of the complex, multi-dimensional relationship between Africa and her Diasporas. My specific focus here is Bode Sowande's *Tornadoes full of Dreams*, a little known play which re-visions the experiences of the trans-Atlantic slave trade and its continuing ramifications on black people located in the Americas as well as the homeland.

It is perhaps necessary to, before I go on; make it clear that I do not myself subscribe to an absolutist perspective of cultural identity. I draw back clearly from any view that holds individual cultures to be intact, seeing them as hermetically sealed from each other. No individual tradition is sacrosanct, in my view. Just as differences exist, so do points of contacts and mutual inter-meshing. Actually my problem with Gilroy's position stems from this belief that identities are simultaneously continuous with, and different from, each other. As I have earlier pointed out, the author of *The Black Atlantic* seems to place total emphasis on "routes" while completely jettisoning that of "roots," its sound-alike. Gilroy celebrates "homelessness," stressing the idea of travel, of voyage. This would have been no problem, to be sure, had he realised that even a ship has a place of origination, that as it sails from one point to the other, it carries with it memories of its initial point of departure.

In emphasizing questions of memories and continuities and, as well, those of differences and ruptures in my conception of identity then, I derive a lot of inspiration from Stuart Hall. In his very short but well-cited essay "Cultural Identity and Diaspora," Stuart Hall projects identity as a process both of "being" and "becoming". To him, identity issues from the past as much as it belongs to the future. It is not a fixed phenomenon, immutable to time, place and history. As he argues, cultural identities "come from somewhere, have histories." At the same time however, and "like everything which is historical, they undergo constant transformation."

Hall exemplifies his thesis with Black Caribbean identity insisting that its construction rests on two poles; the first being that of "similarity" and "continuity", and the second that of "difference" and "rupture." Because it ensures a relationship with the past, the pole of similarity and continuity constantly reminds a typical Caribbean of the manner of his/her arrival at his/her contemporary location. The second pole, on the other hand, emphasises the "broken" nature of this continuity. Even before their departures from Africa, differences existed among the slaves. They belonged to different cultures and societies, spoke different languages and practised different religions. They were also of different sexes and age grades. The moment they entered the Middle Passage however, these differences became blurred, and the links that the individual slaves had with their roots became ruthlessly severed.

In my view, Africa remains important to all black people (dis)located in different parts of the world, but it is an Africa that is no longer the same as it was four hundred years before. Rather, it is an Africa that has become transformed in different ways, which has been translated into different languages but which nonetheless remains the point of origin, *not* in the literal – it ought to be emphasized – but *only* in the inspirational sense.

This seems to be Okpewho's point in *Call me by my Rightful Name*. The problem that confronts his protagonist in the novel occurs because of his failure to establish a proper relationship with his past. After undertaking a voyage back to his roots in Africa, Otis is now able to locate a place for himself in America. His vision is clearer; he can now take steps into the future.

But even when African writers thematise the question of a physical return to the homeland, they still find a way of articulating the extreme difficulty involved in such a choice, making it clear that the Africa their hero(in) has chosen to return to differs very remarkably from the one from which his/her ancestors were uprooted four hundred years before. Ama Ata Aidoo, the Ghanaian novelist and playwright, makes this statement with force in *The Dilemma of a Ghost*, her play which was first produced in 1964 when the author herself was still an undergraduate student at the University of Ghana, Legon. At the centre of the play, are a young couple, Ato and Eulalie Yawson. Ato is Ghanaian, and has just returned from America where he studied for a degree. His wife in turn is an Afro-American (the term is specific to the time of the first production of the play) and it is the first time she would be stepping on an African soil. Prior to this coming, all that Eulalie knew about Africa were what she picked up in tourist brochures and such other documents.

At the opening of the play, Aidoo actually makes the audience witness the couple's last moments in the United States, and Eulalie is shown nursing romantic dreams of Africa, talking about the "palm trees, the azure sea, the sun and golden beaches..." (9) On her arrival in Ghana, Eulalie also reminisces about her days in the US. She recalls the words of her late mother as the latter admonishes her never to "curse me and your Pa every morning you look your face in the mirror and see yourself black." (24) The young woman announces with pride to her dead old woman that she has even surpassed her expectation by coming "to the very source. I've come to Africa and I hope that where'er you are, you sort of know and approve." (24) It does not need too close an observation to realise that Eulalie will get into trouble given her uncomplicated identification with the homeland. Africa may be the source, is indeed the source, but the matter cannot be this simple for somebody who had been born and raised in the West. Thus it happens that Eulalie experiences great difficulties blending into her new cultural environment, and her case is not helped by the fact that Ato, her husband, is not a particularly careful, clear – headed and mature person. By the time the play ends though, Eulalie has already begun to adjust. The final stage instructions state that as she returns home on the day her crisis attains a climax, she crashes into the hands of Esi Kom, her mother-in-law, and the latter, still supporting her, leads her into the wing of the compound occupied by Ato's old people.

It is the story of the manner of departure of Eulalie's ancestors from the African homeland as well as the indescribable agony they underwent both while on the voyage and after their arrival in the New world that Bode Sowande dramatises in his own play *Tornadoes Full of Dreams*. The dramatist is a prominent member of the second generation of the Nigerian dramatists of English expression, the generation immediately following that of Wole Soyinka, the Nobel laureate. Sowande had studied French at the University of Ife (now Obafemi Awolowo University), Nigeria, and had proceeded thereafter to the University of Sheffield, Britain, where he obtained a PhD in Dramatic Literature in 1977. He taught Theatre Arts at the University of Ibadan before resigning in 1992 to go into full time playwriting and theatre production.

In 1989, Sowande had been approached jointly by the French Embassy in Lagos and the Ministry of Culture, Paris to write and produce a play as part of the activities put together in celebration of the bicentenary of the French Revolution. Accepting the commission, Sowande had, at the same time, adopted a very complex approach to his assignment. The ensuing work thus, of course, affirms the legacies of the revolution, the legacies that is, of freedom and enlightenment, and the ideals of equality, egalitarianism and human rights. As it does this however, it also takes pains to lay bare the huge ironies and contradictions associated with this mega-text of revolutions. For example, just as the wheel of the revolution oscillated in full motion, France, at the same time continued to pursue its interest in the Atlantic slave trade. Indeed, San Domingo, the largest slave colony in the Americas at the time was owned by the country. As C.L.R James informs us in his classic work, *The Black Jacobins*, this particular West Indian colony actually "supplied two – thirds of the overseas trade of France and was the greatest individual market for the European slave – trade." (vii) When the over five hundred thousand slaves who produced the enormous wealth of the colony then demanded their freedom, France did not hesitate to come out against it. The slaves were then left with no other choice than to wage a war for their freedom. It was an epic struggle, lasting ten full years but they triumphed in the end.

*Tornadoes full of Dreams* also makes a statement on the process of identity transformation of blacks in the Diaspora. Its action centralises the story of a young Sango priestess who was captured from Oyo Ile and sold into slavery. It weaves through the experiences of these unfortunate girl and those of others caught along with her in the Middle Passage, going on until the story reaches a crisis point twenty – five years after in a plantation in San Domingo. The woman ultimately attains her freedom, having poisoned her master but rather than undertake a return journey to her original home in Africa following this development, she chooses, together with her children, to identify with the struggle for freedom being waged by the slaves in San Domingo at the time.

The work stands then as this paper's centre of focus. In it, this paper that is, I explore Bode Sowande's representation of the tragic encounter between the peoples of Black Africa and those of Europe during the trans-Atlantic slave trade, the playwright's statement on the mutual culpability of all the parties involved in the trade, and his visionary articulation on the dimensions of the relationships between his beleaguered continent and the blacks of the Atlantic world.

As already stated, *Tornadoes Full of Dreams* centralises the travails of a young daughter of a Sango priest, the Yoruba god of thunder, lightning and restorative justice. The girl is about fifteen years of age when the play opens, and she has grown up to a woman of about forty years by the time the drama winds up. Herself a priestess of the same god, she is captured in a raid by Akinlade, a warrior of the tropical forest who has now brought her together with other captives to the desert to be sold to Arab slave traders. The play actually opens with an encounter between Akinlade and Abubakar, an Arab slave merchant and clearly a regular customer of the former. The two haggle over the price of the "merchandise" that Akinlade has brought but just as they are about to wrap up the deal, the girl is suddenly caught in a fit of possession, going into a trance. Recognising the presence of Sango in her, Akinlade instantly revokes the deal he has struck with Abubakar, insisting on the need to carry out some rituals before he could sell off the girl; and he also makes it clear that, following the propitiation, he would not be returning to the desert. Rather, as he also states clearly, he would be heading for the coast where he hopes to establish a trading partnership with the white slavers from across the Atlantic. Hard as Abubakar tries to persuade him to avoid engaging in a deal with those he describes as "white Christians" who, as he adds further, are "worse than the fox of the desert, (and) deadly like the serpent" (14), Akinlade would not listen. With his mind set on the huge profit that would start accruing to him henceforth, the "jungle warrior" heads for the coast.

As it happens, Akinlade himself ends up being captured at the coast by Sidney, the captain cum sailor, and taken on deck as a slave together with the Sango priestess. They are both shipped to San Domingo and sold to different masters, losing contact henceforth. They are to meet again at the point where the drama attains a climax and the encounter proves fatal to Akinlade.

But as a way of building a critique of modernity and the Enlightenment project into the play, Sowande raises two historical figures from the world of the dead, making them preside over the actions of the play, engaging each other in dialogue in the process. The first of these is Kwame Nkrumah, first president of Ghana; a generally acclaimed man of great vision and a friend and ally of renowned intellectuals of the black Diaspora including C.L.R James and George Padmore. The second is Napoleon Bonaparte, brilliant war commander and Emperor of France between 1804 and 1812.

The two characters contemplate each other with respect and dignity throughout, and the views they exchange are consistently profound and wide - ranging. Part of it, include the issue of, as stated earlier, who of the two principal parties involved in the slave trade should be held responsible for what no doubt represents a terrible crime against humanity. While Bonaparte finds it difficult to understand how Africans would "go to war only to sell their own people," Nkrumah fires back by asking whether "there (was) no conscience in Europe when she came to Africa." (39) The engagement also touches on the rationale - or lack of it - behind wars of conquest and territorial expansion, and the contradiction inherent in the action of an emperor - Bonaparte that is - whose country gave the world a revolution powered by the ideals of liberty, equality and fraternity but would not hesitate to pull out his army when a colony of slaves rose up to fight for their own freedom.

The slave revolt in question took place in San Domingo and was led by Toussaint L'ouverture. L'ouverture was a son of a chief of Dahomey kingdom who was captured in a war and shipped to San Domingo. He was bought by a planter who luckily treated him with some measure of respect. He became a catholic, got married to another slave who bore him eight children the eldest of which was L'ouverture. The boy grew up under some measure of relative freedom, a situation which made it possible for him to acquaint himself with the ideas of a few great thinkers, not least of which was Abbey Raynal, the author of *Philosophical and Political History of the Establishments and Commerce of the Europeans in the Two Indies*. Toussaint L'ouverture did not fail to put his knowledge to practical use when an opportunity presented itself, leading as it were an extremely backward people to defeat four powerful European nations in a row, following which he became a leader of the independent state of San Domingo. Sowande resolves the multi-dimensional conflict generated in the *Tornadoes* in the context of this revolution.

Now, to move back a bit, the Sango priestess is re-named Magdalena in the Middle Passage by Sidney, the captain of the ship after having violated her sexually. On arrival at San Domingo, she is sold to Talbot, a rich French planter and the relationship produces three children. Indeed, when Talbot and Sidney are first brought together in the play, the main purpose is to sell off the girl to the former. The two Europeans are not to encounter each other again until after another twenty five years, by which time the two are already in their sixties. Magdalena herself has grown to about forty years in age. But what is perhaps more important is the fact that, by now, things are no longer at ease.

Again, Sowande keeps very close to C.L.R. James' *The Black Jacobins* in dramatising the tension that characterises this period. The slaves have heard of the French Revolution, have learned of the three important words that powered it, and have decided to appropriate its spirit. Britain has also discovered India, realised that the labour that produces sugar in that country of the East is cheaper than that of the slaves of the West Indies and, taking this to be a great blessing, especially since it comes so soon after losing America, decided to abolish the slave trade. Sidney makes this clear to Talbot in so many words in the play and, frightened, he takes a decision to sell off his property and re-locate to France. Talbot's property in San Domingo includes, of course, all his slaves and, equally, Magdalena and her three children. Determined against being treated as chattel once again, Magdalena poisons her master and, together with her three children, escapes to join the war of freedom which was going on at the time.

What Bode Sowande's *Tornadoes full of Dreams* evokes then is the history of the making of the African Diaspora in the Western hemisphere. The details of how African men, women and children were captured and sold into slavery are vividly enacted in the dramatic work. The audience is taken through the horrors of the Middle Passage, and the dehumanising experience the slaves undergo in the New World. The enactment can be taken to represent a demonstration of the first crossing in what Paul Gilroy would later come to describe as the Black Atlantic.

Anticipating, as it seems, an argument that was to come four years later, Sowande's position seems to be that while the notion of "routes" is important, it is only so to the extent that it links up with the question of "roots." The heroine of Sowande's play was born an African and she grew up as a Sango priestess. The process of her identity transformation commences at the point when she sets feet on the deck. It deepens when she is re-christened Magdalena by Sidney, having first had his way with her, and intensifies even more the moment she is adopted by Talbot as a mistress, producing three children in the process. By the time she attains her freedom at the age of forty, she has lived in the Diaspora for twenty – five good years and produced grown up children who have known no other lives beside the ones they have lived in San Domingo. It seems normal therefore that the thought that comes to her head at this point, and in spite of her obvious attachment to her roots, is not one of returning to her land of birth but rather, that of joining the liberation struggle of other African slaves in San Domingo. Almost a hundred and fifty years later however, her descendants in the English – speaking parts of Caribbean Islands would migrate in droves to the "mother country" in search of economic fulfilment. This journey represents the second crossing and with it, the construct that would later be known as The Black Atlantic becomes fully configured.

## References

Adamafio, Tawia. *By Nkrumah's Side: The Labour and the Wound.* Accra: Westcoast Publishing House, 1982.

Aidoo, Ama Ata. *The Dilemma of a Ghost.* Essex: Longman, 1985.

Davidson, Basil. *Black Mother: Africa and the Atlantic Slave Trade.* Middlesex: Penguin, 1980.

Davidson, Basil. *Africa in Modern History.* London: Allen Lane, 1978.

Equiano, Olaudah. *The Life of Olaudah Equiano or Gustavus Vassa, the African: Written by Himself.* Essex: Longman, 1988.

Gilroy, Paul. *The Black Atlantic: Modernity and Double Consciousness.* London: Verso, 1993.

James, C.L.R. *The Black Jacobins: Toussaint Louverture and the San Domingo Revolution.* London: Secker & Warburg, 1938.

Haythornthwaite, Philip, J. *Napoleon: The Final Verdict.* London: Arms and Armour, 1996.

Hill, Errol. *The Trinidad Carnival.* London: New Beacon, 1997.

Klein, Herbert, S. *The Atlantic Slave Trade.* Cambridge: Cambridge University Press, 1999.

Osundare, Niyi. *Thread in the Loom: Essays on African Literature and Culture.* Trenton, NJ: Africa World Press, 2002.

Sowande, Bode. *Tornadoes Full of Dreams.* Lagos: Malthouse, 1990.

Wa Thiong'o, Ngugi & Mugo, Micere Githae. *The Trial of Dedan Kimathi.* London: Heinemann, 1977.

# Complicating the Truth of
the Truth Commission
- Kirsten Holst Petersen

*I understand you, he said, I understand completely.*
*And because he spoke with compassion, the old man wept, and Jarvis*
*sat embarrassed on his horse. Indeed, he might have come down from*
*it, but such a thing is not lightly done. But he stretched his hand over*
*the darkening valley, and he said, One thing is about to be finished,*
*but here is something that is only begun. And while I live it will con-*
*tinue. Umfundisi, go well (pp. 248-9)*

I guess we all recognise the sentiments and the tone of his short section from near the end of Paton's 1948 novel *Cry the Beloved Country*,
in which the father of the murdered white boy pledges his support
to the community of the father of the black boy who committed the
murder, and who will be hanged on the following page. This (both
the novel and the sentiments) became pivotal in South African literature all through the Apartheid period. Most texts, both those
expressing black anger and resistance and those expressing white
guilt, pitted themselves against the tenor of *Cry the Beloved Country*,
with increasing vehemence as the political horizons hardened, and
the oppression deepened. Paton's liberal ideals, defined by him as 'a
generosity of spirit, a tolerance of others, an attempt to comprehend
otherness, a commitment to the rule of law, a high ideal of the worth
and dignity of man, a repugnance for authoritarianism, and a love
for freedom' (Coetzee, 2001, p. 320), combined with his deep faith
in the power of Christianity, were increasingly seen as naïve and
powerless in the face of Afrikanerdom. Liberalism became a word of
abuse. Novel after novel pointed out the impossibility of this reconciliation across the colour divide. It is the main theme in Gordimer's

early writing: from the impossibility of friendship across the divide in *A World of Strangers* (1958) to the impossibility of a love relation across the colour line in *Occasion for Loving* (1963) to Rosa's spells in prison in *Burgher's Daughter* (1979) to Maureen Smale's panicky race towards the chopper to get away from her black benefactors in *July's People* (1981). The tone darkens visibly as the apartheid regime grows more violent and it reaches a depth of horror with Coetzee's novel *Waiting for the Barbarians* (1980), a horror in the face of which the values of the main character, a liberal magistrate are both help-lessly ineffective and bordering on the pathological. On the black, or protest, side the torture scenes which begin and end Alex la Gumas's novel *In the Fog of the Season's End* (1972) are a clear indication that those who actively opposed the regime were under no illusions as early as the late 60s.

Between fighters, opponents and guilt-feelers there was an agre-ement that the colour divide could not be crossed and a humane society established with the help of humanist and Christian values. The literary texts reflected very accurately the thoughts and feelings of the major sections of South African society.

And yet, in 1995, with the setting up of the Truth and Reconcilia-tion Committee, this is exactly what was attempted. The purpose of the TRC was to work towards a national reconciliation by creating a public record of human rights violations. The reconciliation would come about as a result of setting the record straight, of creating a new narrative of the nation, publicly acknowledging the suffering and bravery of the victims and the crimes of the perpetrators.

The TRC consisted of three sub-committees: The Committee on Human Rights Violations, the Committee on Amnesty and the Com-mittee on Reparation and Rehabilitation, and after an extensive tour of public hearings the final report was delivered on October 29, 1998. The sessions of each Committee created their own responses, but the Committee on Amnesty created the fiercest opposition. Perpetrators of crimes violating human rights could gain amnesty if they confes-sed their crimes, revealed all the facts and proved that the crimes were committed in pursuit of political goals. As Susan Gallagher writes, 'Given the amnesty provisions, there is no doubt that many murderers, terrorists, and torturers will go free' (Gallagher, 2002,

p. 117). It was made clear that amnesty did not imply forgiveness, and neither were the perpetrators required to show contrition or penitence. Despite this, however, the agenda of the TRC was heavily overlaid by Christian humanist ideology and rhetoric. Desmond Tutu opened the first gathering of the TRC on December 1995 with these words: 'We will be engaging in what should be a corporate nationwide process of healing through contrition, confession and forgiveness' (Susan Gallagher, 2002 p.118). Thus, victims were – and were not – asked to forgive, and perpetrators were – and were not – asked to repent. This meant that reconciliation, based on the confessions of perpetrators, came to cover a wide area of possibilities, from reluctant acceptance of necessity to forgiveness on the part of victims, and reluctant revealing of evidence which could not be destroyed anyway, to remorse on the part of perpetrators. This wide scope of possible responses, variously referred to as a 'patchwork' or 'a multiplicity of partial versions and experiences' (Ingrid de Kok, quoted in Shane Graham, 2009, p. 11), grounded in individual confessions, precludes closure, which in this case would consist of establishing 'an official truth', and it keeps open the possibility for an ongoing discussion about the moral, ethical, psychological, etc. options which offer themselves in answer to the challenge of reconciliation. Literature, whether fictional, semi-fictional or autobiographical, is eminently suited to this important task. Andrè Brink has called for the enquiries of the TRC to be 'extended, complicated and intensified in the imaginings of literature', otherwise 'society cannot sufficiently come to terms with its past to face the future' (Andrè Brink, 1998, p. 32).

With this we are back in the discussion about Paton's discredited dream solution to the South African problem, and the topic which has haunted South African literature all through apartheid times: the possibility, or not, of reconciliation continues under the new dispensation. Whilst the answer of the literature written during the apartheid period was overwhelmingly 'No', the new political dispensation means that reconciliation is a necessity, and Paton's ridiculed, 'powerless' humanist answer has been elevated to the central principle of the TRC. True, Mr Jarvis has climbed off his high horse and the present Umfundisi is a good deal less humble, but the meeting of black and white across the dead bodies of loved ones in an effort to cultivate the land is again a viable possibility in South African literature. A parallel to Paton's vision can be found in the conclusion of W.P.B. Botha's 1997 novel *A Duty of Memory*: the lesbian lover of a murdered Afrikaner woman sits in her office in London and listens to telephone calls on her answering machine from the mother of the African servant who was also killed in the same police conspiracy. Lettie, who was also a servant on the farm where the action took place, tells Beth in London: 'Good news. Jomana Enterprises has put a bid for Leefontein [the ancestral farm, now up for sale]. Two of my sisters whose husbands are businessmen are putting up some of the money, along with a few members of my sister's church. Also Sergeant Muller [the honest Afrikaner policeman] is contributing 15%. So Beth if you still would like to join us in our venture...I will ring back later...The phone rings. She puts out her hand' (p. 227). As Paton dreamed: something ended, something new is about to begin, and that 'something' certainly calls for the values he extolled: ''Generosity of spirit and an attempt to comprehend otherness,' and it also relies on a larger than life capacity for forgiveness. There is, of course, a reversal: These qualities are now asked of the black side of the reconciliation process, thus throwing the burden of guilt, remorse, gratitude and humility on to the white side.

Some of the hearings which attracted the most interest were the hearings of notorious perpetrators, like the Vlakplaas five, a group of former security policemen, engaged in abductions, torture and murder. This group did repudiate their earlier beliefs and embraced the ideology of 'reconciliation, forgiveness and understanding,' as it was advocated by President Nelson Mandela, but their statement was carefully worded in such a way that the repudiation could also be read as an explanation or an excuse (apologia). It runs along the lines of: 'We were brought up to believe that...Apartheid was sanctioned by God through the church...We were brought up to believe that... We have come to realize that these beliefs were wrong...' (TRC website).

This formula leaves space for discussion of the precise nature and degree of guilt which can be attributed to the group and to all other applicants for amnesty with the same background, and a prize winning novel, Mark Behr's *The Smell of Apples* from 1995, carries this discussion into the realm of literature. The novel was contemporary with the TRC hearings, and as such it functioned as an argument in the ongoing discussion in which the whole nation took part through daily broadcasts.

The novel's very genre begs the question of guilt at the same time as it forces the reader to form an opinion. Using the literary genre of a first person narrative, told by an 11-year-old boy, it approximates the testimonies of the TRC hearings in form and at the same time offers an explanation for how the Apartheid ideology could take root in an average child. It turns the reader into a TRC committee member and thereby demands a verdict, but it also turns the reader into a child care officer whose duty it is to protect abused children. And it is the child care officer who wins, thus exonerating the future officer in the South African army from his participation in South Africa's secret war in Angola. In the course of performing this complex task the novel offers a devastating criticism of the Apartheid ideology and state, and in the light of the author's admission to having spied for the government whilst a student at Stellenbosch University in the 80s, this deceptively simple novel becomes a tangle of ethical questions.

Marnus is 11 years old in 1973 and living with his father, the youngest ever Major General in the South African Defence force, his mother, a beautiful Jewish ex opera singer, and his 16-year-old sister, who in the course of working through her adolescent rebellion, is waking up to the injustices of Apartheid. Most of the novel is taken up with Marnus' innocent description of his upper class Afrikaner environment, endorsing its ideology. He is a well-adjusted, sensitive child, thus paradoxically likeable and at the same time accepting the warped version of reality offered to him: an innocent racist. The Apartheid world view which he innocently and dutifully reveals may appear parodic ('Once the communists from Peking began indoctrinating the blacks the blacks took over Kenya and Tangenyika, and the Masai and other tribes were too stupid to see that Mao-Tse-Tung was taking them on a wild goose chase. Where have you ever heard of a Masai or a Kikuyu or a Wachagga that knows anything about running a farm?' (p. 37). 'This is our place given to us by God…' (p. 124)), but critic Rita Bernard who writes that she grew us as a child of the Afrikaner elite in the same period (70s), sees the novel as being 'a veritable compendium of the sayings, stereotypes and justifications that made up the everyday banality of Apartheid' (Bernard, 2000). This insight furthers the apologia aspect of the novel: the socialisation of a racist, carefully explained through a meticulous and correct depiction of his background and upbringing. There is a genre, or a group of novels, sometimes referred to as 'complicity novels'; they start off as an account of apartheid ideology and repressions, but turn into a narrative of conversion, centred on the awakening of the main character. This does not happen here. Marnus does have a rude awakening, ending his idyllic childhood. He realises that his mother, whom he adores, is having an affair with a visiting Chilean general, and he watches his father rape his best friend, who is on a school holiday visit. This punctures the myth of the Christian family and throws the boy into turmoil as he has internalised the close connection between evil, sin and hell of the Dutch Reformed church. Concomitant with this breakdown on the private front the boy is exposed to the evil of apartheid. Their servant's son, a year younger than himself is horribly burnt by some white men for stealing charcoal, and the sight of the wounded boy in a hospital bed prompts him to ask his mother whether it was really white men who did it. Her answer: 'Yes, but that won't heal little Neville. And it probably wasn't right of him to steal charcoal' (p. 138) does not satisfy him, and he forces her into more subtlety than she likes 'But all white people aren't Christian… Remember there are also lower class whites' (p. 139). The boy's response to this is not to object, but to retreat into nightmares. Outwardly, he carries on being well-adjusted, suppressing his new insights. No explanation is given for that, other than that which is implicit in his socialisation into the male universe of white Afrikanerdom and his unconditional love and admiration for his parents.

This lack of external reactions on the part of the boy is implicit in the text and is thereby viewed as, if not inevitable, then at least a very understandable reaction, thus furthering the aspect of apologia in the novel.

The narrative is punctuated by italicised sections, at first seen as snatches of a diary, kept by the adult Marnus caught in crossfire on a hopeless mission somewhere in war-torn and devastated Angola, but increasingly more surrealist and at the end representing his thoughts as he lies dying. They repeat his childhood dilemma, still unsolved, but now acknowledged, 'I feel dad's face against my chest and my arms around his head, and I feel safe. But now it is a different safety. Death brings its own freedom, and it is for the living that the dead should mourn, for in life there is no escape from history' (p. 198).

It is definitely a victim, not a perpetrator, who dies here, and the message: that there is no escape from history seems to perform two tasks: it exonerates the main character of guilt, but it also sees reconciliation as an impossibility. Death is the only possible outcome for a character like Marnus caught in the crossfires of this particular history.

This closure is not the whole story, however. There are chinks in the Apartheid armour: the usual suspects who manage to act on their insights: the teenage sister, or the unmarried aunt, who is a feminist, smokes and objects to apartheid and for all those reasons is barred from visiting the family. Added to this are Marnus' nightmares in which he substitutes the burnt coloured boy for his abused friend in a wild horse ride along the beach, thus at least subconsciously acknowledging his affinity with him. And of course the author himself is still alive to tell the story, despite his complicity in the system, and judging from the number of prices this novel has won it seems a reasonable assumption that its treatment of the topic of reconciliation touches a deep need in South African society: It can function both as an explanation for how things could get as much out of hand as they did on the Afrikaner side and as an exposition from the inside of the evils of apartheid to its victims. It begs the question of guilt by refusing a straight answer, and in this lies a tension between the purpose of the TRC and much of its literary responses. Whilst the TRC strove to 'put South African society on a sound moral basis'…,' 'to put across the idea of moral responsibility,' (Antjie Krog, 1998, p. 9), the literature works to complicate this concept.

The pivotal text in the immediate literary responses to the TRC is Antjie Krog's *Country of My Skull*. The text is a discussion about TRC's ability to steer the country away from the brink of civil war and engender reconciliation through a country-wide discussion of guilt, redemption, forgiveness, shame, inevitable lying and plain obstruction and hostility.

It consists of a seemingly random succession of genres which are not normally found in the same text and which transgress both the journalistic rules of objective reporting and the literary convention of artistic independence of reality checks. Krog reported the Truth Commission's hearings for the national radio, travelling with it all over the country, during which time (244 days) it conducted more than fifty public hearings. She sat in on the hearings and conducted interviews with the key people involved. This provides the journalistic aspect of the text which consists of selected transcripts of the hearings and verbatim quotes from interviews. The more personal aspect of this direct reportage is found in her role as a witness to the proceedings with their highly emotionally charged atmosphere. This falls well within the brief of a reporter who reports with sympathy and involvement the horrors of the victim stories, but at the same time she conducted a personal and very intense soul searching process about her own position as a person deeply rooted in Afrikaner culture. This aspect takes the form of personal memory, confessions and discussions about the moral and ethical dilemmas involved. The subject is her own position in South African society as an Afrikaner with a love for the country and a strong dislike for the apartheid regime: the dilemma of a reluctant traitor, a lose-lose situation. This departure from reporting into personal agonising shades into pure fiction. She invents an infidelity which allows her to stage a very intimate reconciliation scene in which she outlines all the difficulties, in fact the near impossibility of a complete reconciliation in a personal relationship. Although this has no place in her journalistic duty to report truthfully on what she hears, it acts as a very timely reminder of the difficulties involved.

Added to the objective reporting, the subjective agonizing and the pure fiction is a fourth feature which shapes the text: the juxtaposition of the incidents, whether historical, personal or fictional. The sequence tells its own story, at times acting as a commentary on the text: the transcription of part of an interview with the minister of justice about the form and purpose of the TRC, centring on the idea of moral responsibility, is followed by a report of a 'row and an underhand TRC deal' (p. 9), is followed by a memory/fictional tale of cattle rustling and increased violence disturbing the paradise of her childhood home on the family farm, followed by the reportage of a visit by the English queen, who refuses to apologize for the atrocities during the Boer war as her visiting schedule is full: High-mindedness and political manoeuvrings on the black side, lost in-nocence and beauty, and British hypocrisy blurring the picture of the Afrikaners as the only perpetrators of evil.

The mixed genre is eminently suited to convey 'a patchwork of all the view points of the country' (p.14), which was the brief of the TRC when it was set up, but it also allows for a deeper involvement in one person's struggle with the complexities.

Krog's *Country of My Skull* performs the same double speak as *The Smell of Apples*, but with a much sharper insight into the con-tradictions and dilemmas it involves: she hates and exposes, but loves and feels guilty for betraying by exposing, and goes back to hating, etc., all this with a nail biting, nerve tearing intensity which precludes any thought of hamming. The dilemma is not only real, it is intense. Faced with a group of what she refers to as 'The Afrika-ner manner (those who call their sons 'my old bull')' [which is what happens in *The Smell of Apples*] she feels only aversion: 'the night-mare of my youth. The bullies with their wives – the chatty women with impressive cleavages and well behaved children … Aversion. I want to distance myself. They are nothing to me. I am not one of them. I find myself overcome with anger. Anger for being caught up in their mess' (p.113). And yet, on reporting on the Vlakplaas Five, she admits to herself that 'I am powerless to ignore what vibrates in me – I abhor and care for these five men' (p.122).

'Why do I want to give evil a human face?' she asks herself, and yet her broadcasting immediately brings angry phone calls from Afrikaner listeners who accuse her of suggesting that all Afrikaners are murderers (p.122). Feeling contempt for the leader of the Natio-nal Party, who denies knowledge and responsibility for Apartheid atrocities, she feels closer to the actual murderers, like the Vlakplaas five, and longs for a simple moment of unambiguous peace, an apology. She dreams it up, arriving at a pure moment, echoing Paton, 'We are so utterly sorry. We are deeply ashamed and gripped with remorse.' The moment ends with a plea, which is also an affirmation of her – and the Afrikaners' status – as natives of South Africa, 'But hear us we are from here. We will live it right – here – with you, for you' (p.125). The purity, or closure, of this moment is seriously disturbed by her inability, or unwillingness to put words to her feelings about the Vlakplas five and in particular Dirk Coetzee. The image she chooses about the Vlakplaas five is that they 'have walked a road, and through them some of us have walked a road' (p.125), and similarly, with Dirk Coetzee. He was 'just an Afrikaner who, for whatever reason, decided to walk a certain path. And to pay the price for it' (p. 88). The 'walking a certain path' image puts a lid on the soul searching, keeps a distance at a point where it is truly difficult, or perhaps impossible to get any closer. It forestalls closure.

This is a strength, rather than a weakness, in the text. The form of *Country of My Skull* allows for this depth and variety of both intellectual and emotional fluctuation. Basically, it asks all the difficult questions and attempts to suggest answers, but by doing so partially, with uncertainty or not at all, it tries out the many definitions of reconciliation which Krog refers to as 'her daily bread. Compromise, accommodate, provide, make space for. Understand, Tolerate. Empathize. Endure…Yes. Piece by piece we die into reconciliation' (p 50). She follows up these insights with a nervous breakdown and asks Wilhelm Verwoerd, a philosophy professor who works for the TRC commission for an answer, and he, not very helpfully, comes up with the piece of advice that 'we must make space for ambiguity' (p.126). Not knowing what to do with this she marvels that he is the grandson of Hendrik Verwoerd, the architect of apartheid, and she ends the chapter with a victim testimony in which a man holds his dying mother after she has been summarily shot by the South African police, a scene which does not exactly invite a response, tempered by ambiguity. And so it goes on, each stop on the way forcing its own opposite possibility in a seemingly endless regression. Complexity and ambiguity are built into both form and content of *Country of My Skull* and more surprisingly also into *The Smell of*

*Apples*. It would not be difficult to carry on the same line of investigation in such texts as Coetzee's *Disgrace* and Riad Malan's *My Traitor's Heart*. Here I shall just suggest that those texts are mainly concerned with the dilemmas of reconciliation, and their intention is to problematize the concept through precisely ambiguity.

The post Apartheid texts that I have dealt with, or mentioned here, take a complex and bleak view of reconciliation, and the difficulties that the participants experience with it centre around their doubts about the efficacy of the humanist and Christian values upheld by Alan Paton in 1948, denied by most of the literary responses to Apartheid all through its period, but reinstated as both an ideal and a working necessity in the charter for the Truth and Reconciliation Committee. Paton's liberal humanism expressed in his beloved cry to his country turned out to be a universally applicable culture that was only begging to be applied to the South African situation, and its derivative literature.

**References**

Antjie, Krog. *Country of My Skull*, Three Rivers Press, 1999.

Behr, Mark. *The Smell of Apples*, Abacus, 1995.

Bernard, Rita. "The Smell of Apples, Moby-Dick, and Apartheid Ideology." Modern Fiction Studies Vol. 46 no.1 (2000), 207-226.

Brink, André, "Stories of History: Reimagining the Past in Post-Apartheid Narrative." *Negotiating the Past: The Making of Memory in South Africa*. Ed. Sara Nuttall and Carli Coetzee. Oxford: Oxford UP, 1998. 29–42.

Coetzee, John M. *Strange Shores: Essays 1986- 99*, Secker and Warburg, 2001.

Gallagher, Susan, V. *Truth and Reconciliation: The confessional Mode in South African Literature*, Heinemann, 2002.

Graham, Shane, *South African Literature after the Truth Commission: Mapping Loss*. Macmillan, 2009.

# Chomtengure: CONSTRUCTION OF THE SUB-ALTERN IN ZIMBABWEAN SONG-DRAMA
## - Robert Muponde

In this article I discuss Zimbabwean culture with particular reference to two Shona song-dramas whose construction and vision border on the timeless and mythopoetic. The two songs, *Chomtengure* (the turning wheel of the ox-drawn cart) and *Uyo Ndiani* (Who is that one?) are indeed the construction of a worldview, and are, paradoxically, epitomes of the indestructibility and vulnerability of master narratives of identity and history. They represent what George Kahari, in his extended, catch-all critical prolegomena titled *The Rise of the Shona Novel* (1990), thought could be termed "the matter of Zimbabwe", that is, a core of folklore which is central to a people's system of values. This core becomes a touchstone of future growth and elaborations of culture. It underwrites sensibilities that constitute a cultural imagination. In a conservative sense, it could be used to hold down culture, to become its definitive content. In a revolutionary sense, it might represent the perennial search for a sense of identity, spirit, place and nationhood in contemporary Zimbabwe. The two songs I will comment on shortly represent the creative possibilities of this tension that ripples the rather viscous content of "the matter of Zimbabwe", especially as currently understood and represented by intellectual adherents of the "patriotic history" project of Robert Mugabe's beleaguered political party.

**Chomtengure (the turning wheel of the wagon)**
Chomtengure
Chomtengure
It is now the endless turning of the ox-wagon wheel
Woye woyee

You call me an ox-wagon driver, why?
Woye woye
I have seen your pants wet with dew
Woye woye
Why are you calling me ox-wagon driver?
Woye woye
I have seen the grease of the wagon all over your clothes
Woye woye

The wife of the wagon driver jump into the wagon
Woye woye
And disembark only when the wagon has a break down
Woye woye
The wife of the ox-wagon never goes without peanut butter
Woye woye
Because she takes the wagon grease as her butter
Woye woye

Chomtengure (the turning of the wheel)
Chomtengure (the turning of the wheel)

This song-drama, often mischaracterized as a labour protest song which emerged at the beginning of the last century, is as old as imagination itself. Because it dramatizes in song-form the tedium and nomadism that characterize the black ox-wagon driver's life in colonial Zimbabwe (then Rhodesia), and the attendant poverty, critics such as George Kahari have often tied the song-drama to political protest. Protest as a genre is founded on the idea that its graphic and forceful descriptions of oppression and suffering could raise awareness and moral shock in the oppressor, leading to an amelioration of the conditions that give rise to the outrage in the first place. It is also very easy for critics to limit the genre of protest to the articulation of the relationship between the weak and the po-werful, the oppressor and the oppressed, the abused and the abuser. In this case, the song-drama *Chomtengure* establishes what become the rules of engagement between abuser and abused, and provides song as part of a cache of arms in the sole possession of the abused.

It is not clear what the abuser sings in celebration or consolidation of his/her own position or relationship to the abused. The abused is armed with song, with the expressive armoury of the weak, with the hope that the articulatory and expressive potential of the song-drama would revivify the humanity denied the abused other. This strategy succeeds in a highly developed moral economy. Colonial Zimbabwe (Rhodesia) was far from being an ideal place for such songful supplications, as the stock response to protest song was often prison, censorship and banishment from the community. Alec Pongweni (1982) compiled a book of what he calls songs that won the liberation struggle in Zimbabwe, and these songs were composed around the celebration of armed action. An ad hominem attack on the abuser through song alone narrowed the possibilities of protest literature. At best, the protest song became a form of social and political entertainment: at worst it lost all value and became an instance of art which cannibalizes social situations for art's sake. In other words, it is possible to seek a social stimulus for one's artistic content and expression, in order to feed the conventions of a genre, and not necessarily in order to right the wrongs of a political establishment. Poverty and suffering, for instance, become just the ingredients that the protest genre requires to perpetuate itself. The social submits to the dictates of the form. Critics begin to look for these ingredients as central to the full description of a genre. George Kahari, a victim of such critical tropism, where certain social, artistic and experiential signifiers point to the adequate description of a form or genre, was quick to call *Chomtengure* a protest song. It is a protest song, but not only in Kahari's sense of the political.

It is a song that evolved from a particular social and political milieu of oppression. That is true. But it morphed into something beyond the master narrative of oppression and liberation. It found its place in colonial classrooms, where of course it was sanitized of its political content. I remember that when I was a pupil at one of the good primary schools in colonial Zimbabwe, we used to dramatize it, and the echoic chorus "woyee woyeee!" used to fill our ears, and we would rock our bodies to its rhythm with delight. In the Shona primary school textbook, there was an illustration of the ox-wagon driver with a pipe in his mouth, a long coat on his back, a cowboy hat on his head, and a long whip in his hand. The reddish/yellowish colours of the illustration painted a distant world of travel and a hardy character. We had seen this character in cattle herders in our village. I always thought *Chomtengure* referred to one wealthy and mean villager who owned lots of cattle and many fields, and would whip any little boy who allowed his father's cattle to stray into his fields or mix with his own better fed ones. I was often that small boy who was the beneficiary of the largesse of this rich villager's dung-soaked whip. I always thought the singing persona in *Chomtengure* was my mother, pleading with this man bent on skinning me like a skunk, mocking him for his neglect of his own household in pursuit of large herds of cattle and lush fields of maize and millet. There was something wasteful about the ox-wagon driver. In the song, he is mocked. His pants are wet with dew (because he is on the road all his waking and sleeping life), and dirty with wagon grease (he hardly has time to wash his clothes because of his calling). His wife, against all expectations of prosperity which come with a travelled husband, cannot afford peanut butter, and has to resort to using wagon grease! This is not political protest per se. It is a social satire applicable to many situations in the various professions, where some people give up their lives for a particular trade (whether they are employed by someone else to do the job, or they are self-employed) to the detriment of their personal and family health. For example, in Zimbabwe bricklayers are often the butt of many jokes. They are known to be proud of their professions, and are also known to point to impressive edifices as monuments to their talents, but often live in shacks themselves. *Chomtengure* immortalizes the experiences of itinerant professions and point to the social dislocation that, ironically, an uncritical broader view of the road might occasions.

One other function of the song-drama which is often missed is its analeptic value in situations of labour. Because of its rhythm, the song was often used to coordinate labour in collective activities such as *Nhimbe* where the whole community helps to thresh corn or millet. It energizes the community in the processes of production, and renews and consolidates communal ties. *Chomtengure* becomes an occasion for irony. If its roots are in labour protest, it actually celebrates the net value of labour by being reanimated in sites of collective, regenerative labour. It constantly reminds the community of the possibility of engaging in unrewarding labour, hence by being actualized at a labour site, it acts as a reminder to the community to avoid expending energy and talents in destructive occupations. There is always the possibility of one or two known members of the community, often present at the *Nhimbe*, whose lives go round and round like the wheel of the wagon, until they are worn out and discarded by fate. While their lives are full of events, cumulatively, these events amount to a cyclic experience of negative growth.

*Nhimbe* is also not only an occasion for socially productive labour, but a place for the rehabilitation of social miscreants. Participants at *Nhimbe* have been known to "thresh" their opponents, enemies and detractors verbally or physically, directly or indirectly. *Nhimbe* is a magical place of healing and restitution. What happens there ends there. For instance a wronged person might 'thresh' his enemy's legs 'accidentally', often without retribution from his/her victim, because the victim 'gets the message' immediately, and rests assured the debt has now been repaid, and therefore the matter rests there at the *Nhimbe*. No one is expected to take the fight or altercation to the home. Thus the song of abuse could easily be reconditioned by society into a song of social redemption, whether there is an employer or not, a white oppressor or not. It is the ability of the erstwhile 'protest song' to get a life that eludes critics who are bent on restricting the song to a cyclopean and fixed vision of dispossession and suffering in politics and labour. The sightings of suffering and dispossession are then used by these conservative critics as a fixative which holds together the graphics of this song-drama and pins it down to a single meaning and purpose. Yet, a multifocal reading of the song-drama might produce verifiable instances of the many lives and possibilities of *Chomtengure*. These range from protest at labour sites to play and entertainment in the classroom; restoration of the moral and social order through direct and indirect rebuke of those who wrong others or indulge in unproductive social activities; and the meting out of instant, socially approved justice by victims of social miscreants in the enabling environment of *Nhimbe*. Society regains itself, and moves on, and *Chomtengure* is but one instance of the protean nature of cultural products which gather and discard meanings and purposes originally designed for them, and from them. These cultural products do not play with identities, but manufacture their own, independent of their originators' intentions. Reading cultures, and cultures of receptions may also return cultural products to positions they no longer speak from, or speak of. Or they may increase the possibility of life for cultural products and practices by tracing the particularities of the environments in which they animate their vibrant migrancies. While migrants do have some starting points, they are not solely defined by where they have been, or where they go. The incessant turning up of dust behind their feet is good enough starting point not only to enquire about where they come from, and why they come from there, but where they are, and what they do where they are. The turning wheel of the wagon could therefore be studied *in medias res*, and traces of travel gathered on it could be read not as 'grease' and wear and tear, but hints of the depth and breadth of life possible. This reading has been denied the song-drama by cultural nationalists in Zimbabwe, who celebrate stasis as stability, and traces of travel as stains.

**Uyo Ndiani? (Who is that one?)**
Who is that one?
Who is that one who herds cattle?
That one with cattle
The one with cattle where will he take them?
Where will he take them?
Where will he take the cattle?
Why do you ask? What has happened to the cattle kraal?
What has happened to the cattle pen?
There is a girl
There is a girl (in the cattle pen)
There is a girl who has rejected men
She has rejected suitors
She has rejected them because she wants Dhimba (a small sweet-singing bird)
She says she loves Dhimba
She says she loves Dhimba
But you Dhimba refuse her

Dhimba you must reject her too
Dhimba you must spurn her so she can be embarrassed
So we can see her ashamed
Ashamed like a big man
Like a very big man
A very big man sitting on a log
Sitting on a log
A decayed log
A decayed log
A log that will break up the Tonga people
Tear down the Tonga
Tear up the Tonga people
Where have the white people come from?
Where have the white people come from?
The white people have come from the valley
They have come via the valley
In the valley are girls
There are girls there
These girls have big breasts
They have big breasts
Very big breasts full of fat
Full of fat
Full of fat oh please we ask for some
We ask for some fat
We ask for some fat please so we can rub on our heads
So we can rub our heads
Our heads which are the colour of guinea fowl
The colour on guinea fowl
And of scabs....

*Uyo ndiani* (who is that one?) celebrates the beauty and potential of shifting and mixed perspectives. If *Chomtengure*'s persona suggests the making of the mythopoetic nomad in Zimbabwean culture, *Mufambi rombe*, the proverbial stone that gathers no moss, the subject of *Uyo ndiani* is even more peripatetic in terms of content and perspective.

The song-drama opens with an attempt to identify a roving subject ('Who is that one who herds cattle?'). The cattle herder is taking cattle to a pen that is occupied not by other domestic animals, but by a girl who has spurned many suitors in favour of a poor man ('Dhimba', the beautiful, tiny and meatless bird). The song encourages 'Dhimba' the favoured poor suitor to ditch the proud girl and shame her, and expose her the way a hollow and decayed log cannot sustain the weight of a big man and will give up on him in the most embarrassing fashion when it collapses. The collapse of the hollow and decayed log is compared to what may or should happen to the Tonga people, who presumably deserve the same treatment as the proud little girl. The Tonga, or the mention of the Tonga (whose crime is not stated), conjures the arrival of the white settlers on the land, and the image of well-fed and big-breasted girls (as opposed to the 'Kasikana' – a small/slender girl - in the second stanza of the song). The nubility and breasts of these girls, who live in the direction the white man has come from, can be used to cure scabs on the heads.

The dramatic beginning is matched with the equally dramatic ending. The identification of a solitary and wandering herd boy who is looking for a cattle pen does not logically lead to the story of fat breasts and scabs on the head which the community suffers from.

To some extent, it is a pastoral romance. Nothing much, in terms of what is expected of the pastoral genre is revealed. The rustic background and activities are present, without the bliss and songs of enchantment. The romantic affair is not between the herd boy and the girl in the cattle pen. In fact, the girl stands as an obstacle both to the cattle which must come 'home' to rest and to communal processes that require that a good girl is one who brings cattle into her father's kraal by marrying a good man. Thus, figuratively speaking, the girl stands in the kraal and prevents cattle from getting into the homestead, denying a whole community wealth and self-regeneration. By choosing a poor man, Dhimba, over other suitors, she is unilaterally authorizing her own quest narrative which disrupts communal and patriarchal ethos. There is the possibility of love and its excitements and entanglements. The heroine, standing there in the kraal, lovesick and defiant, presents herself as the suffering victim of societal intolerance. The kraal is a double paradox. For her, it is the space of equanimity and reconstitution of the self, as well as a site of rebellion. It also presents a founding dilemma both for her and her society. Without her, there are no cattle in the kraal, and by extension, no community. With her in the kraal, there are no cattle in the homestead, hence an uncertain patrimony and lineage. The kraal is an allegory of oppression where her ambitions are concerned, and a metaphor of her liberation when she identifies it not just as the graveyard of African womanhood, but a potential site of resurrection by staunching the flow of communal symbols of control and wealth. She finds herself lone-rangering against a society that actually views itself as the victim of her arrogance and insensitivity. The community conjures the white men, the Tonga people, girls with fat breasts and scabs in a story of unrequited love, or frustrated ambition, to indicate its deep sense of betrayal by the little girl. There is tragedy looming somewhere when the community fails to put down the insurrection. It could be the beginning of the end of an era or ethos. So, the seemingly nonsensical song-drama, with its unpredictable concatenation of events, is actually not just a pastoral romance, but a cumulative allegory of changing times. It is a ballad of the times. But there are ways in which it refuses to abide by the terms of each genre: cumulative tale; pastoral romance; ballad; nonsense; quest narrative; allegory; etc.

As an allegory, it works well, but not as one would have predicted. It is more helpful to view the cumulative fragments as instances of unfinished allegorical stories. For instance, one narrative contract which characterizes narratives hitched to the anti-colonial struggle would invariably suggest that the story is an allegory of the disruptive influence of the white settler, and the need to unsettle him, etc. But no, what we have is the suggestion that fat-breasted 'foreign' girls are an answer to local health problems. An allegorical reading of the ending suggests sexual overtones, that the diseased 'head' which is full of scabs is malnourished because it lacks the 'fat' from the 'foreign' girls. It becomes an allegory of domestic oppression and abuse as well as xenophobia. In any case, the male suitors have been rejected by the proud little girl, so salvation comes from afar. It is a story of revenge with misogynistic tendencies. The misogyny undermines the romantic quest narrative. Here, the little girl who loves Dhimba, never gets fulfillment. The cumulative tale does not advance her plot. It muffles her voice, marginalizes her views and feelings, and curtails the journeys she could have undertaken, and at the end of the song-drama, her experience amounts to nothing. There is no qualitative transformation of her status and experience, nor is her pain and suffering rewarded. The object of her quest is not secured. The blocking characters still reign. There is no triumph, except of her ill-wishers. The promise of the love ballad is undermined by the elegiac tone that creeps in at the end, and the vengeful motives that drive the plot. The intended humour of the nonsense song-drama cannot lighten the sad image of a lorn, and isolated lovesick girl, and the possibility of a crude liposuction of the fat breasts to cure scabs.

The good thing about this song-drama is that it suggests the possibility of a creative bricolage which writers like Dambudzo Marechera later attempted when confronted with questions of genre, convention and canon. Thus in 'the matter of Zimbabwe' one finds a song-drama like *Uyo ndiani* which suggests future creative elaborations and refinements. The rolling of fragmentary incendiary plots, endlessly new sets of characters in rapid sequences, and an unpredictable accumulation of disjunctions and narrative abruptions, and an attempt to make a grim story of oppression look hilarious, and the milking of fat from women's breasts look like harmless misogyny, presents us with what can only be called a postcolonial dreamlore.

The aesthetic of vulgarity that Achille Mbembe (2001) says characterizes the relationship between the powerful and the powerless in the African postcolony, is here also given a new meaning. It is the thing to make lullabies and ballads from. Yet the rapidly shifting and mixing perspectives allow a more complex appreciation of the song-drama than *Chomtengure* permits.


## Conclusion

While the two songs teem with visions of the nomadic, the rootless, the cyclic and powerless, they do not in themselves 'play with identities'. They deploy these seemingly continuously mutating identities in a particular way in order to instil a sense of balance and autonomy in the 'margins' and a sense of instability at the 'centre'. The 'voiceless' are the values that give 'voice' to the 'centre', and it is the centre that plays with the identities of the voiceless in order to maintain its power base. It is this tension between the two inter-dependent poles that shapes *Chomtengure* and gives it its sense of perpetual revolution and cyclical habits. The vigil-like alertness of *Uyo Ndiani* underscores the need to define power and its execution in relation to the margins, and to see identities as continually being reconstituted. *Uyo Ndiani* occupies therefore both a complementary and oppositional vantage point in relation to *Chomtengure*. The lack of conclusive closure in both songs is in itself an admission of the complexity of post-colonial identity formation, and is an image of open-enddedness in social processes. This endless vista of struggle and transformation is a counter proposal to the one enforced by the ruling party in Zimbabwe where destiny (individual or national) starts and ends with the Party and the land.

*Chomtengure* ("Going round in circles") is indeed an epic of the disempowered. It is as much contemporary as it is historical and timeless. The song has stood the tides of fashion and continues to de-scribe and inform national character – even though it has escaped the populist attention of contemporary music critics. The only critic who has tried to give the song meaning is George Kahari (1981). But he fell dutifully into the trap of ascribing an anti-colonial, protest value to any art form produced in the colonial era. The intentional ambi-guity of *Chomtengure* also made it vulnerable to the colonial masters who quickly transcribed it into school textbooks as an example of the prosperity of their Uncle Tom *kaffirs* (derogatory for black sub-jects) because its persona is a man who earns a living by driving an ox-drawn cart for the White master. While Kahari views the song as a protest against unfair labour practices, he does not appreciate its mythopoetic possibilities – and its evolution into a symbol of the quest for identity which culminated in the armed struggle. Beyond that, Kahari does not see how this seemingly innocuous song begins to assume even more frightening lineaments in the post-colonial situation, because it continues to critique the values of the ruling class and society at large while positing counter proposals that go beyond the five-year development plans of the national govern-ment. This cultural and intellectual drought (Zimunya, 1982) in the Zimbabwean ruling elite is the cause of *Chomtengure* (purposeless wandering) in national vision.

*Uyo Ndiani*, is a song-drama which gives a panorama of identities and places undergoing rapid transformation in kaleidoscopic fashion. It is difficult to define and fix in time any description or personality as change assaults society. Identities are only apprehended momentarily only to be disputed by inflows of new personas, genres and conventions. So, *Uyo Ndiani* (Who is that one?) undermines the certainty that is also the bane of contemporary society. It affords even the 'voiceless' the critical awareness of their rank, and the possibility of difference in the same rank. Now, this self-diagnosing is a habit absent in most of the despairing musicians in Zimbabwe.

Alice Kwaramba (1997) tends to view all the Zimbabwean musicians as being defined in terms of their opposition to alienating authority. What is absent in the musicians is the capacity to sing *past* present authority. They seem to derive social identity from the existence of oppositional relations in the public sphere, which they critique. Once the dichotomies of power and powerless, rule and misrule disappear, they lose their very *raison de'tre*. This is how the tenuousness of the existence of the subaltern mentality is constructed in the Zimbabwean musician. And in *Chomtengure* and *Uyo Ndiani* we see prefigured and rehearsed the very character and predicament of denizens of the frontier or margins.

# Appendix

## Chomtengure

*Chomtengure*
*Chomtengure*
*Chave chomtengure vhiri rengoro*
*Woyee woyeee*

*Wanditi muchairi wandionei?*
*Woyee woyee*
*Ndakuona mabhurukwa azere dova*
*Woyee woyee*
*Wanditi muchairi wandionei?*
*Woyee woyee*
*Ndati ndaona girisi rawakazora*
*Woyee woyee*

*Mukadzi wemuchairi kwira mungoro*
*Woyee woyee*
*Wozoburuka ngoro yachona*
*Woyee woyee*

*Mukadzi wemuchairi haashayi dovi*
Woyee woyee
Anopota achinombora girisi rengoro
Woyee woyee

## Uyo Ndiani? (Who is that one?)

*Uyo ndiani?*
*Uyo ndiani ane mombe dzake*
*Ane mombe dzake*
*Ane mombe dzake anodziisepi?*
*Anodziisepi?*
*Anodziisepi?*
*Mudanga munei? Mudanga munei? Mudanga munei?*
*Mune kasikana.*
*Mune kasikana*

*Mune kasikana karamba varume*
*Karamba varume*
*Karamba varume kati ndoda dhimba*
*Kati ndoda dhimba*
*Kati ndoda dhimba iwe dhimba ramba*
*Iwe dhimba ramba*
*Iwe dhimba ramba tione kunyara*
*Tione kunyara*
*Tione kunyara kunge rumeguru*
*Kunge rumeguru*
*Kunge rumeguru rigere pamutanda*
Rigere pamutanda
Rigere pamutanda
Pamutanda nyepfu
Pamutanda nyepfu
Pamutanda nyepfu nyepfura vaTonga
Nyepfura vaTonga
Nyepfura vaTonga
Varungu vabvepi
Varungu vabvepi
Varungu vabvepi?
 Vabva nekumapani
Vabva nekumapani
Vabva nekumapani
Kune zvisikana
Kune zvisikana
Kune zvisikana zvine zvizamu
Zvine zvizamu
Zvine zvizamu zvizere mafuta
Zvizere mafuta
Zvizere mafuta
Tinokumbirawo
Tinokumbirawo
Tinokumbirawo
Tizore misoro
Tizore misoro
Tizore misoro yakachena hanga

Yakachena hanga
Yakachena hanga nemaronda zvose…..

**Acknowledgement**
I would like to thank Dr Maxwell Kadenge, an expert in Zezuru phonology, for discussing with me my translations of the two song-dramas into English.

**References**


Kahari, George, 1990. *The Rise of the Shona Novel*. Gweru: Mambo Press.

Kahari, George, 1981. *Aspects of the Shona Novel*. Gweru: Mambo Press.

Kwaramba, Alice, Dadirai. 1997. *Popular Music and Society*. Oslo: University of Oslo.

Mbembe, Achille. 2001. *On the Postcolony*. Berkeley: University of California

Palmberg, Mai and Annemette Kirkegaard. Eds. 2002. *Playing with Identities in Contemporary Music in Africa*. Uppsala: Nordic Afrika Institute.

Zimunya, Musaemura, 1982. *Those Years of Drought and Hunger*. Gweru: Mambo Press.

# STORIES OF FROZEN WORLDS: THE PASSAGE OF TIME IN THE NOVELS OF CHENJERAI HOVE
## - Ranka Primorac

'[T]his country and its forests, animals,
even snakes and mosquitoes belongs to us.'

Robert Mugabe (cited in *Sunday Mail* 4 April 2004)

'If the birds and insects refused to sing,
What would the forest be?'

Chenjerai Hove (*Bones* 76)

## ZANU (PF) and the Arrow of Time

This essay aims to describe the concept of the passage of time as imagined and represented in the English-language novels of Chenjerai
Hove (*Bones*, *Shadows* and *Ancestors*), and to set this concept against
the idea of time implied in the notion of history currently disseminated by the official mythology of Zimbabwe's ruling party. Chenjerai
Hove is one of Zimbabwe's best-known writers: apart from novels,
he has also authored several volumes of poetry, and non-fiction (see
Rooney forthcoming, for a discussion of his poetry). The political
essays he published as a regular column in a weekly newspaper
(collected in Hove, *Palaver Finish*) set him on a collision course with
the Zimbabwean authorities, and he now lives outside Zimbabwe. A
broad outline of recent activities of ZANU (PF), Zimbabwe's ruling
party, is also well known. Having come into power in 1980 after a
bloody civil war and a protracted series of negotiations, ZANU (PF)
experienced the first serious challenge to its hegemony in 2000. As a

response to this challenge mounted by a constellation of agents and alliances (see Alexander 2003 and Chan 2003), it instigated a violent take-over of Zimbabwe's privately owned agricultural land.

This process, known as 'the fast-track redistribution of land', led to the collapse of Zimbabwe's economy and an increase in political repression. It is, however, officially represented as the pinnacle of Zimbabwe's history as an independent nation: the final instalment of a protracted liberation struggle, the triumphant third *Chimurenga* [uprising]. The official narrative of a continuing anti-colonial war entails a reinscription of the nation's past which, in turn, rests on a certain understanding of the passage of time. Chenjerai Hove's fictional narratives anticipate, interrogate and challenge both this understanding and the cluster of official meanings attached to it.

It has been argued elsewhere that, in the context of an enforced polarisation of political discourse in Zimbabwe, fictional literature may be seen as a repository of concepts and identities that resist easy appropriation, and that it can make a contribution to the debate on central issues such as land (Chan and Primorac 2004). For reasons that will become apparent below, this is especially true of the 'experimental' or aesthetically dominated novelistic tradition (see Kaarsholm forthcoming; Primorac 2002; 2003), of which Chenjerai Hove is a key representative.

The narrative of three dovetailing *Chimurenga* has become the backbone of the official Zimbabwean version of history – the so-called 'patriotic history', described in detail by Terence Ranger (Ranger 2004). Both Ranger and others have commented on a seeming paradox contained in the Zimbabwean government's rhetoric: although the take-over of farmland was meant to represent a 'fast-track' movement of Zimbabwean national identities into the *future*, the official discourse has often evoked a sudden return into the *past* - reviving the emphasis on the importance of liberation war 'veterans' in the political process and using war-time methods, including violence, to draw the Zimbabwean population to its cause. Writing about this paradox, Christine Sylvester notes how this kind of historical imagination blots out the *present* – so that the national 'now' is seen as being either unimportant or non-existent in view of the grand advancement of future-in-the-past that is still to come: 'By looking backwards as a way of managing an unpopular present, ZANU (PF) hoped to write a ticket to the future, and to do so with its everyday failings as a government in full public view' (Sylvester 30).

And yet there is, in fact, an underlying logic beneath ZANU (PF)'s temporal hard-headedness. Minimising the importance of the present, through references to the unfinished business of the past, points to a view of history as something that unfolds in time that is imagined as relentlessly *linear*. Speaking of 'patriotic history', Ranger himself has described it as offering 'a highly selective and *streamlined* version of anti-colonial struggle. It is a doctrine of "permanent revolution" leaping from *Chimurenga* to *Chimurenga*. It has no time for questions or *alternatives*' (Ranger '[Doctrine of Permanent Revolution]'). The simple, uni-directional quality of 'patriotic history' highlighted in this description overlaps neatly with 'the representation of time as moving from the past forward into the future, according to the well-known metaphor of the arrow of time', as Paul Ricoeur (1980) puts it – omitting, significantly, to mention the present. 'Patriotic history' is selective, streamlined and future-oriented because it is teleological – and, thus is, I would argue, inevitably grounded in a linear, arrow-like understanding of time.

In the present context, this is perhaps best illustrated through the writings of Alexander Kanengoni, whose complex and moving works of fiction contrast sharply with his recent texts written in defence of ruling party policies. In a 2003 newspaper article, the former freedom fighter and present-day farmer, Kanengoni - claiming to refer to personal memory – stresses the steady and unchanging character of Robert Mugabe, whose decades-old plans for Zimbabwe with regards to land have now been put into practice: 'For me, programmes like land reform and affirmative action (…) are all part of the focus that he told us during that time [23 years ago]' (Kanengoni 2003). Even more strikingly, another personal/historical narrative directly links the 1888 Rudd Concession and the author's taking possession of a Centenary farm in 2002, subsuming the symmetrical narrative of dispossession and subsequent repossession under the metaphor of a unidirectional, goal-oriented journey. The final words of the text emphasise the idea of a cause-and-effect chain, as well as a multiple arrival reached through a linear temporal progression: 'Once again I looked down at my piece of land. Yes, the war was over. Therefore, all arms must go to the armoury because the war was over'. (*The journey too;* Kanengoni, 2004). In contrast to the implied foresight of ZANU (PF), the opposition is on occasion represented as emphatically backward-looking. Tafataona Mahoso has written: 'The MDC was born already weighed down by dog-tired ideas, trying to repackage for Zimbabwe some 1920s clichés in the twenty-first century' (Mahoso 2004).

This idea of an untrammelled, although slightly retarded progress - a neat, if violent, unfolding of the movement of colonial occupation, and the gradual counter-movement effecting restitution - is resisted by the fiction of Chenjerai Hove. Far from imagining the passage of time as a flying arrow, Hove's novels question the possibility of emergence of new identities in postcolonial Zimbabwe. The sections that follow will argue that the complex works of Hove: *Bones*, *Shadows* and *Ancestors,* imagine Zimbabwean lives as taking place in environments that are still and unchanging, and may be described as *frozen*.

**The Liars of the Land**
This section seeks to highlight the key configuration of commonalities in form and meaning, relevant to the discussion of time in Hove's work. Hove's writing deserves more critical attention than it has received. Although *Bones*, his first novel in English, is well known and has attracted some debate (mostly to do with its style, and attitude towards nationalism and the nation), *Shadows* and *Ancestors* have, to my knowledge, been less widely discussed, despite sharing several important textual traits with their better-known predecessor. I will briefly discuss each of these traits in turn.

All of Hove's novels in English identify themselves as unofficial histories – that is, as stories of those who were close to recorded historical events, but whose participation in them has gone unnoticed, or has been deliberately erased from official memory. Hove's main theme in all three novels is the suffering of Zimbabwean peasants, and especially the women among them. His relationship to official historical discourses is made most explicit in *Shadows*, whose prologue starts with the words:

> For those looking for fiction, go elsewhere, there is none here. For those looking for tall tales, find the story-tellers of the land to tell you the cock-and-bull stories. For those in search of history, go to the liars of the land (p. 9).

In contrast to the lies told by historians, *Shadows* claims to contain a version of historical truth otherwise overlooked. Similarly, a key character in *Ancestors* – Miriro, a woman who has been silenced - asserts: 'A story untold is a story of death. One who has a story inside them and does not tell it means they are harbouring death in their hearts, in their souls.' (pp. 19-20). As for *Bones*, the critic Rooney has described it with the following words:

> *Bones* is close to the concerns of many non-literate or semi-literate, non-elite Zimbabwean women of a certain generation. That is, it addresses the sufferings of (…) *women who have been forgotten*, and it engages with the need for consolation, mourning and remembrance, and for the paying of respects (Rooney 1995: 120; emphasis added).

Furthermore, all three of Hove's novels are written in what may be termed an 'unofficial' kind of English – a kind of 'in-between' language that obeys the grammatical and syntactic rules of written English, but employs repetition, certain kinds of figures of speech and certain kinds of imagery to create an impression of spoken Shona. In all the novels, events are narrated through relatively short sentences and clauses, and narrators draw their metaphors, symbols and imagery largely from the world of nature. They also incorporate Shona sayings, folktales and folk songs. The final result amounts to what Dan Wylie (1991) has called an 'inter-language': a richly creative *illusion* of Shona-ness, which nevertheless – precisely through *not* being Shona – draws readers' attention to its own linguistic artificiality. The following paragraph from *Bones* provides an illustration:

> He really wants to keep her like a mother baboon keeping its
> little one. They are now like pot and fireplace, always together
> like a tree and a leaf. Do you know that some women know
> how to please their husbands more than anything else? Never
> mind their bad cooking and all that, but when night comes,
> they know the language of the night. They make a man swear
> by his ancestors never to leave her (p. 8).

Although Hove's work has been described as 'polyphonic' (Boeh-mer 1993), ideological and other differences between characters in his fiction are diminished by the fact that all or most of them (as well as the novels' impersonal narrators) use a similar sort of ritualistic, sonorous[1] linguistic register. The stylistic similarity among the characters' voices and the fact that, in all the novels, their words intersect and complement one another may leave readers with the impressions that, in Hove's worlds, the bearers of unofficial histories groups share a communal and *unchanging* language and voice (see also Veit-Wild, 'Dances with Bones').

The stylistic peculiarity of Hove's work also belies the fact that, in all of the novels, there are multiple narrators and/or multiple narrative perspectives. In addition to that – and this has a direct bearing on the texts' construction of time - the ordering of events in the novels is not chronological. Instead, the narratives jump back and forth between various speakers and various points of narrated time, leaving readers to work out for themselves both the temporal and the causal links between events. This, however, is not always possible. The fifteen chapters of *Bones*, for example, are told by five different narrators. For three of those narrators (Marume, Chisaga and the unknown woman), it can be stated with some certainty that each of their sections issues from a different point in narrated time - although it is not always possible to relate those different points to one another chronologically. One of the other two narrative voices (the voice of the spirits) speaks from a non-human temporal dimension, whereas the fifth voice (Janifa) is capable of being given at least two different interpretations with regard to the relationship of narrated time and time of narration (see chapter on Hove in Primorac 'The Place of Tears'). All this results in a high level of temporal indeterminacy, which further contributes to creating the effect of stasis. Hove uses similar technique in both *Shadows* and *Ancestors*.

Such an approach to chronology is likely to be familiar to readers of modernist novels, and indeed, in many formal aspects, Hove's works may be termed neo-modernist. This is important in the present context because it points to a further temporal characteristic of Hove's work. In terms of historical time as a *theme*, all three novels deliberately avoid emphasising the officially accepted markers of historical *progress*. The key example of this is the year 1980, the date of the arrival of independence and majority rule. Although all three novels span the pre-independence and post-independence eras, the exact moment of its coming is deliberately 'submerged' in the texts. By this I mean that, although the texts contain enough information for the readers to be able to discern that some parts of the story take place before 1980, and others after, there is nowhere in Hove that a compositional break marks individual sections of the text as being 'before', and others 'after' The key national event – the formal transition from Rhodesia to Zimbabwe and the national temporal benchmark in all versions of nationalist history of Zimbabwe – is not textually represented or singled out in any way. It should be stressed that this textual strategy is unusual among post-independence novels in English. Other key texts such as Tsitsi Dangarembga's *Nervous Conditions*, or Yvonne Vera's first four novels, all take place entirely before 1980; alternatively, novels such as *The Stone Virgins* or Shimmer Chinodya's *Harvest of Thorns* make it very clear where the text itself is divided into pre- and post- independence sections. This rejection of the officially accepted segmentation of national time is yet another aspect the unchanging quality of Hove's worlds.

In contrast to this deliberate temporal vagueness, *Bones*, *Shadows* and *Ancestors* insist on clarity when it comes to drawing an important *spatial* distinction: that between urban and rural areas. But in Hove's worlds, space also participates in obstructing change and impeding growth. The stories of all three novels take place in part on commercial farms, and in part in cities. Yet all three texts stress the enormous difficulties that the peasant characters encounter in crossing the space that separates cities from the rural areas; that is, in *traversing* the land that has been the source of so much historical motivation. This is not to say that ownership of the land itself is unimportant in the stories told by Hove's texts. *Bones* features (and condemns) the character of a cruel and exploitative white commercial farmer; both *Shadows* and *Ancestors* tell stories of men who, before independence, long to become *Matenganyika* – buyers of land – and who go through enormous sacrifice just to attain that status. But once they have attained it, the texts make it clear that without the right to direct one's own movement across the land, and without the right to leave it and/or return at will, the ownership in itself becomes meaningless.

This difficulty in effecting spatio-temporal movement may be further linked to violence. Some key events related by Hove's novels are very violent: the novels tell stories of rapes, beatings, deaths, murders and suicides. Although characters often seek to escape such violence by relocating, they soon discover that the violence is everywhere. 'Every place is the place of tears', says a narrator in *Ancestors* (180). Thus, although the two kinds of space are clearly distinguished from each other, the omnipresence of violence diminishes the difference between country and city.

All this is to say that, in Hove's worlds, social change cannot be imagined as taking place as a matter of course in linearly conceived time – and neither can it be effected by a relocation in space, or by violence. The worlds of *Bones*, *Shadows* and *Ancestors* are static and constricting, as if frozen – and in this they resemble the silent forest evoked by Hove in the sentence from *Bones* cited at the outset. This, however, does not mean that the passage of time is imagined in an identical manner in each individual novel. In *Bones*, time is seen as causing those that dare show agency (expressed as movement) to be literally *swallowed* by space. In *Shadows*, the passage of time demands of the characters *silence* and *endurance*. And in *Ancestors*, the movement of time is *uneven*, and it favours those in positions of power. The following section looks in more detail at each of the texts in turn.

### Stories of Frozen Worlds

Marita, the heroine of *Bones*, is a peasant who lives on a large, white-owned commercial farm during the war of liberation. After independence, nothing changes in the relationship between the cruel white farmer and his workers. He continues to exploit and abuse them, saying: "There is nothing that the [new, independent] government can do [to me]. I rule here (…). If your government wants to run this farm, let them bloody take over. Then we will see if they can run a farm' (99-100).

Marita decides to challenge this man: she wants to go to the city, to see if, at a government office, she can find whether her guerrilla son is alive. In effect, she is testing the space of the city – the seat of the newly-independent government - to see if it is capable of countering the farmer's taunt. She is also challenging the temporal aspect of the idea of independence to live up to its meaning of emergence, social change and progress. But she fails: when she reaches the city, she dies mysteriously and literally disappears from the view of both readers and other characters. Contrary to what some critics have claimed, Marita is not (unlike the unknown woman) killed in the novel. Readers are not told how she dies. She never returns to the farm and is not or is able to find her son: it is as if the city has, literally, swallowed her.

The novel places great emphasis on the difficulty Marita encounters in leaving the farm and travelling to the city. She has to take the bus, and in order to get to the bus stop, she has to walk through:

> large farmlands which nobody farms. The owners are frenzied or vicious when they see someone walking through these unspoiled forests that are their farms. But there is no bus or car to take the walker away from the roads through the farms. So, one does not know how to leave the farmlands and reach the bus stop (69).

It is as if, between settler farmland and the city, there is a spatial vacuum, and a vacuum of ideology and of power. Just as settlers control the 'unspoiled forests' outside the city, so the key holders of power in the city itself are government bureaucrats. It has been written that pre-colonial African imagination of political spaces visualises such spaces in the shape of concentric circles radiating from the core (Mazarire, 'Changing Landscape 707). In *Bones*, the two poles of the represented world – the farm and the city – may be imagined in a similar manner, as if they exerted a gravitational pull on those who inhabit them. This is because whenever the characters of *Bones* leave either the farm or the city, they are, conspicuously and near-instantaneously, *replaced* by others. On the farm, Janifa is loved by Marita in place of her absent son; she is also raped by Chisaga in place of Marita. In the city, the unknown woman's dead body replaces Marita's as the unclaimed corpse at the mortuary. Both spatial poles of *Bones* draw people like magnets, then work towards keeping them, literally, in their place. The bi-polar world that results is frozen in the sense that it works towards preventing movement between the poles. Such movement is difficult, especially for a multiply disempowered person - a black female peasant - like Marita.

In such a world, time is like a voracious beast: it annihilates, literally, everything that moves. Even the rebellious Marita cannot imagine herself participating in an end-oriented sequence of events, immersed in arrow-like time. In the future, she says, she will no longer be working on the farm (30). But when her friend Janifa asks what she would do should she find her son, it turns out that the only plan she has is encapsulated in the words: 'I will be happy' (43). Marita's son, the veteran of the liberation war (the second *Chimurenga*), cannot do this, either, and is, at the novel's end, rejected by Janifa. The only voices that can fully record the difficulty and injustice that occur in the frozen world of *Bones* are those of the ancestors, who speak from a parallel spatio-temporal realm. However, although they have the power to express moral outrage, they are powerless to directly intervene: 'Nobody will come to claim [Marita's] body from the house where they keep corpses so that they do not gather worms' (103).[2]

In *Shadows*, however, even the ancestors are silent. Towards the end of the novel, there is an episode in which armed dissidents – the Ndebele, former guerrillas, unhappy with their treatment in independent Zimbabwe - abduct and kill a villager during the post-independence war of the 1980s, and leave his body in the open countryside. But the centre-piece of *Shadows* is a family, a story of the forbidden love between a young woman named Johanna, the daughter of a black farmer who has managed to obtain a plot of land in a 'native purchase area', and a farm hand called Marko, of whom her father disapproves. This love affair is marked by patience and silence: Marko has waited for a long time for Johanna to return his love, neither of them can express the love in words, and both go silently to their deaths when faced with forced separation. Meanwhile, Johanna's father struggles to turn the poor soil on his farm to profit, and is forced to flee to the city when freedom fighters accuse him of being a sell-out.

In executing the difficult movement between rural and urban spaces, Johanna's father resembles Marita from *Bones*. Unlike Marita, he manages, after much suffering, to *return* to the farm. However, he comes home only to be killed by dissidents – and he leaves his wife and children to a fate of unspoken suffering.

For the peasants of *Shadows*, the passage of time represents the necessity for *silent endurance*, its movement separating survivors from the loyalties and constancies of the past, and taking them into an uncertain future. The link between endurance and silence is emphasised by the novel's closing paragraph:

> Johanna's mother hears the echoes of the new lullabies from the lips of the mothers carrying silent children. She hears them sing about the red moon is blood, the eye of the bull is a bullet, the girl's long neck is a needle. She hears it all in the silence of this house of death where life would have to start anew, like the dead leaves that would have to rise again from their death (*Shadows* 108).

Like *Shadows*, *Ancestors* also features a peasant family who moves out of the crowded 'tribal trust lands' into a new farm in a 'native purchase area.' But *Ancestors* ignores the theme of public politics almost completely: it mentions national political events only once, in passing.[3] Instead, it focuses on the gendered politics of family relationships.

Sometime after the move to the new home, the father of the family disowns and sends away one of his wives, because she has, in his view, defied the ancestors by crying during a family ritual. But it is the father himself – the bearer of the 'official' version of family history – who has caused ancestral unrest, by suppressing two family narratives of the cruel treatment of women. One is the story of Miriro, a deaf and dumb woman who, in pre-colonial times, killed herself when forced to marry against her will. The other is a similar story of Tariro, the daughter of one of the farmer's wives, given away to an older husband in Lusaka, then Northern Rhodesia.[4] This set of intertwined stories is told to Mucha, the exiled woman's son, by Miriro herself, who comes to him in dreams.

Temporally, *Ancestors* is especially interesting. The novel is divided into three parts. Each chapter within these parts bears a temporal designation marking the historical location of narrated time (for example: '*1850 – Birth of a Deaf-and-Dumb Child*,' or '*1960 – Father (the Hearer Hears)*'). The chapters are not arranged in chronological order, but because they take place on different dates, a chronological sequence may be recovered. Because the passing of historical time brings change (the emergence of new truths and identities), the space-time of *Ancestors* may be seen as having overcome (albeit with great difficulty) the static, 'frozen' condition of the worlds of *Bones* and *Shadows*. But the historical grounding of the narrative should not be mistaken for an attempt at historical 'objectivity.'

For one thing, there are large gaps – places of indeterminacy – between the dates: many pieces of the temporal 'jigsaw puzzle' are missing (it should be noted that 1980 – the year of independence – falls within one of those gaps). For another, some of the dates (e.g. '197-,' '198-') are deliberately not fully articulated, whereas others ('2 July 1970') are more specific than others: this may create an impression of the passage of time as *uneven*. And finally, in combination with the novel's division into parts, the historical details create a temporal hierarchy of events which is not based on chronology.

The three parts of *Ancestors* are entitled: 'The Hearer Hears of Fathers,' 'Women' and 'Children,' respectively. In Part One (to do with fathers), the chapters are both chronologically ordered and marked by a fully articulated date. In Part Two ('Women'), the chronological ordering is gone (in the text, '1966' is followed by '1958' and '1968'), but the full articulation of dates remains. In Part Three ('Children'), it is impossible to establish the exact chronology of chapters because three of the dates are not fully spelt out. The blurring of chronology and temporal specificity mirrors the decrease in the relative power of characters: men and adults are more powerful than women and children: the more powerful groups control the movement of the less powerful, and different groups are associated with different ways of articulating historical time.

In the end, Miriro actively intervenes in family by guiding a group of children – the least empowered characters in the novel – safely to their home in physical space. In addition to thus encouraging and aiding movement, she also encourages speech. She tells her descendants: 'You have a story within you, and I am the story. It is that story which has made you live. Not to tell it is death' (*Ancestors* 20). Chenjerai Hove's novels do not deny that spatio-temporal movement is possible, or desirable. But they recognise that, in a post/colony, it is also likely to be complexly executed and fraught with difficulty, aided by dialogue and brought to a standstill by silence.

## Of destiny as Language and Movement

I have tried to give some indication of how, in Hove's novels, the passage of time is neither straightforwardly linear, nor can it be unambiguously related to the 'patriotic' nationalist narrative of gradual advancement towards liberation. In the article on narrative time in which he described the idea of time as an arrow, Paul Ricoeur stresses that such a mechanical and abstract understanding of time cannot claim genuine historicity (181). According to Ricoeur's understanding, the key temporal element that is absent from Zimbabwean 'patriotic history', with its insistence on absolute continuity of identities (exemplified in Kanengoni's insistence on the constancy of Mugabe) is the idea of incomplete repetition, or of *a becoming*.

Ricoeur writes: 'when we speak of *becoming*, either in the field of nature or history, we imply an indefinite extension of duration *both backwards and forward*.' (181; emphasis added). He is here speaking of the need to overcome the arrow-like orientation towards the future of linear time, and to reconnect retrospection to anticipation in the forging of new identities. This implies an awareness of one's positioning in the present, and it seems to me that Hove gives poetic expression to just such a process when he refers to the creation of a new consciousness, to which he dedicates *Bones*. He writes: 'to the making of a new conscience, / a conscience of bones, blood/ and footsteps/ dreaming of coming home some day/ in vain' (*Bones* 5). It is only this, temporally complex, kind of transformation that will help to 'unfreeze' the static Zimbabwean worlds of which he writes. Hove's writings repeatedly call for dialogue and speech as a means of aiding this process. But that is not all. Apart from the need for dialogue, his novels also suggest another set of conditions which need to be fulfilled in order for the passage of time to become associated with genuine emergence.

*Bones*, *Shadows* and *Ancestors* construct their own versions of the passage of time – time as devourer, time as a test of endurance, and time as an indicator of power relations - as variants of the theme of *curtailed movement*. In doing so, these novels may be taken as articulations of, and demands for, certain basic spatio-temporal rights, whose realisation may be seen as going hand in hand with envisaging the forging of a new Zimbabwean consciousness. These rights have to do with the seemingly simple actions of traversing, or not traversing, physical space, and I would name three of them. They are: (1) the right to *leave* and to *arrive* – denied, for example, to Marita in *Bones*; (2) the right to *stay in place* – not to initiate spatial movement at all (this is denied to Johanna's father in *Shadows*); and (3) the right to *leave, arrive* and *return* – denied to Mucha's mother and sisters in *Ancestors*.

These rights may sound simple, but they are not easily obtained in Hove's novels, in many other Zimbabwean novels, or indeed in Zimbabwe itself. (Among the various kinds of reports and testimonies that have come out of Zimbabwe in the past few years, for example, Maldrum's *Where we have Hope,* Buckle's *African Tears* and Chenga's 'Zim's Land Reforms still on Track,' and Wasosa's 'Jokonya Kicks Out New Farmers,' it is not difficult to find stories of individuals and groups forced to leave, forbidden to leave, or forbidden to stay in various locations, or stories of those who monopolise the privilege of movement, especially in vehicles.) In Chenjeai Hove's novels, a desirable future is inextricably linked to these rights, as opposed to any kind of simple ownership of things or resources.

In his non-fictional texts, Hove has himself referred to some of the spatio-temporal rights outlined above. In his 'Europe and Us ...' a book chapter about the socio-spatial relationship between Africa and

Europe, he speaks of the unacceptability of granting Africans '[t]the right to depart [from Africa], without the right to arrive [in Europe]' (59). In the collection of political columns, *Palaver Finish*, he describes ease of movement as indispensable to the spreading of democracy:

> The best way to keep the nation ignorant is to deprive them of roads so that new ideas do not cross certain boundaries. That is why the ruling party's strategy has often included beating up those who were able to move from the city to country with ease (14).

Finally, in a co-authored text on the importance of tradition, there is a sentence which seems to me to sum up both Hove's poetics and his credo as an intellectual: 'People shape their destiny through language and movement' (Hove and Trojanow's *Guardians of the Soil* 9). In contemporary Zimbabwe, few have access to shaping their destinies in this way. Hove himself has left his country of birth, and may well feel that he cannot at present return. In the easy official political classification of today, he has been branded a 'traitor', for insisting on (in his texts), and executing (personally), the right to speech and movement which he holds so dear (Maruma, 'Chenjerai Hove Now a Sellout'). He has, however, continued writing, and a recent collection of poems contains lines of both despair and hope. A short poem about the passage of time, entitled 'tomorrow', reads like a comment on the ruling party's refusal to attach importance to the present moment, and returns to the motif of destiny: 'outside tomorrow/ and yesterday/ there is still another day/ called destiny' (*Blind Moon* 54). If, in the nineteen-eighties and the nineties, when *Bones*, *Shadows* and *Ancestors* were first published, historians and literary critics had examined these novels' representations of movement and time, perhaps they would have been able to glimpse some of the silence and stillness that is now the fate of so many in Zimbabwe.

**Notes**

[1]This descriptor was used by Flora Veit-Wild in 'Dances with Bones'(8). See also Dan Wylie's parallel with Haggard in 'Language Thieves.'

[2]For a more detailed discussion of the realm of the ancestors, and the relationship between the living and the dead in Hove, see R. Primorac, *The Place of Tears*.

[3]'War was all over the place. A friend had warned you that you could easily die if you walked into the areas where guerrillas were fighting the white man to free our land' (*Ancestors* 185-6).

[4]The Shona verb, *kumira*, means 'to be still,' but also 'to wait.' The text of *Ancestors* suggests that Miriro's name means 'the one who is awaited' (p. 45; see also the more elaborate explanation on p. 143). George Kahari translates the name as 'significance, symbolism' (219). Both Kahari's Shona Dictionary, and Hannan's translate 'Tariro' as 'hope, expectation' (see Kahari 285, and Hannan *Standard Shona Dictionary*).

**References**

Alexander, Jocelyn. '"Squatters," Veterans and the State in Zimbabwe.' *Zimbabwe's Unfinished Business: Rethinking Land, State and Nation in the Context of Crisis*. Ed. A. Hammar, B. Raftopoulos and S. Jensen. Harare: Weaver Press, 2003. 1-47. Print.

Boehmer, Elleke. 'The Nation as Metaphor in Contemporary African Literature.' *English Studies in Transition*. Robert Clark and Pieiro Boitani. London: Routledge, 1993. 320-331. Print.

Buckle, C. *African Tears: the Zimbabwe Land Invasions*.' Johannesburg: Jonathan Bull Publishers, 2001. Print.

Chan, Stephen. *Robert Mugabe: A Life of Power and Violence*. Ann Arbor: The University of Michigan Press, 2003. Print.
--- and Ranka Primorac. 'The Imagination of Land and the Reality of

Seizure: Zimbabwe's Complex Reinventions.' *The Journal of International Affairs at Columbia University* 57.2 (2004): 63-80. Print.

Chenga, N. 'Zim's Land Reforms still on Track.' *The Herald* (Harare), 7 April 2004. Print.

Hannan, M. *Standard Shona Dictionary*. Harare: College Press, 1996. Print.

Hove, Chenjerai. *Shadows*. Harare, Baobab Books, 1991. Print.
---. *Bones* (Harare, Baobab Books, 1994 [1988]). Print.
---. *Ancestors*. Harare, College Press, 1996. Print.
---. 'Europe and Us: "Please Mind the Gap"' *Images of the West*. (Ed, not stated). Harare: Baobab Books, 1996. Print.
---. I. Trojanow. *Guardians of the Soil: Meeting Zimbabwe's Elders*. Harare: Baobab Books, 1996. Print.
---. *Palaver Finish*. Harare, Weaver Press, 2002. Print.
---. *Blind Moon*. Harare: Weaver Press, 2003. Print.

Kaarsholm, Preben. 'Coming to Terms with Violence: Literature and the Development of a Public Sphere in Zimbabwe,' in R. Muponde and R. Primorac (eds), *Versions of Zimbabwe: Literature, History and Politic*. Forthcoming.

Kahari, George. *Plots and Characters in Shona Fiction*. Gweru: Mambo Press, 1990. Print.

Kanengoni, Alexander. 'One Hundred Days with Robert Mugabe.' *Daily News*, Harare, 12 April 2003. Print.
---. 'The Long Way Home: One Man's Story.' in D. Harold-Barry (ed), *Zimbabwe: The Past is the Future*. Harare: Weaver Press, 2004. 47-51. Print.

Mahoso, Tafataona. 'MDC Born Senile, Living in Denial.' *The Sunday Mail*, Harare, 4 April 2004.

Maldrum, A. *Where we have Hope: a Memoir of Zimbabwe*. London: John Murray, 2004. Print.

Maruma, O. 'Chenjerai Hove Now a Sellout.' *The Herald* (Harare), 8 April 2004.

Mazarire, G. 'Changing Landscape and oral Memory in South-Central Zimbabwe: Towards a Historical Geography of Chishanga, c. 1850 – 1990.' *Journal of Southern African Studies* 29. 3 (2003): 701-715. Print.

Primorac, Ranka. 'Iron Butterflies: Notes on Yvonne Vera's *Buttefly Burning*,' in R. Muponde and M. Taruvinga (eds). *Sign and Taboo: Perspectives on the Poetic Fiction of Yvonne Vera*. Harare: Weaver Press, 2002. 101-108. Print.
---. 'The Novel in a House of Stone: Recategorising Zimbabwean Fiction.' *Journal of Southern African Studies* 29.1 (2003): 49-62. Print.
---. *The Place of Tears: The Novel and Politics in Zimbabwe*. London: I. B. Tauris. Print.

Ranger, Terence. 'Nationalist Historiography, Patriotic History and the History of the Nation: the Struggle over the Past in Zimbabwe.' *Journal of Southern African Studies* 30.2 (2004): 213-233. Print.
---. '[Doctrine of Permanent Revolution in Zimbabwe].' Lecture delivered at the University of Uppsala, May 24 2004.

Ricoeur, Paul. 'Narrative Time.' *Critical Inquiry* 7.1 (1980): 169-190. Print.

Rooney, Caroline. 'Re-Possessions: Inheritance and Independence in Chenjerai Hove's *Bones* and Tsitsi Dangarembga's *Nervous Conditions*,' in A. Gurnah (ed), *Essays on African Writing 2: Contemporary Literature*. Oxford: Heinemann, 1995. Print.
---. 'Against the Corruption of Language: the Poetry of Chenjerai Hove,' in R. Muponde and R. Primorac (eds), *Versions of Zimbabwe: Literature, History and Politics*. Harare: Weaver Press. Forthcoming.
*Sunday Mail*, "Muzenda's commitment should be emulated: President," *The Sunday Mail*, Harare, 4 April 2004. Print.

Sylvester, Christine. 'Remembering and Forgetting "Zimbabwe": Towards a Third Transition,' in P. Gready (ed), *Political Transition: Politics and Cultures*. London: Pluto Press, 2003. Print.

Veit-Wild, Flora. 'Dances with Bones: Hove's romanticized Africa', *Research in African Literatures* 24.3, 1993. Print.

Wasosa, M. 'Jokonya Kicks Out New Farmers.' *Zimbabwe Independent*, 2 April 2004. Print.

Wylie, Dan. 'Language Thieves: English-Language Strategies in Two Zimbabwean Novellas.' *English in Africa* 18.2, 1991: 39-62. Print.

# Some Ambiguities in the Treatment of Homosexualities in African Literature and Film
## - Marc Epprecht

Beginning in the early 1950s, a diverse group of African authors pushed the limits of conventional representations of African sexuality by creating fictional African characters who engaged in same-sex practices or expressed same-sex desire. The first critical discussions of this literature by Daniel Vignal (1983) and Chris Dunton (1989) found that African novelists often treated same-sex sexuality in didactic or schematic ways. In this, they largely conformed to the prevailing consensus among ethnographers and other experts developed over many decades, viz., homosexuality was a) non-existent or insignificant in African traditional cultures until b) introduced by Europeans or Arabs, and c) was a social pathology that Africans could and should resist as with other forms of imperialism or moral corruption. In Dunton's terms, "homosexual practice is almost invariably attributed to the detrimental impact made on Africa by the West" (Dunton, 1989, p.421). Both Dunton and Vignal, however, also noted exceptions and ambiguities in the texts that they analysed, and concluded that African artists were not consistently and dogmatically homophobic or heterosexist in their work. Indeed, Vignal went so far as to suggest an element of "homophilia," meaning that he discerned sympathy or respect in some authors' treatment of the issue. Despite sometimes ham-handed "explanations" of non-normative sexualities, authors such as Lanham and Mopeli-Paulus (1953), Ouologuem (1971), and Njau (1975) recognized the possibility of love, dignity and "moral honesty" (Maddy, 1973, p.90) in same-sex relationships. They also used homosexual characters to make critical observations of hegemonic gender relations and Eurocentric or African nationalist assertions about African-ness.

The two decades plus since Vignal's and Dunton's essays witnessed the appearance and maturation of the HIV/AIDS pandemic, the rise of political homophobia in many African countries, and the emergence of an African gay rights movement. Along with these developments has come an explosion of writing about non-normative sexualities and gender role non-conformity in Africa. Gay characters also began to appear in film and theatre by African directors who profoundly challenge longstanding clichés about African sexuality. In this chapter, I trace that trajectory through key works in literature and film since the 1990s. The goal is to ask, how do these works contribute to contemporary debates about sexual rights and sexual health on the continent, bearing in mind the very significant frustrations that continue to be encountered in struggles against gender-based violence and HIV/AIDS in much of Africa (see Johnson, 2007, for example)?

Small, fractious gay rights groups first emerged in South Africa in the early 1980s. Then, in November 1987, future President Thabo Mbeki made an explicit promise that the ANC was firmly committed to combating homophobia along with all other forms of discrimination in a future democratic South Africa (Tatchell, 2005). The stage was set for the emergence of what Elleke Boehmer (2002) has called a "restorative queer aesthetic," that is, fiction and film by African authors that aimed to heal African masculinity and femininity from the crippling stereotypes of hegemonic masculinity and anti-racism conventions in the literature. As Vignal and Dunton observed, a staple of the latter was the portrayal of African men reduced to metaphorical boyhood or even raped by racist whites or Arabs. The "remasculation" of African men in this literature was achieved through sometimes heavy-handed portrayals of African men's virility, including through the sexual domination of white women. African women's anti-colonial credentials were meanwhile asserted through a virtuous maternalism that largely negated the possibility of erotic desire in women outside of service to – and penetration by – men (see Stratton, 1994, among others, for a critical assessment of these conventions).

*The Invisible Ghetto* (Krouse, 1993) was a ground-breaking achievement in that respect, being the first book wholly devoted to gay and lesbian writing in Africa. As well as short-stories and poems, it included a memoir by one of South Africa's first black gay activists, Simon Nkoli, plus interviews with heterosexual men who enjoyed sexual relations with younger men or boys. This was followed the next year by *Defiant Desire* (Gevisser and Cameron 1994), a scholarly collection of histories, memoirs, and literary criticism. Among the editors' most impressive accomplishments was to give voice to such a wide range of subjectivities by race, class, gender and sexual orientation. Several provocative chapters not only overturned received wisdom about sexuality in South Africa, but directly challenged conventions of euphemistic language that enabled the dominant culture to deny homosexualities (Achmat, McLean and Ngcobo, for example).

The work of Tatamkhulu Ismail Afrika also represented an often discomfiting challenge to the "macho" constructions of masculine sexuality in this period of political transition (Dunton, 2004). A recurrent conflict in his short stories involves male characters who wrestle with self-doubt about racial identity and sexual desire. In "The Quarry" (Afrika, 1996) for instance, the narrator starts off explicitly refuting that he is gay but then spends the rest of the story obsessing about the love life of a younger, bisexual, coloured man (Buddy). It includes one startling scene where he gently probes the sleeping Buddy's anus, ostensibly to soothe Buddy's aching hemorrhoids. In "The Vortex" and its sequel "The Treadmill" (1996), the white protagonist, Colin, is victimized (or is he saved?) by blacks, beginning with a vicious gang rape by black men in prison, followed by a long-running love affair between Colin and a black inmate. The re-assertion of approved white masculinity outside prison proves difficult for the confused Colin to achieve, however, and ultimately it takes another black man, Mjozi, to bring clarity. In a long and difficult process of developing the inter-racial friendship between Colin and Mjozi, homoerotic desire is hinted at constantly (shared showers, shared prostitutes, notably). The tension finally breaks when Mjozi learns of Colin's prison past and takes that knowledge as license to roughly sodomize him.

Outside of South Africa, the 1980s and early 90s also witnessed a wave of political transitions. The end of one-party regimes and military dictatorships took place in the context of economic neoliberalisation which in many cases brought severe unemployment and a turn to "survivor sex." The tired and implausible machismo of so much of the first generation of post-colonial writing was vulnerable to a queer deconstruction in this context. Senegalese author Ken Bugul (pseudonym for Mariétou Mbaye) provides an early and startling example. In her semi-autobiographical novel first published in French as *Le Baobab Fou* (1983), she created a female Wolof character who reflects both on the traditional role of homosexual men known as *gor-djigen* and of female-female intimacy in her village. Ken Bugul describes such intimacy as indicative of the "healthier approach to sexuality" in traditional culture compared to the confused sexual and bisexual relationships in Europe (Ken Bugul 1991, 50, 58, 84-85). Calixthe Beyala's *Her Name Shall Be Tanga* also takes pointed aim at some of the central tropes of African nationalist mythology around gender and sexuality. Not only does she portray her central character's mother as abusive and exploitative, but Tanga, the African girl, as the active seducer in a lesbian encounter with a woman in prison. She adds the further twist of making the passive partner in that encounter European. Tanga offers sex to the humiliated Anna-Claude as comfort in the dismal aftermath of the latter's failed relationship with an African man (Beyala 1986, 44-5).

The real inspiration for the emergence of a queer African aesthetic outside of South Africa, however, was the emergence of wave of homophobic demagoguery by politicians to distract public attention from economic malaise and their own poor governance. The President of Zimbabwe, Robert Mugabe, launched a series of denunciations of gays and lesbians in July of 1995, soon echoed in Namibia and elsewhere with prominent leaders inciting citizens to vigilantism. In Zimbabwe this led to a number of gay-friendly interventions in opposition, including GALZ (1995), a collection of autobiographical accounts and short stories written by Zimbabwean gays and lesbians. The highly respected author Charles Mungoshi entered the fray the next year with a short story in the popular magazine *Horizon* (republished in Mungoshi 1997). At a time when the state-controlled press, political and church leaders were all attempting to construe homosexuality as an alien threat to the nation; "A Marriage of Convenience" depicted an affair between two indigenous Shona men hiding behind the façade of marital respectability.

The rise of political homophobia drove many African lgbti deeper into the closet or to seek asylum in the West. Yet, it also stimulated the formation of gay rights associations that coalesced in the late 1990s as a nascent pan-African sexual rights movement (Epprecht 2004; GALZ 2008). A proliferation of new scholarship and gay-friendly literature and visual arts both reflected and pushed these changes. The bulk of this material continued to come from South Africa, including several anthologies of lgbti writing, plays, magazines, and websites.

However, it was two films from West Africa that broke the mould in the production of gay-positive cinema. Mohammed Camara's feature film *Dakan* (1997), first, focused on a love affair between two young African men in Conakry, Guinea. *Dakan* is notable for its sensitive treatment of the theme as well as the first male-male erotic kiss ever to be shown in African cinema. But this is not a celebration of coming out in the Western sense. On the contrary, there is a strong affirmation of family in customary terms of marriage, children and extended family. So, while it is true that the lovers Manga and Sori eventually leave their respective wife and girlfriend, presumably to live the gay life abroad, there are long scenes preceding this that establish how difficult that break from family can be, including Manga shown affectionately cradling his baby.

*Woubi Chérie* (Brooks and Bocahut 1998) was released soon after. A documentary, it revolves around interviews with trans-identified individuals (*woubis*) in Abidjan, Côte d'Ivoire. The focus is on their efforts to create an association to protect their rights, culminating in a big party and expressions of big hopes for the future. The anticipated political and social transformation away from homophobia is to be achieved, in the *woubis'* view, in part by proselytising gay lifestyles and identities in Africa.

*Woubi Chérie* was the first of a series of documentaries that questioned old orthodoxies about African essential heterosexuality. This cinema as a whole was often unabashedly didactic: to prove the existence of homosexual desire among blacks in the African past, or to stimulate open debate about the full range of human sexuality that might help in the struggles against HIV/AIDS. A common trope has been to demonstrate continuities and compatibilities between traditional extended family values (*ubuntu*) and new expressions of non-normative sexuality in Africa. In *Dark and Lovely, Soft and Free*, for example, both the mother of a transgender Xhosa man and the female co-wife of a transgender Mosotho polygynously married to a bisexual mine worker emphasize that family loyalty trumps sexual preference in African culture. The point is underscored that hatred and intolerance (rather than homosexuality) are the real offense against *ubuntu* (Alberton and Reid 2000). The play *After Nines!*, to give an example from another medium, was based directly on oral history gathered in the black township of Soweto and aimed to undercut the notion that African societies are intrinsically homophobic (Colman, 1998). Here, the ghosts of historical African characters return to advise the modern parents to show charity, love and respect for their gay children. This, they suggest, would be truer to the spirit of African humanism than dogmatic and coercive notions of heteronormativity embedded in modern ideas around social respectability.

Another milestone in the treatment of homosexuality in African cinema was when it moved beyond documentary and didacticism to entertainment, in effect to normalize same-sex relationships in the pursuit of titillation and profit. *Karmen Gei* (Ramaka, 2001) distinguishes itself in that way. Not only is it the first feature film by an African director to feature an African woman who is voraciously bisexual in her desires, it is also remarkable for the explicit eroticism depicted on screen – tasteful and discreet by Western standards but daring by African cinematic traditions. *Karmen Gei* casts two stunningly beautiful women in the roles of the primary lovers. Angel is a light-skinned prison warden hopelessly bewitched by the radiantly black but scheming Karmen. Karmen uses Angel sexually to escape from prison, and then dumps her in favour of a succession of men. When the broken-hearted Angel kills herself, however, there is no doubt that Karmen feels a deeper emotion than anything she displays for her male lovers.

Homegrown lesbianism is also treated with ambiguity in a Nollywood film set in contemporary urban Nigeria but marketed throughout the continent and diaspora. The Nigerian film industry is characterized by its cheaply produced and heavily moralistic melodramas that set idealized traditional, patriarchal family-oriented values against modern, sexually loose and money-oriented values. *Emotional Crack* (Imasuen 2003) appears to be the first to use female-female sexuality as representative of the latter and as a hook to draw in audiences. The film centres on a sexual triangle between an abusive and philandering husband, his unhappy wife, and her bisexual seducer (also his lover). The title itself forewarns of a calamitous break (crack, chasm) or uncontrollable addiction (crack, the drug), and indeed, horror, anger and seeming insanity culminate in the lesbian seducer's suicide. On the surface, heteropatriarchal norms are re-established. "Nonetheless," according to one Nigerian film critic, "the depiction of Camilla and Crystal's affair tends to imply the possibility and potential of same-sex love, even when society disapproves so strongly" (Oloruntoba-Oju, 2008). The sound track adds to the effect by refusing to pull homophobic strings. Demurring musical comment or comparison between the different types of love affair, it seems to suggest that love is blind and can conquer everything.

The cultural impact of *Emotional Crack,* and of the gay rights associations noted above, should not be overstated nor, conversely, should the damage and pain of homophobic backlash be minimized. Yet the growing profile of lgbti in public discourse does suggest that an audience has emerged in Africa that can appreciate relatively sophisticated treatments of same-sex issues. Indeed, the Caine Prize for best short story published in Africa in 2007 went to Monica Arac de Nyeko's "Jambula Tree," a poignant love story between two young Ugandan women that casts a poor light on the neighbourhood busybodies who enforce propriety. This is not as surprising as might be inferred from the extreme homophobia of political and religious leaders in Uganda and some of its neighbours in recent years. The present generation, after all, is the first to have been born and to have come of age under the shadow of the HIV/AIDS pandemic and its imperative to talk about sexuality in ways that traditional taboos strongly discouraged. Moreover, migration to the West and observation of Western society are no longer the preserve of elites and intellectuals. Satellite television now brings the foibles and frivolities of the West, along with serious debates about society and culture, directly into millions of African households daily.

The first three novels by African authors to deal substantively and sympathetically with gay themes engage those debates as they play out in diverse contemporary urban contexts. Sello Duiker's *The Quiet Violence of Dreams*, first, is set in post-apartheid Cape Town where a group of young people test the limits of inter-racial love and sex, drug use, fashion, and rapidly changing gender roles and identities. Duiker's main character is a university-educated Xhosa man, Tshepo who, we learn, was anally raped at age 17 during a horrific act of gang violence that also resulted in the rape and murder of his mother. His abusive and homophobic father was complicit in the crimes. Tshepo's confusion about his adult sexuality is exacerbated first by drugs, and then an infatuation with his coloured roommate, Chris. Chris, it transpires, is a volcanic stew of misogyny, homophobia and class rage. Eventually he and two of his friends anally rape Tshepo, coming out as members of a notoriously violent homosexual gang.

Up to this point, not much in the novel distinguishes it from the old associations of homosexuality with coloureds, foreigners, criminality and/or insanity, and the portrayal of Africans as victims of homosexual rape or exploitation. In a remarkable transition, however, the just-raped Tshepo takes up a job as a "stallion," the local term for a black male sex-worker at an elite massage parlour. There, he listens and learns about the meaning of masculinity from his diverse clients and fellow sex workers. There are loving, erotic scenes between many of the characters, as well as frankly commercial exchanges that the author presents in a non-judgemental manner. As Tshepo becomes more aware of his homosexual orientation, he also becomes emotionally liberated and stable. The first time he allows a client to penetrate him anally is a turning point, allowing Tshepo mentally to break from his family and the oppressive expectations of men in African culture. Duiker also uses some of these male-male sexual encounters to defend Africa against the assumption of primitiveness (atavistically, essentially homophobic) by Westerners. For example, one of the sex workers extols the absence of homophobia in rural, customary Xhosa society and blames the European missionaries for introducing the intolerance encountered today. In another scene, Tshepo pointedly chastises an African-American who condescendingly worries about "the whole tribe thing" (which he incorrectly presumes makes it hard to be black and gay at the same time).

Far from the kind of tragic end that sexually transgressive characters tended to meet in the earlier generation of African novels, Tshepo eventually experiences an epiphany that leads to a better life and the fulfilment of African humanist ideals. Significantly, this epiphany occurs while being penetrated by a gangster character who had picked him up wandering the streets of an impoverished black township. Tshepo decides to leave his life on the fringes of the mostly white Cape Town elite. He moves to Johannesburg where he takes up residence in the inner city district of Hillbrow. Duiker's choice of locale for this conclusion is surely no accident. Hillbrow is the historical centre of black gay life in South Africa and, today, is the overcrowded slum that provides refuge for economic migrants from all over the continent. Tshepo finds a sense of happiness and self-esteem as an out black homosexual doing social work among poor, despised migrants from the rest of Africa.

*Femme nue Femme noire* (Beyala 2003) offers no such happy ending. The absurdist plot is little more than a vehicle to set up a series of more and more outlandish sexual adventures and hence to tear at the stereotype of African women's passivity and subservience to men's needs. The female characters here both enjoy and actively seek out clitoral orgasms even if excised, frequently independently of men, and by a wide variety of techniques described in frank, erotic, and quirky detail. The young narrator, Irene, is meanwhile sketched with both an aggressive, "masculine" sexuality and a deep maternal instinct. This seeming contradiction allows Irene (and us) to reflect on oppressive gender roles and hypocrisies in African and Islamic culture as they exist (indeed are exacerbated) under contemporary neo-colonial conditions. Whites appear only by allusion, not for their homosexual decadence or exploitation of African sexuality, but for their role as the foreign experts who pushed structural adjustment on Africa. It is the consequent poverty and corruption that fuels the crises of sexuality and family dynamics which Beyala satirically deplores.

Much of the eroticism in the novel is lesbian or bisexual, including tender encounters between Irene and her elder co-wife. But

Beyala also includes one comedic scene that portrays a male-male sex act in a somewhat positive light. This involves a man who had once been a boy-wife to a career soldier but who is now married in proper fashion to a very beautiful woman. He deeply regrets that he is unable to make his wife pregnant. After many years of impotence, however, his virility is restored through the act of being anally penetrated by another man. The main male character, Ousmane, also recalls that boredom and frustration with his sex life within marriage was cured after discovering "the pleasures of sodomy" among other unleashed passions.

Irene watches, listens and to some extent inspires the various activities and unexpected confessions of the other characters. They, in return, regard her as insane or perhaps possessed by a powerful spirit. The danger lies in Irene's ability to reflect honestly on the meaning of desire and not to impose moral judgments on others, exposing the mendacity of respectability in the process. It ends badly for her. Beyala seems to be saying that the achievement of pleasure and sexual self-knowledge, by whatever combination of partners or orifices, is a radical and necessary political act in the wider, insane context of postcolonial, AIDS-ravaged Africa.

Finally, Jude Dibia's *Walking With Shadows* is Nigeria's first gay-themed novel (Dibia 2005). Dibia wrote it at a moment when Nigeria was starting to supersede Zimbabwe as the source of the harshest homophobic political rhetoric on the continent. Indeed, while the film *Emotional Crack* noted above raised a tentative element of doubt about heteropatriarchal certainties, the dominant discourse in Nigeria since the late 1990s had swung dramatically in the opposite direction. Competing Christian and Islamic fundamentalisms were not only demanding a return to imagined moral rectitude but represented a terrifying danger of civil war. Politicians scrambled to co-opt or to appease those fundamentalisms in part by scapegoating homosexuality (Gaudio, 2009). In such a context, Dibia's novel is a bold, ambitious attack on many of the staples of homophobic politics and culture in Africa generally.

*Walking with Shadows* keeps close to novelistic conventions of realism, making its almost systematic overturning of "common sense" all the more powerful. The narrative follows the journey of Ebele Adrian

Njoko from effeminate, confused, and persecuted boy to a man who, through tragedy, comes to understand and accept his adult sexuality. As a young man, Adrian first discovers his capacity to love (and be hurt by) men. He then tries to hide and repress his desires within a normal-appearing marriage to Ada. He is successful to the extent of maintaining his fidelity to Ada for eight years and in fathering a child with her. A vengeful co-worker, however, plunges everything into turmoil by outing his secret from years ago. Much emotional pain ensues, but Adrian ultimately brings himself and his wife to a mature acceptance of the fact of sexual difference. True, he and Ada will still be getting divorced, but they promise to remain friends and to discuss the issue honestly with their one child together. It would be a triumph except for the fact that such honesty is not feasible in contemporary Nigeria. The novel ends with Adrian pondering whether to emigrate to England so that he can be true to himself as a person.

*Walking with Shadows* is full of dramatic inversions and ironies. For example, rather than looking admiringly to the West, Dibia casts the main European character as a betrayer who is irrationally, recklessly and self-destructively promiscuous. Rather than portraying Africa as an angry victim of foreign sexual intrigues, Dibia portrays a variety of African homosexuals and bisexuals comfortably at ease with themselves. This includes Abdul, a Muslim man in a mutual loving relationship with another man, Femi, plus several men who have sex with men but publicly claim to be heterosexual. Their wives either do not know or are not really bothered by it. The only significant foreign influence is Christianity, which, through the character of a Pentecostal minister and his followers, is portrayed as introducing a brutal homophobia (they attempt to beat the effeminacy out of Adrian). Even in conceding that many Nigerian homosexuals are promiscuous, Dibia pushes his presumably heterosexual audience to reflect on their role in creating that situation. Because homophobia in the dominant culture makes it almost impossible for homosexuals to share an enduring emotional attachment, they turn to multiple partners as "an emotional trump" against expected disappointment.

Adrian, the African homosexual, emerges in this way as an advocate for sexual monogamy and emotional stability, and as a powerful voice against the hypocrisies and intolerance of the dominant heteropatriarchal cultures.

## Conclusion

Depictions of same-sex sexuality in African fiction and film have both increased in frequency and changed in character since Vignal and Dunton first raised the issue. The change in tenor reflects the profound shifts that have occurred in Africa since the 1980s, including the spread of HIV/AIDS with all its attendant implications for hegemonic gender and sexual cultures, the rise of political homophobia and a gay rights movement in opposition, new historical and ethnographic research, and Africans' increased exposure to globalized culture industries. The fading of the pall of colonialism has also freed up African imaginations to move beyond anti-colonial conventions in the literature. Uzor Maxim Uzoatu puts this development succinctly in his foreward to *Walking with Shadows*. Summarizing three generations of Nigerian literature in its engagement with Eurocentric constructions of African sexuality, he writes, "The grandfather [Chinua Achebe?] may have won his plaudits for his holy celibacy only for his son [Ayi Kwei Armah?] to earn his mark as a libertine of the heterosexual mode; then comes the grandson [Dibia] who sees no greater gain than homosexual love" (Uzoatu, 2005). For Dibia's character Adrian Njoko, the gain is clear insight into both homophobias in contemporary Nigerian society and self-indulgence and recklessness in a Western gay identity.

The African artists reviewed here do not on the whole portray same-sex desire as necessarily incompatible with conjugal and extended family obligations. On the contrary, most of the African men who have sex with men and women with women do so while maintaining heterosexual relationships, including marriage. They desire children and, significantly, do not always rupture from parents, children, friends or even wives and husbands on account of their same-sex preference. Some of the most sympathetically drawn gays and lesbians are also strongly family and child-oriented. In some cases (Beyala, Duiker, and Dibia, notably) they are seeking to recover from abusive and violent upbringings in heterosexual families by building healthy, loving families of their own or in surrogate.

African artists, in short, at least in the principal English and French language publications and films that touch upon the topic, do not uniformly share the view that homosexuality and bisexuality are non-existent, insignificant, or always stigmatized in Africa south of the Sahara. Nor did they agree that homosexuality is an unalloyed threat either to the African family or to African dignity. For a small but a growing number of artists, diverse homosexual or bisexual characters facilitate a powerful critique both of contemporary African society and of Western presumptions about (and prescriptions for) Africa. In line with Boehmer's notion of a "restorative queer aesthetic," this imagination of diverse sexualities may open the door to more creative and effective interventions against gender-based violence and sexual ill-health than evidently still prevail in so much of Africa.

**Notes**
[1]This is also one of the arguments of *Heterosexual Africa?* (Epprecht 2008), from which this chapter is adapted. Here I owe a debt to the pioneering interventions on sexual rights in Africa by Mai Palmberg, notably Dunton and Palmberg (1996) and Palmberg (1999). See also critical assessments of non-normative sexuality in African literature and film studies by de Waul (1994), Hayes (2000), Migraine-George (2003), Veit-Wild and Naguschewski (2005), Eke (2007), Stobie (2007) and Hoad (2007). With respect to terminology, I use the short-hand lgbti, msm, and wsw in lower-case to refer to people whose sexuality does not conform to heterosexual norms. Further to this issue, see Steyn and van Zyl (2009).

[2] See Joint Working Group (2006) for an anthology of lesbian writing, and the Linx link on www.mask.co.za for some of the many gay-friendly websites out of South Africa. Key works of scholarship include Murray and Roscoe (1998) and Morgan and Wieringa (2005).

[3]Achmat and Lewis (1999), Njinje and Alberton (2002), Ditsie and Newman (no date), and Tilley (2001), among many examples.

## References

Achmat, Zackie. 1994. "My childhood as an Adult Molester: A Salt River Moffie." In Gevisser & Cameron, *Defiant Desire*, 325-341

Achmat, Z. & Jack, L. (dir/prod). 1999. *Apostles of Civilised Vice*. Muizenberg, South Africa: Idol Pictures.

Afrika, Tatamkhulu. 1996. *Tightrope*. Cape Town: Majibuye Books. Alberton, Paulo & Graeme Reid (dir.). 2000. *Dark and Lovely, Soft and Free*. Johannesburg: Gay and Lesbian Archives.

Arac de Nyeko, M. 2007. Jambula tree. In Ama Ata Aidoo (ed.) *African Love Stories*. Banbury: Ayebia Clarke Publishing.

Beyala, C. 1996. *Your Name Shall be Tanga*. Portsmouth NH: Heinemann.

Beyala, C. 2003. *Femme Nue, Femme Noire*. Paris: Albin Michel.

Blair, D. S. 1976. *African Literature in French*. Cambridge: Cambridge University Press.

Boehmer, E. 2005. Versions of Yearning and Dissent: The Troping of Desire in Yvonne Vera and Tsitsi Dangarembga. In Flora Veit-Wild & Dirk, N. (eds). *Versions and subversions in African literatures I: Body, sexuality and gender*. Rodopi, Amsterdam, 113-128.

Brooks, P. and L. Bocahut (dir). 1998. *Woubi Cheri*. Paris and Abidjan: ARTE France, 1998.

Camara, M. (Dir). 1997. *Dakan*. Conakry: ArtMattan.

Colman, R. (Dir.) 1998. *After Nines!* (unpubl. Play transcript and Oral History Research, Gay and Lesbian Archives, AM 2894).
De Waul, S. 1994. A Thousand Forms of Love: Representations of Homosexuality in South African Literature. In Gevisser & Cameron (eds.). *Defiant desire*. pp. 232-245.

Dibia, J. 2005. *Walking with Shadows*. Lagos: BlackSands Books.

Dunton, C. & Palmberg, M. 1996. *Human Rights and Homosexuality in Southern Africa*. Uppsala: Nordiska Afrikainstituet.

Duiker, S. 2001. *The Quiet Violence of Dreams*. Cape Town: Kwela Books.

Dunton, C. 1989. Wheyting be dat? The treatment of homosexuality in African literature. *Research in African literatures*, 20, no.3: 422-48.

Dunton, C. 2004. Tatamkhula Afrika: The Testing of Masculinity, *Research in African literatures* 35, no 1: 148-161.

Eke, M. N. 2007. *Woubi Chéri:* Negotiating Subjectivity, Gender, and Power. In Ada U. A. & Maureen, N. E. (eds.) *Gender and Sexuality in African Literature and Film*. Trenton NJ and Asmara: Africa World Press.

Epprecht, M. 2004. *Hungochani: The History of a Dissident Sexuality in Southern Africa*. Montréal: McGill-Queen's University Press.

Epprecht, M. 2008. *Heterosexual Africa?: The History of an Idea from the Age of Exploration to the Age of AIDS*. Athens: Ohio University Press, Scottsdale: UKZN Press.

GALZ. 1995. *Sahwira*. Harare: Gays and Lesbians of Zimbabwe

GALZ. 2008. *Unspoken facts: A History of Homosexualities in Africa*. Harare: GALZ, and Ann Arbor: African Books Collective.

Gevisser, M. & Edwin, C. (eds.). 1994. *Defiant desire: Gay and lesbian Lives in South Africa*. Johannesburg: Ravan.

Hayes, J. 2000. *Queer nations: Marginal Sexualities in the Maghreb*. Chicago: University of Chicago Press.

Hoad, N. 2007. *African Intimacies: Race, Homosexuality and Globalization in African Literature and History.* Minneapolis: University of Minnesota Press.

Imasuen, L. (dir). 2003. *Emotional crack.* Emem Isong and Bob Emeka Eze (story) and Emem Isong (screenplay). Lagos: RJP Productions.

Johnson, C. A. 2007. *Off the map: How HIV/AIDS Programming is Failing Same-sex Practicing People in Africa.* NY: International Gay and Lesbian Human Rights Commission.

Joint Working Group. 2006. *An Anthology of Lesbian Writing from South Africa.* Johannesburg: Triangle Project and Umzantsi Publishers

Ken B. 1991. *The Abandoned Baobab.* Trans. Marjolijn de Jager. Chicago: Lawrence Hill Books.

Krouse, M. (Ed.). 1993. *The Invisible Ghetto: Lesbian and Gay Writing from South Africa.* Johannesburg: COSAW.

Lanham, P. and Mopeli-Paulus, A.S. 1953. *Blanket boy's Moon.* London: Collins.

McLean, H. and Linda N. 1994. *Abangibhamayo bathi ngimnandi* (Those who Fuck me Say I'm tasty): Gay Sexuality in Reef Township. In Gevisser & Cameron, *Defiant desire,* 158-185.

Maddy, Y. A. 1973. *No Past, no Present, no Future.* London: Heinemann

Migraine-George, Thérèse. 2003. Beyond the 'internalist' vs. 'externalist' debate: The Local-Global Identities of African Homosexuals in Two Films, *Woubi Chéri* and *Dakan. Journal of African Cultural Studies* 16, no. 1: 45-56.

Morgan, R. & Saskia, W. (eds.). 2005. *Tommy boys, Lesbian Men and Ancestral Wives: Female Same-sex Practices in Africa.* Johannesburg: Jacana.

Mungoshi, C. 1997. Of Lovers and Wives. In *Walking Still*. Harare: Baobab.

Murray, S. O. & William, R. (eds). 1998. *Boy Wives and Female Husband Studies in African Homosexualities*. NY: St.Martin's Press.

Njau, R. 1975. *Ripples in the Pool*. London: Heinemann.

Njinje, M. & Paolo, A. (dir.) 2002. *Everything Must Come to Light*. Johannesburg: Out of Africa Films.

Nkoli, S. 1993. The Strange Feeling. In Krouse, *The Invisible Ghetto*, 19-26.

Nkoli, S. 1994. Wardrobes: Coming out as A Black Gay Activist in South Africa. In Gevisser & Cameron, *Defiant desire*, 249-257.

Oloruntoba-Oju, T. 2008. A Lesbian Affair on Nigerian Video (A film review). In GALZ. *Unspoken facts: A History of Homosexualities in Africa*. Harare: GALZ, and Ann Arbor: African Books Collective.

Ouologuem, Y. 1971. *Bound to Violence*. London: Heinemann

Palmberg, M. 1999. Emerging Visibility of Gays and Lesbians in Southern Africa: Contrasting contexts. In Adam, B. D., Jan W. D. & Krouwel, A. (eds) *The Global Emergence of Gay and Lesbian Politics: National Imprints of a Worldwide Movement*. Philadelphia: Temple University Press, pp. 266-292

Ramaka, J. G. (dir.). 2001. *Karmen gei* Dakar: Les Ateliers de l'Arche. Stobie, C. 2007. *Somewhere in ihe Double Rainbow: Representations of Bisexuality in Post-apartheid Novels*. Scottsville: University of Kwa-Zulu-Natal Press.

Stratton, F. 1994. *Contemporary African Literature and the Politics of Gender*. London and NY: Routledge.

Steyn, M. & Mikki van, Z. (eds.) 2009. *The Prize and the Price*. Cape Town: Human Sciences Research Council.

Tatchell, Peter. 2005. The Moment the Anc Embraced Gay Rights. In Neville, H., Karen M. & Graeme R. (eds.) 2005. *Sex & Politics in South Africa*. Cape Town: Double Story, 140-147

Uzoatu, U. M. 2005. Forward. In Dibia, J. *Walking with Shadows*. Lagos: BlackSands Books.

Vignal, D. 1983. L'Homophilie dans le roman Négro-Africain d'Expression Anglaise et Française, *Peuples Noirs, Peuples Africains*. XXXIII: 63-81.

# RELIGION AND SEXUALITY IN TWO CONTEMPORARY AFRICAN NOVELS
## - Chima Anyadike

An exploration of the relations between the development and expression of sexual awareness and the empowerment of young women in two African novels, *Purple Hibiscus* (Chimamanda Adichie, 2003) and *The Heart of Redness* (Zakes Mda, 2002), provides an occasion for suggesting that the pre-colonial and traditional moral and religious orders constitute healthier contexts for women's sexual development and empowerment than the imported ones. The suggestion is strongly supported by scholarly and field studies of a pre-colonial African society.

The pre-colonial and Christian/Islamic moral and religious orders in Africa are in different ways and degrees repressive of private and public expressions of sexual and erotic desires especially by women. While it is true that there are variations, even contradictions within each order, it seems that we can make tenable distinctions between on the one hand, the traditional belief systems and practices regarding women sexuality and on the other hand, sexual codes and practices based on religions imported and imposed upon Africa from elsewhere. Such distinctions allow us to explore the question of which moral and religious order is more supportive of a healthier development of female sexuality and social empowerment in contemporary Africa. Our exploration is based on the fictitious African situations created by African novelists in general but in particular, Chimamanda Adichie of Nigeria in *Purple Hibiscus* (2003) and Zakes Mda of South Africa in *The Heart of Redness* (2000). These two novels are not wholly representative of the multicultural situations in Nigeria and South Africa, not to mention the entire African continent, but they explore basic and important common features which can be used to stimulate thought and discussion on female power and sexuality in Africa. Such discussions are important in the overall project of correctly understanding and presenting the evolving cultural images of Africa.

On the distinctions between the traditional and the contemporary religious orders, we may begin by observing that although each is constituted by a cluster of beliefs interpreted and implemented according to individual lights and situations, imported religions, unlike traditional ones, have codified in holy writs, norms of sexual behaviour which can be accurately referred to. The few traditional religions with written codes, like the Yoruba Ifa tradition, do not have long and extensive traditions of commentary, interpretations and translations all of which clarify dogma and guide scholars and devotees. Related to this is the remarkable absence of proselytization or itinerant preachers among the traditional believers. Religious principles are disseminated by family members, elders, diviners and priests when consulted. Another important distinction has to do with how the imported religions stress the other-worldly, the sinful nature of man and the world from which believers must seek to triumphantly escape as against the this-worldly emphasis of traditional religions. Ancestors, spirits and gods are there to help man live a better life in this world. There are no heavens and eternal hell fires waiting as ultimate rewards or punishments. The implications of all these for strict obedience and application of rules, especially those related to sexual behaviour, are only too obvious.

Unfortunately, the colonial impositions, urbanization and globalization have stifled the growth and development of the traditional perspectives, leading the majority of Africans to the dogmatism of Christianity and Islam. There are probably still a good number of Africans who retain some beliefs from their traditional order but have no problems with embracing the imported religions. This abandonment, rather than development of traditional religions, often based on social and economic reasons and notions of superiority, has not augured well for personal integration and total development of African societies. As we shall see from the discussion of the novels, Africans may have become more socially mobile, more 'modern' and even freer, thanks to the social and technological advances in the western world, to express their sexuality; but they have also by the same token, become less morally rooted in and committed to any culturally defined trajectory of development. They do not appear willing to draw lessons from how the Japanese, the Chinese, the Indians, Jews, indeed all other peoples of the world cannot conceive of development that is not culturally directed. The point here is that social mobility and freedom of sexual expression that are not integrated with genuine cultural development can only lead to individual alienation often coupled with social stigmatization.

Be that as it may, female sexuality is one way African writers throw up for reflection, the confused and frustrating nature of neo-colonial consciousness as it manifests itself in all kinds of power play Men often find it useful when they want to compensate masculinities battered by forces arising from personal failures, unjust social arrangements and exploitative international economic order; women use it to gain advantages including political and economic ones; children may depend on it for their very survival. However, the general portrayal of the strong, assertive and progressive woman in the contemporary African novel has more often than not, been associated with promiscuity, prostitution or at best, a negative view of feminism.

In Jagua Nana of Ekwensi's novel of the same title, Penda of Ousmane's *God's Bits of Wood*, Lucia in Dangarembga's *Nervous Conditions*, Wanja in Ngugi Wa Thiong'o's *Petals of Blood*, Adaku in Emecheta's *Joys of Motherhood*, Esi in Ama Ata Aidoo's *Changes*, to name a few, we are presented with women who have freed themselves from the stranglehold of the patriarchal institutions in order to freely express their sexuality and take control of their lives. Since these writers are a mixture of Christians, Moslems, traditionalists, men and women, one is tempted to conclude that the road to female sexual freedom and empowerment must go through the process of the rejection of socially approved rules of sexual conduct. Esi in *Changes* for instance, can no longer accept that a husband has the right to make love to his wife whenever he so desires and so divorces her husband for marital rape, a new 'feminist' offence in her society.

However, there are other strong women depicted in the African novel who manage to escape the taint of promiscuity, prostitution and 'alien' feminism. Let us look briefly at three of them: Cheikh Hamidou Kane's The Most Royal Lady in his *Ambiguous Adventure*; Beatrice in Chinua Achebe's *Anthills of the Savannah*, Wariinga in Ngugi wa Thiong'o's *Devil on the Cross*. As her name implies, the Most Royal Lady is an impressive figure in Kane's novel, wielding as she does, enormous political and cultural influence, but we are told absolutely nothing about her sexuality and marital status. Achebe's Beatrice adheres to the socially approved norms of sexual conduct and empowers herself through education to take up an influential position in government, but her role in the novel is really nothing more than that of mopping up operations after the major battles have been fought by the men around her. Ngugi wa Thiong'o on his part subjects Wariinga to a series of events designed to lead her on to the acquisition of a revolutionary consciousness. Although she was sexually abused by men and she finally comes to recognize in Gatuiira, the man she wants to marry, issues of sexual rights are really not central to *Devil on the Cross*. The question therefore is this: Why don't we often come across in the African novel, women who, without attracting to themselves the stigma of promiscuity, prostitution, or negative feminist branding successfully combine the power and influence of the Most Royal Lady or the culturally rooted but educated sense of gender rights of a Beatrice with the sexual freedom of a Lucia or Esi? That is the question we must now address as we look at the relationship between religion and sexuality in *Purple Hibiscus* and *The Heart of Redness*.

Kambili in Adichie's novel grows up in her father's closed world of fundamentalist Catholicism. It is a world in which Eugene, her father, freely uses physical and mental torture as instruments of imparting religious faith and maintaining 'manly' control of the home. Traditional culture and religious beliefs, according to him, are "the remnants of ungodly traditions" (73), from which he did everything to protect his children. His own father, who refused to convert to Christianity, was not allowed to come to his house; he in turn did not visit him, being content with sending money to him through a driver from time to time. When his father dies, Eugene gives money to Aunty Ifeoma, his sister, for funeral expenses since according to him, he "cannot participate in a pagan funeral" (189). Kambili's mother, Beatrice takes in all the assault and battery that her husband Eugene metes out to her because she appreciates how he stuck with only her despite the fact that as she puts it: "many mothers pushed their daughters at him" and "asked him to impregnate them, even, and not to bother paying a bride price" (250). She therefore refuses to raise her voice as Eugene, often put up in the church by Father Benedict as an exemplary catholic, violates her and their children physically and emotionally and on more than one occasion, destroys a baby in her womb.

It is not surprising that in such an environment, Kambili cannot develop a healthy sense of her sexuality. And so the author moves her and her brother Jaja, at least for a brief period from their father and Father Benedict to a more liberal Catholicism as represented by Father Amadi and Aunty Ifeoma's household. As if to demonstrate that the problem is not with the religion but with the practitioners, especially as there appear to be many women who believe that they are both feminists and devoted Christians, it is Father Amadi who awakens in Kambili, powerful erotic and sexual energies. It is a great transition from the point when on arriving at Nsukka, Kambili tells the reader that as her cousin Amaka undressed in their room, "I quickly averted my gaze. I had never seen anyone undress: it was sinful to look at another person's nakedness" (117), to when not too long after that, she took great delight in how her chest was heaving at the sight of Father Amadi and " liquid fire was raging inside me" (174), making her to feel guilty because she "could not focus on [her] sins, could not think of anything else except how near he was" (175). All of this led her to think "with a fierce unreasonable sadness, how Father Amadi's smooth skin would not be passed on to a child, how his square shoulders would not balance the legs of his toddler son who wanted to reach the ceiling fan" (180)

When Kambili's fathers bizarre 'purification' by hot boiling water lands her in the hospital and Father Amadi travels to Enugu from Nsukka with Aunty Ifeoma to visit her, Amaka observed that Father Amadi's concern "wasn't just priestly concern" (219) and Kambili confesses to her on further interrogation that the word 'crush' "did not come close to what I felt".

The love that has been awakened between Father Amadi and Kambili will remain platonic because Amadi is a good catholic priest. If Kambili is lucky, she will meet another man with whom she can develop sexual love in other directions. What is important for our purposes here is the nature of the awakening of sexuality in her and the agents of that awakening. Father Amadi, Aunty Ifeoma and her daughter Amaka are the important agents. It is significant that these three characters do not deny some of the merits of traditional culture and religion even though they are Christians. Indeed an important aspect of Father Amadi's appeal for Kambili, has to do with how different he was from Father Benedict in often rejoicing with the singing of traditional songs. However, being Christians, they cannot take any active interest in developing those traditions. They will continue to suppress the development of a part of themselves or at best live double lives. When Amaka for instance, refuses to take a foreign name for her confirmation rite in the church, Father Amadi admonishes her with "Nobody has to use the name. Look at me. I have always used my Igbo name, but I was baptized Michael and confirmed Victor". In other words, rather than insist on names that mean something to you, just take names you will never use. There are serious limits to what these agents can do to help Kambili fully acquire a developed sense of the kind of sexuality and power she desires and for which she has the means. It is therefore not surprising that when they reached their limits at the end of the novel, they are relocated to other places. However, the author does not fail to indicate that while in these places, they remain unfulfilled as something in them continues to long for home.

As they prepare to leave for America, Amaka tells Kambili: "I won't be happy in America. It won't be the same" (266). While there, she writes her to say that although "there has never been a power outage and hot water runs from the tap…, we don't laugh anymore… because we don't have time to laugh, because we don't even see one another" (301) Aunty Ifeoma, who holds on to two jobs to make ends meet, we are told, " writes about things that she misses and things she longs for, as if she ignores the present to dwell on the past and the future" (301). As for Father Amadi, now in Germany, Kambili reports that "He never responds with a yes or a no when I ask if he is happy. His answer is that he will go where the Lord sends him. He hardly even writes about his new life except for brief anecdotes such as the old German lady who refuses to shake his hands because she does not think a black man should be her priest or the wealthy widow who insists he has dinner with her every night… His letters dwell on me" (303).

At the end of the novel therefore, Kambili's development of her sexuality is frustrated; she reverts to offering masses every Sunday for her father, wanting to see him in her dreams. She and her mother write, according to her, "huge checks…for bribes to judges and policemen and prison guards" (297).

Clearly, things, for Chimamanda Adichie, have continued to fall apart for the Igbos, for Nigeria and indeed for Africa and female sexuality and empowerment is the worse for it. We have seen that part of the reason for this state of affairs, as the author sees it, can be located in Christian (catholic) fundamentalism and its practice of hypocritical celibacy. Eugene's catholic faith makes him lead a double life which on the one hand makes him want the best for his family and his nation and on the other hand prevents him from tapping the indigenous resources that can lead to the realization of such noble desires. Father Amadi, the would-be liberator of the positive sexual energies in Kambili, hitherto suppressed by Eugene's draconian catholic rules, is himself limited by the catholic celibacy that in the end frustrates the sexual awakening. Adichie's indictment of the inhibiting power of the catholic faith as practiced by Eugene is underscored by her portrayal of Papa Nnukwu, his father. Papa Nnukwu's relationship with his grandchildren, especially his daughter's children, brings out the best in them. As Kambili puts it:"Amaka and Papa Nnukwu spoke sometimes, their voices low, twining together. They understood each other, using the sparest words. Watching them, I felt a longing for something I knew I would never have"(165). She knew that part of what was responsible for that 'something' may have to do with Papa Nnukwu's organic relationship with his traditional religion. After she watched him do his morning ablution or itu-nzu, she observed that "He was still smiling as I quietly turned and went back to the bedroom. I never smiled after we said the rosary back home" (169). Unfortunately, Aunty

Ifeoma and her children, being Christians, are unable to build on that 'something' and have to go away at the end, leaving Kambili to fall back, frustrated, on what is left at her home.

Zakes Mda provides in his novel *The Heart of Redness* a similar fictional representation of the situation except that he also provides some hope for a way out through the healing power of a traditional worldview. The novel, in some sense, begins from where *Purple Hibiscus* ends: Camagu, the main protagonist, has spent over thirty years outside his country, South Africa, serving as a consultant for UNESCO in Paris, FAO in Rome and the International Communications Union in the US. At the beginning of the novel, he is visiting home at the end of the apartheid era in response to a desire to find out what he can contribute to his country's development. After a very frustrating period of looking for a suitable job, because he was seen as not part of the freedom struggles or as they put it, he does not know how to do the freedom dance, he prepares to travel back to the United States. A chance meeting with a woman who excites in him a certain interest delays his departure. In the process of looking for this woman in order to get to know more about her, he encounters two other women who become interested in having a serious relationship with him at the same time: Xoliswa Ximiya, a Christian and Qukezwa a very traditional young woman. He also becomes in the process, very involved in a series of projects in the community of Qolorha, where these women live; a situation which helps him to develop a culturally oriented view of development that the author clearly wishes to present as a more viable alternative to the globalized, capitalist view represented in the novel by a naturalized alien, John Dalton.

It is therefore understandable that Qukezwa exercises almost a magical seductive power over Camagu. In what appears to be both an appropriation and an interrogation of the western myth of woman as the seducer and the initiator of the original sin of the forbidden fruit, Qukezwa is portrayed as a young woman without any sexual inhibitions. Camagu is taken aback by her blunt offer of herself to him for consideration as wife at their first meeting and how much she draws from the traditional lore and knowledge of herbs and other foods pertaining to sexuality. The message here seems to be that there is no reason why a woman should not propose marriage to a man she likes or refuse to avail herself of what knowledge there is that enhances the pleasures and objectives of sexuality. Rather than being portrayed as shameful sins of the fallen woman or prostitute, this is seen as a positive asset for a woman who wants to ensure that her man has nothing to look for in another woman. The author also rethinks the notion of chastity and virginity before marriage by bringing these to accord with Qolorha traditional emphasis on fertility. Qukezwa insists that she and Camagu ride stark naked on horse back and becomes pregnant because Camagu reaches a climax from the experience which did not involve a physical intercourse. The writer therefore has it both ways: he can have Qukezwa chaste or technically a virgin before marriage and yet have her demonstrate her ability to conceive a child. It is significant that when there are signs that she is pregnant, the old women examine her and certify her a virgin and yet do not question her about the 'mystery' of her pregnancy. The more subtle point is that there is more to sexuality than sexual intercourse. Camagu, who used to be the man about town, finds that there is so much to learn from Qukezwa about sexuality, especially female sexuality. It is important to note that there is an important distinction to be made between what the author wants Qukezwa to represent and Qorloha notions of promiscuity, infidelity and prostitution. That distinction is established by the fact that Noma Russia, the woman who inspires Camagu's quest in the first place, had got into an affair with Qukezwa's father and remained throughout the novel, under the curse of Quezwa's mother.

Placed against all these however, Xoliswa Ximiya, Quekzwa's rival for the love of Camagu, makes such a poor showing. Although the pride of her parents and indeed the whole community, having risen to be the principal of the community high school, a devoted Christian and 'progressive' thinker, she considers the problems of the community to be that of backwardness or redness. The community constitutes the heart of redness. As she sees it "It is a part of our history of redness…a backward movement…All this nonsense about bringing back African traditions" (160) When she learns of the affair between Camagu and Qukezwa, her former student, she confronts him: "Is it true what I hear about you and that child? " When Camagu says among other things, in reply " That child as you call her, is not dismissive of beautiful things; where you see darkness, witchcraft, heathens and barbarians, she sees song, and dance and laughter and beauty" (189), Xoliswa's final comment is "You believe in that mumbo jumbo? You are a disgrace to all educated people"(190).

But Qukezwa knows a lot more than song, dance, laughter and beauty; she is much more than a sexual symbol. She, for instance, single-handedly carries out a campaign against the foreign poisonous trees that threaten the indigenous productive trees of Qorloha and persuasively defends her action before a committee of elders. She not only knows the history and values most cherished by her community, she knows what constitutes a danger to its genuine development. So, not satisfied with making her a composite of Qolorha's versions of Eve and the Virgin Mary, Zakes Mda crowns her with the honour of being the mother of a future saviour of the people. The son of Camagu and Qukezwa is named Heitsi, a name the narrator explains is after "Heitsi Eibib, the earliest prophet of the Khoikhoi ... the one who parted the waters of the Great River so that his people could cross when the enemy was chasing them. When his people had crossed, and the enemy was trying to pass through the opening, the Great River closed upon the enemy. And the enemy all died." The narrator continues "Camagu smiles to himself when he remembers how he learned all this from Qukezwa when she was teaching him about the sacred cairns. He also learned that the Khoikhoi people were singing the story of Heitsi Eibib long before the white missionaries came to these shores with their similar story of Moses and the crossing of the Red Sea." (249-50).

The novel ends however by pointing out that this new Heitsi, is afraid of the sea "This boy does not belong in the sea! The reader is told "this boy belongs in the man village" (227). He will presumably inherit and advance the co-operative work between the women and men his parents have developed in Qolorha against the capitalist invasions of the western world and their home allies. Therein lies for this modern day Hetsi or Moses, the "business of saving his people" (227).

We may therefore conclude by observing how, if we accept the findings of Nkiru Nzegwu in her book about the Igbo of Nigeria, (Nzegwu, 2006), we will find that the fictional Qolorha of Mda's novel has so much in common with the pre-colonial Igbo, especially in regards to female sexuality. Nzegwu argues from the evidence of her research and field work that contrary to conventional scholarship on the matter, that if patriarchy "stands for lack of autonomy of wives, most crucially the lack of sexual autonomy", then "This was not the case in Igbo society, where wives retained control of their creativity, possessed the right to engage in economic pursuits and to provide the consumption needs for themselves and their children. Contrary to the patriarchal stance that women had no place in civil society, or public realm, Igbo women as wives and daughters participated in political activities and established political groupings both in the family and the community at large ( Nzegwu, 44).

The task before those interested in the reconstruction of the usable past from that society for purposes of empowerment of the present one should be directed towards understanding "by what processes and in what ways Igbo societies changed…from a society that encouraged the growth of women's capacities and full flourishing to one that constricted their life objectives" (62). Ify Amadiume, another well known Igbo female scholar, after recognizing "that a great deal of what anthropologists and western feminists were saying about African women's lack of power was incorrect…decided to go home and, with the help of Nnobi people themselves, write our own social history, especially from the women's point of view". The results of that effort, which Nzegwu's study largely corroborates, led to the publication of her book, *Male Daughters, Female husbands* (1987) written, in her view, to challenge "the new and growing patriarchal systems imposed on our societies through colonialism and western religious and educational influences" (9).

I have tried to show in this paper how two recent novels about contemporary African societies so far apart geographically as Nigeria and South Africa have explored those processes and ways, locating the main source of the problem in imported moral and religious orders which men opportunistically appropriated thereby unwittingly alienating themselves and the women from a healthier moral and psychic environment. The fictional picture of Qolorha women in pre-colonial Xhosa society as can be reconstituted from Mda's novel gets a scholarly validation from Nzegwu's book about women in pre-colonial Igbo society. It is a picture which is so much more inspiring than the Christian Igbo world Adichie recreates in her novel. Does Kambili have a good chance of meeting an Amadi who is not a priest? If, and when Aunty Ifeoma and her daughter Amaka decide to go back to Nigeria, will they, like Camagu, find men with whom they can work to transform their society into a re-cognizably Igbo/African modern society? In other words, how can female sexuality receive healthy and integrated development and empowerment in Africa? The novels suggest that these are a very difficult questions; but through one of them, *The Heart of Redness*, Zakes Mda, in the characterization of Quekzwa, indicates that this is a difficulty that should not kill the enthusiasm of those who consider an affirmative answer not only desirable but also worth working for.

**Works Cited**

Achebe, Chinua. *Anthills of the Savannah*. London: Heinemann, 1987.

Adichie, C. N. *Purple Hibiscus*. New York: Random House, 2003.

Amadiume, Ify *Male Daughters, Female Husbands: Gender and Sex in an African Society*, London and New Jersey: Zed Books, 1987.

Dangarembga, T. *Nervous Conditions*. London: Women's Press, 1988.

Ekwensi, C. *Jagua Nana* [1961] Oxford: Heinemann, 1987.

Emecheta B. *The Joys of Motherhood*. London: Heinemann, 1980.

Kane, C. H. *Ambiguous Adventure* [1962]. New York: Walker and Co., 1963.

Mda, Z. *The Heart of Redness*. New York: Farrar, Straus & Giroux, 2002.

Ngugi wa Thiong'o, *Petals of Blood*. London: Heinemann, 1977
---- *Devil on the Cross*. London: Heinemann, 1982. Nzegwu, Nkiru *Family Matters: Feminist Concepts in African Philosophy of Culture*. Albany: State University of New York Press, 2006

Chilivumbo, Alufeyo B. "Malawi's Lively Art Form: Chioda Dancers Mirror their Changing World in a Traditional Frame." *Africa Report* 16 (1971): 16-18.

Chirambo, Reuben M. "Culture, Hegemony, and Dictatorship in Malawi: Song, Dance, and Politics in Malawi, 1964-1994." PhD. Diss. University of Minnesota, 2005.
_____. "Traditional and Popular Music, Hegemonic Power, and Censorship in Malawi, 1964-1994." In *Popular Music Censorship in Africa*. Eds. Michael Drewett and Martin Cloonan. England: Ashgate Publishing Ltd., 2006. pp. 109-126.

Fairclough, Norman. *Discourse and Social Change.* Cambridge, United Kingdom: Polity Press, 1992.

Foucault, Michel. *The History of Sexuality.* Vol. 1: And Introduction. London: Vintage Books, 1990.

Gibbs, James. "Of Kamuzu and Chameleons: Experiences of Censorship in Malawi." *The Literary Half-Yearly* 23.2 (1982): 69-83.

Gilman, Lisa. "Purchasing Praise: Women, Dancing, and Patronage in Malawi Party Politics." *Africa Today* 48.3 (2001): 43-64.

Hall, Stuart. "Notes on Deconstructing 'the Popular'." In *Cultural Theory and Popular Culture: A Reader.* Second Edition. Ed. John Storey. London: Pearson Prentice Hall, 1998.

Hayward, Fred M, and Ahmed R. Dumbuya. "Political Legitimacy, Political Symbols, and National Leadership in West Africa." *The Journal of Modern African Studies* 21.4 (1983): 645-671.

Kaspin, Deborah. "Chewa Visions and Revisions of Power: Transformations of the Nyau Dance in Central Malawi." *Modernity and Its Malcontents.* Eds. John and Jean Cornaroff. London: 1993. pp. 34-57.

Kasule, Samuel. "Popular Performance and the Construction of

Social Reality in Post-Amin Uganda." *Journal of Popular Culture* 32.2 (1998): 39-58.

Lemke, Jay L. *Textual Politics: Discourse and Social Dynamics*. London: Taylor and Francis, 1995.

Le Vine, Victor T. "Changing Leadership Styles and Political Images: Some Preliminary Notes." *The Journal of Southern African Studies* 15.4 (1977): 631-638.

Lwanda, John L. *Kamuzu Banda of Malawi: A Study in Promise, Power and Paralysis*. Glasgow: Dudu Nsomba Publications, 1993.

Mapanje, Jack. "Censoring the African Poem." *Index on Censorship*. 9 (1989): 7-9, 11.

Mazrui, Ali A. *Cultural Engineering and Nation-Building in East Africa*. Evanston, IL: 1972.

Mbembe, Achille. *On the Postcolony*. Berkeley: University of California Press, 2001.

Mkamanga, Emily. *Suffering Silently: Dancing with Kamuzu Banda of Malawi*. Glasgow: Dudu Nsomba Publications, 2000.

Phiri, Kings M. "Dr Banda's Cultural Legacy and its Implications for a Democratic Malawi." In *Democratization in Malawi: A Stocktaking*. Eds. Kings Phiri and Kenneth Ross. Blantyre, Malawi: CLAIM, 1998. pp. 147-167.

Semu, Linda. "Kamuzu's Mbumba: Malawi Women's Embeddedness to Culture in the Face of International Political Pressure and Internal Legal Change." *Africa Today* 49.2 (2002): 77-99.

Young, Cullen and H.K. Banda, eds. *Our African Way of Life*. London: United Society for Christian Literature, 1946.

# Part III
# Music, Dance and Media in the Construction of African Identities

# Primitive - Essence – Fusion:
## White Approaches to Black Dance
## - Carita Backström

Visualize a classical ballet dancer: body in vertical alignment, erect spine, knees straight, pointed feet, the whole energy reaching upward as if lifting from the ground.

Visualize an African dancer: bare feet in solid contact with the floor, knees flexed, torso slightly bent forward, a fluid movement passing from one part of the body to another, body units moving separately and poly-rhythmically.

Two different aesthetics, not too long ago valued very differently; the classical ballet considered the height of elegance and sophistication, the African dance looked upon as primitive and simple.

Not so any longer, at least not amongst dancers and choreographers. They borrow freely; the modern and contemporary dance is a mix and remix, on both sides. In dance history however, not much is said about how black dance has influenced white (today often many-coloured) contemporary dance.

I will in the following present three "white" ways of approaching African dance, three very different approaches from different times, touching upon questions of form, meaning and respect.

**The Negro Ballet**
"It will be the only Negro ballet, the only possible Negro ballet in the world, and it will stand as a model for the genre" (Näslund, 328). With these proud words the French painter Fernand Léger wrote to Rolf de Maré, leader of Les Ballet Suédois. The year was 1923, the place Paris, and the ballet he writes about was *La creation du monde*. And it was indeed to become the first big *scenic* manifestation of the growing interest (in Europe) in African art and sculpture.

This interest was not completely new in Paris; the breakthrough had come some ten years earlier with painters like Vlaminck and Derain, Picasso and Braque who had found African sculpture and recycled its forms into what was to become cubism. But it was only after the First World War that the influence spread and became influential. That year also saw the first exhibition of so called primitive art, Première Exposition d'Art Nègre et d'Art Océanien, organized by Paul Guillaume who also arranged a Fête Nègre at Rolf de Marés theatre, Théâtre des Champs-Élysées.

Rolf de Maré is not a well-known name, but has recently been splendidly introduced in a book by Erik Näslund, the director of the Swedish Dance-museum.[1] Rolf de Maré belonged to one of Sweden's richest families and became a passionate patron of the arts. In 1911, twenty-three years old, he went on a world tour, a Bildungsreise that took him to India, the Far East, China, Japan and America. During this journey he saw ceremonial and traditional dance performances and gathered a big collection of masks, instruments and dresses. This - collecting objects and documentation belonging to dance from different cultures - was to become his lifelong occupation, and resulting in the unique Museum of Dance in Stockholm, which he founded in 1953.

Two men were crucial to Rolf de Maré's further development: the painter Nils von Dardel and the ballet dancer Jean Börlin. Dardel was his first great love and a lifelong friend. He introduced de Maré to modern painting and the artistic circles in Paris. Börlin was his second love, and it was in order to give Börlin a chance to develop as a dancer and a choreographer that Rolf de Maré founded Les Ballet Suédois in Paris 1920.

Börlin's first evening at Théâtre des Champs Élysées consisted of his own solos, inspired by different cultures. One of them was called *Sculpture nègre*, and expressed the contemporary interest for "primitive" form. Börlin wore a bodysuit and his hands and face were masked by angular constructions that made him look like a wooden sculpture. From the pictures one can also see that his knees are bent or flexed in what the choreographer and researcher Alphonse Thierrou from Ivory Coast calls *dooplé* and which is a basic characteristic of African dance. This was not recognized by the critics (probably not by Börlin himself either) at the time, but his dancing was considered new, marked by certain heaviness and different from the classical ballet and also from the virtuosity of the Ballet Russe.

The writer Blaise Cendrars wrote to Börlin: "Mon vieux, tu ne sais pas danser. Comprends-moi bien: tu es sur le même plan que les matelots, les soldats, les mulâtres, les nègres, les hawaïens, les sauvages, et c'est ce que j'admire le plus en toi. Avec tes pieds de paysan suédois, tu danses aux antipodes des Ballets Russes, tu bouscules la tradition ballet français…" (557-558). ('My friend, you don't know how to danse. Understand me correctly: you are on the same level as the sailors, the soldiers, the mulattos, the negros, the hawaians, the svages, and that is what I admire most in you. With your Swedish peasant feet you are on the antipodes of the Ballets Russes, you turn the tradition of French ballet upside-down…' - my translation) A sailor, a negro, a Swedish peasant…images of primitivism and authenticity far from the rigid classicism, and also from the traumas of the First World War (Cendrars lost his arm in the war).

In 1920, the same year that de Maré founded les Ballets Suédois, Blaise Cendrars published *Antologie Nègre*, a collection of folk tales and legends from all over the African continent. Professional ethnologists at the time did not consider it scientific enough, but the writer and ethnographer Michel Leiris saw its value, appearing as it did at a time when few people, apart from some specialists and painters, saw the richness of African art: "Son action, sur le plan de la poésie et de la culture, est aussi remarquable que celle des artistes qui, une dizaine d'années avant, découvrait le poid de l'art Africaine. Plus qu'un livre, c'est un acte…" (Cendrars, 555). ('His achievement in the realm of poetry and culture is as remarkable as that of the artists who some ten years earlier discovered the importance of African art. More than a book, it is a deed…' – my translation).

From the beginning, and very much thanks to Nils Dardel and his friends in Paris, the Swedish ballet collaborated with the avant-garde amongst French artists: Paul Claudel, Jean Cocteau, Arthur Honegger, Erik Sati, Francis Picabia, René Clair…Blaise Cendrars moved in the same circles, as did his friend Fernand Léger. So when Cendrars proposed his "Negro ballet" it was natural that Léger (who had already collaborated with the Swedish ballet in Claudel's *L'homme et son désir*) would do the design and the costumes. Together they chose for composer Darius Milhaud who was happy to be able to use elements of the jazz music he had heard and fallen in love with in Harlem, New York. The Choreographer was of course Jean Börlin, but it seems that it was the vision of Cendrars and Léger which dominated the production.

What did the ballet look like? I quote from Erik Näslund's description: "*La creation du monde* was a kind of African *Rite of Spring*, beginning when heaven and earth have just been separated and the three big creators of the universe have created the world. Upstage hang Léger's characteristically heavy, cubist clouds and underneath was a solid, formless mass that gradually came to life. Forms arouse from chaos and began to move. Behind them the three Gods of Creation grew up in the shape of three gigantic figures in ghastly masks. Apes with long arms began to dance, melancholy pensive insects crawled between the legs of the gods. Gigantic birds came wading from the swamp and after them the messengers of the gods on high stilts. The animals and the creatures united in a slow dance. Suddenly one could distinguish human forms in the mass. It was the man and the woman, the last to be created. They recognized each other. In convulsive movements this strange couple performed the mating dance of spring. Stillness fell, the figures disappeared, leaving the man and the woman in a tender embrace. Stars lit, the moon appeared. This was the spring of mankind" (Naslund, 332-335).

Obviously *La creation du monde* was a piece of multimedia art long before the term was coined. But what makes it a "Negro ballet"? The story is based on Cendrars's *Anthologie Nègre*, but it could be any creation story. According to Darius Milhaud, Léger was inspired by the animal costumes that African dancers wear at religious ceremonies. From the reconstruction one can well imagine this being so, even though they are translated into the personal aesthetic of Léger. When it comes to the actual dance we are obliged to imagine what it looked like with the help of descriptions like the one above. It seems that most of the dancers were hiding behind the figures, creeping on the floor or moving on stilts, more like mobile sculptures – or dance masks - than human beings. It is also obvious that this dance is far from the classical ballet, closer to Börlin's "peasant feet" and also closer to basic features of African dances; bare feet in contact with the earth, masks. As I see it *La creation du monde* could be looked upon as a modernist rendering of a classical African mask dance, but translating only the forms of the dance, stripped of its local and possibly sacred meaning. I also suspect that for Léger the form and the aesthetic experiment were far more important than the "Negro" component. And as such *La creation du monde* is a milestone in the history of performing arts.

### Searching for an Essence

Sixty years after *La creation du monde*, in1983, the Swedish dancer and choreographer Birgit Åkesson published a book called *Källvattnets mask* (The Mask of the Spring Water).

Birgit Åkesson was a legendary dancer who in the 1940s and 50s created a deeply original free dance and in the 1960 choreographed epoch-making ballets together with modernist composers like Karl-Birger Blomdahl and Sven Erik Bäck. Then something happened.

"I was in want of something in our culture. Something inside me was looking for deeper roots for the dance. I chose to look for it in Africa, south of Sahara. It took me seven years of travelling in different African countries and after that as many years before I could form an idea of what I had seen" (Åkesson, *Källvattnets Mask*, 5).

*Källvattnets Mask* is the result of these seven + seven years of looking for deeper roots, and it was something of a sensation at the time. My first contact with the book was through Birgit Åkesson herself when she lectured about her African experience. She was a charismatic lecturer and I was absolutely bewitched by her passion for her cause. Reading the book (or browsing through it, for it is that kind of book) I was first all impressed by the way she watched the dances and described them: in great detail, very exact – a professional watching a fellow professional. "What I saw was concrete in choreographically unexchangeable forms," she states (5). I choose a random example to show her way of registering what she saw: Penenga – a dance by men at a burial, (Tanzania):

The talking drum is calling. The two other drums follow. Four elders lead Penenga. They dance side by side followed by the

18 other dancers in two rows. At the head are those that have been dancing the longest, those who are to hand over Penenga to the others. With procession like gravity Penanga proceeds. The whisks sweep through the air in strange calligraphic veins, rhythmically adventurous and perfectly controlled. The steps are slow. They rise up on their toes and linger until the whisks return. The talking drum is heard. The dance becomes more intense and does not advance. The whisks float in the light grips, and the men, with the leap of the leopard in their hearts keep the leap of the whisk in a slow return and fulfil the movement. The drum stands aside. Penenga moves forward.

After the description (which in the book is much longer) Birgit Åkesson adds that Penenga is danced at midnight. "It wants to re-establish the balance before dawn. It wants to drive away evil. Like the wind it gives coolness and cleanses the mind" (93-96).

I think that this professional attitude is one of the great qualities of the book. And I would add the poetical streak; "with the leap of the leopard in their hearts". Hard facts imbued with impressionistic images; original and inspiring and unique, but also problematic.

Perhaps the first person to venture a cautious criticism of Birgit Åkesson is Wilhelm Östberg, social anthropologist and curator at the Ethnographic museum in Stockholm. In connection with an exhibition of a collection of masks belonging to Birgit Åkesson he edited a book together with Ann-Cathrine Lagercrantz: *Dansmaskens berättelser, Birgit Åkessons resor i Afrika*. He gives her just credit; the book is fascinating, she opens up new ways of seeing. But there are problems; her descriptions might be exact but her interpretations are a mixture of times and places leading to a synthesis she calls Africa. And this Africa of hers is far from the changing society of today, or even from the society of the 1960s and 1970s when she travelled:

Urbanization and modernity were there already when Birgit Åkesson travelled in Africa but those were not her interest. When you read her you are reminded more of the Africa which fascinated Brancusi, Braque, Picasso and other pioneers of modernism; the direct contact with spiritual worlds and what was then called instincts, the untamed nature, the astonishing masks and sculptures so different from the academic painting they themselves had been schooled into. In *Källvattnets Mask*, Joseph Conrad's Africa feels closer than, say, Nelson Mandela's" (Östberg & Lagercrantz, 128).

That is certainly true, but Birgit Åkesson's intention was not to look for Mandela's Africa or the urbanized modernity. Nor for Conrad's Africa. She looked for the essence of dance – all dance - and found it in Africa: "When I had understood what dance in Africa included, I could get an idea of what dance in other cultures has signified and see the relation between dance and society" (Åkesson, Källvattnets mask, 311).

She was not the first to have this experience. In 1977, the Senegalese president Senghor invited the legendary choreographer Maurice Béjart to found a dance school, Mudra Afrique, in Dakar, and Béjart later wrote: "The dance in Africa was a revelation to me; I felt with a gratifying certainty, that here I had found true dance in its purest and most extensive expression, which at the same time is the most human and closest to REALITY".[2]

Unlike Béjart, Birgit Åkesson never turned any of her African knowledge into dance; she wrote her book.

I once asked Birgit Åkesson if we could meet and discuss contemporary African dance (for a work I was doing). Her answer was short and categorical: "African dance is dead". This to me was a surprising answer. How could this brave avantgardist, once called "the Picasso of dance", dismiss the exiting, innovative contemporary dance that was emerging in different African countries? There are plausible explanations; perhaps she connected the notion of contemporaneity with the folkloristic "airport" dance, created to amuse presidents and tourists, perhaps she was not *à jour* with the new trends, or perhaps she had found *her* Africa and did not want to change her essentialist interpretation. To her the only valid African dance was the traditional dance with a specific social function, and - at the same time - a universal essence, in her mind linking it to Japanese No or Greek antiquity.

The first person to introduce Birgit Åkesson to the fieldwork in

Africa was the Finnish anthropologist Marja Liisa Swantz, based in Tanzania.[3] Swantz writes warmly about their mutual research journeys and their growing friendship, and concludes that Åkesson's book, when it came out, fell between the disciplines: "Anthropologists were not prepared to accept it and artists were not ripe for an intercultural handling of basic artistic phenomena. Perhaps time now is ripe to give Birgit's work the credit it deserves" (Östberg & Lagercrantz, 39).

## Fusion

In 1991, the South African dancer and choreographer Sylvia Glasser created a work called *Tranceformations*, a seminal work in the history of dance. As the name elegantly implies, the piece deals with trance and change.

The history behind *Tranceformations* is one of passionate and serious research. In an article called "Transcultural Transformations," Sylvia Glasser presents herself thus: "As a white, middle-class South African, I was brought up in a typically privileged fashion separated socially and in school from black South Africans. Atypically, the attitude of family, teachers and friends led me to believe apartheid was wrong. Furthermore, I was interested in and admired African dances and music at a time when the prevailing attitude of most white people (and many black people) towards African traditional cultures was one of disdain or disinterest" (Glasser, *Transcultural Transformations*, 287). This attitude and interest led Sylvia Glasser in 1978 to establish a non-racial dance company, Moving Into Dance. Right from the beginning her dance ideology was one of fusion. "By cultural fusion I mean the synthesis or integration or combination of two or more cultural forms of expression which have their roots or sources in different traditions or different countries" (Glasser, *Appropriation and Appreciation,* 3). Today the concept of fusion is more or less self-evident; choreographers borrow and fuse, traditions spread back and forth from east to west, from north to south, and nobody thinks this in any way strange. But in the 1970s in South Africa it was a daring political and aesthetic choice to make - even though fusion to some extent was taking place in practice on an unconscious level, and more and more so with the growing globalization. In Sylvia Glasser's case the choice was deeply conscious and personal; to a person coming from a liberal Jewish family all forms of ghettos were of evil.

But she had to make a long journey in order to reach the stage where she could create *Tranceformations*, which is based on bushman (san) rock painting. For three years she studied social anthropology and came in contact with Professor David Lewis-Williams, head of the Rock Art Research Unit at the University of the Witwatersrand. He asked questions which forced her "to think of the choreographic project in a totally different way. Did I realize that I was dealing with the religious beliefs and sacred symbols of the Bushmen? Did I realize that rock art was part of the religious symbols of these people"? (Glasser, *Transcultural Transformations*, 288). He also acquainted her with the actual trance dances and with the dispossession of contemporary Bushmen, themes that she integrated into the choreography.

Her cast consisted of ten black African and two white African dancers, all urbanized and brought up with schoolbooks, which described the Bushmen as "primitive, simple-minded, childlike and dishonest". This meant they all had to work hard to overcome the derogatory myths and reach an understanding of what was for them a totally foreign culture.

The finished choreography is a beautiful piece of sophisticated contemporary dance. In every movement (torso bent forward, arms extended backwards, hunting positions…) you can recognize the expressive lines and figures known from the rock paintings, and at the same time what you see is a dance which is absolutely modern, combining African and western movements. One can sense that the dancers have integrated the meaning of the dance and linked it to the movement in an organic and respectful way.

To Sylvia Glasser the whole process of choreographing *Tranceformations* was of great importance: "The dance epitomized the fusion I had been searching for – not just between Africa and the West, but between fragmented aspects of self and spirit so important to artists in any medium" (306).

Moving Into Dance is today a school from which many internationally renowned dancers and choreographers have emerged. One of them is Vincent Mantsoe who has learned the art of trance from his *Sangoma* mother and aunt, and who can use it as a method in his own dance. Mantsoe has by now his own company with African, French and Japanese dancers, continuing the tradition of fusion based on respect for the "other" culture. To him also the work with *Trance-formations* was a revelation: "It changed my attitude towards other cultures. I wanted to appreciate other cultural beliefs and it also affected the way I do my own choreography. *Tranceformations* did wonders to me: it put me in the "other" mood; I was possessed; I was somebody else, I was new; my face, eyes, feet, nose, fingertips, hair, chest and back had incredible power. The whole of the atmosphere changed for me. It brought me a new life as the spirits of the Bushmen taught me how to respect the rituals of other cultures" (306).

**From Exotic Form to Fusion**

When Cendrars, Léger and Börlin created their "Negro ballet" African culture was considered primitive by the general opinion. But to the artists, "primitive" was a fine concept, something they could use in their fight against old and petrified forms. In their eyes it was authentic and wild, like the jazz music, which was electrifying the Parisian public. They used the forms, not bothering much about their possible original meanings, and they turned them into modernist art.

When Birgit Åkesson went on her expeditions to Africa it was to look for the essence of the continent's culture. She searched for what she considered pure ancient forms of rituals, not contaminated by modern life or other cultures. She did not consider the dance primitive, on the contrary, but to her, as to the artists of the 1920s, the foreign culture served as an alternative to the dance of her own civilisation.

Sylvia Glasser too looked for alternatives and found it in the oldest of artistic forms in South Africa, the rock paintings. She studied their meaning and she made her dancers study as well. Thus they were able to appropriate the forms of the paintings and of the trance dance. This basically respectful approach made the fusion possible: Sylvia Glasser could combine ancient and modern forms without violating or trivializing the origin. She could combine the classical ballet with the African dance in firm contact with the earth. Visualize the dance: it is contemporary.

## Notes

[1]Näslund's richly illustrated book will be published also in English and French.

[2]Acogny, p. 8. Béjar's school has been lead by Germaine Acogny, the grand old lady, choreographer and teacher of contemporary dance in West Africa.

[3]Åkesson does not refer to people she worked with in Africa, but she includes Swantz' *Ritual and Symbol in transitional Zaramo Society* in the bibliography. Åkesson is full of contempt for anthropologists in general.


## References

Acogny, Germaine, *Danse Africaine* (Fricke Verlag, 1988)

Åkesson, Birgit, *Källvattnets mask, Om dans i Afrika* (Bokförlaget Atlantis, 1983).

Åkesson, Birgit, *- att ge spår i luften -* (Kykeyon, 1983).

Cendrars, Blaise, *Anthologie Nègre*, (Buchet/Chastel, 1947).

Cendrars, Miriam, *Blaise Cendrars* (Editions Balland, 1984).

Glasser, Sylvia, *Appropriation and Appreciation* (paper given for the International Society of Dance History Scholars, New York 1993).

Glasser, Sylvia, *Transcultural Transformations*, (in Visual Anthropology, Vol. 8, 1996).

Lagercranz, Ann-Cathrine and Wilhelm Östberg, Dansmaskens berättelse, Birgit Åkessons *resor i Afrika* (Etnografiska muséet, 2007).

Näslund, Erik, *Rolf de Maré, konstsamlare balettledare museiskapare* (Bokförlaget Langenskiöld, 2008).

# Dancing BANDA'S Dictatorship:
## The Cultural-Political Discourses of Power in Traditional Dance Performances in Malawi
### - Reuben Makayiko Chirambo

**Dance Performance as Discourse**

Traditional dance performances at political functions of the various political parties in Malawi are a constant and integral feature of the political functions. While they are presented as traditional forms of entertainment at the functions, and indeed across the country traditional dances are an everyday entertainment, they are also forms of political discourses relating to power politics in Malawi understood within the sense in which Foucault describes discourse and power. Foucault describes discourse as "the general domain of all statements, sometimes as an individualizable group of statements, and sometimes as a regulated practice that accounts for a number of statements" (1990: 80).

What I suggest as discourse of dance is what is produced by a corpus of the dance performance that includes the body movements (corporeality), songs, drums, audience participation, the setting, among others, in a totality that could be read as a text or statements of the performance. What constitutes text is not just the lyrics of the songs, but the various statements of the dance performance in its totality, including the non-verbal expressions that give meaning to the dance. As Lemke explains, meanings "get made in contexts where social expectations and non-linguistic symbols play a role," arguing that "when speaking of the *text* produced on that occasion, [we need] to add to verbal record of the discourse as much as we can of the visual and actional signs and symbols that contribute to its potential social meanings" (1995: 8) (italics in original). Though Barthes was primarily concerned with the written text as a sign that signifies meaning (32-4), it is possible to extend his insights to argue dance performance as a signifying text that produces meaning. As text, dance performances produce meanings that constitute or contribute to discourses of power or, in Foucaultian terms, are a discursive practice. Fairclough argues that "discourse contributes first of all to the construction of what are variously referred to as 'social identities' and 'subject positions' for 'social subjects' and types of 'self'" (1992: 64). Secondly, discourse helps to construct social relationships between people (ibid). Discursive practice, which is the very act of discourse, is "constitutive in both conventional and creative ways: it contributes to reproducing society (social identities, social relationships, systems of knowledge and belief)" (65).

In Malawi, in the case of traditional dances at political functions, the discourse of dance is intrinsically linked to the cultural politics, where such politics involves appropriation of cultural artefacts, including traditional dances and praise names for political purposes by the regime. In this paper one is interested in the relationship between discourse and power where the discourses reveal and express or represent the power relationships in the traditional dance performances at political functions. Of particularly interest is how dance discourses contributed to the legitimation of the dictatorship of President Banda and the MCP in Malawi between 1964 and 1994. I argue that the most effective and pronounced discourses of political power of the dictatorship of former president for life and dictator, Dr. H.K. Banda and the Malawi Congress Party (MCP) that ruled Malawi from 1964 to 1994 were produced and articulated in the dance performances in which Banda himself often participated as singer and dancer. This political power should not, as Foucault argues, be seen as emanating from a single point at the apex of the state, in this case the apex being Banda and his political establishment. Rather, political power also resides and is reproduced in discursive practices that involve the interaction between the leadership and the ordinary people in our case in the dance performances.

The discussion of dance discourse in Malawi here will focuses on the dance performances during the reign of the dictatorship of Banda and the MCP in Malawi. These dance performances were done at the political functions of the MCP in which Banda routinely participated by singing and dancing with various groups that staged dances for him. I use examples of the *Mbotoska*, *Chimtali*, *Chimdidi* and *Ingoma* dances to illustrate that dances constituted a discourse of power by contributing to and being a part of the political discourse of Kamuzuism. The term 'Kamuzuism' was coined from President Banda's middle name, Kamuzu, and was presented to Malawians as a specific ideology or philosophy of Banda. Among the ideas, beliefs, and values that formed this ideology was the suggestion that Banda was a God-sent Messiah endowed with unsurpassed wisdom, therefore, making it easy for him to assume life presidency. This also meant that his authority could not be challenged, let alone criticised. All forms of dissent were severely punished by, among others, detention without trial, torture and even by death. (See Africa Watch and Amnesty International Reports for details).

Banda devised four cornerstones that became lynchpins of Kamuzuism: Unity, Loyalty, Obedience, and Discipline. He argued that the party (MCP) and the government of Malawi were founded on these principles. Any questioning, criticism or complaint against Banda or the Party was considered an act of disobedience, as it was indiscipline and threatened national unity, besides showing disloyalty to the party, government, and Banda. Since the majority of the people of Malawi internalized these ideas of Kamuzuism, which became the basis for their everyday lives, even the harsh punishment meted out to errant individuals were lauded, for example, in the songs that accompanied the dances done for Banda (Chirambo 2006). It can be argued that Kamuzuism was a hegemonic ideology of Banda's leadership, and as a dominant ideology was the source of the ideas that formed the discourses of power in Malawi during his reign. Banda mobilised the consensus of a large section of the people of Malawi to subscribe to this ideology and his political leadership. The political discourse of Kamuzuism was therefore concerned with Banda and his position as leader, and expressed the ideologies that the nation was required to know and use as the basis of conduct.

The ideology of Kamuzuism that was the source of the notions in the political discourse of the dances was mainly propagated and expressed in the praise names and titles given to President Banda and used in the dances. Praise names and titles for political leaders in Africa and Malawi in particular should be understood within the cultural politics of political symbolism and how this informed the political conduct of the leaders and the people. Hayward and Dumbuya explain that,

> The importance of political symbols rests on what they evoke in the minds of the people – whether pride, hostility, satisfaction, reassurance, or support – because they are associated with particular events, types of action, deeds, benefits. It is not so much the symbols themselves that are significant, but the meanings that people attribute to them. (1983: 648)

Most praise names/titles of leaders in Africa have cultural connotations that provide meanings for both the people and those to whom they are given or are used for. Le Vine goes further to suggest that political symbols adopted by political leaders in Africa relate to the political roles, styles, and images that the leaders adopt.' These symbols are directly related to people's expectations of the leaders and the norms by which they should operate. Therefore, Le Vine argues that any leader must "cope with a given image of his role by attempting to satisfy the sum of the norms and expectations of performance, as well as finding the appropriate acts to give personal expression to the role" (1977: 632). The choice of praise titles, Le Vine observes, is based on the "evocative power" of the symbols where such names/ titles will help to "create or maintain affect between [the leaders] and their followers, to induce submission, acquiescence or support, as well as to satisfy their [leader's] own role-cognitions" (1977: 632). Praise names used for Banda evoked his historical roles and defined his relationship with his followers with the aim of creating affection between Banda and his supporters.

The praise titles given to Banda in Malawi included *Ngwazi* (Conqueror), *Nkhoswe* (Guardian and provider), *Mkango* (Lion), and *Moto* (Fire), referring to his role in the liberation struggle against colonialism. The titles are in the mode of "revival of warrior tradition" which Ali Mazrui (177) suggests is the trend in modern African politics. The tendency is to cast modern leaders within the warrior tradition or conquest that typified empire builders of the kingdoms in the past. For modern African leaders, their conquest was the winning of independence for their countries from colonial powers as well as the sometimes brutal suppression of opposition in post-independence Africa. The meanings of Banda's titles went beyond the historical roles Banda played by referring to personal traits or qualities of Banda that explained his leadership style in the post-independence. Banda was 'conqueror' even of his critics and opponents after independence. He was also perceived as invincible.

The title *Ngwazi* is a praise name among the *Ngoni* people of northern and central regions of Malawi. It means Conqueror. It was given to Banda after independence for vanquishing colonialists in order to win independence for Malawi. The title also evoked the idea that Banda was invincible, unconquerable even beyond winning independence. The other titles such as *Mkango* [Lion] and *Moto* [Fire], refer to shrewdness and ferociousness as attributes of Banda, all qualifying him to be leader for Malawi. Among the *Ngoni* and indeed in Malawi in general, bravery and valour are cherished qualities for a leader. Banda was also the fiery fire that consumed or destroyed federation and colonialism to get independence for Malawi.

Banda was also called *Nkhoswe* No. 1. The term *Nkhoswe* explains a relationship between men (*nkhoswe*) and women siblings (*mbumba*) particularly in the matrilineal society of the Chewa of central Malawi where Banda himself came from. However, the idea is not limited to the Chewa. Similar notions exist amongst the Tumbuka and Tonga of northern Malawi and among other ethnic groups in the south such as the Sena of Nsanje and Chikwawa districts. Young and Banda describe the relationship between *nkhoswe* and *mbumba* as follows: "All the male members of a Chewa family on the mother's side are *nkhoswe* to all the female members on the mother's side." (13)

The women to whom the males are *nkhoswe* form what is called *mbumba*. Young and Banda explain the implications and responsibilities of the *nkhoswe* to his *mbumba* as follows:

And being *nkhoswe* to them [*mbumba*] you, as a male and no matter how young you are, are a Responsible Relative….When you say "They are my *mbumba*", or, "She is my *mbumba*", you *are* admitting a responsibility in law; you are *not* claiming them or her as particular sort of relative such as aunt, cousin, sister or daughter. All *nkhoswe* are responsible in law not only for the well-being but also for the good conduct of their *mbumba*...*nkhoswe* [is] an "advocate" and a "sustainer" of his *mbumba*. (13)

Young and Banda explain that it is the *nkhoswe*, for example, who is sued for offences committed by his *mbumba*. Also, the *nkhoswe* sues if his *mbumba* is wronged. The *nkhoswe* is therefore the guardian, protector, and in case of need, the provider for his *mbumba*. He is sometimes called *Mwini-mbumba*, (literally, the owner of *mbumba*). Thus, when Banda became *Nkhoswe* No. 1, it was an appropriation of a specific cultural tradition and extended it over the entire nation. Now all women in Malawi and by implication those associated with them were Banda's *mbumba*. Through this, Banda placed women in Malawi under his direct tutelage and protection, guiding their lives and providing for their needs as necessary. Banda took his responsibility as *nkhoswe* literally. It was never just a symbolic title.

Others explain the relationship of *nkhoswe* and *mbumba* between Banda and women of Malawi as one of exploitation and indeed of oppression (Lwanda 1993, *Kamuzu Banda*; Mkamanga 2000; Gilman 2001; Semu 2002). They emphasize the fact that not all women may have liked the objectifying position of *mbumba* to Banda, particularly because of the obligations this entailed such as supporting Banda without questioning and singing and dancing for him whenever he appeared in public. However, it is a relationship that served Banda well in establishing him as a culture hero. It also earned him grassroots support, legitimacy and popularity.

The four traditional dances and their accompanying songs, three done by women, *Mbotoska, Chimtali, Chimdidi* and one mostly by men, *Ingoma* drew upon some of the ideas expressed in the praise names. These are a representative sample of the many dances that were featured at political functions in Malawi in the reign of Banda and the MCP.

It should be mentioned that while traditional dances, which are forms of popular culture, were sites of hegemonic influence as discursive practices, as Stuart Hall observes, "popular culture is [also] one of the sites where [the] struggle for and against a culture of the powerful is engaged…[i]t is the arena of consent and resistance (Hall 1998: 453). In other words, the dances and songs above and what follows in this discussion do not suggest that all the discourses simply affirmed Banda's position, legitimising and popularising his regime. Oppositional discourses in the dances and songs often contested the singular authority of Banda and the MCP, but often in subtle and cryptic ways for fear of reprisals such as detention without trial and torture for the critics (Gibbs 1981, Kaspin 1992, Mapanje 1995).

### *Mbotoska* Dance Performance

*Mbotoska* is a traditional dance done by women and sometimes girls, most commonly in Rumphi district of the northern region of Malawi. It is an entertainment dance for all ages. Women form a circle around a set of two or more drums, which are beaten by men though in recent times women also beat the drum. The dancers go round with the circle dancing to the rhythm of the drums and songs. *Mbotoska* seems to have borrowed a lot from *Chiwoda* and *Chimtali* dances, with which it has almost everything in common. The dance became prominent in the 1970s with its inclusion among dances at political functions for Banda. Their songs outside the political functions are usually about social issues of the communities or simply playful entertainment. What I examine here are efforts to give a specific rendition of *Mbotoska* dance to dramatize Banda's cultural politics, as *nkhoswe*. This dramatisation involved mainly body movements, song and drumming that I suggest constituted a specific meaning in the political discourse of the dance. Dancing and singing in most African societies are in themselves dramatic renditions that involve a lot of innovative styles suited to the particular occasion and sometimes to achieve specific meanings.

The message of this specific performance of *Mbotoska* is about the aeroplanes that Banda bought for the women and the plane rides abroad he allowed some of the women to undertake. In his role as *nkhoswe* of all the women in Malawi whom he referred to as his *mbumba,* Banda sent his women on study tours to countries such as Britain and Scotland, Germany, Israel and Taiwan. He also bought aeroplanes in which women and other party functionaries travelled on duty within the country. He also built houses for some of the most active women in the party. In this case, the women are expressing their appreciation for travelling abroad and for the aeroplanes he bought for women in Malawi. Plane rides were obviously novel experiences for most ordinary women; hence, they repeatedly referred to them in their songs, thanking Banda profusely for the experiences. However, the question was always how to thank Banda enough or show appreciation more tangibly for his work as their *nkhoswe*. While for most dances the easiest way to accommodate politics was through their songs or costume, adapting the style of dancing as *Mbotoska* dance did was by no means easy. Women of Rumphi district in their performance of *Mbotoska* presented themselves as a 'plane' to say thank you to Banda.

"Ndege" [the plane] as they called the performance, was quite an ingenious innovation to *Mbotoska*. The "plane" was how the group entered into the dancing arena. Most groups often had an opening song which they sang as they filed into the centre of the dancing arena in front of Banda. When dancing the "plane," *Mbotoska* dancers entered the dance arena in the manner of a descending plane about to land at an airport. Instead of simply filing into the arena, they more or less 'landed' into it. To do this, they formed a long line about 20 or so metres away from the centre of the dance arena and then while dancing to the beating of drums, they edged their way into the arena. The lead dancer and singer, Mai NyamNyasulu, danced backwards while facing the line and together they stretched out their hands, flapping them, bending lower each time to imitate a descending plane. By the time, they formed full circle around the microphone and drums they would be more or less crawling, suggesting the plane has landed. All along the lead dancer would shout, *Iyo ndege, yawa ndege* ['Here is the plane; the plane has landed.'] Other than this shouting, there was no singing, only the drums. In this way, the dance performance expressed and enhanced the meaning of their experience of riding aeroplanes while demonstrating thankfulness to Banda more profoundly than songs would have done.

In "Ndege," the body movements constituted the message that speak of the plane and express gratitude to Banda their *Nkhoswe* for enabling them to ride in aeroplanes. The meaning of "ndege" in the dance both in reference to the actual aeroplanes and as a symbolic representation of the "thank you" message to Banda are within larger and dominant political discourse of power in which Banda was the *Nkhoswe* – provider and guardian of his *mbumba*. His *mbumba*, here *Mbotoska* dancers, were beneficiaries of the *Nkhoswe's* political largesse. Such gestures on the part of Banda won him popular support of the women and the grassroots in Malawi as well as legitimise him in his adopted traditional role as *Nkhoswe*. Banda occasionally danced with *Mbotoska* dancers.

**Banda's Singing and Dancing**
Banda routinely danced and sang with as many groups as possible during functions that could be read as discursive practices within the formulation of discourse and power (see Fig 1).

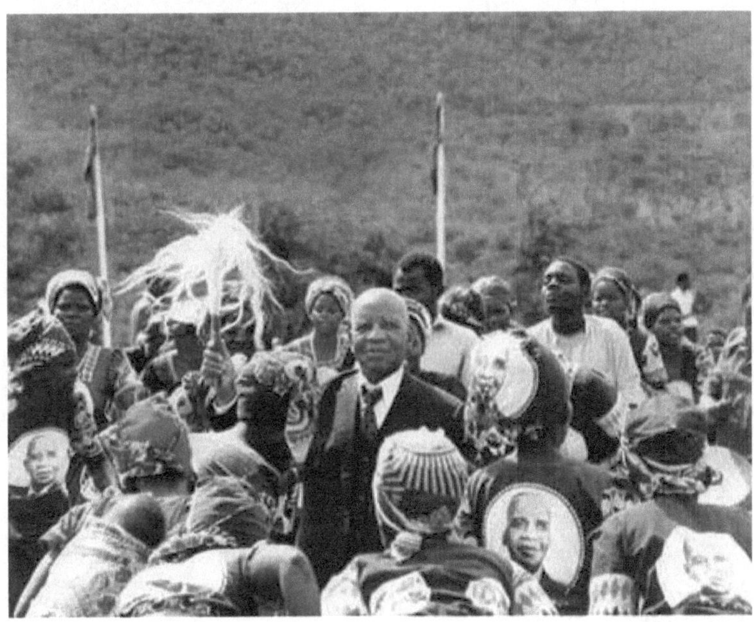

Fig. 1: Banda routinely danced with many groups

As a discursive practice, Banda's dancing with the women in *Chim-tali* dance above is textual, involving visual and actional signs and symbols, as Lemke above suggests In other words, this performance involves what Fairclough says is "text production, distribution, and consumption" (1992: 78); in this case, Banda was involved in the production of the text. By placing himself in the midst of the performance as a singer and a dancer, Banda engendered specific meanings that directly relate to the power relationships that discourse is concerned about. Arguably, therefore, in this combination of song and dance, the active involvement of President Banda constitutes a discursive practice. The totality of the dance performance is the story of their relationship which affirmed their subjectivities – for Banda, his leadership position, and for the other dancers, their subordinate and subservient position to him, their elevated *Nkhoswe* and Leader. The songs too, as part of the totality of the dance performance, articulated the discourse of the power relationship between Banda and his supporters. The three songs below essentially illustrate the dialogue between Banda and his supporters done while performing *Chimtali*.

**Banda**: *Inu azimayi, ulendo waku Ulaya munakwera chiyani?*
**Women**: *Tinakwera pa ndenge pa ndege ya Malawi, oyiya*
**Banda**: *Azimayi nyang'ani*
**Women**: *Oyiya*
**Banda**: *Munyadire ufulu Ufulu wa Malawi*
*Mkango wa Malawi*
*Likulu ku Lilongwe*
*University ku Zomba*
**Women**: *Aaa oyiya*
*Tinyadire a Ngwazi*
*Awo akhala pampando waufumuwo*
**Banda**: You women, on your trip to Europe, what did your ride?
**Women**: We rode Malawi's plane, o yes
**Banda**: Women be proud
**Women**: Yes
**Banda**: Proud of the freedom
Freedom in Malawi
The Lion of Malawi

Capital City in Lilongwe
University in Zomba
**Women**: Yes
Proud of *Ngwazi*
He is seated on the throne.

Once the lead singer of the women dancers started this song and Banda signalled he was going to lead the singing by moving towards the microphone, he would assume the lead vocalist position for the song while the women simply backed him. While the women danced round the microphone Banda would stand by the microphone to lead the singing, dancing and waving his flywhisk in the air as in the photo above. While in the *Mbotoska* dance above the women of Rumphi district dramatised their "thank you" to Banda for plane rides, here Banda and the women in a question and response format sang about the plane rides for which the women expressed gratitude. Banda urges the women to be proud of the plane rides and other achievements he has made and the women respond by enumerating the various developmental achievements including getting independence for the country. In the last two lines, the women affirm Banda as their king seated on the throne.

Similar dialogue goes on in the song below where again Banda assumes the role of lead vocalist and leads his women into singing an affirmative song about the women subject position and his own leadership position.

| | |
|---|---|
| **Banda**: | *Amayi nyang'ani, nyang'ani, nyang'ani nawo inu* |
| **Women**: | *Tinyang'e nawo ufulu wa Ngwazi mMalawi* |
| **Banda**: | *Mumakwera?* |
| **Women**: | *Timakwera ndege ya Malawi* |
| **Banda**: | *Mumabvala?* |
| **Women**: | *Timavala salu ya Malawi* |
| **Banda**: | *Mumavala?* |
| **Women**: | *Timavala wotchi ya Malawi A Ngwazi ee* |
| **Banda**: | Women, be proud |
| **Women**: | We're proud of *Ngwazi's* freedom |
| **Banda**: | What do you ride? |

| Women: | We ride Malawi's planes |
| Banda: | What do you wear? |
| Women: | We wear Malawi's cloth |
| Banda: | What do you wear? |
| Women: | We wear Malawi's watches |
| | Here is our *Ngwazi*. |

Again Banda urges his women to be proud of what he has done as *Ngwazi* and *Nkhoswe* to which the women respond with assurances that he is their *Ngwazi*. In the song below, the occasion is a visit to Banda's palace at Sanjika in Blantyre City. The palace is a magnificent building more or less carved out of the mountainside overlooking the city. Banda used to invite his women to take turns sightseeing at the palace and in turn perform dances to thank him for the magnificent building.

| Banda: | *Inu ndinu ayani, yani nanga?* |
| Women: | *Ife ndife amayi* |
| Banda: | *Ochokera?* |
| Women: | *Ochokera ku Mwera* |
| Banda: | *Mwangowona?* |
| Women: | *Tangowona nyumba ya Ngwazi yamangika ku Sanjika.* |
| Banda: | Who are you? |
| Women: | We are women |
| Banda: | Where are you coming from? |
| Women: | We are coming from the South |
| Banda: | What have you seen? |
| Women: | We have just seen *Ngwazi's* palace built at Sanjika. |

The dialogue in these songs and dance is entirely about Banda as *Nkhoswe* and *Ngwazi*. The dialogue enumerates development programs and recounts the trips abroad that Banda enabled. Banda literally and physically planted himself at the centre of the dance to sing and dance. The seemingly simplistic message where Banda and his supporters dance to entertain themselves should be read within and as a discourse of dance performance. The discourse was meant to affirm their existing relationship even as it helped popularise and legitimise the dictatorship. Though the dialogue in the songs above is about development programs Banda achieved for the country and the improvement he brought to individual people's lives, the most important fact is that Banda and the people sang about such issues together in the dance arena, reproducing their social identities and defining their political relationship.

Besides singing songs with a political message, Banda also danced and sang songs that had nothing to do with his own praise, particularly *Chimdidi* songs done by women from his home district, Kasungu. While the group adapted some of their songs into praises for Banda, whenever Banda joined in the dance, he insisted on and led singing those traditional songs that were not his praises such as "*Bwere n'bwereke.*" This song is about a woman who lives by borrowing from her neighbours because her husband is never at home to provide for her. Another favourite was "*Inde inde yaya kade,*" advising a woman that a man is not for one woman. When he joined the dance, Banda sang the solo parts and determined the order of the songs. Although he often sang in complete discord with the group, he nevertheless persisted to lead the songs and the dance. In the circumstances, the women did their best to keep in accord with his singing and they danced accordingly. It was part of the fun of singing and dancing with their leader. The beauty and meaning of this performance was no longer in how well Banda and the women sang and danced but in the fact that Banda danced with them. Banda loved these songs and the dance not for the meaning of the songs but as part of his childhood world. But in performing them with his *mbumba,* as their *nkhoswe,* the text produced relates to the power relationship between them.

What took place in these songs was not simply monotonous enumeration of development programs in Malawi and praise for the man who made them happen. This was a dialogue in the dance arena where a leader and his people together performed a discourse of the power relationship and not just political entertainment. The women were not simply offering praise and worship to a leader seated on the platform far away from them. He was in their midst with them, singing and dancing among them. His presence and participation in dance arena helped establish a rapport in their relationship that would otherwise not have been possible. Whenever Banda joined in the singing and dancing, he certainly aroused the emotions of his dancers into frenzy (See Mkamanga 2001: 37). Their joy and enthusiasm increased and was quite obvious. He too was often visibly excited as he sang and danced among his people. For this reason, his people often courted him with songs they knew he would not resist wanting to dance and sing.

Another dance in which Banda participated with immense vigour and pleasure is *Ingoma*. In the *Ingoma* dance, the nature of the discourse is not so different from the other dances above. *Ingoma* is originally a traditional warrior dance of the Ngoni people of northern and central Malawi. Though Banda could not sing their songs, he enjoyed dancing with the dancers at the so many occasions. The dance involves stamping feet on the group simulating a war stampede. The dancers brandish a spear and a shield, their instruments of war. In the case of *Ingoma* from Mzimba district in the picture below, where the dancers line up in formation like an army parade, they treated Banda like their commander-in-chief. After all, *Ingoma* is a war dance that in the past celebrated war victories. Once they were ready for him to come in, their leader, Inkosi Mzukuzuku, marched up to the VIP stage and bowed once just as a guard commander would invite the president to inspect a guard of honour. Banda would then get down the VIP podium taking with him his shield and spear that had been presented to him earlier on as *Ngwazi* - Conqueror. It is the Ngonis of Mzimba who bestowed on him the title of *Ngwazi*. When leaving the dancing arena, often Inkosi [Chief] Mzukuzuku escorted him back to the VIP podium. But as can be seen from the picture below, Banda and Mzukuzuku sometimes engaged in animated conversation or chatter and laughter. Banda in the picture is holding the shield in his hand while Inkosi Mzukuzuku points to the sky above. Banda seems to be looking up too. Whenever Banda joined the dance, all other dancers put away their spears and shields at the back of the formation for what I gather were security reasons. Authorities could not take chances to have the president amidst armed dancers.

What is most significant perhaps in this dance performance again is the personal relationship that both Banda and the performers developed through a discourse of subjectivities and power. Through dancing, they cultivated a personal relationship that allowed them to take liberties that included telling him when to come in and dance. There was also a joking and casual informality to their relationship because of the dance. However, Banda's elevated position as the only bearer of the shield and spear and the manner of his invitation to come and dance confirmed his position as *Ngwazi*, the Conqueror. Again, as Fairclough argues that "discourse as a political practice establishes, sustains…power relations, and the collective entities between which power obtains" (1992: 67). Banda and his people sustained their power relationship in these dances. And since discourse is ideological and "discursive practice constitutes, naturalizes, sustains … positions in power relations" (Fairclough 1992: 67), this dance performance reified political power relations, and legitimised and popularised the dictatorship of Banda and the MCP.

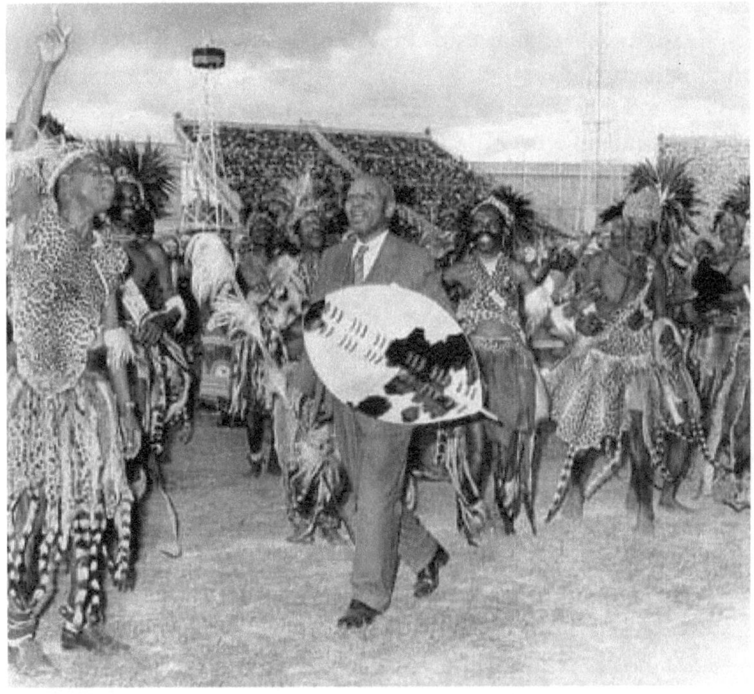

Fig. 2 - Photo by Department of Information, Blantyre, Malawi

## Conclusions

In sum, Banda's performances with his people was a discursive practice, whose discourse had profound meaning on his relationship with those ordinary people, adding a measure of informality that helped establish a rapport of mutual endearment between himself and the people. In other words, Banda cultivated intimacy with his people that the often cold and hurried handshakes from the podium could not achieve. This is because during the performance of the songs and dances, Banda came, face-to-face, eye-to-eye, body-to-body, word-to-word, in the closest possible manner to the people. Banda showed that he loved to be with and among his people and the people seemed to enjoy his company and participation.

From as early as 1958 when he returned to Malawi, Banda danced with his people and sang as a matter of habit. It is on this account of singing and dancing that George Nurse suggests that for the people, Banda's visit to them was "a visit of not merely a politician, a transient leader…but a glamorous occasion, the passing [and walking] among them of a symbol that transcends them but yet is not so remote as to be beyond their reach" (105-6). He was both the leader and a man, one who could move, dance, and sing freely and with dignity everywhere and with everyone. For the people, Banda was "not someone set too far apart, on a pedestal" (106). He was there with them, and as Nurse concludes, "an apotheosis and a projection of themselves and they acclaim[ed] him not with slavish deference but with the joy and enthusiasm they feel in the epiphany of their own importance" (ibid). By his presence in the dance arena, he gave them a feeling and a sense of their own importance and involvement not just in the political discourse, but also in the entire social political order that we call Kamuzuism. They identified with him and him with them. The physical presence in the dance arena promoted his physical presence, appealing to the collective imagination of Banda in his image as *Nkhoswe* and *Ngwazi*.

As Foucault and other commentators suggest, discourse and discursive practice is constitutive of, making possible and promoting certain kinds of political and social relationships while constricting others. In discourse, subject and leader positions as well as political identities are formed and sustained. It is arguable, therefore, that in dance performances described above, the nature of the discourse enabled or constituted and sustained social and political relations in the power politics of Banda and the MCP's dictatorship.

The dance performances should be seen in their totality as constituting a display of political power and authority for Banda, and as institutionalising his regime, giving it legitimacy and popularity, that is, enabling its hegemony. The significance of performance in politics is as Samuel Kasule suggests; it adopts "popular cultural performances and idioms as a means of politicizing society at the grass-roots level." (42). This is because, Kasule suggests, it is "the most viable form of entertainment, education, and conscientisation. Its prominence arises from the fact that it draws on people's performance cultures (music and dance and other forms), beliefs, and aesthetics for specific political and cultural reasons" (ibid). In Malawi, dance performances at political functions were the greatest manifestation of and a means for the creation of a relationship of hegemonic power between Banda's regime and his subjects. It went beyond being simply "occasions that state power organizes for dramatizing its own magnificence; [or] ceremonial displays through which it makes manifest its majesty" (Mbembe 103). They were occasions where the discourses of power in the dances helped naturalise and sustain Banda's dictatorship.

## Notes

[1]Chilivumbo in "Malawi's Lively Art Form" shows how *Chiwoda* and several other dances performed in the north and central Malawi influenced each other. Dancers learned from or copied each other's styles and sometimes even songs, making the dances seem like varieties of the same dance.

## References


Africa Watch. *Where Silence Rules: the Suppression of Dissent in Malawi.* New York: Africa Watch, 1990.

Amnesty International. *Malawi.* London: Amnesty International, 1976.
______. *Malawi: Human Rights Violations 25 Years after Independence.* New York: Amnesty International, 1989.
______. *Malawi: Prison Conditions, Cruel Punishment, and Detention without Trial.* New York: Amnesty International, 1992.

Barthes, Roland. "Theory of the Text." In *Untying the Text: A Post-Structuralist Reader*. Ed. Robert Young. Boston and London: Routledge and Kegan Paul, 1981

Chilivumbo, Alufeyo B. "Malawi's Lively Art Form: Chioda Dancers Mirror their Changing World in a Traditional Frame." *Africa Report* 16 (1971): 16-18.

Chirambo, Reuben M. "Culture, Hegemony, and Dictatorship in Malawi: Song, Dance,
 and Politics in Malawi, 1964-1994." PhD. Diss. University of Minnesota, 2005.
_____. "Traditional and Popular Music, Hegemonic Power, and Censorship in Malawi, 1964-1994." In *Popular Music Censorship in Africa*. Eds. Michael Drewett and Martin Cloonan. England: Ashgate Publishing Ltd., 2006. pp. 109-126.

Fairclough, Norman. *Discourse and Social Change*. Cambridge, United Kingdom: Polity Press, 1992.

Foucault, Michel. *The History of Sexuality*. Vol. 1: And Introduction. London: Vintage Books, 1990.

Gibbs, James. "Of Kamuzu and Chameleons: Experiences of Censorship in Malawi." *The Literary Half-Yearly* 23.2 (1982): 69-83.

Gilman, Lisa. "Purchasing Praise: Women, Dancing, and Patronage in Malawi Party Politics." *Africa Today* 48.3 (2001): 43-64.

Hall, Stuart. "Notes on Deconstructing 'the Popular'." In *Cultural Theory and Popular Culture: A Reader*. Second Edition. Ed. John Storey. London: Pearson Prentice Hall, 1998.

Hayward, Fred M, and Ahmed R. Dumbuya. "Political Legitimacy, Political Symbols, and National Leadership in West Africa." *The Journal of Modern African Studies* 21.4 (1983): 645-671.

Kaspin, Deborah. "Chewa Visions and Revisions of Power: Transformations of the Nyau Dance in Central Malawi." *Modernity and Its
Malcontents*. Eds. John and Jean Cornaroff. London: 1993. pp. 34-57.

Kasule, Samuel. "Popular Performance and the Construction of
Social Reality in Post-
 Amin Uganda." *Journal of Popular Culture* 32.2 (1998): 39-58.

Lemke, Jay L. *Textual Politics: Discourse and Social Dynamics*. London:
Taylor and Francis, 1995.

Le Vine, Victor T. "Changing Leadership Styles and Political Images:
Some Preliminary Notes." *The Journal of Southern African Studies* 15.4
(1977): 631-638.

Lwanda, John L. *Kamuzu Banda of Malawi: A Study in Promise, Power
and Paralysis*. Glasgow: Dudu Nsomba Publications, 1993.

Mapanje, Jack. "Censoring the African Poem." *Index on Censorship*.
9 (1989): 7-9, 11.

Mazrui, Ali A. *Cultural Engineering and Nation-Building in East Africa*.
Evanston, IL: 1972.

Mbembe, Achille. *On the Postcolony*. Berkeley: University of California Press, 2001.

Mkamanga, Emily. *Suffering Silently: Dancing with Kamuzu Banda of
Malawi*. Glasgow: Dudu Nsomba Publications, 2000.

Phiri, Kings M. "Dr Banda's Cultural Legacy and its Implications
for a Democratic Malawi." In *Democratization in Malawi: A Stocktaking*. Eds. Kings Phiri and Kenneth Ross. Blantyre, Malawi: CLAIM,
1998. pp. 147-167.

Semu, Linda. "Kamuzu's Mbumba: Malawi Women's Embeddedness to Culture in the Face of International Political Pressure and
Internal Legal Change." *Africa Today* 49.2 (2002): 77-99.

Young, Cullen and H.K. Banda, eds. *Our African Way of Life*. London:
United Society for Christian Literature, 1946.

# Culture and Yoruba Popular Music in Nigeria
## - Bode Omojola

Contradictory notions in modern African popular music highlight the challenge faced by African musicians in dealing with received European cultural practices and the complexity of locating these cultural practices in relation to the African cultural heritage. Olaniyan (2004: 158) reflected on this ambivalence in his study of Fela Anikulapo-Kuti's afro-beat music, and observed that, on the one hand, Anikulapo-Kuti's music reacts against European cultural practices by seeking to promote "authentic African paradigms and institutions" but, on the other, it often patronizes European musical elements and performance practices. Kofi Agawu has also argued that, even where much of the raw musical material used in African popular music emanates from European cultural sources, their use by African musicians often resonates with a new register and form (Agawu, 2003:148-149).

It is in this sense that modern African popular music registers simultaneously as a resister and symptom of imposed Western cultural practices emanating largely from colonial rule. Thomas Turino, focusing on musical practice in Zimbabwe, analyzes this phenomenon from the perspective of cosmopolitan global formations. Although cosmopolitan styles "are widely practiced in many parts of the worlds," they are often "restricted to certain segments or social groups of the population in particular areas" (2006: 6). In addition, they are dynamic because they are continuously reworked within the constrictions of specific cultural environment, and as defined by emerging challenges and needs. Turino's discussion stresses the critical importance of the element of adaptation as a creative strategy.

The application of the concept of cosmopolitanism to the discussion of African popular music thus helps to direct attention to the resilience of African musicians, and the capability of subdominant societies to engage and rework "global" elements and ideas according to the demands of their immediate environment. Christopher Waterman has similarly observed that the process of reworking foreign musical material by African musicians is illustrative of how they have adapted to the progressively urbanized nature of their environment (Waterman, 1990: 9). On the Yoruba people of western Nigeria, Waterman notes that African musicians are "characteristically adept at interpreting multiple languages, cultural codes, and value systems, skills which enable them to construct styles that express shifting patterns of urban identity" (Waterman, 1990: 9). He describes the musicians as "master syncretizers" of modern Africa who work with musical material and deal with issues that emanate from African and non-African sources, especially those that emerged from colonial rule and globalization.

This article examines the ways in which Yoruba modern musicians rework Western and indigenous elements in a manner that illuminates the social dynamics and the constantly shifting social and political landscape of their environment especially since the latter half of the 20th century. By social dynamics, I refer to the flux that characterizes cultural, religious and social life in Nigeria notably in the colonial and postcolonial era. And by political landscape, I refer to Nigeria's modern political structures, governance and institutions as shaped during and after the colonial era. My objective here is to assess how Yoruba popular musicians have interrogated social and political issues of their social environment in their music, while also reworking foreign musical elements to suit the local cultural environment. My discussion derives from an extensive fieldwork in Nigeria, comprising interviews with Lagbaja and Victor Olaiya, and participation in popular music events in cities like Ilorin, Ibadan, Oshogbo and Lagos (some of the major Yoruba cities where modern popular music receives its greatest patronage).

**Yoruba Popular Music and Social Dynamics in Nigeria**
The development of modern Yoruba popular music is tied strongly to colonial rule, the nationalist struggles leading to independence and the myriad of social and political issues emanating from these

events. Western music and musical practices were introduced through mission schools and through the Christian church especially from the mid-19th century, leading to the adoption of European musical instruments, the incorporation of European music liturgy and the gradual entrenchment of Western tonal harmony. By the beginning of the twentieth century, some Yoruba professional musicians had become quite proficient in performing and interpreting Western music, constituting the filter through which Western musical practices would permeate to the more ordinary people. The introduction of European church music would later provide the impetus for the development of modern popular music genres in Nigeria. For example, pioneering figures of modern Yoruba popular music like Victor Olaiya, Bobby Benson and Adeolu Akinsanya, who were trained in the church or missionary schools, later adapted their knowledge of Western music to the process of writing and performing highlife, a transnational musical genre that was popular in the 1950s and 60s in countries like Ghana, Nigeria and Sierra Leone.[1] As Akin Euba has explained, the growth of highlife and allied syncretic forms like *asiko* and *juju* was also linked to the cultural impact of returning ex-slaves and their descendants (Euba 1989: 119).

Highlife music was in its early years the music of the elite. Indeed, the name *highlife* evolved as a descriptive label used by the less privileged to describe the elitist orientation of the music (Collins, 1976). In Nigeria, in spite of its status as a cross-cultural musical form that was accessible to people of different ethnic backgrounds, highlife appealed largely to the socio-aesthetic taste of the emerging political elite of the colonial era. Its cross-cultural appeal was somehow undermined by its tendency to polarize along socio-economic lines, thus providing a symbol of the considerable social gap between Nigerian leaders and their followers.[2]

As illustrated in Victor Olaiya's 50s and 60s songs like *Labalaba* ("Butterfly"), *Fami Mora* ("Draw Close to Me"), and *So Fun Mi* ("Tell Me"), recently repackaged in the album *Leading Gentleman*, highlife music is typified by the use of European harmonic and tonal elements consisting essentially of the primary chords of I, IV and V. These chords are performed in a cyclic manner, functioning rather like ostinato patterns and much like the rhythmic patterns of the clave, the rattle and the bell – three prominent percussion instruments used in the music. The clave usually plays the Yoruba *konkolo* rhythm as played by the bell or any of the secondary drums (*omele*) in a Yoruba drum ensemble. Other percussion instruments include the *conga* drums, and much later, Yoruba *dundun* hourglass drums. The orchestration of highlife is also evocative of the American big band tradition, which was aired on colonial radio stations and made available through recordings during the colonial era. In Yoruba highlife music, the percussion instruments mentioned above provide rhythmic support for wind and brass instruments as well as guitars, the instruments which provide harmonic direction.

The syncretistic musical language of highlife speaks to the ways in which Yoruba and indeed Nigerian musicians in general responded to the imposition of Western musical practices in the country. Although many Yoruba and Nigerian musicians, including Bobby Benson, Victor Olaiya, Samuel Akpabot and Roy Chicago, did imitate Western musical genres like the foxtrot and waltz at the beginning of their careers, many later began to experiment with a new musical style that reworked received and imposed musical styles. Highlife, the first musical evidence of such adaptations, could thus be described as a musical response to European cultural domination during the colonial era. By reworking Western harmonic elements in a manner that conforms to the cyclic character of Yoruba drumming, by adapting Western-type melodies to suit the tonal and inflectional features of Yoruba language, and by incorporating indigenous musical instruments into their musical performances, musicians like Olaiya sought to "own" Western musical resources while laying the foundation for the emergence of a new popular music tradition that would speak more coherently to the social conditions of an emerging African social, political and urban experience. It must be noted however that the experiments provided in highlife music represented only the beginning of the process of such a creative synthesis. For in spite of the incorporation of Nigerian elements, highlife music continued to bear Western influences, notably in its heavy reliance on European tonal elements and musical instruments, and in the nature of its performance contexts: dinner parties, expensive night clubs, cocktails and studio-produced recordings.[3]

It is also important to note that while the highlife music of Olaiya and his ilk spoke to the social and aesthetic needs of the elite, some other equally syncretistic musical genres were tailored to the taste and social conditions of the then emerging Yoruba urban working class. These alternative traditions are often discussed under the rubric of "palm wine" music,[4] which refers to the informal nature of such performances at drinking "joints" that were patronized by working class communities in Lagos in the 1930s, 40s and 50s. Palm wine bands often comprised of the acoustic guitar or its indigenous Yoruba equivalent, notably the agidigbo—the Yoruba *mbira*.[5] As Afolabi Alaja-Browne has observed, the man who pioneered this tradition was Tunde King, who, in the 1930s, led a group of musicians to entertain at a drinking joint located in the Olowogbowo part of Lagos (Alajah-Browne, 1989:231). Lagos at this time had begun to grow into a cosmopolitan centre harbouring a considerably varied ethnic and cultural demographic comprising European missionaries and colonial officers as well as traders; returnee ex-slaves and their descendants from places like Brazil, Cuba and the United States; and Nigerians of different ethnic backgrounds. Musical instruments like the *sekere* (rattle), guitar, maracas, tambourine, conga and banjo were available in the city and had become familiar in musical performances taking place there.

Tunde King's career illustrates the multi-cultural and cosmopolitan setting that provided the fillip for the syncretistic orientation of palm wine music in the early decades of the 20th century and its subsequent evolvement into a national and international genre later in the century. Born in Lagos in 1910, King attended a Methodist school where he was introduced to the guitar. His music was contrastive to the elitist orientation of highlife, since he performed for the less privileged residents of Lagos. King's ensemble would grow from an informal music group to a more structured band, featuring banjo, the rattle and the tambourine. In its predominant reliance on the percussion, his music provided the ground for the emergence of a modern form of juju music as shaped initially by Isaac Kehinde Dairo in the 1960s, and later, by Ebenezer Obey, Sunny Ade and Shina Peters in the 1970s and 80s. As Alaja-Browne has explained, Dairo made a significant contribution towards the elevation of juju music from an evening pastime of beer-drinking "rascals or area boys," into a pan-Yoruba musical genre notably in the 1960s and 70s (Alaja-Browne, 1989: 231). As illustrated in songs like *Elele Ture*, and *Ekunrere Mo Wa*, Dairo's music incorporates musical and linguistic resources from the more provincial parts of Yoruba land, notably Ekiti and Ijesha, thus broadening the cultural appeal of juju beyond the urban vicinity of Lagos. His provincial adaptation of King's juju provided a model for the works of non-Lagos musicians like Dele Ojo and Wale Glorious in the 1970s; as well as for that of Sunny Ade, the man who took juju music to the global stage in the 1980s. Dairo's *juju*, noted for its distinctive accordion sound, also relied on a limited use of the Yoruba *dundun* talking drum, thus preparing the ground for Sunny Ade's expansive neo-traditional experiments of the late twentieth century and beyond.

**Yoruba Popular Music as a Neo-traditional Form**
The incorporation of the dundun drum in *juju* music by Dairo represented only the beginning of a vigorous neo-traditionalist approach of modern Yoruba popular music. In the early 1970s, juju music provided one of the most successful contexts for that approach. The development of juju music by musicians like Ebenezer Obey, Sunnny Ade, Idowu Animasaun and Shina Peters (who initially formed a band with Segun Adewale) was informed by a strong incorporation of traditional Yoruba performance practices and styles in a manner that fundamentally differs from what obtains in *highlife* music. The music of Sunny Ade illustrates the strong neo-traditional basis of the classic *juju* form. Born in 1946, Sunday Aladeniyi (alias King Sunny Ade) formed his juju band in 1966, at the beginning of the Nigerian civil war. The forced emigration of Igbo musicians from the Yoruba prime cities of Lagos and Ibadan to their home states in eastern Nigeria as a result of the war helped to create a less crowded social and cultural space for Yoruba musicians like Sunny Ade and Ebenezer Obey during the war. Sunny Ade's juju was initially modeled after that of Tunde Nightingale, notably in its sonorous singing, solemn sound and slow beat, and the use of melodic material and style incorporated from Christian hymnody. This however became modified later when Sunny Ade enlarged his ensemble through the addition

of more traditional Yoruba percussion and traditional Yoruba folk songs, and the use of a praise-singing style rooted in traditional Yoruba *oriki*. Sunny Ade's juju, as illustrated in albums like "Ariya Special" and "Togetherness/Kajose" remains essentially grounded in this Yoruba derived neo-traditional style.

Instrumentation is at the centre of the differences between juju and highlife. Firstly, juju music dispenses with wind and brass instruments. In its place is a battery of Yoruba *dundun* hourglass drums. Secondly, the number of guitars used in the classic juju style of Sunny Ade increased to three, with further support from the steel-Hawaii guitar, which Sunny Ade introduced to his ensemble. More significant however is how these stringed instruments are used. Unlike highlife music, in which guitars are used to provide harmonic direction, their use in juju is essentially rhythmic. They are made to provide layers of ostinato thus generating a polyrhythmic texture, which is the hallmark of Yoruba instrumental music.

Thus, in spite of the fact that Christian and Western-type vocal melodies continue to characterize juju, instrumental accompaniment does not necessarily outline the harmonic and tonal direction suggested in the melodies. The lead guitar, usually played by the bandleader, is employed to generate improvisatory parts that are similar to those of *iyaalu* in the Yoruba drum ensemble. Thirdly, traditional Yoruba praise poetry, *oriki*, is used as a major tool of performance designed to eulogize juju patrons for monetary reward. Oriki is often interspersed between songs that may include indigenous folk songs based on traditional proverbs and other types of figurative expressions. Fourthly, the expanded instrumental section is matched by a much larger chorus of singers than found in highlife. The band leader often acts as lead singer with support from a chorus that comprises the same people playing the instruments. The percussive and rhythmic character of juju provides the basis for an invigorated dancing style. Juju musicians often dictate the nature of such dances by dancing in addition to singing and playing instruments. The incorporation of these indigenous elements highlights the neo-traditional conception of modern Yoruba popular music.

Popular music genres like *apala, sakara, waka, and fuji*, which are associated with Islam, reflect even stronger influences of indigenous

Yoruba music than both *highlife* and *juju*. As Euba (1989) has discussed in his extensive study of these idioms, *apala, sakara, waka, and fuji* are performed mainly by Muslims and often carry Islamic themes. *Apala*, popular since the 1940s, is associated with musicians like Ayinde Bakare, Ligali Mukaiba and Haruna Ishola. Its neo-traditional conception is reflected in the use of Yoruba instruments like *adamo* (pressure drums), *akuba, agidigbo* (Yoruba variant of *mbira*), *sekere* (guard rattle) and *agogo* (iron gong). *Waka*, a genre exclusive to female musicians, grew, like *fuji*, out of *were*, informal performances rendered during Islamic Ramadan fasting seasons by young men and boys. The major exponents of *waka* have included Batile Alake (from late 1950s to 60s) and Salawa Abeni (mainly in the 1980s and 90s). Like *apala*, *waka* employs Yoruba instruments such as *sekere, akuba*, and *agidigbo*.

*Sakara*, though originated in the second decade of the second century, became extremely popular in the 1970s and 1980s mainly through the music of Yusuf Olatunji. In spite of its association with Muslim musicians, its Islam-themed lyrics, *sakara* is also neo-traditional in conception both in the use of traditional musical instruments and in the employment of traditional vocal practices. For example, it is dominated by a call and response format featuring a male solo and a male chorus, all singing to the accompaniment of *aha* (calabash drum) and *goje* (one-string bowed lute). Its sparse instrumentation matches its contemplative, solemn and stately character, as well as its focus on philosophical lyrics which often affirm the power of Olodumare (Almighty God) as the controller of human destiny as illustrated in his song *Oba Oluwa Loni Dede* (Our Life is in God's Hands).

## Yoruba Popular Music and Politics

Mark Mattern's essay titled "Theorizing Political Action in Popular Music" (2006) provides interesting perspectives on how music responds to social and political issues. He identifies three forms of political actions in music, namely confrontational political action, deliberative form of political action and pragmatic political action. Confrontational political action is radically oppositional and propelled by a "perception of incompatible interests' between different ideological groups. Zimbabwe's pre-colonial musical genre, *chimurenga* and Fela Anikulapo's post colonial *afro-beat* readily come to mind here.[6] Musical activity that preaches a deliberative or dialogical approach, on the other hand, is propelled by a dialogical objective towards reconciliation. Pragmatic political action is illustrated in the use of musical performances to achieve a common objective by a group of people who share the same interests (Mattern, 2006: 374). Yoruba highlife music, which I discussed earlier, rarely directly addresses political issues in the ways analyzed by Mattern. As I have explained elsewhere, however (Omojola, 2009: 260), the music of Yoruba highlife musicians, like those of their ilk from other parts of the country, though generally apolitical, conformed to the desire of the Nigerian political elite of the colonial era to achieve national unity in a country populated by various ethnic groups and nationalities. In an album titled *Wazobia*, for example, Roy Chicago, a popular highlife musician of the 1960s, introduced the term *wazobia* to articulate a vision of a united Nigeria. Chicago formed the word *Wazobia* from syllables derived from each of the three main Nigerian languages as follows: *wa* (from Yoruba), *zo* (from Hausa) and *bia* (from Igbo). Each of these three words translates as 'come' in English. *Wazobia* thus symbolically proposes a form of unity amongst Nigerian ethnic groups. Chicago's unifying concept of *wazobia* typifies the political orientation of most Nigerian highlife musicians towards promoting a sense of unity and national consciousness, an orientation considered an appropriate response to the divide and rule policy of the British colonial regime.

The most politically directed of all Yoruba popular music genres, however, was Fela Anikulapo-Kuti's afro-beat. Although Fela Anikulapo-Kuti had started leading an ensemble as far back as the early 1960s while a student in England, it was not until after his visit to the United States in 1969 that his music evolved into a strong anti-establishment political expression. Born in 1938, Anikulapo-Kuti embraced the radical ideology of his mother, a political activist with strong ties to Kwame Nkrumah, Ghana's first president. Anikulapo-Kuti also belonged to a musical family. His father and mother were among the pioneering composers and performers of Yoruba church music during the colonial era. In 1958, Anikulapo-Kuti went to Eng-

land to study music, returning to Nigeria in 1963, and working briefly with a government radio station in Lagos before going into full
professional career in music. Like his mother, he embraced the pan
African political philosophy of Nkrumah and other leading African
nationalists of the colonial era. Anikulapo-Kuti believed that most
of the problems that African countries faced in the postcolonial era
could be directly linked to European colonization of the continent.
He advocated a revival of what he regarded as authentic African
traditions as practiced, drew connections between the struggles of
the Black peoples in the Diaspora and the dilemma of the African
postcolonial era, and blamed Africa's leadership crisis for the per-
sistence of that dilemma.

 The political orientation of Anikulapo-Kuti's music thus contrasts
very sharply to the pro-establishment orientation of juju music.
Furthermore, this contrast illustrates the ways in which musicians
respond differently to the same social and political phenomenon
and how stylistic choices made by musicians may be linked to a
specific political ideology. The reliance on performance and stylistic
elements derived from traditional Yoruba ceremonial music, notably
*oriki* and indigenous Yoruba drumming by juju musicians speaks
to the predominant conception of their music as praise music. Juju
musicians like Ebenezer Obey, Sunny Ade and Shina Peters are
renowned for the use of these two performance elements to praise
their patrons for handsome monetary compensation. The conception of juju music as a song of political and social praise is not unrelated to the historical circumstances within which the music grew
in the 1970s and 80s, a time now often referred to as the oil boom
era when Nigeria made significant amount of money from its vast
oil resources. The time witnessed the rise of corrupt politicians and
businessmen and women as well as government contractors who
provided cash rewards to juju musicians for singing their praise
and for providing the social contexts for the display of their wealth
and influence in the society. But while juju musicians responded
patronizingly to the social dynamics and politics of the oil boom
era, Anikulapo-Kuti's afro-beat was carved as a critique of the same
social phenomenon. In songs like "Zombie," "Mister Follow Follow"
and "VIP: Vagabonds in Power," to name just a few, he condemned

inept leadership, official corruption and mismanagement of resources. In his "ITT" (International Thief Thief), he condemned the activities of multinational institutions who Fela believed colluded with Nigerian corrupt leaders to exploit the nation's resources to their own advantage and with total disregard for the masses. Although he attributed some of the woes of Africa to the destabilizing effects of colonialism and slavery, he ascribed much of Nigeria's economic and social problems to the lack of creative leadership on the part of Nigeria's leaders. While songs like "Zombie" and "Mr Follow Follow" constitute a direct attack on the Nigerian military class, they must also be seen as a metaphorical disparagement of Nigerian leaders for being perpetually subservient to European political leadership. Anikulapo-Kuti's music is grounded in a form of political activism that goes beyond the confines of musical performance. For example, he attempted to contest the presidential elections in 1979. His activities at the 'shrine,' as Fela named the night club that hosted his regular performance, and his self-styled Kalakuta Republic, his commune, musical studio and abode, where he lived with members of his band as well as his wives who doubled as dancers and singers, were guided by a libertarian political philosophy that perpetually undermined the authority of the Nigerian government. The alleged predilection of Fela and members of his band for Indian hemp smoking was used by the Nigerian police as an excuse to invade the place and effect Fela's arrest on many occasions. *Kalakuta Republic* was in a sense a dissident "state" within the Nigerian state

However, in forging a musical aesthetics suited to conveying his radical political ideology, Anikulapo-Kuti integrates Yoruba musical elements like call and response mode of singing, folklore, dance and drum language with African-American elements of jazz, soul, and a modal melodic quality that simultaneously references Yoruba vocal music and jazz. The sole pioneer of afro-beat, Anikulapo-Kuti also integrated highlife, which he had played while working with Victor Olaiya prior to going to England, into his music. Anikulapo-Kuti's music, in spite of the multiple sources of his musical material, does not however amount to a patchy form. Rather, what we see in his music is an organic synthesis in which these various elements assume their roles uniquely within a vibrant afro-beat style.

As Olaniyan has observed in his extensive discussion of Anikulapo-Kuti's music, Anikulapo-Kuti rejects the Yoruba oriki mode, which constitutes a major stylistic tool for the work of Yoruba juju musicians like Ebenezer Obey and Sunny Ade, as I mentioned earlier. This he substituted with songs of abuse (*yabis*) directed against Nigerian leaders (Olaniyan, 2004: 144). In traditional Yoruba contexts, such songs function to admonish misbehaving kings and chiefs as well as individual members of the society who cross lines of decent social relations. Such songs are the mainstay of Anikulapo-Kuti's politically charged music that landed him in trouble on many occasions, spending weeks, months and even years in Nigerian jails.

The music of Lagbaja, a relatively recent Yoruba musician who always wears a mask whenever he performs, also fits squarely into a discussion of music as a form of political narrative.[7] Lagbaja's music navigates a middle-ground terrain between the radical politics of Anikulapo-Kuti's music and the nationalist orientation of highlife, but is definitely devoid of the conservative and pro-establishment orientation of juju. It is interesting to note that, although his music does not wholly subscribe to the political philosophy inherent in any of these musical genres, it draws on musical elements from all three. The folk element of juju and fuji, the cyclic harmonic style of highlife, the singing style and afro-beat orientation of Anikulapo-Kuti's music: all these elements are to be found in ample proportions in Lagbaja's music. One or more of these elements often feature more strongly in a particular song. His "Nothing for You," for example, maintains a strong affinity with highlife in its harmonic style and romantic theme, recounting a romantic negotiation between a young lady and an insistent "sugar daddy," who seeks a relationship with her; while his "Skentele Skontolo" provides a witty gender discourse expressed in traditional folk songs. Lagbaja's "Suuru Lere" is more eclectic in style, drawing on elements of highlife, afro-beat, Yoruba folklore, and American funk. As I have explained in another study (Omojola 2009), the song focuses on a broad range of political issues, including electoral malpractice and political instability. In the song, Lagbaja enjoins all Nigerians to work together to overcome all these problems. It is noteworthy that Lagbaja's music also relies heavily on the use of traditional instruments, notably *gangan, akuba* and other percussion instruments like *sekere* and *agogo*. These are often combined with Western instruments like guitars, saxophone and the keyboard.

**Culture, Message, Music: "Mister Follow Follow"**

Fela Anikulapo-Kuti's "Mister Follow Follow" is an interesting example of the manner in which the musician integrates social, cultural and political contexts within his music. The main theme of the song is the culture of uncritical followership or uncritical obedience to the commands and directions of authority figures. Reverence of elders and authority is a cultural fact in Africa and especially in the Yoruba sub-region that was home to the musician. However, Anikulapo-Kuti was not about to accept the attitude of unquestioning obeisance to established patterns, as he felt this could never lead to progress in any society.

The immediate context for "Mister Follow Follow" is provided by the Nigerian military institution and especially the case of soldiers and policemen who, by the very nature of their job and training, mandatorily follow instructions given by their superior officers. Anikulapo-Kuti questions such a tradition because, according to him, following instructions blindly cannot but lead to fatal errors especially when the original instruction is based on a faulty premise and is not motivated by noble considerations. Anikulapo-Kuti's relationship with the Nigerian military class makes this immediate context more appreciable. Indeed, his running battles with Nigerian military authorities provide the background for understanding the meaning many of his songs. It should be remembered that his house was raided on many occasions by soldiers and policemen acting on orders "from above."

"Mister Follow Follow," like "Zombie," is significant in a profound way because it also adumbrates the hierarchical structure of the military as a way of drawing attention to the unequal relationship between the Nigerian political class and the former colonial masters. The music articulates Anikulapo-Kuti's strong belief that African leaders have been perpetually subservient to their old colonial masters. In "Mister Follow Follow" (see the appendix for a transcription of the lyrics), Anikulapo-Kuti urges his listeners to open their "eyes, mouth, sense and ears" so as to avoid falling into a pit of "rats, roaches, termites, and darkness."

This thematic rally against the culture of uncritical followership is carefully amplified by a systematic musicality that is characteristic of Anikulapo-Kuti's corpus. There are four identifiable sections in "Mister Follow Follow" as shown in Figure 1.

The first section is the longest, lasting for over seven minutes of the song's total duration of about 13 minutes. The first section is entirely instrumental as is often the case in Fela's songs. The section illustrates some familiar elements of Anikulapo-Kuti's music. These include a gradual build-up of instrumental density that begins with the ostinato patterns of rhythm guitars, drums and rattles, and those of the bass and brass instruments. With the groove well established, the music continues with series of improvisation-like phrases and strophes of straightforward melodies.

The instrumental section continues for about seven minutes before voices come in. The relatively slow tempo of "Mister Follow Follow" matches the gentle counseling tone of the song, and provides a contrast to the agitated character of "Zombie," a song which explores the same theme and attacks the culture of uncritical followership in a more aggressive tone.

*Fig. 1: Fela Anikulapo-Kuti's "Mister Follow Follow": Outline of Form*

| Time Indicator | Section | Features | Formal Design |
|---|---|---|---|
| 00-7:20 | Extended instrumental opening | Gradual build up of density; groove layout; melodic strophes and improvisations | A |
| 7:20-10:52 | Solo voice and chorus on "Mr Follow Follow" | Basic groove continues with a reduced instrumental activity; entry of voices | B |
| 10:53-12:20 | Return of opening instrumental section | Ostinato patterns; melodic strophes and improvisations | A (abridged) |
| 12:21-12:57 | Extended closing cadential device | Reduction of instrumental density | Coda |

Framed by instrumental sections, the vocal section of "Mister Follow Follow" lasts for just about three and a half minutes. How should one, considering the short duration of the vocal section, interpret the relatively long opening instrumental section? Should we hear it as a mere introduction or as an integral part of the piece?

There is no direct evidence from Anikulapo-Kuti to suggest that the instrumental sections of his music are conceived as some kind of program following Western models of the Romantic era. I would however like to suggest that the instrumental sections, which account for over seventy percent of the piece, provide the necessary musical context for contemplating the main message of the piece and that the entire music can be seen as an integration of musical cultures.

There is a sense in which the opening instrumental section entices and enchants, creating in the listener the disposition and the urge to listen to, and even identify with the central message of the music as contained in the vocal section. The captivating power of the instrumental sections resides in its leisurely pace, its engaging groove (comprising of layers of ostinato patterns, each of which is made distinct melodically and through the use of different instruments), the dialogical relationship between the different components of the orchestration, and the entrancing power of Anikulapo-Kuti's improvisation. All these seem to prepare and condition the listener towards identifying with the message contained in the ensuing vocal section. The vocal section and the instrumental sections thus work together to articulate the central message of the song.

Following the end of the relatively short vocal section, Anikulapo-Kuti brings back the opening instrumental section, albeit in an abridged form, lasting from 10:53-12:20, but retaining the main themes and the improvisatory-like material of the opening section. The remaining section of the piece functions like a coda in which Anikulapo-Kuti decreases the momentum and the energy of the piece through a reduction in the density of musical material, and by slowing down the tempo in the very final moments.

The complementary relationship between the purely instrumental sections and the section in which voices are heard shows that Anikulapo-Kuti paid close attention to the musical and non-musical themes of his songs. The oratorical effectiveness of his politically-directed tirade against the culture of uncritical followership is hinged on his superlative musical craftsmanship.

## Conclusions

Emerging from my discussion is the fact that Yoruba popular music derives from multiple ethnographic contexts, and that the musical material used in its various genres emanates from multiple cultural sources. By singing in a variety of languages, including English, Yoruba and the Nigerian pidgin English; by disseminating their music electronically and through recordings; and by touring different parts of the world, performing to non-Yoruba listeners; it is clear that Yoruba popular musicians conceive of their music to be enjoyed well beyond the confines of the Yoruba society. This performance perspective inevitably invests their works with some degree of musical autonomy. This autonomy is defined by the capacity of modern Yoruba popular music genres, often products of both local and global resources, to communicate even in situations in which not all their cultural and historical ramifications are immediately available or accessible to the listeners.

However, given the demonstrable capability of Yoruba popular music to penetrate boundaries, the continual projection of identifiable elements of the Yoruba identity is also a definitive hallmark of its praxis. Yoruba musicians tend to reconfigure foreign elements according to their own perception of their immediate communities and of the nature of the relationship between such communities and the outside world. The political significance of such a process of musical reconfiguration must be seen first, in terms of how Yoruba popular music challenges assumptions about the overbearing hegemony of globalization; and second, in how the music attempts to bridge cultural gaps and promote national consciousness by facilitating harmonious relationship amongst various ethnic groups in Nigeria.

Above all, Yoruba popular music speaks to different social and political developments and issues as obtained in the colonial and postcolonial periods. The careers of Yoruba musicians constitute a "lived experience" that is shaped by and is insightful of critical developments in Nigeria's political history. The history of Yoruba popular music was shaped in response to vagaries of the political history of Nigeria itself. The engagement between these three temporalities (career spans of individual musicians, the history of Yoruba popular music and the political history of Nigeria itself) draws attention to the multi-dimensional factors at work in the development of musical styles, and in the shaping of specific musical works. The intersection of these temporalities also provides insights into the enduring relationship between specific musical practices and general social and cultural values, an issue at the heart of ethno-musicological investigation.

**Appendix**
**"Mister Follow Follow" (From "Zombie" by Fela Anikulapo-Kuti and the *Africa 70*, 1976)**

Solo: Mister follow follow
Chorus: Follow follow o follow follow follow follow
Solo: Mister follow follow
Chorus: Follow follow o follow follow follow follow
Solo: Some de follow follow dem close dem eye
Chorus: Dem close eye pin pin pin
Solo: Some de follow follow dem close dem mouth
Chorus: Dem close mouth pan pan pan
Solo: Some de follow follow dem close dem ear
Chorus: Dem close ear gboin gboin gboin
Solo: Some de follow follow dem close dem sense
Chorus: Dem close sense gbirin gbirin
Solo: Some de follow follow dem close dem eye
Chorus: Dem close eye pin pin pin
Solo: Some de follow follow dem close dem mouth
Chorus: Dem close mouth pan pan pan
Solo: Some de follow follow dem close dem ear
Chorus: Dem close ear gboin gboin gboin
Solo: Some de follow follow dem close dem sense
Chorus: Dem close sense gbirin gbirin

Solo: I say dem close sense, say dem close sense
Solo: If u de follow follow, make you open eye, open mouth, open sense,
Solo: If you de follow follow, make you open sense, open ear, open mouth
Solo: Na da time, na da time you no go fall]2ce
Solo: If you de follow follow dem wish

Chorus: Na inside cupboard you go quench
Solo: If you de follow follow dem wish
Chorus: Na inside cupboard you go quench
Solo: Cockroach de, rat de, ikan de, darkness de
Chorus: Na inside cupboard you go quench
Solo: My brother make you no follow book o
Solo: Look common go your way
Chorus: Follow follow
Solo: If you de follow follow
Chorus: Follow follow
Solo: Make you open eye
Chorus: Follow follow
Solo: If you de follow follow
Chorus: Follow follow
Solo: Make you open sense
Chorus: Follow follow
Solo: If you de follow follow
Chorus: Follow follow
Solo: Make you open eye
Chorus: Follow follow
Solo: If you de follow follow
Chorus: Follow follow
Solo: Make you open sense
Solo: My brother make you no follow book o
Solo: Look common use your sense
Chorus: Follow follow
Solo: If you de follow follow
Chorus: Follow follow
Solo: Make you open eye
Solo: If you de follow follow
Chorus: Follow follow
Solo: Make you open mouth
Chorus: Follow follow
Solo: Make you open eye
Chorus: Follow follow
Solo: Make you open sense
Chorus: Follow follow

**Notes**

[1] Highlife, a transnational urban popular music, originated in Ghana. Emmanuel T. Mensah, Ghanaian highlife's most important musician, toured a number of West African cities in the 1950s and helped to popularize the music in countries like Nigeria, Sierra Leone and Gambia. It must be noted however that highlife music was already being performed in Nigeria by musicians like Bobby Benson and Victor Olaiya prior to Mensah's tour.

[2] The polarizing status of highlife has however waned significantly in the course of history. Seen now generally as the music of yesteryears, highlife music today evokes the nostalgia of independent struggles and the euphoria that greeted national independence in 1960. The relevance of highlife music in contemporary times however goes beyond its nostalgic connotations. Highlife musical style has, for example, become popular amongst Nigerian Christian gospel artists who employ the harmonic language and the singing style of the music to convey Christian themes both within the context of worship during church service as well as in recorded music on CDs.

[3] See also Waterman (1990), Veal (1995 and 2000), Turino (2000), Agawu (2003) and Muller (2004).

[4] Palm wine is a sweet alcoholic beverage found in tropical West Africa, and is generally associated with working class consumption, as a local alternative to imported wine, hence "palm wine music."

[5] The Yoruba *agidigbo* employs a much smaller number of pitches, and is much bigger than the Shona *mbira*. It often functions like a bass instrument producing melodic patterns that are comparable to those of the bass guitar in a modern band.

[6] Developed by Fela Anikulapo in the late 1970s and noted for its radical political ideology, afro-beat is defined by a musical style that reworks highlife, jazz and traditional Yoruba musical elements.

[7] For more detailed studies on Lagbaja's music, please see the following: Omojola, Bode. 2009. "Igbadun in Yoruba Performance: History, Social Discourse and Indigenous Aesthetics in the Music of Lagbaja."*Journal of Popular Music Studies* 21 (2):170-191; and Waterman, Christopher. 2002. "Big Man, Black President, Masked One: Models of the Celebrity Self in Yoruba Popular Music in Nigeria," in Mai Palmberg and Annemette Kirkegaard (eds.) *Playing With Identities in Contemporary Music in Africa*. Uppsala: Nordiska Afrikainstitutet: 19-34.

**Selected Discography**
Ade, Sunny
1982. *Ariya Special*
1984. *Togetherness/Kajose* SALPS 42

Anikulapo-Kuti, Fela
1975. *Zombie* and *Mister Follow Follow*. CRLP 511
1979a. *VIP: Vagabonds in Power.*
1979. *ITT: International Thief Thief.* K203554

Lagbaja.
2001. "Suru Lere," in *We Before Me*. BOOOO5K129 Indigedisc,
2001. "Nothing for You," in *We Before Me*. BOOOO5K129 Indigedisc,
2005. "Skentele Skontole," in Africano: The Mother of Groove. MM0507.

Olaiya, Victor.
N.d. *Leading Gentleman*. Vols. I & II.; (Audio CD). Premier Music, Lagos, Nigeria

Dairo, Isaac Kehinde.
1962. *Elele Ture*. NWA 5079
1965. *Ekun Rere Mo Wa*. (Second release: in Salome OHRLP 44 CD, 1992.)

Olatunji, Yusuf
*Oba Oluwa Loni Dede*

**References**

Agawu, Kofi. 2003. *Representing African Music: Postcolonial Notes, Queries, Positions*. New York and London: Routledge.

Alaja-Browne, Afolabi. 1989. "A Diachronic Study of Change in Juju Music." *Popular Music* 8 (3): 231-242.

Collins, John. 1976. "Ghanaian Highlife." *African Arts* 10 (1): 62-72.

Euba, Akin. 1989. *Essays on Music in Africa 2: Intercultural Perspectives* Lagos and Bayreuth: Elekoto and Iwalewa-Haus.

Mattern, Mark. 2006. "Cajun Music, Cultural Revival: Theorizing Political Action in Popular Music." In *Ethnomusicology: A Contemporary Reader*, edited by Jennifer C. Post, 371-381. New York and London: Routledge (Taylor and Francis Group).

Muller, Carol A. 2004. *South African Music: A Century of Traditions in Transformations*. Santa Barbara, California: ABC CLIO

Olaniyan, Tejumola. 2004. *Arrest the Music!: Fela and His Rebel Art and Politics*. Indianapolis: Indiana University Press.

Omojola, Bode. 2009. "Politics, Identity, and Nostalgia in Nigerian Music: A Study of Victor Olaiya's Highlife" *Ethnomusicology* 53 (2): 249-276.

Omojola, Bode.. 2009. "Igbadun in Yoruba Performance: History, Social Discourse and Indigenous Aesthetics in the Music of Lagbaja." *Journal of Popular Music Studies* 21 (2): 170-191.

Turino, Thomas. 2000. *Nationalists, Cosmopolitans, and Popular Music in Zimbabwe* Chicago and London: The University of Chicago Press.

Veal, Michael. 1995. "Jazz Music Influences on the Music of Fela." *Glendora Review*, vol.1:8-13.

Veal, Michael. 1995. 2000. *Fela: Life and Times of an African Musical Icon*. Philadelphia: Temple University Press.

Waterman, Christophe. 1990. *Juju: A Social History and Ethnography of an African Popular Music*. Chicago and London: The University of Chicago Press.

Waterman, Christophe. 2002. "Big Man, Black President, Masked One: Models of the Celebrity Self in Yoruba Popular Music in Nigeria." In *Playing with Identities in Contemporary Music in Africa*, edited by Mai Palmberg and Annemette Kirkegaard, 19-34. Uppsala: Nordiska Afrikainstitutet

Wikipedia. "Tunde King." http://en.wikipedia.org/wiki/Tunde_King. Accessed May 28, 2010.

# Finding One's Feet in Modernity: Young Women and the Global Media in Dar es Salaam and Harare
## - Hilde Arntsen and Ylva Ekström

The mediascapes in many African countries have changed dramatically in the last decades, as they have in other parts of the world.[1] In popular discourse, the global media, and in particular, mediated popular culture, are often accused of being threats to so-called 'genuine' and 'traditional' African cultures and identities. It is sometimes argued that mediated popular culture is influencing young people, especially young women, in negative ways. Youth themselves, on the other hand, often regard the popular culture media as a 'window to the world', and they may be keen on using select parts of the global media products to negotiate their own identities as young and modern people in cultures in transition. The tension between such opposing perspectives is by no means new. In Tanzania and Zimbabwe, for instance, the authorities have attempted to use the media to forge particular forms of desired national identities at the expense of international influence, and introduced strict legislative measures to maintain tight control of the media scene. Despite this, certain aspects of national media cultures are influenced by global media formats and content. In a world increasingly marked by the concurrent processes of globalisation, increased differences between rich and poor, rising nationalism and infringements on the rights of individuals, the use of global media texts raise interesting questions in this terrain of conflicting developments.

Based on our research among young women in Dar es Salaam and Harare in the late 1990s and early 21st century, we will here argue that mediated popular culture may constitute significant factors in the lives of these young women despite parents' or authorities' efforts to restrict their access to particular media products which are not considered to be suitable to them. The young women who read, watch or listen to the products of contemporary global media cultures may use these encounters as sources of identity negotiation, and ways of navigating into adulthood. That does not mean, however, that the youth embrace the media content's worldview wholeheartedly. As we will show here, the global media offer resources for further negotiation as well as elements that the youth dismiss as irrelevant.

## Challenges to Globalisation

We will not speculate on the logic(s) that are behind the processes of globalisation. However, regardless of whether one may understand globalisation as a single driving force, as does Immanuel Wallerstein (1990) in his world systems theory, or ascribing to the more multifaceted approaches of Anthony Giddens (1990) or Roland Robertson (1992), we note that processes of globalisation are contested and unevenly experienced around the world. There are several weak points in these grand theories of globalisation, however. First and foremost, there is a definite Western dominance in terms of the empirical examples with which many authors of globalisation argue their case. Second, there is a relatively weak emphasis on culture or cultural products in their sweeping arguments about globalisation processes that impact on both the global marketplace and on local societies. Taking a more empirical approach, Herman and McChesney in the book, *The Global Media: the New Missionaries of Global Capitalism* (1997), chronicled the global actors in the media markets, and argued for their wide-reaching impacts. We are in no doubt that these global media actors have possibilities of impact across the globe, and even in Africa, as several African commentaries argue. On the other hand, we cannot subscribe to the cultural or media imperialism thesis that was prominent in international media research in the 1970s, and which continues to find advocates even in contemporary public debates. The understanding behind media imperialism was that there was considerable ideological impact emanating from the media products, and that the seemingly innocent commercial entertainment was linked to political forces seeking global impact (see e.g. Schiller 1969, Boyd-Barrett 1977).

It follows from here that we are of the opinion that the grand theories of globalisation will benefit from being supplemented with approaches that are not at the systemic level, but rather at the level of individuals. This level is often missing in the debate on the impact on the global media in Africa. We will thus relate our analyses of young urban women's engagement with the media to the ongoing theoretical debates regarding globalisation and modernity. Rather than adopting the position that all foreign media content is bad and that such material have detrimental influences on Tanzania and Zimbabwe, as is a position adopted by some critics and scholars when dealing with the influence of particularly Western media in African countries (see e.g. Tomaselli (2009) for a discussion about this, and Mkandawire (1998) for an example of such arguments), we will approach the media as content with which the youth engage in a variety of ways. We will look into how the flow of symbolic forms and images that constitute the changing mediascapes may provide the young women with imaginative resources through which they may be able to negotiate their own positions in the world and in the societies in which they live. This is consistent with the Cultural Studies tradition within media studies, in which the individual media user or audience member is regarded as competent to make informed readings of the media in question, and that the cultural and ideological representations inherent in the media content offer resources that the said individuals use creatively. Moreover, we will argue that with studies based in the concurrent analysis of multiple elements such as media structures, media content and media audiences, one may be able to arrive at a more multi-faceted understanding of the processes at play, in line with the approaches of Ulf Hannerz (1990). To be able to grapple with the complexities and the fluidities in this situation, Arjun Appadurai's notion of mediascape is a term that will guide our analyses here. Mediascapes, Appadurai argues, may encompass the large and complex repertoires of images and narratives circulating through the media, in which the "world of commodities and the world of news and politics are profoundly mixed" (1995:35). Viewed in this way, investigating global media is no longer merely a case of investigating entertainment commodities in the global market, but rather one way of understanding cultural complexities in actual societies.

## Questions in Media Anthropology

Within media studies, there has recently been a shift in focus from the study of media audiences to the study of media cultures, through media ethnographic work (see e.g. Alasuutari 1999, Ang 1996, Gray 2003). Parallel to this, the field of media anthropology has risen within anthropology (see e.g. Askew & Wilk (eds.) 2002, Ginsburg *et al.* 2002, Abu-Lughod 1999, 2005, Fuglesang 1994, Kottak 1990, Lange 2002). In these two closely related research traditions, recent developments have not stopped short of investigations into the reception of certain media texts by particular audiences (Liebes & Katz 1990, Arntsen 1993), but moved to "get a grasp of our contemporary 'media culture', particularly as it can be seen in the role of the media in everyday life, both as a topic and as an activity structured by and structuring the discourses within which it is discussed" (Alasuutari 1999:6). Studies of popular culture in Africa show that this is indeed a vibrant field with several and often conflicting research traditions (see e.g. Barber (ed.) 1997, Zilberg 1995, Nyamnjoh and Page 2002, Nyamnjoh 2008). Even the relatively recent tradition of youth culture research (see e.g. Vered & Wulff 1995, Ekström 2010) contributes to this field.

Citizens of contemporary media-saturated societies, even those who do not read the newspapers, listen to the radio or watch television, can hardly avoid hearing about the latest news thanks to the everyday media discourse, as media scholar Ien Ang (1996) exemplifies. In the urban areas of contemporary Tanzania and Zimbabwe, however, people's lives are structured by different and fundamentally uneven mediascapes. We must remember that not everyone, even in the cities of Dar es Salaam and Harare, have direct access to the whole ensemble of media and information technologies that are often taken for granted by theoreticians and publics in the West. Uncritically applying theories and concepts developed in the West to other areas of the globe with a number of structural differences may thus not be such a fruitful exercise (Tomaselli and Shepperson 2000). Despite this, the globally distributed popular culture products are there to be consumed by great numbers of people also in these cities. It can be argued that this is the case not only for those privileged few that have direct access to all the modern communication technologies. Personal communication from one individual to another may ensure that people keep themselves abreast of key events taking place, even if they are not be able to watch the news on television, listen to news bulletins on the radio and talk-back radio programmes or watch the latest entertainment programme on television.

**Changing Mediascapes**
According to Göran Hydén and Michael Leslie in *Media and Democracy in Africa*, the rapid growth of independent media became a reality in most of Sub-Saharan Africa in the 1990s. Despite the fact that economic decline and general decreasing standard of living occurred at the same time as the media expansion, they comment "there has been an unmet demand for information and entertainment in these countries" (Hydén & Leslie 2002:11). Tanzania and Zimbabwe have also been part of this continent-wide development, but there are important differences in the development of media in the two countries due to significantly divergent political situations in the two particular contexts.

In Tanzania, as a consequence of the so-called *mageuzi* process,[2] increased development towards democratic and free media became an important dimension in the 1990s (Brennan & Burton 2007). The new constitution in 1992 that paved the way for a multiparty system also became the starting point for an increasingly diversified mediascape compared to the limited number of media titles that were the result of the restrictive cultural politics during the previous *ujamaa* era - the post-independence socialist regime headed by President Julius Nyerere.[3] While the media in the years between the early 1960s and the mid-1980s were mainly supposed to disseminate party propaganda, and to serve as a tool for development of the nation and for education of the people, the media boom that took place during the last decade of the 20th century undoubtedly opened the door for more democratic structures. The transformation has given the media more autonomy in the Tanzanian society, and as media scholar Jill Johannessen (2006) argues, "the increase in media channels allows for the articulation of problems and the dissemination of knowledge, along with the presentation of different priorities and views than those of the state-owned media" (Ibid:99). However, fifteen years after the liberalisation of the media "steps towards a free press are still gradual," Lawrence Kilimwiko (2007:78) argues, pointing to the concentration of ownership and lack of journalist professionalism, and to continuous self-regulation and state interference. The state-run *Radio Tanzania* that had enjoyed the broadcasting monopoly for more than twenty years, saw the competition from a handful of commercial television stations and around twenty private radio stations at the turn of the century.[4] Although the content initially consisted primarily of re-broadcasts of foreign material, radio has eventually provided the already vibrant music scene of Dar es Salaam with a new arena from which to reach its audiences (Perullo 2007, Ekström 2010), and television paved the way for a new era of 'traditional' local drama production (Lange 2002, Johannessen 2006). Furthermore, the mushrooming of printed publications has turned the Dar es Salaam-centred newspaper market into one of the fastest growing media markets on the continent (Hydén & Leslie 2002).

In Zimbabwe, on the other hand, the authoritarian media structure that existed at Independence in 1980 continued largely unchanged, despite certain efforts to democratise it (Rønning & Kupe 2000, Moyo 2004). The main pro-government newspapers, the news agency Ziana and the broadcasting monopoly Zimbabwe Broadcasting Corporation were considered to be key actors in building the new nation (Skare Orgeret 1998) and in curbing political criticism. Political opposition has been clamped down hard upon ever since independence, and in particular through the *Gukurahundi* massacres of political opponents to the ruling party in the Matabeleland province in the early 1980s. Despite this, the early 1990s saw traits of budding media pluralism. New independent newspaper titles were established, and a commercial broadcaster, Joy TV, was allowed to broadcast via the ZBC frequencies for a short while in the late 1990s before suddenly being forced off the air. Draconian media legislation introduced throughout the 1990s which stifled press and media freedom, the forced shutting down of independent newspapers, and harassment of editors and practicing journalists who asked politically inappropriate questions, all contributed to the once budding media freedom turning sour (see e.g. Zaffiro 2002, Rønning 2003, Ndlela 2003, Moyo 2006). Commercial media waged a precarious existence, with the number of titles being drastically reduced. Well-to-do subscribers in the urban areas were to some extent able to circumscribe some of these restrictions: It was possible to subscribe to South African satellite television services M-Net. The Zimbabwean mediascape in the late 1990s was thus characterised by hard official restrictions and creative individual solutions to get access to the media. The onset of the Zimbabwean crisis around the turn of the millennium, with withdrawal of foreign investment, mismanagement of public funds, hyperinflation, record-high unemployment figures, escalating HIV/Aids crisis, political unrest and human rights abuses further characterise the Zimbabwean situation at the time when the interviews reported here were conducted.

## Some Points on Methodology

The two case studies which form the empirical basis for our discussion here, investigate the changing mediascapes in two African metropolitan cities around the turn of the millennium. The Dar es Salaam case is based on studies of the media culture and youth in Dar es Salaam at several occasions between 1998 and 2005. Specifically, it draws on ethnographic work carried out in a group of upper secondary school students in a girls' school in Dar es Salaam during two phases in 2002 and 2003.[5] The young women originate from different places in Tanzania, with various backgrounds in terms of ethnicity, class and religion. They came to attend the secondary school in Dar es Salaam, where they studied and lived in a girls' hostel for two years. Similarly, the material from Harare is based on fieldwork at various times throughout the 1990s, and on interviews with students from two senior high schools in Harare in 1997 and 1998.[6] The interviews concerned the students and their everyday lives, their media use, their media preferences and their thoughts about coming of age in a time of transition and conflict.

The two studies were not designed to be comparable, but there are a number of significant similarities between them; the focus on the role that mediated popular culture play in the lives of youth in the city, the attempts to understand wider processes of globalisation through local appropriation, and the negotiation of gendered identities at the intersection of modern lifestyles and traditional and moral values. Both apply a selection of qualitative methodologies such as ethnographic approaches to the study of individuals and analysis of specific media texts. In this article we have chosen to focus on one particular young woman from each of the cities, in order to shed light on what role their engagement with media in general and with television and soap operas in particular, play in their negotiation of gender, relationships, and lifestyles. In order to secure their anonymity, the names of the schools and those of the students remain undisclosed, and key biographical characteristics have been changed.

## Linda in Dar es Salaam

One of the young women in the Dar es Salaam case, let us call her Linda, is from Moshi, a town in the northeast of Tanzania, towards the border to Kenya and close to Mount Kilimanjaro. She has grown up in a middle class neighbourhood with her mother and her step-father, her grandmother, an older sister and her little daughter, and two younger brothers (the sons of her step-father). Her father has passed away. She is one of the few girls at the hostel who does not spend the holidays studying or taking extra tutorials, but travels by bus to see her family as soon as she gets the opportunity.

Linda's family is a bit better-off than the average Tanzanian family. In their home in Moshi, they have a television and Linda loves to follow soap operas and watch films.[7] In her opinion, traditions and customs, ways of life and people's views of the world have changed particularly through the recent access to television. She compares the culture of contemporary Tanzania with the time when her mother was young, and argues that values and attitudes have changed as a result of the increased access to media images from the world. She also argues that there are differences between the urban and the rural areas of Tanzania. In an interview she explains her view:

> Linda: Especially the case of TV has made the young [people] in the cities to know early what's happening in the world. But it takes a long time for those young [people] in rural areas to know what's happening in the world. In Dar es Salaam, TV has changed much the lifestyles of young people. Because they see

how people from other countries do, the way they live, so they copy those lifestyles. They have changed the dressing styles of young people in Dar es Salaam. You can find a girl with a tight mini-skirt and people don't care about it. But this is not seen much in rural areas of Tanzania. Also the hair dressings of young people in Dar es Salaam has changed due to medias as when they copy when they see the young people in TVs, videos or magazines dressing their hair in different styles. (Dar es Salaam, 10 March 2002.)

Linda often wears trousers and a large T-shirt, sometimes a blouse, but rarely skirts – except for the compulsory light blue school uniform skirt she wears every day in school. She seldom plaits her hair, but rather oils it in order to get a straight-looking style. Compared to many of her friends, Linda thinks that she has a more 'traditional' African body, but she isn't very happy with it. Striving to become a *dada ya kisasa* (modern sister), she admires the 'international' body ideal promoted through music videos, soap operas, beauty contests and by Miss Tanzania.

When staying at the hostel during the school terms, Linda and her school friends have limited access to media. There is a television in the matron's house that they are only allowed to watch on certain occasions. Some of the girls have transistor radios that they listen to at a low volume at night. They follow the lives of the local and international celebrities, and read about the latest episodes of the soap operas on TV in the popular *magazeti ya udako* (gossip tabloids) that they can buy for the price of a soda (approx 100-150 Tanzanian shillings at the time of this study) on their way back from school. Some of them, Linda being one, pop into an internet café a couple of times every week to communicate with friends and relatives abroad. In the final school year, 2003, Linda has been given a mobile phone by her mother to be able to keep better in touch. Her uncle who lives in Dar es Salaam provides her with 'credits' (top up vouchers) every week, and although this puts her in a dependency position in relation to him, Linda feels more independent because of her mobile phone. The phone gives her a higher position in the hierarchy of the girls at the hostel, and the phone is sisterly shared among them to 'beep' friends and relatives, to receive calls, and to send text messages. She says she feels different and even more like a *dada ya kisasa* after she got her phone: "I feel so different because when I see somebody here with a cellphone I feel so happy that I am also one… And the first person to call was D [giggling] (Dar es Salaam, 4 April 2003).

We here see how both mediated symbolic material and the usage of communication technologies function as ingredients and status markers in the process of positioning oneself as a modern person in Dar es Salaam. The idea that (foreign) media influence fashions and lifestyles of especially young people is widely spread in Tanzanian popular discourse. One example is the *Bongo Flava* rap "Bongo Dar es Salaam," which was very popular in 2002 and 2003.[8] In the lyrics, the musician Professor Jay indicates that the soap opera *Isidingo* has influenced the people and places in the affluent areas of Dar es Salaam.

> No problem, anything the heart desires you'll get. Bongo Dar es Salaam is good time and success. Go to Bongo's great areas and be amazed, and pass by Slipway, Blue Palm or Mambo Club. If you aren't used to it, you might break your neck, things like in *Isidingo*, people with Nokia Ringo. You can't tell who's a gate-kid or who's a hooker. They all shine like they've been out there, my friend. […][9]

*Isidingo*, mentioned in these lyrics, is a popular South African soap opera that has been aired daily in South Africa since July 1998, and that has been re-broadcast on Tanzanian *ITV* since some time around 1999/2000.[10] The soap has gained great popularity in Tanzania, and it was mentioned by all the young women in the Dar es Salaam study as one of their favourite television programmes.[11] Several of them regarded it as much better than both the local productions (Swahili dramas) and series originating in the West. Indeed, most series broadcast on Tanzanian television are from the US, e.g. *Passions* and *Days of Our Lives*. But, contrary to what is often assumed to be the case in 'cultural imperialism' thinking or in popular debate about foreign influence, the influence from 'global media' in Tanzania does not necessarily come from the North (such as the US or Europe). The influence might just as well come from the South. Thus, to paraphrase Appadurai (1996), in Southern and Eastern Africa 'South Africanisation' might be a much more actual threat than the so-called 'Americanisation'. Indeed, the dominant position of South African media and communication technology on the continent has been pointed out by several media scholars (see e.g. Tomaselli 2009), and is one of the manners in which the debate on globalisation may become more nuanced.

Irrespective of whether the origin of the media is from the US or South Africa, the question of foreign influences is often imbued with a combination of fascination and fear. The rap by Professor Jay warns that "If you aren't used to it, you might break your neck" in the prosperous locations of the city, because you will be so amazed by all the things that are "like in *Isidingo*." In the rap, *Isidingo* stands for 'up-to-date' habits and manners, and 'modern' ways and lifestyles, and status symbols such as "Nokia Ringo" (mobile phones) connote *watu wa kisasa* (modern people). People of all walks of life look like they have "been out there," meaning that they look as if they have travelled to or lived in Europe, South Africa, Asia or the US.

When asked to write an essay about the role of the media in their everyday lives,[12] Linda wrote about the role that *Isidingo* plays in her life, and she shows that the influence goes beyond the issue of lifestyles and looks:

> The piece of media output that has been of certain significance in my life is a TV show called *Isidingo the Need* acted in South Africa. […] From this, I've learned that a black man or woman can be married to a white woman or man without any problem. People think that it's difficult, but through this TV show we've seen it's possible. […] Also in this show there's the way young ladies live, there are students [while] others are not students and they live in a friendly way. This makes me feel happy b'coz I dislike those who see that those who are not educated cannot be their friends. […] In this TV show also there are characters who are HIV positive. The ways they got HIV and their lives after being affected we see they are still friends with those who are not affected, and they get advices from others and they live in no difference with those who are not affected.[13]

As is the case with other soap operas, *Isidingo* presents a glorified version of reality. In this case it is an optimistic vision of how the post-apartheid South Africa could have become rather than of how things really are. *Isidingo* is just one of many media products dealing with issues of relationships between people of different sexes, races and classes in the Tanzanian mediascape, and it is not the only one that has HIV/AIDS as one of its topics.[14] There are, however, very few representations of sexual relations that these young women can relate to; the locally produced dramas have been very restrictive in representing sexual relationships, and the American soap operas are portraying relationships between people that are far removed from their everyday lives to be considered relevant. *Isidingo* thus re-presents a community of modern urban African people with which Linda and her friends can identify.

That Linda in her essay expresses a fascination that people living with HIV/AIDS "are still friends with those who are not affected" does not mean that she necessarily thinks that this is the way it really is in South Africa. Rather, the series feeds her imaginations with the idea that this could possibly be the case. Similarly, when she says "I've learned that a black man or woman can be married to a white woman or man without any problem," this does not mean that she is not aware of the fact that inter-racial marriages are uncommon. But, *Isidingo* contributes to her understanding that this could be possible, contrary to what she sees in most other media representations (and in her own reality) where black and white people are still represented as segregated. The perceptions she makes of relationships between people of different classes, ethnicities and sexes, of romantic love and of the soap's portrayal of people living with HIV/AIDS may well be romanticised and un-realistic. But they seem to serve as imaginary resources Linda can make use of when negotiating her own position in the urban Tanzanian reality.

Linda and her friends can be regarded as *watoto wa geti kali* in Swahili, meaning 'children behind a strict gate' (or 'gate-kid' as formulated in the rap lyrics above), in the sense that during their stay at the girls' hostel they are under strict orders to stay inside the hostel walls from 6 pm every evening until it is time to go to school in the morning. During the day they are only allowed to move between the hostel and the school, unless they ask for permission for other excursions at the hostel matron. Thus, they are in many ways cut off from the urban culture outside the walls of the school and the hostel. Despite these restrictions, they are inspired by the popular culture media in their construction of their own modern female identities; they copy hairstyles and outfits from the fashion pages of popular magazines, and when they get the chance to access the media, they select bits and pieces that can teach them about *wanawake na maendeleo* (women and development) in different parts of the world (see further discussion in Ekström 2010).

The portrait of Linda serves as an illustration of that for young women in modern urban Tanzania, particularly for those that live far away from their mothers and other older female relatives, the media may in many ways serve to guide them towards womanhood, the role that mothers, aunts and grandmothers used to play at a time when many girls went through 'traditional' initiation rites.

## Mary in Harare

At many levels, the situation was not much different when interviewing young women in a government secondary school in urban Harare some years earlier, in the late 1990s. The young women tell about a rather highly routinized and restricted everyday life, especially for those who are far away from their homes and have to be boarders on the school premises. During school terms, the school impose strict rules of conduct, regarding movement out of the school premises and regarding with whom the students are able to socialise. While the day scholars are free to leave the school once the day's instruction is over, the boarders are not allowed outside of the school gates, except on Sundays and even that only if it has been sanctioned by the parents. The media available to the students is restricted. Some students have small transistor radios with them in the school hostel, but batteries are scarce (there are no electrical sockets to plug in the radios), so even a radio in working order is hard to come by. The few radios around are shared with friends, and if played in the dorm, the 17 or so other people belonging to each dorm have no choice but to listen, too. (Each hostel is divided into several sleeping halls, dorms, where 18 –

20 students have their beds.) Most often, they tune in to Radio 3 which broadcast a mix of international popular music. Only a few prefer Radio 2 with its fare of Zimbabwean music. The hostel matron has placed her own small TV set in the hostel lounge area for the students to watch, and instructed the rules for its use: During the week, it can be turned on only after the schoolwork hours are over. During weekends, there are more possibilities for viewing, but the television can only get the ZBC television channel. If some students misbehave, however, it is not uncommon for the whole hostel to be losing their television privileges. The school subscribes to the pro-government daily newspaper, *The Herald*, but to none of the independent newspapers. The students who take computing have access to a computer at school, but without internet access. At the time of the study in Harare, not many of the young women had computer access elsewhere either.

The day scholars are also living in a tightly controlled environment, at home or with relatives close to the school, although they have a somewhat freer lifestyle than the boarders. During term time, schoolwork and household chores take up much of the weekdays. Radio listening thus becomes the favourite pastime during the week. On the weekends, however, television viewing and watching of often pirate-copied videos seem to be most popular. Some students may ccasionally visit to the movie houses, but that requires transportation and cash which is hard to come by. This can be solved by having boyfriends who can take them out, or by meeting their parentally approved friends at home. Even here in the urban area of Harare, few of the day scholars report regular access to any of Zimbabwe's independent newspapers.

Nineteen-year old "Mary," is a student in a government-run upper secondary school in Harare. When we meet outside of school hours, she is wearing jeans and a T-shirt, and a few times she is even donning a wig. It is brown and very stylish, and Mary wears it with great pride. Other times her hair is straightened and gelled, or plaited. Often, she is wearing bright orange nail polish on the fingernails on her left hand and a bead bangle around her wrist. Clearly, she is bending the dress code in the school a little bit. In the dorm there is an informal dress competition. She comments:

Mary: In my dorm we are only girls. There is a kind of a competition among us, people will want to be dressed up, you know, even though we are only girls. So that you, guys, the others, will say oh she is wearing something nice. Even though there is no one to attract or something like that. That is why I am wearing the wig, you know, to fit. (Interview in Harare, 27 September 1998.)

Mary is an avid fan of the Zimbabwean soccer team Dynamos, and she tries to watch their matches on television. She will be sitting for her A level exams in a few weeks time after the study is made. Twelve years of schooling will soon be over, and while this is a busy time in preparing for the exams, there are also anxieties about what will happen after school. She admits that her options depend on how well she performs at the exam table, as well as on the contacts she has abroad through her sister. Although she chose her subjects in order to qualify for legal studies, she has now changed her mind. This happened partly after watching television series such as *LA Law*:

Mary: I'd like to do something on banking or accounting. They are my subjects. With my subjects one might think that I might want to be a lawyer. I do history, literature and geography. But ah no, I don't want to be a lawyer. I discovered that later. I want to do something with accounting. I just admire the atmosphere of the accounters (sic), compared to being in a court room.
Hilde: Have you been in a court room?
Mary: No, I haven't. But there used to be *L.A. Law* and the like [laughter]
Hilde: But is *LA Law* how it usually is in a courtroom?
Mary: No, I don't think so, it's exaggerated, but you get an idea, […] and I've been hearing from other people. But I don't want to be associated with criminals and the like. (Interview in Harare, 27 September 1998.)

Although she has given up the dream of becoming a lawyer, Mary feels the family pressure to do well at the exams. "They all expect me to do wonders," she laughs. Amid reports of rising unemployment, sky-rocketing inflation and rather bleak prospects of pursuing further education or landing a secure job, the mediated popular culture provides material with which Mary can dream about the future. This is a situation she shares with her fellow school mates. They also source many of the ideas of how to behave as a young woman from the television series or films, in particular the foreign ones.

> Mary: These films you know, *Santa Barbara*. There's *Knots Landing*, *Capitol*, and I also like *Beverly Hills*. And some comedies, I don't like those action packed films. And I like the ZimNet movie, it's big, and some comedies like *Family Matters*, *Fresh Prince of Bel-Air*, *Golden Girls* and the like, and musicals like *Music Box* and the local you know. […] You are trying to ask me which one I would choose? Ah, I'd go for *Santa Barbara*. [Hilde: Yea?] Yes, and especially *Beverly Hills*, I'd go for that one. (27 September 1998.)

She knows a lot about the various series and films that have been broadcast or shown in Zimbabwe over the past years, and regrets that some of her favourite series are no longer broadcast. It is not easy, however, to behave and dress like the actors on the screen. "The *ambuyas* [grandmothers] don't like," Mary says often, whenever she talks about cultural practises that are deemed not entirely culturally acceptable or indecent in Zimbabwe. That might be wearing a too short a skirt, or taking one's boyfriend home before getting ready to marry him. Her own attitudes to the cultural practices she experiences in the soap operas she has been watching are ambivalent:

> Mary: I know that is their culture [on *Beverly Hills*]. We have our own culture and we have to live by that. There are some people like here, […] they are now beginning to accept that Western culture you know, whereby they allow their daughters [more leeway in decency and dress], but still they are very few, ah, they are very few who accept [these influences].

Most of the young women in the Harare study are very clear about the global fiction media material as being just that – fictitious. Some students explicitly draw the parallel between what happens in the various television series and what happens in their own lives, or what could happen in their lives. Mary's mother has left the high-density area where the family stays and spends most of the time in the rural homestead. Because of that, Mary does not confide in her mother or her parents regarding matters about the future or more everyday matters of the heart. She trusts very few friends with such conversations. Providing advice to girls and young women in love matters is something that traditionally was taken care of by the *tete*, an aunt or an elder member of the extended family. Although the advisory role of the *tete* is loosing ground in current Zimbabwe, above all in the urban areas, the parents do not seem to take over this advisory role. In fact, Zimbabwean media scholar Winston Mano (2005) argues the popular call-back radio format on ZBC functions as a *tete* in contemporary society.

Issues of realism and plausibility are among the reasons given when they are asked about what they enjoy watching in the television series. To many, it is the presumed realism of the various television shows that make them enjoyable. To others, it is rather the opposite: The further removed it is from their own everyday life, from their cultural environment, the more enjoyable it becomes.


**The Young Women in Dar es Salaam and Harare**
Linda in Dar es Salaam and Mary in Harare, and the rest of the women in our two studies offered us valuable insights into the world they were living in and into their thoughts about the global media. Their comments also relate to the questions addressed by media anthropology and media studies. Although our case studies in these two cities are qualitative in focus and thus not designed to be representative of the population of young women in these cities, their comments are relevant and valuable.

Many young women who are still in school and living in big cities such as Dar es Salaam and Harare are tightly controlled in terms of their physical movement, their physical appearance and in terms of their access to the media, television in particular. Not all students in our studies have access to a television set at home or in school lodging. Those who do not make creative arrangements to be able to watch at friends' or relatives'. They arrange for friends to tell them the latest developments in their favourite soap operas, and they go to great lengths to accommodate others who are less fortunate than themselves and have less media access. Although many of these women appear to have little contact with the global popular culture products, they make up for the lack of access with intensive involvement with the media content they happen to have access to. There is thus no reason to argue that their social environments which place restrictions on them are in any large way successful.

Hints of fashion trends, clothes and hairstyles are picked up from movies, television series or magazines. Limited financial resources may restrict their possibilities of purchasing many of the items they dream about, but it may also encourage the women to become more creative about how they go about styling themselves, how they make dresses moulded on clothes they have seen on the screen or in a magazine, or how a hair-do can be made, for instance. They are using the popular culture as a resource when negotiating the notions of decency through an ongoing dialogue concerning cultural acceptable ways of behaviour. Taking influence from the media in how to behave, speak, dance, even using a mobile phone or how they attempt to appear as if they have been out travelling, are other elements where they draw heavily on mediated popular culture. The media may constitute one of several influences for their career choices or elaborations on further education. Despite living in far from media-saturated environments, the young women in these two urban areas to a large extent grow up together with radio and television, and build knowledge of the world, construct their cultural and gender identities through interaction with mediated popular culture products. Uneven possibilities notwithstanding, keeping the positive influences of growing up in the changing mediascapes is just as important as being aware of factors which are considered to be not decent or appropriate in a particular culture, not to mention the tensions in politics and current affairs.

As already indicated, the mediascapes of Dar es Salaam and Harare have gone through profound changes in the past decades. Arjun Appadurai's term mediascape concentrates on "image-centred, narrative-based accounts of strips of reality" which offer to their users "scripts which can be formed of imagines lives" (1990:299). The term thus encompasses media texts published by a multitude of interests and ideological positions. These must be taken into account. We have highlighted some of the positive changes it entails for young women, but we acknowledge that the situation is more multifaceted than what we have been able to illustrate here. One of the assets of media studies as we see it, is that we have been able to ask the young women themselves about their understandings of and associations with the media, and not merely rely on the often derogatory and negative impressions which can be found in the discourse of the authorities and the parental generation regarding the so-called detrimental influences of the media on the so-called innocent minds of the youth.[15] The young women in Dar es Salaam and Harare aptly illustrate the power of the individual to make sense of these new strips of reality and turn them into pleasures as well as spurs for future action.

As for most young women growing up, particularly those in urban areas, the process of becoming a woman is surrounded by conflicting ideas, expectations and ideals. Media and popular culture play, as we have seen in the cases of Linda and Mary, a central role in their everyday lives, in a variety of ways, in this period of life. It is safe to argue that the women source imaginations and fantasies from the mediascape around them, and bring with them these experiences into finding their new roles as young women in urban life. Because the parental generation might not offer the role models they are seeking, the media become central in the process of carving out new ways of becoming and being modern.

### Finding one's Feet in a Global Modernity

Our studies in Dar es Salaam and Harare suggest that the question of young women and modernity may well provide a link between the grand narratives of globalisation on the one hand and media studies or media anthropology on the other. Arjun Appadurai argues that mediascapes, i.e. the conglomerate of media channels and their various texts, are a way of making sense of the globalisation processes which may be both disjuncted and uneven. We will add that it is through the engagement with media texts and the discussions of these with peers that the young women in our studies in Dar es Salaam and Harare find their feet in modernity. It is through their active engagement and their attempts to make sense of the mediascapes around them that these women arrive at increased understanding of the position they occupy in contemporary society, in family relationships and among friends. Through engagement with the media texts, the young women negotiate their present and their future. That society around them may place restrictions on their possibilities for realising these dreams is another issue. What is significant is that the young women's agency in dealing with the media texts seems to help prepare them for the coming of adulthood, or womanhood, and for the choices to be made. The ambivalences they may experience are turned into resources with which they elaborate on their life situations.

It is not surprising that the young women creatively use and make sense of the mediascapes in which they live. It is also not surprising that the global media have a reach well into life situations where their impact is sought to be restricted by authorities or the parental generation. We would like to argue that the study of global media and processes of globalisation is not a choice between 'good' and 'bad' cultural processes. As we see it, it is also not a question of either accepting or rejecting the global popular media. Rather, the point is to contribute with more nuances to the debate on processes of globalisation in Zimbabwe and Tanzania, as well as on a wider scale.

## Notes

[1] Arjun Appadurai (1996:35) uses the concept mediascape to indicate both the "distribution of the electronic capabilities to produce and disseminate information (newspapers, magazines, television stations, and film-production studios), which are now available to a growing number of private and public interests throughout the world, and to the images of the world created by these media."

[2] *Mageuzi* means transformation in Swahili, and has been used to describe the political and economical transformations that took place in the country from the mid-1980s as a result of de-regulation and liberalisation of the economy and the move towards democratic politics with the first multiparty elections in 1995.

[3] *Ujamaa* literally means familyhood in Swahili, and was used as the name for the African socialism that was the first President Julius Nyerere and TANU's post-independence politics, driven by the key words nation-building through self-reliance and "modernization through traditionalization" (Hedlund & Lundahl 1987).

[4] Television was prohibited on the Tanzanian mainland until 1992. Four private stations started in 1994, and the state-run television TVT (Televisheni ya Taifa) came on air in late 1999.

[5] These studies were carried out for research reported in Ekström (2000) and Ekström (2010), and financed by a minor field study grant from Sida (1998-99), Anna-Maria Lundin's scholarship foundation (2002 and 2003) and by a travel grant from the Nordic Africa Institute (2003). Research permit to Tanzania was obtained from COSTECH for the research discussed here.

[6] The research was carried out as a part of a joint research project, "Media, Civil Society and Cultural Identities," between the University of Zimbabwe and the University of Oslo, under a programme of cooperation entitled "Media Education and Research in Zimbabwe, 1996 – 1999." Research permit to Zimbabwe was obtained for the research discussed here. Please see Arntsen (2009) for more information.

[7] According to statistics referred to and analysed in Jones and Mhando (2006), 2% of the Tanzanian households were estimated to own a television in 2000/2001, and 6% in 2003/2004. According to the same sources, only 11% of the population had electricity in 2003/2004, which was one important reason for the low TV penetration. High costs for TV sets was another reason, and the late arrival of TV in Tanzania a third. Most television households were of course to be found in the urban areas.

[8] *Bongo Flava* is the contemporary local music scene that has developed rapidly over the last years in Dar es Salaam and then spread to the rest of the country. "This genre mixes hip-hop with pop rhythms – locally known as R&B – and also with rumba, taarab and lingala styles," argues Casco (2006:233), who is one of many researchers who have shown a particular interest in this emerging music culture. The radio is considered to have provided the local artists with a new scene from which to reach their audiences.

[9] Translated from Kiswahili by Ylva Ekström with the assistance of Cecy Nzumi and Alex Mwingira: "Hapana matata, kila kitu roho inapenda utapata. Bongo Dar es Salaam ni mpeto wa kutakata. Nenda viwanja vikali vya Bongo ustaajabu Na pita Slipway, Blue Palm au Mambo Club. Kama hujazoea unaweza kuvunja shingo Mambo Isidingo, watu mkononi Nokia Ringo. Huwezi kujua yupi mtoto wa geti, yupi changu. Wote wanameremeta kama Mamtoni, mwanangu. […]." For a more in-depth analysis of this rap, see Ekström (2010).

[10] Transmitted by SABC3 and produced by Endemol South Africa, *Isidingo* is popular all over Southern Africa. *Isidingo* has highest market shares on SABC3, and has been the longest lasting commercial success of Endemol South Africa (Wildermuth 2006).

[11] Wildermuth (2006) mentions similar results from youth in Zambia, indicating that this might be a series widely popular among urban youth in many African countries. Such a position is even supported by an earlier South African study (Strelitz 2004).

[12] This assignment was used as a method where the young women were invited to participate in the research process as co-researchers, by reflecting on the role of media in their everyday lives. They were all asked to write under the headline "Me and the Media," and Linda was one of eight students that volunteered to do this.

[13] Linda, "Me and the Media," August 2002.

[14] Linda and her friends have practically grown up with HIV/AIDS campaigns with the ABC emphasis (propagating that Abstinence, to Be faithful, and to use Condoms is the only way to tackle the pandemic), and they are quite aware of how to protect themselves from getting infected.

[15] The effects research within media studies in the 1950s and 1960s investigated the influence the media had on the minds of individuals. It was generally accepted that people would uncritically accept the media messages. Such allegations of direct influence could not be substantiated in research, however.

### References


Abu-Lughod, Lila, 1999: "The Interpretation of Culture(s) after Television." In Sherry Ortner (ed.): *The Fate of "Culture": Geertz and Beyond*. Berkeley: University of California Press.

Abu-Lughod, Lila, 2005: *Dramas of Nationhood. The Politics of Television in Egypt*. Chicago and London: The University of Chicago Press.

Alasuutari, Pertti, 1999: "Introduction: Three Phases of Reception Studies." In Pertti Alasuutari (ed.): *Rethinking the Media Audience. The New Agenda*. London, Thousand Oaks and New Delhi: Sage.

Amit-Talai, Vered and Helena Wulff (eds.) 1995: *Youth Cultures: A Cross- Cultural Perspective*. London and New York: Routledge.

Ang, Ien, 1996: *Living Room Wars. Rethinking Media Audiences for a Postmodern World*. London: Routledge.

Appadurai, Arjun, 1990: "Disjuncture and Difference in the Global Cultural Economy." *Theory, Culture & Society*, Vol. 7, pp. 295 – 310.
Appadurai, Arjun, 1996: *Modernity at Large. Cultural Dimensions of Globalization*. Minneapolis: University of Minnesota Press.

Arntsen, Hilde [1993] 1997: *The Battle of the Mind: International Media Elements of the New Religious Political Right in Zimbabwe*, Report no. 26, Oslo: Department of Media and Communication, University of Oslo, Oslo.

Arntsen, Hilde, 2006: "Researching popular culture. Notes from the Researcher Network on Studies of Popular Culture in Africa's initial workshop." *Glocal Times*, Issue 5, September 2006. Malmö University College: on, Malmoe. Online journal (www.glocaltimes.k3.mah.se)

Arntsen, Hilde, 2009: *Betwixt and Between: Case Studies in Gender, Culture and the Media in Zimbabwe in the 1990s*, Doctoral dissertation, University of Bergen, Bergen.

Askew, Kelly, and Richard R. Wilk (eds.) 2002: *The Anthropology of Media. A Reader*, Blackwell, Malden (Mass.).

Barber, Karin (ed.) 1997: *Readings in African Popular Culture*. The International African Institute. Bloomington, Indianapolis, Oxford: Indiana University Press and James Currey.

Boyd-Barrett, Oliver, 1977: "Media Imperialism: Towards an International Framework for the Analysis of Media Systems." In James Curran, Michael Gurevitch and Janet Wollacott (eds.): *Mass Communication and Society*. London: Edward Arnold.

Brennan, James R. and Andrew Burton, 2007: "The Emerging Metropolis: A History of Dar es Salaam, circa 1862-2000." In James R. Brennan, Andrew Burton and Jusuf Lawi (eds.): *Dar es Salaam. Histories from an Emerging African Metropolis*. London: African Books Collective.

Casco, José Arturo Saavedra, 2006: "The Language of the Young People. Rap, Urban Culture and Protest in Tanzania." *Journal of Asian and African Studies*, Vol. 41(3): 229–248.

Ekström, Ylva, 2000: *When the Global Meets the Local. Youth and the Media in Dar es Salaam*, MA thesis, University of Uppsala, Uppsala.

Ekström, Ylva, 2010: *"We are like Chameleons!" Changing Mediascapes, Cultural Identities and City Sisters in Dar es Salaam*, Doctoral dissertation, University of Uppsala, Uppsala.

Elteren, Mel van, 1996: "Conceptualizing the Impact of US Popular Culture Globally." *The Journal of Popular Culture*, Volume 30, Issue 1, pp. 47-89.

Fuglesang, Minou, 1994: *Veils and Videos. Female Youth Culture on the Kenyan Coast*. Stockholm: Almqvist and Wiksell International.

Giddens, Anthony, 1990: *The Consequences of Modernity*. Cambridge: Polity Publisher.

Ginsburg, Faye D, Lila Abu-Lughod and Brian Larkin (eds.) 2002: *Media Worlds. Antropolopgy on New Terrain*. Berkeley: University of California Press.

Gray, Ann, 2003: *Research Practice for Cultural Studies: Ethnographic Methods and Lived Cultures*. London: Sage Publications.

Hannerz, Ulf, 1990: "Cosmopolitans and Locals in World Culture." In Mike Featherstone (ed.): *Global Culture. Nationalism, Globalization and Modernity*. London: Sage Publications.

Haram, Liv, 2004: "'Prostitutes' or Modern Women? Negotiating Sexuality in Northern Tanzania." In Signe Arnfred (ed.): *Re-thinking Sexualities in Africa*. Uppsala: The Nordic Africa Institute.

Hedlund, Stefan and Mats Lundahl, 1987: "Kan bönder styras? Det Tanzaniska jordbrukets problem" [Can farmers be governed? The Problems of Tanzanian Agriculture], in Jan-Olof Drangert & Hans Wessgren (eds.): *Tanzania. Krisens ekonomi* [Tanzania. The Economy of Crisis]. Stockholm: Volontärsamverkan, Stockholm.

Herman, Edward S. and Robert W. McChesney, 1997: *The Global Media. The New Missionaries of Corporate Capitalism*. London and Washington: Cassell.

Hydén, Göran, and Michael Leslie, 2002: "Communications and Democratization in Africa" in Göran Hydén, Michael Leslie and Folu F. Ogundimu (eds.): *Media and Democracy in Africa*. Uppsala: The Nordic Africa Institute.

Johannessen, Jill, 2006: *Gender, Media and Development. The Role of the Media in the Cultural Struggle of Gender Transformation in Tanzania*, Doctoral dissertation, Norwegian University of Science and Technology, Trondheim.

Jones, John Muthee and Nandera Mhando, 2006: *African Media Initiative: Tanzania. Research findings and conclusions*, BBC World Service Trust, London.

Kilimwiko, Lawrence, 2007: "Tanzania." In *So This Is Democracy? Report on the State of Media Freedom and Freedom of Expression in Southern Africa 2006*. Windhoek: The Media Institute of Southern Africa (MISA).

Kottak, Conrad Phillip, 1990: *Prime-time Society: An Anthropological Analysis of Television and Culture*. Belmont: Wadsworth.

Lange, Siri, 2002: *Managing Modernity. Gender, State, and the Nation in the Popular Drama of Dar es Salaam, Tanzania*, Doctoral dissertation, University of Bergen, Bergen.

Liebes, Tamar and Elihu Katz, 1990: *The Export of Meaning: Cross Cultural Readings of Dallas*. Oxford: Oxford: University Press.

Mano, Winston, 2004: "Renegotiating Tradition on Radio Zimbabwe." *Media, Culture & Society*, Vol. 26(3): 315–336.

Mbilinyi, Marjorie, 1972: "'The 'New Woman' and Traditional Norms in Tanzania." *The Journal of Modern African Studies*, 10(1972):1, pp. 57-72.

Mkandawire, Richard, 1998: "An Alienated and Disillusioned Youth: The Plight of Young People in Southern Africa." In Patricia McFadden (ed.) 1998: *Southern Africa in Transition: A Gendered Perspective*. Harare: SAPES Books.

Moyo, Dumisani, 2004: "From Rhodesia to Zimbabwe: Change without Change? Broadcasting Policy Reform and Political Control." In Henning Melber (ed.): *Media, Public Discourse and Political Contestation in Zimbabwe*, Uppsala: Nordiska Afrikainstitutet.

Moyo, Dumisani, 2006: *Broadcasting Policy Reform and Democratisation in Zambia and Zimbabwe, 1990-2005. Global Pressures, National Responses*, Doctoral dissertation, University of Oslo, Oslo.

Ndlela, Nkosi, 2009: "African Media Research in the Era of Globalization." *Journal of African Media Studies*, Vol. 1, No. 1, pp. 55 – 68.

Ndlela, Nkosinathi, 2003: *Challenges and Prospects for Press Freedom: Comparative Perspectives on Media Laws in Zimbabwe and South Africa*, Doctoral dissertation, University of Oslo, Oslo.

Nyamnjoh, Francis B, 2008: "Children, Media and Globalisation. A Research Agenda for Africa." In Norma Pecora, Enyonam Osei-Hwere and Ulla Carlsson (eds.): *African Media, African Children*; The International Clearinghouse on Children, Youth and Media, Yearbook 2008. Gothenburg: Nordicom.

Nyamnjoh, Francis B. and Ben Page, 2002: "*Whiteman Kontri* and the Enduring Allure of Modernity Among Cameroonian Youth." *African Affairs* (2002), 101, 607 – 634.

Orgeret, Kristin Skare, 1998: *The Drumbeat of the Nation? A Study of the Zimbabwe Broadcasting Corporation's News at Eight*, Masters Dissertation, Department of Media and Communication, University of Oslo, Oslo.

Perullo, Alex: ""Here's a Little Something Local." An Early History of Hip Hop in Dar es Salaam, Tanzania, 1984-1997." In James R. Brennan, Andrew Burton and Jusuf Lawi (eds.): *Dar es Salaam. Histories from an Emerging African Metropolis*. London: African Books Collective.

Robertson, Roland, 1992: *Globalization: Social Theory and Global Culture*. London: Sage.

Rønning, Helge and Tawana Kupe, 2000: "The Dual Legacy of Democracy and Authoritarianism: The Media and the State in Zimbabwe." In James Curran and Myung-Jin Park (eds.): *De-Westernizing Media Studies*. London and New York: Routledge.

Rønning, Helge, 2003: "The Media in Zimbabwe: The Struggle between State and Civil Society" in Staffan Darnolf and Liisa Laakso (eds.): *Twenty Years of Independence in Zimbabwe: From Liberation to Authoritarianism*: Basingstoke and New York: Palgrave Macmillan.

Schiller, Herbert, 1969: *Mass Communication and American Empire*. New York: Augustus M. Kelly.

Stambach, Amy, 2000: *Lessons from Mount Kilimanjaro. Schooling, Community and Gender in East Africa*. New York: Routledge.

Strelitz, Larry, 2004: "Understanding University Student Media Preferences through the Discourses of 'Realism' and 'Quality.'" *Communicatio*, Vol. 30, No. 2, pp. 36 – 49.

Therborn, Göran, 1995: "Routes to/through Modernity." In Mike Featherstone, Scott Lash and Roland Robertson (eds.): *Global Modernities*. London, Thousand Oaks and New Delhi: Sage.

Tomaselli, Keyan and Arnold Shepperson, 2000: "Sociopolitical Transformation and the Media Environment. Writing Africa into Modernity." *Gazette*, Vol. 62(1), pp. 31-43.

Tomaselli, Keyan G, 2009: "Repositioning African Media Studies: Thoughts and Provocations." *Journal of African Media Studies*. Vol. 1, No. 1, pp. 9-21.

Tunstall, Jeremy, 1977: *The Media are American*. New York: Columbia University Press.

Wallerstein, Immanuel, 1990: "Culture as the Ideological Battleground of the Modern World-System." In Mike Featherstone (ed.): *Global Culture. Nationalism, Globalization and Modernity*. London, Newbury Park and New Delhi: Sage.

Wildermuth, Norbert, 2006: "Isidingo - The Need. A Mainstream Approach to HIV/AIDS Communication?" *Glocal Times*. Issue 5, September 2006. Malmoe University College, Malmoe. Online journal: www.glocaltimes.k3.mah.se

Zaffiro, James, 2002: *Media & Democracy in Zimbabwe. 1931–2002,* Colorado Springs: International Academic Publishers.

Zilberg, Jonathan, 1995: "Yes, It's True: Zimbabweans Love Dolly Parton." *Journal of Popular Culture*, Vol. 29, No. 1, Summer 1995.

# Part IV
# African Culture in Transition

# African Language, Literature and Culture in Transition: The Example of Yorùbá
## - George Sola Ajibade

The quest for nativism in African literature became very prominent after the independence of most African countries. The major concern of the African fiction writers was to reconstruct the colonial and pre-colonial experience in a way that the fictional simulation of native history, culture and language will be preserved and promoted (Adeeko, 1998, pp.1-6). The convergent point for the varying degrees of nativism in African creative writings was that true African independence requires a literature of its own, and that European languages are totally inadequate to express the African philosophical reality (Ngugi, 1981; Kunene, 1992). Within the context of Yoruba studies, Owomoyela (1992, p.93) opined that, "If we wish to assert and preserve distinctly African ways of being and distinctly living, we must cultivate distinctly African ways of speaking." However, many African creative writers also adopted a compromise stratagem by combining elements of both African and European traditions in their creative works. This emergent literary tradition, which was endorsed by many African critics, was appraised in the following terms by Obiechina (1968, p.31):

> Political independence is meaningless without cultural independence, for only the cultural values of a people can inspire them with a national pride, give them a separate identity and something to live and die for. This challenge of culture cannot be met by cosmopolitan culture of the departed colonial powers; it can only be met through the neo-African culture, which is a composite of African and European cultural elements.

Tracking such 'composite' African writing is a continuing challenge, particularly with regard to the writings of Yorùbá people who have a huge heritage of orature and a living tradition of oral literary creativity. This chapter attempts to track the transition of culture as evident in Yoruba literary works from the earliest period. The chapter focuses on the literary output of Kólá Akínládé whose creative works in Yorùbá language could be regarded as taking the lead in using the detective genre to mirror fundamental transitions in the Yorùbá culture and literary tradition.

The emergence of written literature among the Yoruba is clearly a manifestation of foreign influence consequent upon the activities of Europeans in Yorubaland in the middle of the nineteenth century (Babalola, 1985, p.158). The simultaneous and continuing influence of the oral traditions creates a cultural tension that manifests quite visibly in the indigenous literatures. As the brief rundown below indicates, manifestations of western ideas (and languages) brought by colonial experience started showing in the few Yorùbá literatures that were in existence during the colonial epoch, and became more pronounced after independence.

Perhaps, the most significant turning point in early Yoruba literary tradition was the translation of the Holy Bible into Yoruba by the late Bishop Ajayi Crowther and its publication in 1900 by the British and Foreign Bible Society. This event marked an epoch in the transition from orality to literacy among the Yorùbá. In 1911, Reverend David Hinderer translated Bunyan's *Pilgrim's Progress* into Yoruba and this was followed by *Ìwé Kíkà Yorùbá*, Books 1-5, meant primarily for the teaching of school children. Between 1905 and 1906, various collections of poems in the Ègbá dialect of Yoruba were written by Sóbòwálé Sówándé (aka Aróbíodu). The theme of his collections revealed contemporary issues of that time, basically the inception of Christianity in Egbaland and peoples's experiences with this novel religion. In 1930, Thomas wrote the first Yorùbá literature that castigated the western civilization brought by the colonial imperialists with elements that were considered hazardous to the traditions of the Yorùbá people. Most Yorùbá literary productions between 1913 and 1931 were didactic in nature, following the folk tradition of the Yorùbá people.

However, in 1938, there was a remarkable shift in literary productions among the Yorùbá when the Church Missionary Society Bookshop in Lagos published the first novel written by Daniel Olorunfemi Fagunwa titled, "*Ògbójú Ọdẹ Nínú Igbó Irúnmalè*" (trans. by Brave Hunter as *Forest of a Thousand Daemons*). Fagunwa wrote five novels between 1938 and 1961. He intertwined the Yorùbá folk tradition with Biblical injunctions in a way that was appealing to the masses. Only his last novel is different from its predecessors and in one important respect – reduction in fantasy elements in his narratives (Babalola, 1985, p.168).

In 1955, a Yorùbá novelist wrote *Aiye D'Aiye Oyinbo* ("The World has turned into a European World") and *L'Ójó Ojóun* ("In Days of Yore") in 1963. These two novels showed clear departures from earlier Yoruba didactic novels; in that they are historical, but their titles and content are also clear indications of continuing tension between old and new trends in Yoruba literature and culture. The novels merge both the pre-colonial and colonial experiences of the people. Olanipekun Esan's publications in 1965 further manifested the exposure of the Yoruba to the literary world, in that they were translations and adaptations of certain foreign stories.

It was Afolabi Olabimtan who again changed the course of Yorùbá literary tradition by his fictional representations of Nigerian polity in the post-independence era. Most of the post-independence Yorùbá writers follow a similar literary tradition as they carefully wove contemporary issues into their plots while still promoting the Yorùbá language and traditions through familiar themes and subjects. Notable among these writers are Akinwumi Isola, Oladejo Okediji, Adebayo Faleti, T.A.A. Ladele and Kola Akinlade, to mention a few.

Of the works produced by these writers, Kola Akínlàdé's are quite representative in eliciting transition trends in Yorùbá language and culture as represented in contemporary Yoruba literary works. Akínlàdé's works are mainly of the detective fiction genre which only a few Yorùbá creative writers produce. Indeed the only other creative writers who had written detective novels in Yorùbá language are Ọmọyajowo (*Adégbèsan* and *Báyò Ajómọgbé*) and Oladejo Okediji (*Àjà Ló Lẹrù, Àgbàlagbà Akàn* and *Atótó Arére*). While these two writers actually preceded Akínlàdé, their literary orientation is quite distinct from his. The detective novels of Okediji show a *nativist* inclination in the manner his stories focus more on Yorùbá traditional ways of detecting criminals. His criminal characters are crude, raw, and unsophisticated, unlike those of Akínlàdé. That is why it has been characterized as thriller. The main point of Okediji in his detective novels is the increasing crime rate and the incapability of the Nigerian Police Force to effectively contain criminals and prosecute criminal cases; instead, the Yorùbá Vigilante group (*Ojú lalákàn fi n sórí*) performs better. Many scholars have worked on Yorùbá detective novels and they have dealt with the causes of crime in the society and the weaknesses of the police to handle the issue successfully. Among these scholars are: Isola, 1978; Momodu, 1982; Olufajo, 1989; Ogunsina, 1987; 1992, and Adebowale, 1991; 1994.

Akínlàdé's works also set out to prove this same point above about the inefficiency of the Nigerian police to deal with emerging situation in post-independent Nigeria. However, his point of departure is his belief that the solution lies in the police being equipped with modern equipment and Western modus operandi, rather than in quasi cultural outfits like *Ojú lalákàn fi n sórí*, whose methodology consists mainly in the activation of traditional institutions and sensibilities. It is in this promotion of a hybrid approach that we find the kernel and evidence of transition in Yoruba literature.

Kólá Akínládé's works combine European and African traditions, even as he deploys an enormous amount of contemporary Yorùbá expressions. His work is an indication of how Africa more now than ever before is waging battles on several fronts to find a path conducive to economic, cultural, scientific and industrial emancipation. All these endeavours have one aim: the mastery of Western (or modern) knowledge through what Foucault calls an 'epistemological adjustment.' The achievement of this objective is not easy because there seems to be, in each of the areas mentioned above, a fundamental conflict between Western and African values (Kasongo, 1992, p.52). This effect of neo-colonialism and the tension with inbred nativity tendencies manifest at various levels in the detective fictions of Kólá Akínlàdé. Akínlàdé's works include: *Ta Ló pa Omoọba? Ọwó Tẹ Amòòkùnṣìkà, Alòsì Ọlógọ, Owó Èjè, Ajá Tó n Lépa Ẹkùn, Àgbákò Nílé Tété, Aṣenibánidárò, Ṣàngbá Fó!* and *Ta Ló Gbingi Oró?* However, our examples of how they manifest a transition in Yoruba language and culture will be drawn from one of his first novels and one of his latest, *Owó Èjè* and *Ṣàngbá Fó* respectively.

Akínlàdé is noted for his articulation of Yorùbá culture and espousing the aesthetic values of the Yorùbá cosmography. His settings and characters in this regard are revealing. They range from farm settlements peculiar to the Yorùbá people to palm wine shops, *ayò* game meets, family/lineage meeting, recitation of lineage poetry, the *Baálè* (Village head) and *Ọba (Kabiyesi)*, traditional rulers' syndrome, the Yorùbá *babalawo* (traditional medicine man, sometimes wielding *májèlé* (poison) and its coolant), tradition minded criminals and so forth.

Typical Yoruba farm settlement meetings which are on display in *Ajé* village in *Owó Èjè*; *ayò*, a prominent traditional Yorùbá outdoor/indoor game is also on display in the novel (*Owó Èjè pp. 36 & 81-83*). Also, the presentations of a *Ṣàngó*[1] devotee who chants the *oríkì* (lineage poetry) of *Òpómúléró* lineage (*Owó Èjè* pp. 56-58); and that of *Akérékorò* as a Yorùbá traditional healer (*Owó Èjè* p. 59) reveal profound aspects of Yorùbá heritage. Typical Yoruba vestments are also painstakingly described (*Akin wọ ... gáréèjì ní Ondo, nínú èwù agbádá àrán, àti sòkòtò àrán, àti fìlà aṣọ òkè onílà tééré-tééré tó fanimóra* - "Akin ... appeared at the motor garage in Ondo, in a velvet flowing gown, with velvet trouser, and a beautiful cap made with attractive traditional Yorùbá cloth" (54). The use of the gong (*Àjà*) by town criers to convey official information is another traditional Yorùbá practice that is also frequently present in Akínlàdé's work – he actually opens section five of *Ṣàngbá Fó* with this practice. Interestingly, the message of the king of *Àdùbí* town in this section is that the people should desist from partisan politics. Though modern political structures in Nigeria have weakened the authority of the traditional kings, still, Akínlàdé here presents a view that they have their own role and place in the maintenance of law and order within their jurisdiction in the new political structure. The town crier practice itself is a fading culture in Yorùbá but it still occurs in villages and farm settlements. Numerous examples in his works show that Akínlàdé cannot fully depart from the Yorùbá traditions and customs that groomed him. In all of this there is also a definite effort at didacticism, a trait inherited from traditional Yoruba practice of folklore. Akínlàdé's novels were written to teach students in the secondary schools most of whom are ignorant of their cultural heritage due to modernist influences.

At the same time, the use of modern language and modern settings and plots reveal Akínlàdé's capacity to transfer or merge Western ideas into Yorùbá settings. Hotels, beer parlours, pool houses, police stations, courts and State Assembly and National Assembly Houses are all Western traits in his works. It is important to specifically mention here that the detective novels in Yorùbá language emerged after the independence of Nigeria, which also coincides with the era of oil boom and the appearance of various visual Medias. Crime rate escalated. The emergence of Yorùbá detective novels can therefore be traced to a combination of the post-independence agitation for indigenous African literature; the oil boom; introduction of audio, audiovisual and other mass media with their advantages and disadvantages, and the real life escalation of crime rates in the newly independent country. It is therefore a measure of Akinlade's romance with realism that he merges traditional and modern/contemporary perspectives in his novels.

What is clear therefore is that Akínlàdé dances between two worlds of experiences and knowledge – the Yorùbá and the Western worlds. He presents antagonists tendencies and through this presentation endorses a synthetic, contemporaneous and cosmopolitan view. While condemning ritual sacrifices in *Sangba Fo*, western practices such as pools betting are also set up for condemnation in a novel like *Àgbákò Nílé Tété*. That is to say it is not all Western imports that edify.

It is also important to illustrate how Akínlàdé's detective modus shows a clear departure from the traditional Yorùbá mode of investigation. The latter often involves metaphysical means, for example the use of iron implements, or motifs of some deities to swear, usually with disastrous consequences for whoever perjures.[2] In serious cases, investigation would involve a divination process, with the diviner directing suspicion to the culprit who is then pursued relentlessly irrespective of any contrary facts of the case. Needless to say these traditional methods of enquiry sometimes lead to chaos in the community. In his novels, Akínlàdé advocates the use of the Western methods of investigation so as to avoid complications that might arise through the traditional methods of enquiry. Demonstrating a realist orientation, he depicts Yorùbá life and cosmography without recourse to mythical or metaphysical events, or larger-than-life characters, and supernatural interventions. He also introduces the western style jurisprudence in the form of the establishment of a jury; hence his novels indeed reflect a cultural transition at various levels among the Yorùbá people. The deeds, behaviors and the speech of the characters mirror their social positions and what operates in the society after the contact with the Western world, whereby many of the Yorùbá traditional practices are going into extinction.

It has been opined that writing novels in the indigenous languages secludes African writers (like Akínlàdé) from the group of 'language stealers' a moral stigma attached to non-Westerners writing African literature in European or Western languages (Adejumobi, 1999, p.583). Still, Akínlàdé's literary expressions in his detective novels reveal that he cannot depart from the Western ideas and philosophy either. The resulting tension can be seen in some of the motifs deployed in the novels. In *Ta Ló Gbingi Oró?*, for example, during the course of domestic conflicts, Bànáìsì, the mother of Dàpò snatched the husband of Tólá's mother and a Robot was sent to kill Tólá's mother and all her children, while the same Robot takes care of Bànáìsì and her own children. Akínlàdé's introduction of Western idea and equipment here is highly significant because of the apparent rejection of Yorùbá indigenous science and metaphysics in the choice of agent.

Before the advent of the Europeans who colonized them, there were various metaphysical objects and powers that were believed to be efficacious in sending messages from one constituency to the other depending on the objectives of the sender and the nature of the message. Sundry errands could also be effected by deploying the *Ṣìgìdì*[3], a metaphysical robot, either to beat somebody unto death or just to punish the person in some way. That Akínlàdé neglects the use of any of these in his fiction writing with traditional setting, opting instead for the Western technological innovations, is symptomatic of a reorientation of values and of cultural preferences. It also demonstrates the effect of global wave and residual experience of colonization on the writer and the audience of his books. With a largely literate audience, many of whom are in school or in other ways westernized in orientation, the use of globally familiar motifs becomes imperative.

In terms of language, Akínlàdé's works present a hybrid of Yoruba and English. Borrowing is a key feature of this amalgam which manifest in the use of words like: Telephone- *Tẹlifóònù*, Sergeant- *Sájéntì*, Saturday- *Sátidé*, Whiskey wine- *Ọtí wisikí*, Soda Water- *Sódá Wọtà*, bank- *bánkì*, Minister- *mínísítà*, Ward- *Wóòdù*, Engineer- *Ẹnjinià*, Meter- *Mítà*, Mercedez- *Mésídísì*, Volvo- *Fólífò*, Council- *Kánsùlù*, Councilor- *Kánsélò*, and so on. It is noted from these examples that the author has opted for the audio-visual method of borrowing the English language into the Yorùbá language. At times, he tries to translate some English words by describing the particular object in the Yorùbá language. For example, he uses *iná aláfọwótè* – 'the light you press with hand,' for torchlight (Şàngbá Fó: p. 14), *Ìwé Ìròyìn* ('book of news') for 'newspaper, *Àgó ìdìbò* ('tent for casting votes') for 'polling booth.' He has chosen this method of description because of the ambiguity that might arise from borrowing these words directly into Yorùbá language. In any case, he has further developed the Yorùbá language by adding to the diction. His style of code-mixing of English and Yorùbá lexis reveals a major transition from the existing Yorùbá literary traditions.

Akínlàdé also employs literary devices that echo both Yorùbá oral literature and English literary style. An example is the use of parataxis, clauses or phrases arranged in coordinate rather than subordinate constructions in rhetoric. There are many examples in his works but there is a fascinating example in *Şàngbá Fó* (p. 149). This is the description of the incidence after the announcement of the result of presidential election in Àròsọ town[4], when Adeniyi lost the election to Adelanwa of Ẹgbé Ẹléyẹ (Political Party). The description is as follows:

*Ṣàngbá fó!*
*Ìrètí Adeniyi láti di Olóòtú Ìjọba ti ṣàkì*

Akitiyan rè ti jásí asán
*Aápọn rè ti forísánpón*
*Ìṣapá rè ti yọrí sí òfo (p. 149)*

(What an irremediable defeat!
Adeniyi's aspiration to be the President is out of reach
His effort has come to vanity
His struggle amounts to nothing
His endeavour results to zero).

This arrangement and ordering of words makes this passage sound poetic. Akínlàdé also uses metaphors, epigrams, irony, rhetorical words, repetition, parody, metonymy and synecdoche, features that occur in Yorùbá usage but are also reminiscent of English literary style.

Characterization is also an area in which Akínlàdé attempts a western-Yoruba amalgam. It has been observed by (Quinn, 2000, p.50) that:

> Traditional fiction usually includes a physical description of a character's appearance, but many modern and post-modern novels dispense with the physical description and focus on the evident in the character's name. Charles Dickens refined this technique by using names that suggest rather than directly describe the character.

A critical appraisal of Akínlàdé's works shows that he adopts this Western idea. He does not describe his characters but their names suggest the nature of their parts or role in the narratives. Examples include names such as *Túndé Atopinpin* and *Akin Olúṣínà* who are criminal investigation officers in the novels. '*Atopinpin*' means one who pursues a matter to the last point, while '*Olúsínà*' means the one who opens the way or the one who first opens the way. In Akínlàdé's narratives, *Olúsínà* is usually the first person to make suggestions of how to go about investigation when a crime has been committed and *Atọpinpin* is the one who would relentlessly pursue the issue in order to discover the source of the crime committed and make sure that the criminal is arrested.

This idea is very much at home with the Yorùbá belief that the names given to children have social and metaphysical significance in the life of the children. That is why they say, "*Orúkọ ló n ro ọmọ* - - the child behaves in consonance with his name."[5] This also links directly with the prognostication device by which the name already suggests what would happen in the novel or the cause of action of specific characters. Accordingly, a character named *Láfinhàn* (in *Tal'ó Pa Ọmọọba?*) is expected to expose or show something, and he does in the novel; an *Ewégbèmí* ("herbs support me") is likely to be a medicine man, and so he is in the novel; an *Adufe* ('suitors jostle over me') is likely to be subject of amorous contest between suitors, and so it happens in the novel. Names like *Amòòkùnsìkà* – "one who commits havoc under the cover of dark" in *Ọwó Tẹ Amòòkùnsìkà* or *Aṣenibánidárò* - "The enemy who feigns sympathy with the victim" in the novel of the same title are quite telling in their prognosis.

There are many elements of Yoruba rhetoric and language use that are resistant to transition. In most cases among the Yorùbá, ordinary speech sounds like poetry and there is a close connection between the two. Even with the vast influence of the English language and rhetoric, proverbs remain an essential ingredient in the normal conversation of the Yorùbá people. The Yorùbá see the proverb as the 'horse of words'- '*òwe lẹṣin òrò*'. This shows that proverbs are "the meaning-governed expressions whose main function in conversation is to give cultural depth to a speaker's thought" (Adeeko, 1998, p.36). Although, Akínlàdé consciously interpolates between the Western and the Yorùbá traditions, his experience of Yorùbá literary style still rears its head, hence, he weaves his Yoruba-English amalgam with proverbs in order to establish his facts and illuminate his stories. This is also a tool for reflecting Yorùbá socio-cultural milieu. However, Akínlàdé equally weaves the proverbs meaningfully into his Western experience to create a new and contemporaneous view of his people. This accords with the dictum that "the key element in the successful use of proverbs is the ability of the performer to use a proverb whose salient features are compatible in the opinion of his audience with the situation to which the proverb is applied" (Thomas et al, 1986, p.33).

In sum, modern Yorùbá literary productions definitely manifest the reality of colonial contact and continued globalization of cultures. At the earliest stages of this literature some colonized Yorùbá writers demonstrated allegiance to the colonizing powers and authority by writing in English, however garbled their expression might be. This early enthusiasm gave way to a period of nativist commitment when the Yoruba writer wrote in his native language while projecting traditional cultural values and images. The Yoruba literature of the contemporary period shows a dominance of cosmopolitan consciousness. This new literature has been exemplified in the foregoing with the works of Akínládé. The new literature indicates how the Yorùbá creative writer consciously indigenizes and simultaneously westernizes his presentations, thus showing evidence of a culture in transition.

**Notes**

[1]Ṣàngó is the god of thunder among the Yorùbá. He is known as a god of justice who detects and punishes the criminals among them in the past. This practice is fading off and not as common as it used to be in the past.

[2]Iron stands for *Ògún* the god of iron. The Yorùbá believe in Ògún and Ṣàngó as Deities of justice, truth and fair play. No one tries to use their motifs falsely else, these Deities will fight the person which may lead to death or fatal accident.

[3]*Sìgìdì* is a traditional medical object that the traditional medicine men do send an errand to their targeted victims. It can cross borders to deliver the message they send to somebody. In all cases it does evil and harm to the recipients of its action. They use it to fight and kill people. It is important to mention that we have different types depending on the type of message we want to send to people. They usually work after the required incantation has been chanted upon it.

[4]*Àròsọ* is the Yorùbá word for novel or fiction. Here, it is used metaphorically so that his messages in the novel will not look too direct. In the real sense of it, he meant the opposite.

[5]The Yorùbá look at the circumstances surrounding the birth of the child before a particular name could be given to such a child. Not this alone, they aspire to see that the trait of the given name is manifesting in the attitude and behavior of the child.

**References**

Adebowale, Oluyemisi. "Ipò àti Ipa Atọpinpin nínú Ìtàn-Àròsọ Òtẹlèmúyé." 2nd Odujinrin Memorial Lectures, Ogun State University, Ago-Iwoye, Nigeria, 1991.
---. *Style in Yoruba Crime Fiction*. Unpublished Ph.D. Thesis, University of Ibadan, Nigeria, 1994.
--- & Adejumo, G.A. "Ipò àti Ipa tí Obìnrin kó nínú Ìtàn-Àròsọ Ajẹmó Òràn dídá." *Inquiry in African Languages and Literatures*, 1995: 66-77.

Adeeko, Adeleke. *Proverbs, Textuality, and Nativism in African Literature*. Florida: University Press of Florida, 1998.

Adejumobi, Moradewun. "Routes: Language and the Identity of African Literature." *The Journal of African Modern Studies*. Cambridge: Cambridge University Press. 37. 4 1999: 581-596.

Akinlade, Kólá. *Ta L'ó Pa Ọmọọba?* Lagos: Macmillan Nigeria Limited, 1971.
---. *Alòsì Ọlógọ*. Ikeja: Longman Nigeria Limited, 1974a.
---. *Ọwó Tẹ Amòòkùnsìkà* Lagos: Macmillan Publishers Limited, 1974b.
---. *Owó Èjè*. Ibadan: Onibonoje Press, 1976.
---. *Ajá Tó N Lépa Ẹkùn*. Ibadan: Onibonoje Press, 1979.
---. *Àgbákò Nílé Tété*. Ibadan: Evans Brothers, 1980.
---. *Aṣenibánidárò*. Ibadan: Heinemann Educational Books (Nig.) Ltd, 1982.
---. *Ṣàngbá Fó*. Ibadan: Paperback Publishers, 1985.
---. *Ta Ló Gbingi Oró?* Ibadan: Evans Brothers (Nig.) Ltd, 1986.

Babalola, Adeboye. "Yoruba Literature" in Andrzejewski B. W., S. Pilaswewicz and W. Tyloch (eds), *Literatures in African Languages-Theoretical Issues and Sample Surveys*, Cambridge: Cambridge University Press, 1985, pp 157-189.

Fagunwa, D. O. *Ogboju Ode Ninu Igbo Olodumare*. Lagos: Thomas Nelson, 1949.

Isola, Akinwumi. "The Writer's art in the modern Yoruba Novel." Unpublished PhD Thesis, University of Ibadan, Nigeria. 1978.

Kasongo, Kapanga M. *Criticism of African Novel: A Conflict of Discourses*. Ann Arbour: A Bell & Howell Company, 1992.

Kunene, M. "Problems in African Literature." *Research in African Literatures*. 23. 1 1992: 27-44.

Momodu, Oludele. "Ìtàn-Àròso Òtelèmúyé." Unpublished B.A. Long Essay, University of Ife, Nigeria, 1982.

Ngugi wa Thiong'o. *Decolonising the Mind: the politics of language in African literature*. London: James Currey, 1981.

Obiechina, Emmanuel. "Cultural Nationalism in Modern African Creative Literature." *African Literature Today*. 1. 1968: 24-34.

Ogunsina, J. Adebisi. "The Sociology of the Yoruba Novel: A Study of Isaac Thomas, D.O. Fagunwa and Oladejo Okediji." Unpublished Ph.D Thesis, University of Ibadan, 1987.
---. *The Development of the Yoruba Novel, 1930-1975*. Ibadan: Gospel Faith Mission Press, 1992.

Okediji, Oladejo. *Àjà Ló Lẹrù*. Ibadan: Longman, 1969.
---. *Réré Rún*. Ibadan: Onibonoje Press, 1973.

Olufajo, G. Arinpe. "Ìwà Òdaràn nínú Ìtàn-Àròsọ *Òtẹlèmúyé*." Unpublished M.A. Thesis, Obafemi Awolowo University, Ile-Ife, 1989.

Omoyajowo, T. A. *Adégbèsan*. Ikeja: Longman Nigeria Ltd, 1961.
---. *Báyò Ajómogbé*. Ikeja: Longman Nigeria Ltd, 1963.

Omowoyela, Oyekan. "Language, Identity, and Social Construction in African Literature." *Research in African Literature* 23. 1. 1992: 83-94.

Quinn, Edward. *A Dictionary of Literary and Thematic Terms*. New York: Checkmark Books, 2000.

Thomas, Green and William, Pepicello. "The Proverbs and the Riddles as Folk Enthymemes." *Proverbium*. 3, 1986: 33-45.
---. *Itan Emi Segilola, Eleyinjuege (Elegberun Oko L'aiye)*. Lagos: C.M.S. Bookshops, 1930.

# HEALTH AND THE AFRICAN IMAGE
## - Alfred Banso Makanjuola

**Global and African Concepts of Health and Ill-Health**

The HIV/AIDs pandemic has shown that the world has become increasingly seamless as much in terms of diseases and disorders as in terms of economics and culture. High levels of mobility, with many working in one continent and spending weekends in another, means that any uncontrolled or poorly managed infective disorder in one part of the world may quickly pose a threat to other parts. However, while there are some standard global measures to manage both communicable and non-communicable disorders, some measures are peculiar to some races or peoples, These measures, which are closely connected to the peoples' culture and belief system cannot be separated from their attitude to health matters and their corresponding health practices. In this chapter, I would highlight some peculiar features of Africanness in the health behaviour of Nigerians (as patients, caregivers and therapists). The chapter focuses on the influence of culture on health issues, health seeking behaviour, culture and sick role or illness behaviour, attitude to orthodox and non-orthodox treatment, culture and rehabilitation in the Nigerian context. One would attempt to elicit aspects of the African attribute or image and related sociocultural issues that seem to affect health care delivery on the continent, with particular emphasis on traditional mental health practice in the Nigerian/African community.

The attitude of the average African towards health issues can be better appreciated by comparing the concept of 'health' as suggested by global institutions with the related understanding of the concepts by some Africans. The concept of mental health and mental ill-health is a sub-set of the global health concept which would also be explored. The General Assembly of the World Health Organization (WHO) Assembly in 1948 defined health as not just the absence of infirmity but a state of complete physical, mental and social well-being. Mental health is the capacity of an individual, a group and the environment to interact with one another in ways that promote the feeling of well-being. This entails the optimal development and use of mental abilities (thinking, reasoning, understanding, feeling and behaviour) required for normal level of functioning (FMH, 1996). Mental health also entails the optimal development and functioning of the individual, which allows the realization of aspirations and satisfaction of needs as well as the ability to change or cope with the environment (FMH, 1996). Hence, mental ill-health can be defined as the presence of behaviours adjudged to be abnormal by an individual or society and such abnormal behaviour must be persistent and pervasive, causing distress and disability either to the individual or the society.

## Traditional African Concept of Health/Ill Health

While the concept of health in Africans applies to most Africans resident in African nations, it is also applicable to a signifant proportion of Africans in the diaspora such as those resident in Cuba, Brazil and North America. For example, the Yoruba of Western Nigeria and those in Diaspora in South America and the West Indies believe that *Ifa* is the repository of all knowledge and, as a method of divination, it is consulted in all matters, including health (Olatawura, 2007). The African child grows and matures as a product of his/her culture, beliefs, education (teachings, both formal and informal, and religious upbringing), and environment, hence his/her attitude, behaviour and practices are usually determined by these factors. The Yoruba people of Nigeria, and Africa in general, believe that the physical universe consists of a Supreme Being, deities and gods resident in heaven, and human beings, witches and spirits resident on earth. They believe in the concept of unity of life and time. More importantly, they believe there is a continuous communion between the dead and the living, and in a mystical and emotional bond between the natural and supernatural worlds (Olatawura, 2007; Odejide, 1979). The yield of the farm crops can be influenced by forces ranging from direct sabotage by neighbours to anger from supernatural forces (due to offences against gods or ancestors) and preternatural forces (affliction from curses, witchcraft). Consumption of crops that have not been accepted or blessed by the gods may therefore lead to ill-health. The spirit of a family member who was not buried according to the traditional rites may cause ill-health in the society. This, they believe, is possible because there is continous communication between the living and the dead. It can be inferred from the foregoing therefore that the concept of health/ill-health in traditional Africa may not be as simple as obtained, for example, among Europeans or other cultures and as defined by the global institutions. The traditional African may perceive typhoid fever, for example, as an illness which translates beyond the presence of the organism that causes it (*Salmonella typhi*). Even if he/she accepts that the organism is responsible for the observable signs and symptoms such as diarheoa and vomitting, he/she may still believe that there are other forces or reasons why he/she is afflicted with typhoid. This belief tends to explain why, in seeking treatment, the typical pathway to health is to first use home remedies. If this fails, then spiritual help is consulted.

The transmission of this belief system into contemporary/modern health care practice is often an embarrasing fact that attests to the resilience of traditional African'ways of life' notwithstanding the advancement of science and globalism and the pervasive influence of monotheistic religions. Previously, in the *Yoruba* culture for example, spiritual help for ailments is sought from gods such as *Obatala, Sango, Oya, etc*. With the advent of modern religions such as Christianity and Islam, there is a shift towards consulting religious leaders in these faiths with the same underlining principle that ailments are never simply physical. Sometimes, syncretic churches (churches that combine traditional African religion with modern ones) are consulted. If there is still ill-health, a typical patient may then have a last recourse to orthodox hospital or resign to fate. While receiving orthodox hospital care, about 70% of patients still use alternative methods of treatment (Agara & Makanjuola, 2006). It would appear that the visit to the orthodox hospital is to allay symptoms while the use of the alternative mode of treatment is to identify the 'root' cause of the illness. The patient agrees he has typhoid, but why him/her? Why not the neighbour next door? To him/her, someone or forces who do not wish him/her well, or gods that are angry about his children, family (immediate and extended), his clan, or his crops and livestocks, must be responsible. We can therefore against this background appreciate his pathway to treatment, his attitude to drugs given in the hospital and his decision after he has been cured in the hospital to still make sacrifices in order to prevent recurrence or affliction of a family member. We can appreciate why his/her emphasis on prevention, may not be focused primarily on environmental and food hygiene and early identification of symptoms and treatment. We can also appreciate why to have a proper and effective control programme against medical disorders, the community leaders, traditional healers, religious leaders and family heads should be involved in the planning. The role of information, communication and proper education in the language the community understands and using the appropriate cultural and religious principles cannot be overemphasized.

It is important at this stage to place, in perspective, the issue of the expected positive influence of 'school attendance' and other intervening modern institutions on traditional African beliefs needs to be placed in perspective. I have deliberately used the phrase 'influence of school attendance' here instead of the alternative and apparently more appropriate term 'influence of education'. This is because it would originally have been expected that the higher the level of education, the less the influence of superstition on the individual patient. However, Some studies in Nigeria have shown that, in terms of respondents' views on the aetiology of mental illness, there was no significant difference between the beliefs of the literate as compared with those of the non-literate respondents (Erinosho, 1977; Adelekan et al, 2001). A recent study among non-medical workers showed that the higher their level of education, the more they believe that biological factors (such as genetic predisposition and chromosomal abnormalities) could predispose to mental illness. However, educational status did not appear to negate the belief in the influence of supernatural and preternatural forces (e.g. offences against gods or ancestors and affliction from curses, witchcraft) as a causative factor in the aetiology of mental illness (Adewuya & Makanjuola, 2008). It has been reported that many Nigerian home videos propagate a spiritualist world view and depict many occurrences in daily life as having spiritual undertones (Aina, 2004). Studies have shown that there is still a lot of interaction between the public, literate or not, and the traditional healers or religious healers (Makanjuola et al, 2000). The belief in supernatural and preternatural forces in the aetiology of mental illness and other medical illnesses is still very prevalent. The proliferation of religious sects and worship centres in many parts of Nigeria also tends to increase the rate at which people attribute religious reasons to the onset or presence of illness. Often, the phrase, 'spiritual attack,' is used to describe such beliefs (Olatawura, 2007). However, the foregoing should not be seen as implying that education is an antithesis to scientific reasoning in terms of health issues. On the contrary, an intervention study has shown that a structured, purposeful enlightenment of traditional mental health practitioners in a Nigerian State had a positive influence on their attitude and behaviour as regards mental health practice (Adelekan et al, 2001). What is being suggested, rather, is that the type of education given in our schools should be more structured to, among other things, encourage deductive reasoning, influence attitudinal change and dislodge superstitious beliefs that have been ingrained in the subconscious of the traditional African since childhood.

**Sick Role, Illness Behaviour and Stigma in African Culture**
The roles expected of a sick person (including **patient** presentation of illness, attitude to medication, etc) is mostly a function of the culture and the environment of the patient. In the case of mental illness, such roles also involve the collaboration of relations, care-givers and the community. **Patient** presentation of illness (to the hospital) is usually a factor of recognition of the presence of ill-health, availability of means (financial, logistics, transport) to seek the treatment, and absence of distress, disability and stigma to the person or the community concerned. To the traditional African, recognition of ill-health is not difficult, especially when there are physical signs and symptoms such as fever and pain. Recognition of severe mental illness is not difficult either, unlike the minor disorders referred to

as neuroses (Makanjuola, 1997). However, the low level of financial resources due to poverty, absence of means of transportation, bad road networks, lack of promixity to health facilities and stigma are prevailing factors that must be overcome before patients' presence in the hospital. Inability to surmount these challenges often leads to consultation with alternative methods of health care (traditional and religious) in addition to genuine belief in these alternative methods. Sometimes, the patients gets well, especially if the illness is a self-limiting one. However, such success also tends to reinforce the belief in such alternative methods of treatment and the associated belief systems. In reality, alternative methods of treatment such as traditional medicine tend to have some positive results in the treatment of some disorders especially neurotic disorders (Odejide, 1979).

Most cultures, including Africa, expect that a sick person would be excused from certain duties, seek treatment early, take medications and, as soon as he/she is well, return to normal activities. Sometimes, poverty or a non-conducive home environment may prolong illness behaviour, while stigma may influence the pathway to health care. For example, a patient or family with a patient who has symptoms of a highly stigmatized disorder such as mental illness may not be willing to access a health facility because of the stigma. There may be social distancing from the patient and the family, lack of willingness to marry the patient or anyone from his/her family, stigmatization of the offsprings of the patient or family members, withdrawal of rights within the community, e.g. right to be conferred with chieftaincy titles. The consideration of these negative reactions from the society often affects patient's presentation at facilites where the illness would be given a 'label' or classification that is less stigmatizing. Again, such facilities include religious or traditional healer's homes, where the illness is likely to be diagnosed as 'a spiritual attack' from the devil, gods, witches or enemies. It is when treatment fails (usually after months) at these facilities that patient presents in the hospitals (usually a non-psychiatric hospital) and finally a psychiatric hospital. Reports have shown that 70% of patients have received treatment from religious healers, 42.6% from traditional healers while 39.6% had visited general practitioners before presenting at a psychiatric facility (Agara & Makanjuola,

2006). The unfortunate consequences of presentation through this tortous route is late presentation and the attendant problem of poor prognosis.

### *Diagnosis* and *treatment* in African traditional culture

Among the Yoruba speaking people of Nigeria as noted earlier, the hierarchical order in the physical universe consists of the Supreme Being, supernatural forces and human beings in that descending order. The supernatural forces could be malevolent or benevolent; the malevolent ones are responsible for the presence of diseases especially mental illness. Also, it is believed that the means of communication with the Supreme Being is through *Ifa* divination (Odejide, 1979). This explains why in traditional *Yoruba* health practice (including mental health practice), the *Ifa* system of divination is the most common method of divination.

Diagnosis in traditional medicine is quite encompassing and involves not only categorization of the illness, but also identifying the remote cause(s) of the illness. To arrive at a diagnosis, therefore, various methods such as history taking, divination and use of dreams and interpretation are used (Odejide, 1979). The methods of divination include *Ifa* divination system, *Erindinlogun* (16 cowries), *Osanyin* (an extremely dimunitive object who is believed to speak in a voice that closely resembles the human voice and can run errands), *Agbegba* (a mat-like material measuring about 60cm by 30cm which is folded into two.; it is expected to open or close like a book in affirmative or negative response to questions raised by the diviner), and *Omi wiwo* (water gazing). Of all these methods, *Ifa* divination system is regarded as the most important and most reliable (Bascom, 1969). It has been claimed that the descending order of reliability of divining apparatus is *Ifa* divination system using *Ikin* (Palm nuts), *Ifa* divination system using *Opele* (divining chain), *Osanyin, Agbegba* and *Erindinlogun* both rank fourth, while others (water gazing, 'sand cutting' (*yanrin tite*), mirror gazing) rank fifth (Makanjuola, 1997).

The traditional mode of treating medical disorders, including mental illness, is multidimensional. Among the Yoruba of Nigeria, remote causes are first identified and removed through appeasement of the gods, usually through sacrifice to `Esu' (a deity). There may or may not be prescription of `adimu' (sacrifices to other deities such as *Egungun, Orisa*) (Bascom, 1969). Symptoms are then treated with herbs in the form of decoction, concoction, or even locally made soaps which are to be used for bathing. There may or may not be a need for scarification works (superficial cuts or slits made on the skin through which protective herbs or incantations are supposedly passed into the body of the recipient; this is called *gbere* in *Yoruba* language). Topical drugs are also applied to the body, some specifically to the eyes or ears. This is based on one of the concepts in traditional medicine among the *Yoruba* that auditory hallucinations (hearing voices of unseen people) and visual hallucinations (seeing images or objects that do not actually exisit) are real. Complications that could arise from the use of unsterilized sharp objects (used in making scarification marks) include HIV and Hepatitis infections, while otitis media and conjunctivitis could arise from the use of unhygienic or toxic chemicals or liquid extracts to the eye or ear (Makanjuola, 1987).

**Cultural differences in training and patient-doctor relations**
The training of the African traditional healer is usually tedious and lasts between eight to fourteen years but could be more (Abimbola, 1983; Osuntokun, 1975). Generally, the training involves recognition of medicinal plants and animals by their various names, knowing the uses of various medicinal plants and the specific parts that are useful (roots, leaves, bark). This is done through familiarity and practice. Incantations are also memorized especially those required at different stages of herbal preparation and patients' management. Abimbola (1983) described the following stages in the training of *Ifa* priest. The first stage which lasts two to three years is on how to use the paraphenalias of the divining system, such as how to use the divining nuts and the divining chain. The second stage is memorization of *Ese* (verse) from each figure (*Odu*) of *Ifa*. This is done at a steady rate of about one per day. During training, the trainee priest may live with the master priest or goes home to sleep every day. After training, the `graduating' diviner goes through an initiation ceremony which usually takes place in the forest where he is assessed by senior priests. If he is successful, he is allowed to practice on his own. However, the training of a good

priest is continuous and a life long activity. It is at this period that Ifa priests attempt to specialize in the various areas of Ifa divination system. This may involve travels to distant places to learn from other renowned priests (Osuntokun, 1975). Generally, the diviner skillfully relies on a belief system which links all community members to the same set of spiritual forces, which tie the living and the dead together. The healer provides a powerful system of support for the distressed patient by invoking these spirits (Ari Kiev, 1989). Through, the skillful use of various treatments methods such as history taking, divination, community involvement and patient involvement in healing rituals, a traditional healer may achieve some success in some cases of neuroses.

One of the difficult areas for a western trained therapist practising within an African context is the disconnection in their belief systems. While the therapist has been trained about the biopsychosocial model in the aetiology of medical disorders, the typical African patient may not appreciate his/her illness in such terms. Though, he/she believes in the role of genetic factors and poisonous or contaminated food including drug and alcohol, there is also a strong belief in the influence of supernatural forces which *must* be addressed in order to achieve a permanent cure. This lack of congeniality in belief, as opposed to what obtains with the traditional healer, may lead to a setback in the treatment of mental disorders, especially neuroses. The acceptance of patient/therapist role by the patient may not be properly and willingly adopted, leading to poor progress in therapy and even eventual patient drop-out from therapy. Sometimes the therapist may allow his beliefs to influence his clinical judgment and skill because of conflict between his/her traditional and religious beliefs and his medical training (Makanjuola, 2003; 2004).

## Conclusion

In some parts of the world, spiritual and traditional healing goes hand in hand, while in some situations, faith healing has virtually supplanted orthodox medical practices (Olatawura, 2007). In Nigeria, reports showed that 70% of patients have received treatment from religious healers, while 42.6% had received treatment from traditional healers before presenting in the hospital (Agara & Makanjuola, 2006). Even now, faith healing centres are spreading like praire fire all over the world, the western world inclusive (Olatawura, 2007). The practitioners of evidenced based medicine (orthodox practitioners) are members of the society and are therefore not immune from the culturally prevalent belief system (veneration of the seen and unseen forces in all races, the closeness of man to nature in all races), that fosters the growth of these treatment orientations (Olatawura, 2007). Because of the inability of orthodox health care to meet all the perceived needs of the populace (Ehrenreich, 1978), notwithstanding advancement in science, there seems to be a shift by some people towards the use of traditional community health resources which are cheaper and more accessible (Katz, 1983). The expected 'solution' of integrating alternative health care seems to be as efficient as expected in Africa and Nigeria in particular. Richard Laugharne noted that evidence-based medicines is likely to be challenged in the next 15 years, not necessarily because it is invalid, but because it is seen as domineering (Laugharne, 2004).

The foregoing would suggest that the world must prepare for a global crises in terms of the concept of aetiology of ill-health (evidenced-based versus spiritual). It is likely that Africa will be most affected because of its current weak manpower, financial, technological and infrastructural level of development. A good understanding of the culture and image of the African, especially in terms of health concepts, might be a great asset in devising relevant cultural, financial and technological methods of preventing major health crises or epidemics. The solution is not to dismiss this culture, but to understand it.

## References

Adelekan M.L, Makanjuola A.B, Ndom R.J.E. (2001). Traditional Mental Mealth Practitioners in Kwara State, Nigeria. *East African Medical Journal*. 78: 190-196.

Adewuya, A.O. & Makanjuola. R.O.A. (2008). Lay Beliefs Regarding Causes of Mental Illness in Nigeria. *Social Psychiatry and Psychiatric Epidemiology*. Vol. 43 (4): 336-41.

Agara, A.J & Makanjuola, A.B. (2006). Pattern and Pathway of Psychiatric Presentations at the Outpatient Clinic of a Neuropsychiatric Hospital I\n Nigeria. *Nigerian journal of Psychiatry*. 4: 30-34.

Aina, O.F. (2004) Mental Illness and cultural issues in West African films; implications for orthodox psychiatric practice. *Medical humanities* 30: 23-26.

Abimbola, W. (1983) Ifa as a Body of Knowledge and as an Academic Discipline. *Journal of Culture and Ideas*, 1: 1-11.

Ari Kiev (1989) Some Psychotherapeutic Factors in Traditional Forms of Healing. In Peltzer, K. & Ebigbo, P. (1989) Eds. *Clinical Psychology in Africa*. Enugu: Working Group for African Psychology, Department of Psychological medicine, University of Nigeria, Enugu.

Bascom W. (1969) *Ifa Divination: Communication between Gods and Men in West Africa*. Bloomington: Indiana University Press.

Ehrenreich, J (1978). The Cultural Crises of Modern Medicine. *New York Monthly Review Press*.

Erinosho O.A. (1977) Pathways to mental health delivery systems in Nigeria. *International journal of social psychiatry*. 23: 54-59.

Federal Ministry of Health (1999) Mental health handbook for primary health care workers.

Katz, R. (1983/4). Empowerment and Synergy; Expanding Community Healing Resources. *Prevention in Human Services* 3: 2-3.

Laugharne, R (2004) Psychiatry in the Future – the next 15 years: Postmodern Challenges and Opportunities for Psychiatry. *Psychiatric Bulletin*. 28-29; 317-
318.

Makanjuola A.B. (1997) 'Prospects and Problems of Traditional Mental Health Practice in Ilorin Emirate Council Area.' A dissertation submitted in partial fulfillment of the requirement for the Fellowship of the West African College of Physicians, Faculty of Psychiatry.

Makanjuola R.O, Jaiyeola A.A. (1987) Yoruba Traditional Healers in Psychiatry. II. Management of Psychiatric Disorders. Afr. J. Med. Med. Sci. 16 (2): 61-73.

Makanjuola A.B, Adelekan M.L, Morakinyo O. (2000) 'Current Status of Traditional Mental Health Practice in Ilorin Emirate Council Area of Kwara State, Nigeria.' *West African Journal of Medicine*. 19: 43-49.

Makanjuola A.B. (2003-2004) 'Witchcraft and Psychiatry in Nigeria Today.' *Psychopathologie africaine*, XXXII, 2: 189-200.

Odejide O.A. (1979 ) 'Traditional (Native) Psychiatric Practice: Its Role in Modern Psychiatry in a Developing Country.' *The Psychiatry Journal of the University of Ottawa* 4: 297-301.

Olatawura M.O. (2007) 'Orthodox, Traditional Treatment and Faith Healing in Perspective.' Nigerian Journal of Psychiatry. 5: 50-52.

Osuntokun B.O. (1975) 'Traditional Basis of Neuropsychiatric Practice among Yorubas of Nigeria.' Tropical Geographical Medicine. 27: 422-430.

**Part V**
**Book Review, Poems: Culture Miscellany**

# SEXUALITY IN AFRICA: A REVIEW OF MARC EPPRECHT'S *HETEROSEXUAL AFRICA?*[1]
## - Adeyinka O. Banwo

This is a 230 page book on sexuality in Africa written by a historian, Marc Epprecht. The text is subdivided into six chapters, the author attempts to discuss amongst others African sexuality and the phenomenon of HIV/AIDS in Africa.

In this fascinating and controversial work, Marc Epprecht challenges the age long held view on existence of a single African sexuality, and absence of homosexuality or bisexuality in the African continent. He argues that homosexuality has a pre-colonial antecedent and is not a western influenced condition in Africa. In his own words, 'same- sex sexuality and attitudes towards it thus clearly have a history in Africa, just as they do elsewhere in the World." (p.10)

To support his arguments Epprecht draws evidence from Africa's historical past. He further states that the reason behind a determined refusal for non admittance of same-sex sexualities in Africa was homophobia (p.5). Epprecht passes the blame for this on to colonial officials, anthropologists and the African elite of engaging in a determined effort to obliterate the fact about same-sex sexuality in Africa.

Same –sex sexuality in Africa, Epprecht contends, is a source for the spread of the HIV/AIDS virus which remains largely uninvestigated by academics, health workers and researchers Health related professionals activists have focused mainly on three modes of HIV transmission in Africa, i.e. heterosexual intercourse; intravenous injection and mother –to- child transmission (p.2).

He contends that "the idea of an African sexuality and stemming from it, an exclusively heterosexual African AIDS are both wrong and decidedly harmful to struggles for sexual health and sexual rights in Africa and globally".(p.3) Therefore, part of any measure to address problems of HIV/AIDS in Africa must include the admission of same-sex sexuality and its recognition as a source of the spread of AIDS virus.

Nonetheless, he further states, in recent times, African voices in literature and films, including very importantly activists of civil society and gay groups are speaking and writing more boldly on the issue, in an effort to redress previous trends.

Certainly, Epprecht has opened up new grounds of interest and research to historians, social scientists, humanists and health professionals on the theme of sexuality in Africa. His use of historiography and the historical method, in "unraveling" the myth of an exclusively heterosexual African sexuality obviously serves as a major strength of the work.

However, in spite of the strength of this work as noted above, it has also raised some contentious issues. Examples and corresponding deductions in some sections of the work undermines the cultural context and practices amongst some of the African peoples. For instance, the phenomenon of gender variation and gender crossing (pp 45-48; 51, etc) used as evidence to support claim of same-sex sexual relations in part of this work seemed weak and unconvincing. Because in many African societies, men dressing as women and vice versa, or exhibiting mannerisms of opposite sex, does not necessarily translate as evidence of same – sex sexual relations.

In many African societies transgender remarks made by individuals referring to person(s) of similar sex as women/wife or man/ husband may also not be proof of practice of same-sex sexual relations. For a clearer apprehension of such remarks/evidence, a greater insight into the history and forms of cultural expression of such African people(s) becomes imperative. Corroborating European missionary, colonial and anthropological records with accounts from local oral informants in such African societies (which the author admits is not a major strength of this study - pp. 26-27) may shed more light into the nature of these expression/ relations.

In the case of Nigeria, the phenomenon of the *Yan Daudu* as evidence of homo sexuality remains contentious.(p.10) There are scholars who see the *Yan Daudu* as people involved in a socio-economic vocation (productive specialization) rather than as homosexuals (Sinikangas: 2004).[2]

Also, foreign input (western/Arab) to the spread of same sex-sexuality in parts of sub Saharan Africa should not be completely ruled out as the author attempts to imply in some section of his work. The probability of such additional influence may need to be investigated.

The passion exhibited in some sections of this work seems more of an effort to *prove* the practice of homosexuality in Africa,(*you also do it!*) than its claimed objective of drawing our attention to homosexuality as a source for the spread of the HIV/AIDS virus in Africa. This approach and mode of thought obviously has its strong points and weaknesses

Again, however, these observations do not derogate from the importance of this work by Epprecht, which has certainly provided grounds for further research, study and debates on the issues of transgender crossing, third gender, gender variation and same -sex sexual relations in African history and society.

**Note**

[1]Marc Epprecht, *Heterosexual Africa?:The History of an Idea from the Age of Exploration to the Age of AIDS.* Ohio University Press and University of Kwazulu- Natal Press, 2008, pp 230.

[2]Maarit Sininkangas; "*Yan Daudu* - A Study of Transgendering Men in Hausaland in West Africa. M.A. thesis in Cultural Anthropology and Ethnology, Uppsala University, May 2004.

## THE HONOURABLE MINISTER SPEAKS
## (A SESTINA, FOR MAI PALMBERG)
### - John Eppel

Yes, indeed, we have a culture of blame,
which we blame on colonialism;
we have sanctions, which we blame on the West;
we have floods and droughts, which we blame on rich
nations; we have sickness and poverty
and misery, which we blame on the white

settlers who purloined our land ( bled us white!)
by farming it, mining it… and we blame
them for writing poems on poverty
in Africa. Colonialism
has crippled our dear motherland, once rich
beyond riches: north to south, east to west,

you name it. But now, it has all gone west,
finished; our rites, traditions, have been white-
washed. "We gave you football," you say. That's rich!
"There's no accountability. You blame
corruption on colonialism.
Doesn't that indicate a poverty

of ideas?" No, my friend, Poverty,
inflicted on us by your men at West-
minster, reared by colonialism,
nurtured by imperialism, white
on black racism. "'Whatever you blame,'"
you quote, "'that you have done yourself.'" No rich

bitch *murungu* understands or cares. Rich
bitches like you, the queens of poverty,
consumers of black cock - you are to blame.
Like your Hollywood prototype, Mae West,
you want everything! Fuck off, back to White-
all: patron of colonialism,

protector of colonialism,
donator of crumbs, which fall from the rich
man's table. You sicken me, sipping your white
wine, snacking, eyeing my crotch. Poverty
in Africa sustains the greedy West.
*J'accuse*. You, your kith and kin, are to blame.
Yes, colonialism is to blame,
monstrous child of your rich, decadent West.
The crime of poverty is coloured white.

# DEVIL'S FOOD
## - Gabeba Baderoon

*(For Mai Palmberg, who saw the radical and generous possibilities of the
arts for shaping knowledge of Africa, within and outside the continent).*

Pay attention to where you walk
- the filtered light through trees,
the kind of moss underfoot,
the roots of trees, moist and quiet,
where the caps of mushrooms crowd.

Learn which mushrooms are perfect, poisonous,
and which, misshapen, brown, are best of all.
Test the give of the flesh
- too soft means they are bitter and useless for eating.
What's not for eating haunts them all.
Devil's food, says my aunt.

Use your hands.
Feel for the spiky underside of the head
and the soft stem, thinner than your finger.
Probe for the base, push aside
the giving moss, reach
right down, learn by touch alone
when to pull, when it will yield
and come up whole.
Brush off dirt.

Do not eat
until they are cooked.
They taste of the soft metals of the earth,
themselves, not themselves,
the presence of older things.

# The Photograph as Consequence
## - Gabeba Baderoon

On the heaving night the ship *Estonia* sank,
people used the flashes of their cameras
to signal for help against the closing
doors of the sea.

In the end, some of the survivors found
they had taken photographs of the last moments
before the ship went down.

Photographs that are not photographs
but traces of the need to see.

One is of a man sitting on the hull
just before it must have slipped below.

Not waiting.
What was coming was coming.

The stillness of him,
the tilting horizon,
the future there
in the slope of his shoulder.

The photograph contains the accident of translation,
the before and the after.

In the photograph we go back
and he comes forward
to where death had arrived.

*852 people died when the ship Estonia sank in the Baltic Sea on 28 September 1994.*

**Each Tragedy Becomes the Story of a Tragedy
(notes from the final report on the
sinking of the ship Estonia)**

He noticed that the musicians had stopped playing.
The dancers had fallen several times.
Most people remembered their cabin numbers.
Some passengers stood still in the staircases,
and were passed by others.
The ship listed at 30 to 40 degrees.
The sound of the engine suddenly changed.
There was a knocking from the bow
as though something was trying to come in.
He heard a rustling beneath his cabin.
Things fell from the table to the floor.
She took with her an alarm clock which stopped
at two minutes past one.
There was only one public announcement.
It was a woman's voice. She sounded
afraid or injured.
He saw a crack in the ceiling.

The meaning of the words
*pitch*
*roll*
*brace.*

Escaping passengers had to pull
loose the hands of those
who were paralysed with fear
and shout directly in their ears
not to block the way but to run
up to Deck Seven and save themselves.

The meaning of the words
*list*
*heel*
*hold.*

# MEETING OURSELVES IN THE MIRROR
## - Shailja Patel

The matatu I rode into town this morning was blasting Justin Timberlake's *Losing My Way.*

*Can anybody out there hear me?*
*'Cause I can't seem to hear myself*
*Can anybody out there see me?*
*'Cause I can't seem to see myself…*

*Can anybody out there feel me?*
*'Cause I can't seem to feel myself*

My first thought was how ironic the lyrics were, applied to the matatu itself. Pedestrians are invisible on Nairobi's roads – to drivers, that is. As are cyclists, animals, pavement demarcations during rush hour………

But if anything is seen, heard and felt on Kenyan roads, it's matatus. And they know it.

My second thought was that the lyrics feed into some of the responses to my recent performances in Kenya. People say it makes them angry to hear stories of British concentration camps, colonial atrocities, and what are they supposed to do with this anger, this knowledge, why do I have to dredge up this painful enraging history?

I want to respond:

How can we be seen accurately by the rest of the world, known in all our complexity, if we haven't taken in the pain of our own history? If we haven't really looked at, listened to, the schisms and jagged cracks in our own society? Claiming the truth, feeling everything it evokes in us, gives us power to name ourselves. To tell our own stories. To see, hear, feel ourselves, is vital political work.

If I were to define - which I strenuously resist doing in every interview - the current 'trend' in contemporary African art, I would quote from one of my poems that we are *meeting ourselves in the mirror*. We are talking to each other, instead of telling the Western world simplified stories about ourselves. Making work about Africa for contemporary Africans. Work that does not dumb down, prettify, or translate. Art that demands effort, engagement, from the audience.

# ROD OF TYRANNY*
## - Taiwo Oloruntoba-Oju

**(i)      Enter the harem**
It was her *turn to sleep* tonight - Writ,
the royal roster
of carnal responsibility.
The aged *Olorì* has arranged it well
oh she knows, so well, the king's seasonal
Libidinal …
Only an unexpected whim of randy royal lust-al
May alter her careful schedule
Who else would veto the practised judgment of *Olorì Àgbà*, head
Of the royal harem

>       Tonight, new bride it is your turn
>       To accommodate the thrust-y weight, Berth
>       The throbbing undulation
>       Of insatiate royal passion


**(ii)      The Fox, in *redi*-ness**
And the old fox himself?
Already in *ìyẹ̀wù*, arid dome heavily relieved –
Crown, bead, *agbádá* and *sòkòtò* sit, crumpled
An unobtrusive distance.

>       "Open your eyes now, my new bride"

Pronounced the Terror; Tenor
T r e m u l o u s

"Touch, I give you leave…
the body of your husband king
be bold, woman, now you have
my express command and no hindrance"


(iii)      *Asemase … Error!*
And the bride advancing trembling fingers
Glancing, now, coyly, Below. A giggle
Presently escapes her silvery pipe
For, standing at attention
Like a statu(t)e, twixt the great man's thighs
A little scarecrow the size
Of the littlest finger!

          "I did not know, oh, my lord"

Ventured the new bride
Familiarity emboldened

          "When I saw all men tremble and bow
          I did not know this really was
          How much my lord and master was
          Down Below"


(iv)      **Execution (I)**
The king heedlessly executes
His set passion
For this lusty heat first must melt
And other trepidations later be felt

**(v)        Execution (II)**

Summoned!
Same bride, following day
(Silent consternates – others on the carnal row)
Same king, same *ìyẹ̀wù*, different
Presence.


On command she opens the king's
"Present"
Calabashed, dripping fresh and red:
A head that stood
Formerly on her father's neck!

> "This, my bride
> Is why they all tremble and bow
> Not because of the one you saw below"
>
> ----

Oh, the rod of tyranny would pierce, would boom
Silence and acceptance will lead to doom

------

**Glossary**

| | |
|---|---|
| *turn to sleep* | – the "sleeping" turn (when a wife is to occupy the husband's bed) is meticulously organised in traditional Yoruba polygynous culture to avoid conflict |
| *Olorì* | – *"Queen Consort"* (wife to king, prince or chief or title holder in Yoruba culture); |
| *Olorì Àgbà* | – *senior wife to the king* |
| *redi*-ness | – *rèdìí* is a Yoruba slang for coition ("*we ready wo mi rẹ̀dì*" – "If you were not ready you should not have gone *redii-ing*," says the Ijebu (Yoruba) man to his son who has put a girl in the family way but says he is not ready to commit [to] matrimony) |
| *ìyẹ̀wù* | – name for bedroom/inner chambers in Yoruba culture |
| *agbáda; sòkòtò* | – names for traditional Yoruba vestments |

* from *Losses,* a poetry collection by the author

# PANEGYRICS*
## - Taiwo Oloruntoba-Oju

Let me hail you in our communal tongue
In nomenclatures reserved for the mighty
I say let me pour panegyrics on you
In proverbs and indigenous parlance

*Okansoso ajanaku!*

The elephant is one, but see it fill up the woods
The buffalo is one, but see it habitate the grove
I say you are the one, singly
Shakes this institute, *kiji kiji*

*A n pe, a n sa a!*

We invoke her name, we praise her, yet you ask:
"Is she a pauper or a princess?"
We say: "killer of elephant," yet you inquire:
"Is he a farmer or a hunter?"

*Haba*!
Even if you never saw an ocean
Have you never seen the spiralling waves of the sky?
If you never knew the river, *Osa*, have you
Sometimes not tasted its salt … in your stew?

I say even if you never met the lady Mai
Surely, you've heard of culture research, at NAI!

-----

* Adapted from the poem "O yanki yanki" from the poetry collection by the author titled *Losses*

# List of Contributors

**Ajibade, Olusola George**
Senior Lecturer, Dept of Linguistics and African Languages,
Obafemi Awolowo University, Ile-Ife, Nigeria.

**Anyadike, Chima**
Associate Professor, Dept of English, Obafemi Awolowo
University, Ile-Ife, Nigeria.

**Arnfred, Signe**
Associate Professor in the Department for Society and
Globalisation and Head of Centre for Gender, Power and
Diversity. Roskilde University, Copenhagen , Denmark.

**Arntsen, Hilde**
Researcher, Department of Information Science and Media
Studies, University of Bergen, Norway.

**Baderoon, Gabeba**
South African poet. Guest Writer, Nordic Africa Institute,
2005; Assistant Professor of Women's Studies and African and
African American Studies at Penn State, Pensylvania, USA.

**Banwo, Adeyinka**
Visiting Professor, Department of History, Westfield State
College, Westfield, MA. USA.

**Barber, Karin**
Professor, Centre for West African Studies,
University of Birmingham.

Boehmer, Elleke
Professor of World Literatures in English,
University of Oxford, UK.

Chirambo, Reuben Makayiko
University of Cape Town, South Africa.

Ekström, Ylva
Research Fellow and Lecturer of Media Studies, Dept of
Information Science, Uppsala University, Sweden.

Eppel, John
Poet and Teacher, Christian College, Bulawayo, Zimbabwe.

Epprecht, Marc
Professor, Global Development Studies, Queens University,
Kingston, Canada.

Jonsson, Stefan
Associate Professor of Ethnic studies at the University of
Linköping; and Associate professor at Roskilde University,
Copenhagen, Denmark.

Makanjuola, Alfred Banso
Associate Professor, Dept of Psychiatry, Ambrose Alli
University Ekpoma, Nigeria.

Muponde, Robert
Professor of Literature, University of the Witwatersrand,
Johannesburg, South Africa

Nordberg, Karin
Director, Nordic African Institute, Uppsala

Oloruntoba-Oju, Taiwo
Dept of English, University of Ilorin, Ilorin, Nigeria.

Petersen, Kirsten Holst
Associate Professor Emeritus, Roskilde University,
Copenhagen, Denmark.

Omojola, Bode
Associate Professor, Ethnomusicology and African music, Five
Colleges, USA, comprising of Mount Holyoke College, Amherst
College, Hampshire College, Smith College, and the University
of Massachusetts, Amherst.

Primorac, Ranka
Dept of English, University of Southampton, UK.

# Index